FRUIT OF THE SPIRIT

Fruit of the Spirit

Pauline Mysticism for the Church Today

Michael H. Crosby, OFMCap

ORBIS BOOKS

Maryknoll, New York 10545

ORBIS BOOKS
Maryknoll, New York 10545

Fathers and Brothers
MARYKNOLL™

Founded in 1970, Orbis Books endeavors to publish works that enlighten the mind, nourish the spirit, and challenge the conscience. The publishing arm of the Maryknoll Fathers and Brothers, Orbis seeks to explore the global dimensions of the Christian faith and mission, to invite dialogue with diverse cultures and religious traditions, and to serve the cause of reconciliation and peace. The books published reflect the views of their authors and do not represent the official position of the Maryknoll Society. To learn more about Maryknoll and Orbis Books, please visit our website at www.maryknollsociety.org.

I am deeply grateful to Mark Schrauth and Kathy Frymark (ret.) at the Salzmann Library, St. Francis Seminary, Milwaukee, for getting needed books and articles. I also thank Charlotte Prather for her editing as well as my Orbis editor, Jim Keane, for making the book more compact and readable.

Nihil Obstat:
Rev. Francis Dombrowski, OFMCap, STL, Provincial Censor of Books, March 19, 2015
Very Rev. Michael Sullivan, OFMCap, Minister Provincial, Province of St. Joseph of the Capuchin Order, July 1, 2015

Library of Congress Cataloging-in-Publication Data

Crosby, Michael, 1940-
    Fruit of the spirit : Pauline mysticism for the church today / Michael H. Crosby, OFMCap.
        pages cm
    Includes bibliographical references and index.
    ISBN 978-1-62698-154-6 (pbk.)
    1. Bible. Galatians—Criticism, interpretation, etc. 2. Fruit of the Spirit—Biblical teaching. 3. Mysticism—Catholic Church. 4. Catholic Church—Doctrines. I. Title.
BS2685.52.C76 2015
227'.406—dc23

                                                                2015018317

Contents

Introduction

Why This Book at This Time?

If indeed "fools rush in where angels fear to tread," then this attempt to develop a mystical approach to contemporary life based on Paul's authentic letters, especially his Letter to the Galatians, surely applies. I can console myself, however, with the knowledge that being "foolish" also puts me in the company of those to whom Paul wrote this letter in the first place (Gal. 3:1, 3).[1]

A key reason why some might consider this book foolish is the fact that its author is not a formal scriptural exegete. However, I am a student of Scripture. I also am a disciple of the New Testament, attempting to put into practice in my own life and my world of politics, economics, and the church the key message of the gospels of both Jesus and Paul.[2] I decided to write this book because I think I have discovered that Paul has something to say about the gospel as it applies to our Catholic Church today and its members, just as he did to the Galatian church of his day. I recognize the possibility of being critiqued as foolish by formal Pauline scholars, because I do know that (probably more than any other of the actual letters of Paul[3]) almost

---

1. Because so many of the biblical references in this book will be from Paul's Letter to the Galatians, I will not note "Gal." in my citations. Other scriptural sources will have the traditional abbreviations.

2. I discussed the "gospel of the kingdom of God" proclaimed by Jesus and the "gospel" of the death/resurrection/embodiment of Jesus Christ in the church in my most recent book, *Repair My House: Becoming a "Kindom" Catholic* (Maryknoll, NY: Orbis Books, 2012), esp. 80-97 .

3. Paul's actual authorship is disputed regarding the whole Pauline corpus. While this will be discussed later, in summary, the majority opinion has identified Paul himself as the author of the letters to the Galatians, 1 Thessalonians, 1 and 2 Corinthians, Romans, Philippians, and Philemon. For a helpful approach to the chronology of his life and authentic letters see Gregory Tatum, OP, *New Chapters in the Life of Paul: The Relative Chronology of His Career* (Washington, DC: Catholic Biblical Association of America, 2006). See also M. Luther Stirewalt, Jr., *Paul the Letter Writer* (Grand Rapids: Eerdmans, 2003). Even within the seven "authentic" letters of Paul, it is argued, there were later editorial inter-

everything about his Letter to the Galatians has been a matter of debate! I hope this book will generate even more debate, especially because I see it speaking to all of us in the Catholic Church today as it once addressed problems in the Galatian church(es).[4]

Leading Pauline scholar N. T. Wright states that "this epistle has provoked endless controversy at all levels, from details of exegesis to flights of systematic theology."[5] Tatha Wiley goes so far as to say that "contemporary Pauline scholars have challenged virtually all of the historical and theological assumptions embedded in the dominant interpretation of Galatians."[6]

The list of challenges are many. Where does Galatians fit in the chronology of Paul's letters?[7] Was it written before or after the Council of Jerusalem (ca. 51 CE)? To whom was it written: Galatians who lived in the northern or the the southern part of what we know to be modern Turkey? Was/is justification (*dikaiosynē*) its main theme, and, if so, what did Paul mean by the word? Is the "law" to be interpreted according to personal salvation, a stress identified with Martin Luther, or E. P. Sanders's "covenantal nomism,"[8] which says that Paul was not preoccupied with personal

---

polations. See William O. Walker, Jr., "Interpolations in the Pauline Letters," in Stanley E. Porter, ed., *The Pauline Canon* (Atlanta: Society of Biblical Literature, 2004), 189-235.

4. A sense of the abiding applicability of Paul's Letter to the Galatians (as well as to the Romans) is clearly summarized in Pope John Paul II's encyclical on the Holy Spirit in the life of the church and the world, *Dominum et Vivificantem*, no 55: "In the texts of St. Paul there is a superimposing—and a mutual compenetration—of the ontological dimension (the flesh and the spirit), the ethical (moral good and evil), and the pneumatological (the action of the Holy Spirit in the order of grace). His words (especially in the letters to the Romans and Galatians) enable us to know and feel vividly the strength of the tension and struggle going on in man between openness to the action of the Holy Spirit and resistance and opposition to him, to his saving gift. The terms or poles of contrast are, on man's part, his limitation and sinfulness, which are essential elements of his psychological and ethical reality; and on God's part, the mystery of the gift, that unceasing self-giving of divine life in the Holy Spirit. Who will win? The one who welcomes the gift" (http://www.vatican. va).

5. N. T. Wright, *Pauline Perspectives: Essays on Paul, 1978–2013* (Minneapolis: Fortress Press, 2013), 191. Wright describes some of these in the following pages (193-204).

6. Tatha Wiley, *Paul and the Gentile Women: Reframing Galatians* (New York: Continuum, 2005), 10.

7. J. Louis Martyn lists the chronological order of the seven "recognized" letters to be: 1 Thessalonians, Galatians, Philippians, 1 and 2 Corinthians, and Romans, with Philemon being unclear as to the dating. See his *Galatians: A New Translation with Introduction and Commentary* (Anchor Bible; New York: Doubleday, 1998), 20.

8. Until 1977 most scholarship on Paul's writings on justification interpreted it quite individualistically in terms of personal salvation in a way that eclipsed the corporate dimension that stressed the fact that the believers were the fulfillment of the promise

salvation as much as he was about how God has worked to create a unique people? Or is James D. G. Dunn correct in his corrective to Sanders with his "new perspective" insights? Finally, if Paul envisioned a new creation in society between Jew and Greek, slave and free, male and female (3:28), why have twenty-first-century readers not found a way to be free of the residue of the same social patterns of ethnocentricity, domination, and sexism present in Paul's audience?[9] Speaking of audience, why is it that so much time is spent on addressing the "works of the flesh" of the Jewish law when the majority of Paul's Gentile audience might have been more influenced by their pagan background and its worship patterns and rituals than the Jewish law?[10]

This book makes no attempt to resolve the debates, simply because as a popularizer rather than an exegete I am not equipped to do so. Given the

---

made to Abraham to form a people from his "seed," now understood by Paul to be Christ and the church. This changed with the publication of E. P. Sanders's *Paul and Palestinian Judaism: A Comparison of Patterns of Religion* (Philadelphia: Fortress Press, 1977). Sanders argued that Judaism was not a purely legalistic religion, as had been taught until then. He showed that first-century Judaism was not so much a religion of works-righteousness as a religion of grace. His approach to "covenantal nomism" valued the Mosaic law in a way that included God's faithfulness and mercy; however, in practice it led to Paul breaking with Judaism. His "deconstruction" of Paul around "covenantal nomism," highlighting it as a "religion" vis-à-vis others, resulted in a "new perspective" on Paul's concern about the law. Its most articulate proponent has been James D. G. Dunn. Dunn rejected the notion of Paul separating from the Jews. Indeed, unlike Sanders, he argued that Paul was more in continuity with Judaism than separate from it. He argued that "covenantal nomism" was based on its *de facto* notion of the law and holiness as social forms that separated the Jews from others. These "boundary markers," or "social identity markers," in effect, were forms of ethnocentrism with an ideology to justify its dynamics. For further comment on the overindividualizing of Paul at the expense of "his role in the corporate and cosmological view of salvation history," see Joseph A. Fitzmyer, S.J., *Paul and His Theology: A Brief Sketch* (2nd ed.; Englewood Cliffs, NJ: Prentice Hall, 1989), 37.

9. It is important not to read "into" any first-century text a twenty-first-century worldview. The overriding structured relationship that remained uncritiqued at that time and, arguably, dominant at this time was patriarchy. For a good background on this see Jeremy Punt, "He Is Heavy . . . He Is My Brother. Unravelling Fraternity in Paul (Galatians)," *Neotestamentica* 46.1 (2012): 153-71. See also his subsequent "Pauline Brotherhood, Gender and Slaves: Fragile Fraternity in Galatians," *Neotestamentica* 47.1 (2013): 149-69. This complex issue will be discussed at various times in the book. For a broader view on Paul's approach to ethnicity, see Charles H. Cosgrove, "Did Paul Value Ethnicity?," *Catholic Biblical Quarterly* 68 (2006): 268-90.

10. Paula Fredriksen notes that Paul's audience was Gentile converts, not Jewish converts; see "Paul's Letter to the Romans, the Ten Commandments, and Pagan 'Justification by Faith,'" *Journal of Biblical Literature* 133.4 (2014): 804.

narration of just some of the many controversies surrounding Galatians, any attempt by a practitioner like me would truly be foolish! This realization has led me to study the mysticism of Paul and its applicability to us in our day. In this, I hope to be faithful to the insight offered in the preface of J. Christiaan Beker's book discussing the essence of Paul's understanding of God's action "in Christ" among us:

> The controversy about Paul throughout the centuries continues in our own time, evident in the diversity of new perspectives on his person and thought. It is superfluous, therefore, to claim that my delineation of "the essence" of Paul's thought is in any way finalized or fixed. With respect to Paul—as with all other seminal figures in the history of thought—we are always *in via*, "on the way," and must continuously draw new insights from the community of scholarship.[11]

Given these caveats, this book will examine the context of the Galatian world that gave rise to Paul's letter in a way that, I hope, will have relevance for our church today. As a priest in the Roman Catholic Church trying to influence how people navigate their lives in this world and church, I also find a deeper understanding of Galatians and its context can be helpful not only in addressing the challenges we face today of decline of membership and a loss of meaning for so many millions, but how, grounded in a mystical stance nurtured by the fruit(s) of the Spirit, the church might show evidence that it has become a new creation.

How This Book Began

In the 1990s I gave a number of retreats at Queenswood, a retreat center in Victoria, British Columbia, which was sponsored by the Sisters of St. Anne. During one retreat I was asked if I would give a retreat to the Sisters in the retirement center. "These sisters have good will but weak bodies," cautioned the coordinator. "They'll start losing you after twenty minutes."

Being the kind of speaker who takes twenty minutes to get going, my first reaction was "it's impossible." As I considered the retreat theme, I knew I couldn't summarize any of my other retreat conferences in twelve twenty-minute capsules. So I thought it best to develop an entirely new retreat for these senior citizens. But what theme would cover twelve confer-

---

11. J. Christiaan Beker, *The Triumph of God: The Essence of Paul's Thought* (trans. Loren T. Stuckenbruck; Minneapolis: Fortress Press, 1990), x.

ences? First I thought of the Twelve Tribes of Israel or the Twelve Apostles. But I have trouble enough knowing the names of the members of either of these groups of twelve, much less having anything to say about them! Then I thought to do something on the twelve "fruits of the Holy Spirit," about which I had been taught in Catholic grade school. Since the fruit of anything comes only with maturation and good aging, perhaps these women religious might resonate with the topic. But how could I, younger than they by a generation, have anything meaningful to say?

But then reason returned: I am a dues-paying member of the American Association of Retired Persons. Store clerks serving me no longer even ask if I want the senior discount. I can't count how many times I've been asked if I'm retired. When I take the subway in New York, people of all ages offer me their seat. But the final support for this topic rests in a refrain that increasingly comes to me from people who haven't seen me for a long time: "You're looking good for your age." This led me to conclude: If the ground for the Spirit can be cultivated in the young, middle-aged, and those who are retired, then the fruits of the Spirit are not limited to the work of any specific age group. With this affirmation (or rationalization!), I set out to do some preliminary research.

My first concern as I began to study the fruits of the Holy Spirit was how to number them. In his letter to the house church(es) at Galatia, Paul identifies the "fruit (not 'fruits') of the Spirit" as "love, joy, peace, patience, kindness, generosity, faithfulness, gentleness, and self-control" (5:22-23). The fact that Paul says the "fruit" of the Spirit *is* love, joy, peace, patience, kindness, and more invites the reader to decide: is the "fruit" connected with our being in "the Spirit"? Or are all the other "fruits of the Spirit" manifestations of that love about which we read in 1 Corinthians 13 and hear at almost every marriage in a Christian church: "Love is patient, love is kind ..." (1 Cor. 13:4ff.)?

There were other problems with numbering. If Paul numbers the "fruit" of the Spirit as nine virtues, why did I learn in Catholic school that there are twelve (as they still remain enshrined in the latest *Catechism of the Catholic Church*, #1832)?[12] Part of the problem can be traced to St. Jerome. In his Vulgate version of the Bible, he also listed nine but dropped gentleness and

---

12. In the process of writing this book I discovered that even a pope can be confused about the fruits of the Holy Spirit. In his homily on October 17, 2014, Pope Francis identified what Galatians calls the "fruit" of the Spirit as the "gifts" of the Spirit. According to Zenit's account, "Pope Francis reminded the faithful of the gifts that come from a Christian life united with the Holy Spirit. 'Love, joy, peace, patience, kindness, goodness, faithfulness, gentleness, self-control', he stressed, are the gifts that lead us on this path

self-control for modesty and continence. Meanwhile the *Catechism* lists twelve *"fruits* of the Spirit"*: charity, joy, peace, patience, kindness, goodness, generosity, gentleness, faithfulness, modesty, self-control, and chastity.

I decided to use the "Catholic" version so I could get my twelve conferences for the sisters. But my research on the topic found hardly anything. There was little in recent official church teaching on the Holy Spirit, much less the "fruit(s) of the Holy Spirit." The one exception was a 1986 encyclical of John Paul II, "On the Holy Spirit in the Life of the Church and the World." In its opening paragraphs he acknowledged that the Second Vatican Council "brought out the need for a new study of the doctrine on the Holy Spirit" and that "Paul VI emphasized: 'The Christology and particularly the ecclesiology of the council must be succeeded by a new study of and devotion to the Holy Spirit, precisely as the indispensable complement to the teaching of the Council.'"[13] Nonetheless, there has been little development beyond this.

When one searches in Catholic scholarship for something more specific on the "fruits of the Holy Spirit" that is faithful to good biblical scholarship, there was (and still is) almost nothing in English. The great mystic Evelyn Underhill wrote *The Fruits of the Spirit* in 1942, parts of which were compiled and republished in 1982 in a small pocket-size book by Roger L. Roberts.[14] Besides these and an obscure 48-page pamphlet by Josephine Massyngberde Ford, I found virtually nothing in English of any length or substance available in any book, chapter, or article. Not even commentaries on Galatians or articles in scriptural journals had any extended or developed exegesis.[15] The only material on the "fruits" of the Spirit that had been somewhat helpful (but not that scripturally grounded) were

---

towards Heaven." See http://www.zenit.org/en/articles/pope-francis-holy-spirit-gives-us-an-identity-and-inheritance.

13. Pope John Paul II, *Dominum et Vivificantem*, no. 2, quoting from Pope Paul VI, General Audience, June 6, 1973, *Insegnamenti di Paolo*: http://www.vatican.va.

14. Robert L. Roberts, *The Fruits of the Spirit by Evelyn Underhill* (Wilton, CT: Morehouse-Barlow, 1981, 1989).

15. Now that I am writing this book fifteen years later, my conclusion stands regarding the paucity of sources developing a theology or spirituality around the "fruit of the Spirit." One exception (without developing the "fruits" as such) has been the very helpful article by Bernard O. Ukwuegbu, "Paraenesis, Identity-defining Norms, or Both? Galatians 5:13–6:10 in the Light of Social Identity Theory," *Catholic Biblical Quarterly* 70 (2008): 538-59. Unfortunately I also found a paucity of Catholic scholars who developed a more detailed exegesis of Paul in ways that reached the level of many English-writing Protestant scholars and past scholars like Joseph Fitzmyer and Jerome Murphy-O'Connor.

insights in a now-defunct magazine of the Assembly of God called *Paraclete* and some more evangelically oriented books, such as one written by my fellow-Milwaukeean and megachurch pastor, Stuart Briscoe.[16] That was it. It now became clear: except for Gerhard Kittel's *Theological Dictionary of the New Testament*, I was on my own.[17]Accompanying this realization was a sense that I myself had to do a lot of studying and had a lot to (un)learn.

The Current Context (The Situation of Catholicism) and the Text Today (The Fruit[s] of the Spirit)

I believe that Paul's whole theology can be summarized in one word: *gospel*. In Galatians Paul uses the term "gospel" in various forms at least fifteen times.[18] While "gospel" generally means some kind of "good news," Paul's use of "gospel" cannot be separated from either the "gospel" proclaimed by Jesus Christ (as noted in the Synoptic Gospels) or the "gospel" of Caesar's Rome; and it is clear from the Letter to the Galatians that the "gospel" that was even more of a threat for Paul than that imperial gospel was the one promoted by some unnamed agents (1:6-9; see 3:1ff.; 4:17; 5:7-8; 6:7), whom I will call Teachers.[19] They had come from some unnamed place to persuade

---

16. Stuart Briscoe, *The Fruit of the Spirit: Growing in Christian Character* (Fisherman Bible Series; New York: Random House, 1994).

17. Since then Thomas Keating has written a book on *The Fruits and the Gifts of the Spirit* (New York: Lantern Books, 2007) but covers the "fruits" in eight pages (of quite large print). Most other books written on the "fruit(s) of the Holy Spirit" have been written by evangelical authors: Thomas E. Trask and Wade I. Goodall, *The Fruit of the Holy Spirit: Becoming the Person God Wants You to Be* (Grand Rapids: Zondervan, 2000); Stuart Briscoe, *The Fruit of the Spirit: Cultivating Christlike Character* (Colorado Springs, CO: WaterBrook Press, 1984); Jerry Bridges, *The Fruitful Life: The Overflow of God's Love through You* (Colorado Springs, CO: NavPress, 2004).

18. The noun, verb, or compound form of "gospel" is found in Gal. 1:6, 7 (2 times), 8 (2 times), 9, 11 (2 times), 16, 23; 2:2, 5, 7 (2 times), 14; 3:8; and 4:13.

19. These outsiders who spoke against Paul's "gospel" were not given a name by Paul. Various exegetes call them "opponents," "agitators," or the more pejorative "Judaizers." For reasons that will become clearer and more apropos, my identification of covenantal nomism with canonical nomism, and because the proponents of canonical nomism identify their legitimation by limiting the teaching authority of the church to the episcopal, clerical and curial leaders' teaching, I will use the term proffered by J. Louis Martyn: "Teachers." See his *Galatians: A New Translation with Introduction and Commentary* (Anchor Bible; New York: Doubleday, 1997). For more on the "naming" of the opponents a good summary is found in Atsuhiro Asano, *Community-Identity Construction in Galatians* (London/New York: T & T Clark International, 2005), 23-24. A contrary position about the identity of the Teachers is that instead of being Jewish in their background, they

the converted members of the Galatian churches that they needed to incorporate Jewish rituals if they were going to be true Christians, because Jesus was an observant Jew. In Paul's mind, their "gospel" would undermine the integrity of the "gospel" of Jesus Christ that he had proclaimed and that they had once embraced (4:14-15). The "gospel" of these Teachers has come to be identified with a negative consequence of a positive understanding of the covenant and the law (*nomos*). It has been called "covenantal nomism."

In 1977, E. P. Sanders, a Pauline scholar, shook up traditional Pauline interpretation by challenging the traditional (often identified with Martin Luther) understanding of Paul's legitimate concerns connected with law-observance as though he was rejecting it. This put him in opposition to interpretations of Paul as anti-law. Sanders argued that Paul never was against the law or against observance of the law; rather he remained faithful to the Abrahamic covenant and correct observance of the law (*nomos*); thus Sanders's term "covenantal nomism." What Paul did reject was an individualistic notion of personal salvation through the law to the exclusion of good works and also the tendency by some to see themselves in their practice of the Mosaic law as somehow privileged in a way that separated them from other peoples.

Six years after Sanders published his thoughts on "covenantal nomism," James D. G. Dunn tried to honor yet redirect some of Sanders's thoughts with what he called a "new perspective." He concentrated on the key passage from Gal. 2:16: "We know that a person is justified not by the works of the law but through faith in Jesus Christ. And we have come to believe in Christ Jesus, so that we might be justified by faith in Christ, and not by doing the works of the law, because no one will be justified by the works of the law." Insisting (with Sanders) that, contrary to the "Lutheran" interpretation, which meant a virtual rejection of good works associated with faith, Dunn canonized the "new perspective" on Paul as follows:

> Paul's new answer is that the advent of Christ had introduced the time of fulfillment, including the fulfillment of his purpose regarding the covenant. From the beginning, God's eschatological purpose in making the covenant had been the blessing of the nations: the gospel was already proclaimed when God promised Abraham, "In you shall all the nations be blessed" (Gal. 3.8; Gen. 12.3; 18.18). So, now that the time of fulfillment had come, the covenant should no longer be conceived in nationalistic or racial terms. No

---

may have been Gentile converts who believed conversion demanded the full embrace of the Mosaic law.

longer is it an exclusively Jewish *qua* Jewish privilege. The covenant is not thereby abandoned. Rather it is broadened out as God had originally intended—with the grace of God which it expressed separated from its national restriction and freely bestowed without respect to race or work, as it had been bestowed in the beginning. This is roughly the argument of Galatians 3–4, as also developed later in Romans 3–4.[20]

At the heart of authentic covenantal nomism both for Sanders and Dunn is the conviction that all the law(s) of Judaism flowed from the Great Commandment in Deuteronomy 6:4: to love God with one's whole heart. This kind of love practiced by Jesus and Paul involved codified rules and dynamics of "the law"[21] that included ritual practices such as circumcision and the observance of dietary regulations (which they seem to have practiced throughout their lives). However, these were interpreted by the Teachers as a religiously sanctioned form of separation. Their "spin" on the Mosaic law canonized the separation by equating it with the "holiness" that was demanded of Israel by Leviticus 19:1: "Be holy for I, the Lord your God, am holy." Because the God who was holy was believed to be separated from the people, holiness was essentially equated with separation of Israel from its neighbors; an "us" and "them" stance in life. Given his Damascus experience, Paul could no longer tolerate such a separatist idea of holiness; instead, as Gerd Theissen writes, "His 'canon'" would become "the missionizing of the entire gentile world (cf. Gal. 2:9; 1:16)."[22]

Paul needed to be absolutely clear to those who had fallen under the negative "spin" on covenantal nomism as taught by "the Teachers" that the law was not meant to be a source of separation and ethnocentrism but of inclusion and communion. As Paul saw it, the problem with covenantal nomism was not so much the practice(s) of the law as much as something much deeper and more sinister. Those promoting and practicing the law used the law as a boundary marker that set them apart from all others (whether these

---

20. James D. G. Dunn, "The New Perspective on Paul," *Bulletin of the John Rylands Library* 65 (1983). This is available online at http://markgoodacre.org/PaulPage/New.html.

21. Stephen Westerholm notes that a good description of the law as understood by Paul "is the realization that he normally means by *nomos* the divine commandments imparted to Israel on Mount Sinai with their accompanying sanctions. The 'works of the law' are concrete deeds which this legislation manifestly requires." See his *Israel's Law and the Church's Faith: Paul and His Recent Interpreters* (Grand Rapids: Eerdmans, 1988), 220.

22. Gerd Theissen, *The Social Setting of Pauline Christianity: Essays on Corinth* (Philadelphia: Fortress Press, 1989), 52.

others were the Romans, who considered Judaism to be a barbaric superstition, or the gentile converts, who were thought to be deficient because they weren't practicing the law) in an "us" and "them" dynamic of superiority.

While all viable groups have some kind of boundaries to maintain their social identity, the boundaries at play in covenantal nomism at the time of Jesus and Paul, in some circles, had taken the form of what N. T. Wright has called "National Righteousness,"[23] Bruce Longenecker called "Ethnocentric Covenantalism,"[24] and Frank J. Matera called "Cultural Imperialism."[25] Whatever the name, the reality represented continued separatist and exclusivist attitudes behind what Paul declared in Galatians as diametrically opposed to the new created order.[26] Inclusive love, proclaimed in the words and deeds of Jesus Christ, reached their apogee in his self-giving death on the cross and was to be continued in the members of his body, the church, wherein no separatism would exist. The gospel that Paul preached was "the power of God for salvation to everyone who believes." It may have come to "the Jew first," but it was meant for all, including non-Jews, who were called Greeks (Rom. 1:16).

Polarization in the Church, Then and Today

In "The Letter to the Galatians: Exegesis and Theology," N. T. Wright asked, "What then has Galatians to say to the large debates that concern Christian theologians today, living often at the interface of church and world?"[27] Years earlier he shared a similar thought that might be applicable today: "Paul's gospel, like Isaiah's, confronts the tyrants and summons their victims to freedom. If history, theology, and exegesis can join hands at this point, per-

---

23. N. T. Wright, *Pauline Perspectives*, 142.

24. Bruce W. Longenecker, *The Triumph of Abraham's God: The Transformation of Identity in Galatians* (Nashville: Abingdon Press, 1998), 16.

25. Frank J. Matera, *Galatians* (Collegeville, MN: Liturgical Press, 1992, 2007), 11.

26. I do not agree with Tatha Wiley that the "separation" that Paul rejected was defined by gender to the degree that she argues "that the dispute between evangelists over the necessity of circumcision was, in its immediate communal context as well as direct consequence, a dispute over whether the membership of Gentile believers in the Galatian assemblies would be differentiated by gender" because the whole cultural context of Paul (which he did not directly reject) involved structural discrimination against women and slaves (11). Also "gender is at the heart of the Galatian conflict" (15). Paul does seem to reflect forms of separatist thinking in Rom. 16:17 and 1 Cor. 5:9.

27. N. T. Wright, "The Letter to the Galatians: Exegesis and Theology," in Joel B. Green and Max Turner, eds., *Between Two Horizons: Spanning New Testament Studies and Systematic Theology* (Grand Rapids: Eerdmans, 2000), reprinted in N. T. Wright, *Pauline Perspectives*, 204.

haps together they might persuade the contemporary church to rediscover aspects of Paul's message to the world which we, like his opponents, have often enough found it convenient to ignore."[28]

If polarization characterizes what we will see as the two radically opposed notions of a "works of the flesh" approach vs. a "fruit of the Spirit" application of "the gospel" in the Galatian churches, how might N. T. Wright's question speak to our polarized Catholic Church today, especially in English-speaking countries of the West?

Between 1979 and 2013, we Roman Catholics experienced our own form of covenantal nomism, which reinforced separation related to different ways of understanding and living out our Catholicism. However, possibly even more serious than the covenantal nomism of the Jews/Judeans, which involved separation from *others* (*ad extra*), this separation took place within the members of church itself (*ad intra*), again around images related to "*holy*" orders" or priestly and episcopal ordination. One representative articulation of this "us" and "them" division separating the clerics from the laity might be found in a column by Cardinal Francis George while he was archbishop of Chicago. Despite having previously separated himself from both conservatives and liberals in the church who defined "themselves vis-à-vis the bishops rather than vis-à-vis Christ,"[29] he later virtually identified being "Catholic" with the bishops. Thus he wrote in his diocesan paper:

> Theoretically, it is argued that there are Catholic voices that disagree with the teaching of the church and therefore with the bishops. There have always been those whose personal faith is not adequate to the faith of the church. Perhaps this is the time for everyone to re-read the Acts of the Apostles. Bishops are the successors of the apostles; they collectively receive the authority to teach and govern that Christ bestowed upon the apostles. Bishops don't claim to speak for every baptized Catholic. Bishops speak, rather, for the Catholic and apostolic faith. Those who hold that faith gather with them; others go their own way. They are and should be free to do so, but they deceive themselves and others in calling their organizations Catholic.[30]

---

28. N. T. Wright, "Gospel and Theology in Galatians" (1994), reprinted in N. T. Wright, *Pauline Perspectives*, 92.

29. Cardinal Francis George, "Cardinal George's Plan to Evangelize America," interview with John L. Allen, Jr., *National Catholic Reporter*, October 7, 2009, http://ncronline.org.

30. Francis Cardinal George, O.M.I., "What Are You Going to Give Up This Lent?,"

While Paul's opponents believed they were defining Judaism not from what its clerical group necessarily said but what they thought was in the law itself, so, it seems Cardinal George was defining what it means to be "Catholic" not by its official texts (including canon law) and perennial teachings (around conscience)[31] but by his belief that Catholic identity was somehow defined by the bishops alone. The grounds for the assumption underlying this statement is based on his statement that "bishops are the successors of the apostles" and that, as such, they "receive the authority to teach and govern that Christ bestowed upon the apostles." Rather than making the necessary distinctions to interpret such a statement correctly, the cardinal's statement virtually equates sacramental ordination with a sanctioning by God of whatever may be taught by any body of bishops and even, in its most extreme form, by any priest ordained by a bishop.

That Cardinal Francis George could make such a statement without clearer nuances lends support to the consequent "them" and "us" approach to Catholicism that created deep polarization around what it meant/means to be "Catholic." This polarization became identified with two groups at either end of the spectrum of what it means to be "church." Sociologist James D. Davidson termed the poles as "Culture I Catholics" and "Culture II Catholics," describing their differences as

> seeing the Church as a hierarchical institution to seeing it as the People of God; from an emphasis on ordination to an emphasis on baptism; from laypeople passively complying with church teachings to laypeople taking more responsibility for their own faith; and from seeing the world as a place to be avoided to seeing it as a place [in which] we should participate.[32]

Cardinal's column in *Catholic New World*, February 26–March 3, 2012. Cardinal George's teaching in his archdiocesan paper is representative of what might be called "episcopal nomism." I call it "canonical nomism" because of the way this had been *canonized* in the minds of many clerics during the pontificates of Popes John Paul II and Benedict XVI. Such teaching was not shared by all bishops, including the then bishop of Rome. In a September 24, 2011, speech to German seminarians, some of whom would be defined as eager to become clerical promoters of "episcopal nomism," Pope Benedict XVI said that faith cannot be identified with an "us" and "them" approach; rather it "requires that "we do not make ourselves the sole criterion" of what true faith means (http://www.zenit.org).

31. A good discussion of the differences in understanding what it means to be Catholic around authority and conscience can be found in Michael G. Lawler and Todd A. Salzman, "Following Faithfully: The Catholic Way to Choose the Good," *America* 212.3, February 2, 2015, 16-20.

32. James D. Davidson, "Generations of American Catholics," keynote address, in

In a follow-up to this in 2014, Davidson and others outlined the theological construct of Culture I and Culture II Catholics more clearly: "We describe an underlying tension between a compliance-oriented approach that accentuates the authority of the hierarchy and a conscience-oriented approach that emphasizes Catholics' need to follow their conscience, even if doing so means disagreeing with church teachings. This tension is rooted in Catholic theology, tradition and history."[33]

In the above statement, Cardinal George had identified himself as a Culture I Catholic; that is understandable. But he has also equated Catholicism with episcopal teaching in a way that makes him and those who support his thinking *separate from* those who might be Culture II Catholics.

Such a view is evidence of the gradual usurpation of the meaning of "church" to be virtually equated with the male clerics under the cloak of the "official" Magisterium. "Authentic" or "official" teaching often moved well beyond what is theologically and canonically considered "authentic" and/ or "official" to cover almost anything some of those clerics in papal offices, chanceries, and even parishes determined to be "authentic" or "official." Some have called this trend "creeping infallibilism." Often such declarations and decisions and pronouncements would be wrapped in some of the very notions of the separatist kind of "holiness" that Jesus rejected. These dynamics were often reinforced by an ideology of loyalty to such teaching that was virtually equated with obedience to God. In effect, however, because the approach to authority was unilateral rather than dialogical, such a claim to obedience could not be truly "*holy* obedience" when such authority was exercised in a climate of fear. In effect this "obedience" was not characterized by holiness but submission.

When power in any organization takes on the form of a command-control model, violence is invariably the consequence. In a command-control model, the need to dominate takes priority. This not only represents an abuse of authority on the part of those who abrogate the charism of authority to themselves apart from the charisms given by God to all; but

---

Proceedings of the Sixty-Third Annual Convention of the Catholic Theological Society of America 63 (2008): 5.

33. William D'Antonio, James Davidson, Mary Gautier, and Katherine Meyer, "Assumptions in Study on Young Catholics Lead to Unnecessarily Grim Outlook," *National Catholic Reporter* essay, December 6, 2014, http://ncronline.org. The data behind the 2011 study was a follow-up to their once-every-three-year data for the same group covered for over ten years. This is summarized in William D'Antonio, Michelle Dillon, and Mary Gautier, *American Catholics in Transition* (Lanham, MD: Rowman & Littlefield Publishers, 2013).

it also actually subverts the gospel itself. The "obedience of faith," in effect, becomes equated with unquestioning submission to these leaders' authority and their dominating ways rather than the "obedience of faith" to the gospel that is demanded of all the baptized. This exercise of authority actually contradicts the apostolic authority claimed by some of these same leaders.

In a homily at Mass with a group of newly made cardinals in 2015, Pope Francis hinted at what is said above about Culture I and Culture II Catholicism when he talked about the "two ways" church leaders envision how to articulate the Catholic faith.

> There are two ways of thinking and of having faith: we can fear to lose the saved and we can want to save the lost. Even today it can happen that we stand at the crossroads of these two ways of thinking. The thinking of the doctors of the law, which would remove the danger by casting out the diseased person, and the thinking of God, who in his mercy embraces and accepts by reinstating him and turning evil into good, condemnation into salvation and exclusion into proclamation.

What he said next, however, underlines a point being made in this introduction: that Paul's challenge is being replicated in the challenge facing the Catholic Church today:

> These two ways of thinking are present throughout the Church's history: *casting off* and *reinstating*. Saint Paul, following the Lord's command to bring the Gospel message to the ends of the earth (cf. Mt 28:19), caused scandal and met powerful resistance and great hostility, especially from those who demanded unconditional obedience to the Mosaic law, even on the part of converted pagans.... The Church's way, from the time of the Council of Jerusalem, has always been the way of Jesus, the way of mercy and reinstatement.[34]

When the Vatican and/or the bishops "speak for" any part of the church without also "listening to" that part of the church, it is inevitable that there will be an "us" and "them" dynamic that reflects the very covenantal nomism that Paul challenged as violating the gospel. With such a system and ideology, any dissent becomes disloyalty. Hence, if any theologians, especially those in Catholic institutions, questioned any part of the bishops' teaching

---

34. Pope Francis, Homily, February 15, 2015, http://www.zenit.org.

or their interpretation of it, they did so at the risk of losing their jobs and livelihood. A climate of fear thus came to define the underlying dynamic described in the words of Cardinal George: "Bishops speak, rather, for the Catholic and apostolic faith. Those who hold that faith gather with them; others go their own way."

The result of these dynamics in the "official" church has come to be expressed in the dominance of patriarchal clericalism[35] as the form of governance in the church that virtually identified its ordained members with a kind of "holiness" that separated themselves from the rest of the church, ultimately justified by canon law (*nomos*) and practically sustained by *de facto* separation and unaccountability of the clerical group from any outsiders within the church. Canon law and the juridical apparatus of the "official" church thus was exclusively created, interpreted, and administered by a canonically established clergy, entirely male, and hierarchically ordered.

Paul's Covenantal Nomism; Our Canonical Nomism

This contemporary form of the negative (separatist) application of covenantal nomism that Paul challenged as contrary to the gospel he experienced at Damascus and proclaimed everywhere can be called "canonical nomism"; it defines the way church laws have been created, interpreted, and "canonized" in ways that promote clerical separatism in the Catholic Church. In too many places, the clerical, male, hierarchical authority structure and its officials and representatives and initiates have become *de jure* and *de facto* separate from the rest of the church. The result is ecclesiastical apartheid, separating three key groups *within* the Catholic Church in the West: cleric and lay, men and women, and straights and gays (to say nothing of the globalized apartheid between North and South).

Elements of the negative "spin" on covenantal nomism noted in Galatians include Paul challenging the "false brothers" (2:4) who resisted the freedom of those who believed in Paul's gospel and sought instead to "enslave" them in obedience to their own interpretation of the law that would divide them from others rather than unite them. "Elsewhere," Bruce Longenecker writes, "those who promulgate nomistic practice are depicted in terms of self-promotion and the enhancing of one's own reputation" (4:17), and he concludes, "It is little wonder, then, that Paul considers the way of nomistic practice to end in fierce competitiveness and ambitious, cut-throat rivalry

---

35. For a good description of clericalism in the priesthood at all levels, see George Wilson, S.J., *Clericalism: The Death of Priesthood* (Collegeville, MN: Liturgical Press, 2008).

(5:15, 26)."[36] The contemporary reader cannot but find echoes of these dynamics represented in "the sickness and vainglory" of members of the Curia noted by Pope Francis in his December 22, 2014, address to them. Such ways, he noted, occur "when appearance, the color of garments and signs of honor become the primary objective of life, forgetting Saint Paul's words: 'Do nothing from selfishness or conceit, but in humility count others better than yourselves. Let each of you look not only to his own interests, but also to the interests of others' (Phil. 2:1-4)."[37]

Of course, as in any structure, exceptions to this pattern and "nomism" exist, especially at the level of the local parish. Nonetheless, the underlying dynamic of clericalism, careerism, and climbing that often has incurred the censure of Pope Francis has not shown any significant evidence of change since his election.[38] Such behaviors also do not reflect the approach to power that we find in documents of the Second Vatican Council as well as in postconciliar ecumenical documents. "In these texts, there is little emphasis on 'sacred power' conferred upon some groups and withheld from others," Richard Gaillardetz stated in a 2015 address. In reacting to the consequent control of power in the church in the hands of this group, he reminds us that, while such may be justified by canon law and tradition, it is not in the tradition of the Scriptures: "Power is nothing less than the activity of the Holy Spirit manifested in the mutual gift exchange among the various component elements in the church, including the witness of the whole Christian faithful, the normative witness of the bishops and the scholarly contributions of theologians."[39]

---

36. Bruce W. Longenecker, *The Triumph of Abraham's God*, 75. I have found Longenecker very helpful for the development of my thought around the need to develop a new personal and communal *identity* around the "fruit of the Spirit" in this book. Because of this, I wish he would have given the name of his book his subtitle *The Transformation of Identity in Galatians.*

37. Pope Francis, Address to Roman Curia, December 22, 2014 (http://www.vatican.va).

38. As noted above, Pope Francis's challenges to what I have called "canonical nomism" in its Roman curial expression reached a climax in his December 22, 2014, address to the Roman Curia. This was highlighted in the press around the world, as evidenced in the headlines in papers I picked up while traveling from St. Lucia to Milwaukee by way of Toronto: Nicole Winfield, "Pope Francis vs. the Vatican," *National Post,* December 23, 2014; Nicole Winfield, "Pope Gives Curia Public Dressing Down," *Globe and Mail,* December 23, 2014; Deborah Ball and Tammy Audi, "Pope Rebukes Church Bureaucracy," *Wall Street Journal,* December 23, 2014; Josephine McKenna, "Pope Francis: Merry Christmas, You Power-Hungry Hypocrites," *USA Today,* December 23, 2014.

39. Richard R. Gaillardetz, "How Does the Holy Spirit Assist the Church in Its Teach-

From that earlier description by a bishop of the bishops as successors of the apostles who collectively have "the authority to *teach* and govern that Christ bestowed upon the apostles," it may now be clear why I chose the word "Teacher" to refer to those whom Paul believed were undermining his "gospel" of Christ's death, resurrection, and embodiment in all baptized believers.[40] These Teachers, as sincere as they may have been in Paul's time, had become blinded by their conviction that salvation need be connected to their individualistic and separatist interpretation of "covenantal nomism." The same might be said of many of those clerical "teachers" of today who subscribe to a nomism (including issues around governance, canons, liturgical rituals, etc.) that equates Catholic faith with what bishops (and even some priests) teach and how they govern. This "with" the bishops or "outside" of Catholicism attitude that came to dominate during the pontificates of Popes John Paul II and Benedict XVI (even if they personally might not have believed in it), shows, I believe, why Galatians is so important for Catholics as we move from a clerically identified church to one that is being defined by Pope Francis as obedient to the "law of Christ." This understanding was powerfully articulated twenty-five years ago by Jerome Murphy-O'Connor:

> Christians know themselves to be no longer bound by the Mosaic Law with which Paul was so concerned. This can blind us to the fact that his basic principle remains valid with respect to any law. To give blind obedience to any authoritative directive is to place oneself in a state of inauthenticity, because to do so is to surrender one's freedom in an endeavor to escape responsibility.[41]

From reading the Acts of the Apostles as well as Paul's letters, it seems clear that Paul disagreed with Peter's allowing himself to be overly influenced by a negative understanding of "covenantal nomism." Did Paul's differences with two key apostles, James and Peter, make him "not Catholic"? I do not think so, and am strengthened in my belief that the phrase "episcopal nomism" can yield a contemporary understanding of the organizational

---

ing?," The Duquesne University Eighth Annual Holy Spirit Lecture, January 31, 2014 (Pittsburgh, PA: Duquesne University, 2014), 13.

40. See n. 19, above.

41. Jerome Murphy-O'Connor, OP, *Becoming Human Together: The Pastoral Anthropology of St. Paul* (Wilmington, DE: Michael Glazier, 1978), 119. Later Murphy-O'Connor notes, "It would seem to be a logical inference from Paul's position that by enacting binding legislation the church contributes to the inauthenticity of its members" (121).

model of the Roman(ized) Catholic Church, akin to the exclusivistic forms of covenantal nomism rejected by Paul.

While such a statement might seem disloyal to some bishops, it seems quite applicable if we apply to the present ecclesial circumstances the dynamics of what covenantal nomism in its negative aspects meant. We find it in the explanation of James D. G. Dunn, considered by many to be one of the premier Pauline exegetes. "Covenantal nomism," for Dunn, particularly as it applied to the situation impacting the church(es) of Galatia, involved five points:

1. It builds on Sanders's new perspective on Second Temple Judaism, and Sanders's reassertion of the basic graciousness expressed in Judaism's understanding and practice of covenantal nomism.
2. It recognizes that a social function of the law[42] was an integral aspect of Israel's covenantal nomism, where separateness to God (holiness) was understood to require separateness *from* the (other) nations as two sides of the one coin, and that the law was understood as the means to maintaining both.
3. It notes that Paul's own teaching on justification focuses largely if not principally on the need to overcome the barrier that the law was seen to interpose between Jew and Gentile, so that the "all" of "to all who believe" (Rom. 1:17) signifies, in the first place, Gentile as well as Jew.
4. It suggests that "works of the law" became a key slogan in Paul's exposition of his justification gospel because so many of Paul's fellow Jewish believers were insisting on certain works as indispensable to their own (and others?) standing within the covenant, and therefore as indispensable to salvation.
5. It protests that failure to recognize this major dimension of Paul's doctrine of justification by faith may have ignored or excluded a vital factor in combating the nationalism and racialism that have so distorted and diminished Christianity past and present.[43]

It seems quite clear that before and during the conclave that elected Pope Francis, the bishops themselves began to see difficulties with the notion of

---

42. James D. G. Dunn indicates his concern that some exegetes fail sufficiently "to grasp the full significance of *the social function of the law* at the time of Paul and how that determines and influences both the issues confronting Paul and Paul's responses." See his "Works of the Law and the Curse of the Law (Galatians 3:10-14)," *New Testament Studies* 31 (1985): 523-24.

43. James D. G. Dunn, *The New Perspective on Paul* (rev. ed.; Grand Rapids: Eerdmans, 2008), 16-17.

"the new evangelization," a term that had been coined by Pope John Paul II and continued by Pope Benedict XVI. The "new evangelization" became a mantra-like phrase that almost defied description. However, like "covenantal nomism," behind any concrete norms or rituals being discussed there hovered the same separatist approach to being Catholic: an us/them approach that never acknowledged the need to critique the governance structure of the church in light of the gospel proclaimed by Jesus and Paul and solid tradition.[44]

It was the intervention of Cardinal Jorge Bergoglio at the preconclave gathering that influenced the choice to elect him pope. He had bemoaned a "self-referential" church and envisioned a church that was open to the world proclaiming the gospel message of Jesus to the peripheries.[45] The honesty and clarity of his speech contributed to his being elected Bishop of Rome. In his subsequent efforts to move the Catholic Church from being closed in on itself and under the control of clerical and careerist leaders, we seem to be witnessing a clear return to the centrality of Paul's understanding that faith in Jesus Christ is the core belief of Catholics.[46]

Under the previous dynamic of "clerical nomism," the "new evangelization" can be seen as an effort to get people who had left the Western church to return to it without any conversion on the part of the institution or its clerical leaders that would lead it to offer a more inclusive "gospel." Now, Pope Francis is speaking against such clericalism and careerism and inviting us to return to the more inclusive gospel of Jesus Christ. Converting the

---

44. For a fine effort to create the right balance for teaching and governance in the church that is faithful to the scriptural and conciliar understanding of the Holy Spirit, see Richard R. Gaillardetz, "How Does the Holy Spirit Assist the Church?"

45. The Vatican news service, Zenit, has carried Pope Francis's recollection of his talk to his fellow cardinals, which he shared at the request of Cardinal Jaime Lucas Ortega y Alamino of Havana. See http://www.zenit.org.

46. In this sense Hans von Campenhausen writes: "But, for Paul, the Church is not a human, natural entity, but a sheerly miraculous, transcendent phenomenon. The preaching of the Gospel is the only thing which calls to life the Spirit through which the congregation can become what it is. Christians have the Spirit of Christ. Because of this, spontaneity, obedience and love are in fact presupposed and required of the Church as, so to speak, the 'normal' thing. When the Church ceases to be spiritual, that is to say, when within her that which is normal for the world is exalted into a law, then in Paul's eyes she is dead" (*Ecclesiastical Authority and Spiritual Power in the First Three Centuries* [trans. J. A. Baker; London: Adam & Charles Black, 1969], 61). Von Campenhausen also writes, "The congregation lives by the Spirit, and it is a result of the manifold gifts of the Spirit that it develops its various members. Where the Spirit and love are sovereign, it is already "perfect" in Christ, and in need of absolutely no further organization" (32). I doubt whether it is as simple as this; however the sentiment is solid.

Catholic Church from its patriarchal and clericalized "episcopal nomism" to its being regrounded in the life of Holy Spirit within and among all who are baptized in Christ may become the first step in reclaiming the kind of faith envisioned by Paul.[47]

Because this book seeks to promote the cultivation of the "fruit(s)" of the Spirit as a way to develop a mystical theology for the church, we might begin by realizing that, beyond "episcopal nomism," we have other divisions among Catholics, including how we understand the life and functioning of the Holy Spirit in the church today. For instance, I have been surprised at the very different (if not polarized) impressions some people have of how the Holy Spirit operates in our personal, communal, and institutional lives. Oftentimes, it seems the Holy Spirit gets overlooked as a reconciling power in the ongoing, "old order" (see 2 Cor. 5:17) culture wars[48] between Culture I and Culture II Catholics.[49] As a result, the Holy Spirit has little or no breathing room to empower either faction.

The following personal examples might illustrate the problem. In April 1998, I received a letter from a woman who heard me speak five years before at the annual gathering of Call to Action, an organization of Catholic individuals and groups committed to promoting greater justice in our church and society, our world, and the environment. She also was in a program geared to give her certification in the Spiritual Exercises of St. Ignatius. Part of her requirements involved reading my book *Spirituality of the Beatitudes*. In its tenth and final chapter, I noted my experience of attending a meeting of Catholic priests involved in the charismatic renewal and how I had hoped to be given the Spirit's charisms of teaching and prophecy.

She wrote:

> You have written something in the 10th chapter that I never would have associated with Michael Crosby, the presenter, that I have listened to so many times! The revelation that . . . in 1981, you were very impressed with the charismatic gifts of the Holy Spirit. I am

---

47. I am not blind to the fact that Paul himself did not seem to know how to translate his vision of a nonseparatist, new creation way of being "church." This will be evident in the rest of the book.

48. For a good discussion of this, see the interview of Vinnie Rotondaro with Vince Miller, the Gudorf Chair in Catholic Theology and Culture at the University of Dayton, "Rise of Culture Wars Has Meant Ignoring the Common Good," blog, *National Catholic Reporter*, August 9, 2014, http://ncronline.org.

49. Based on data used at an annual meeting of the Catholic Theological Society of America (2008), I discuss these two main stances among many Catholics in *Repair My House*, 32-50.

curious to find out where you are with this now, in 1998? I also dread finding out where you are at with this now because this is something that I have been rejecting since about 1981. Please forgive me; I have never associated the Charismatic gifts of the Spirit with the level you are at, as a scholar and theologian. What worries me is that you were quite an accomplished scholar and theologian when you wrote this book.

It seemed this woman believed that there is a disparity between being Spirit-based and being concerned about justice. However, I soon discovered that she represented only one way of thinking about the Holy Spirit. She may have been on "the left" in the Catholic Church, but many on "the right," concerned about preserving a more patriarchal and clerical "nomism," seem also to want little to do with the Holy Spirit if grounding in this Spirit might challenge their preconceived ideas (and ideology).

I had been asked to be a keynote speaker at the 1998 Sixth Annual San Antonio Catechetical Conference. Before arriving, I had been told by the conference coordinators that a small group was agitating to have me removed as a speaker because of what I had written in two recent books: *The Dysfunctional Church: Addiction and Codependency in the Family of Catholicism* and *Celibacy: Means of Control or Mandate of the Heart.*[50] They had created a website, had distributed flyers attacking me, and had been calling people to get them to boycott the convention. They also planned to picket the convention.

At the convention itself, I was escorted everywhere either by a staff member of the archdiocese or the San Antonio police force. The auditorium had police guarding every entrance. In addition, I was told, a plainclothes policeman sat in the audience near some of the protestors.

Having experienced these two examples of the ongoing polarization in the Catholic Church, I realized that the underlying issue that divided the Galatian church still tears us apart. While having different expressions, they still mirror the underlying debate: ultimately will we as a church be defined by the law or the Spirit, as Paul understood the two terms? Too often, it seems to me, many of us approach our differences so wedded to our ideological stances (that mirror our political positions and ideologies of "left" and "right") that we "do not know God" (4:8ff.). We are bereft of the breath of life that can only come from the Spirit. Without this Spirit in our hearts we become enslaved to our "laws" on the left and the right that

---

50. For a revised edition of this book, see my *Rethinking Celibacy: Reclaiming the Church* (Eugene, OR: Wipf & Stock, 2003).

keep us divided in the household of God, rather than being grounded in the Spirit as sons and daughters of God and, thus, members of one family (4:6-7).

If we are not grounded in the Holy Spirit as the source of our life and ministry in the church, we will not only sow sparingly; we will reap even less (6:7-10). Consequently, being on the right or the left, identifying as Culture I or Culture II Catholics, we will miss the opportunity to apply to our contemporary times the conclusion of Paul that "neither circumcision nor uncircumcision matters." All that matters is that we allow the Spirit in us all to find a way to be a new creation (6:15).

If we remain polarized in our "gospels" of the works we must do that will define us as loyal Catholics we will be little better than the Teachers. Our "gospel(s)" will be just that: *our* gospels. It will not be the gospel taught by Paul that declares even more clearly: "For in Christ Jesus the only thing that counts is faith working through love" (5:6). Consequently, as I develop my ideas in this book it is critical to realize that everything will be viewed from one lens: the gospel of the reign of God as Paul experienced it on his way to Damascus. This is wonderfully summarized by Beverly Roberts Gaventa:

> Paul presupposes from beginning to end that there is only one gospel (1.6-9), the singularity of which consists of the revelation of Jesus Christ as God's son whose crucifixion inaugurates the new age. This singular gospel results in a singular transformation for those called as believers, who are themselves moved into a new identity in Christ alone (2.19-21; 3.26-29) and new life in the Spirit (3.1-4; 5.16-25).[51]

Conclusion

Between 1978 and 2013, many Catholics chafed under the dynamic created by the way many interpreted the teachings of popes John Paul II and Benedict XVI. Since the latter's resignation, which began a kind of demystification of the papacy and the cult that had been propagated to promote it, we now have another kind of chafing being experienced by many, including some seminarians and younger priests. They are having a difficult time accepting the "faith working through love" approach of Pope Francis, one

---

51. Beverly Roberts Gaventa, "The Singularity of the Gospel: A Reading of Galatians," in Jouette M. Bassler, ed., *Pauline Theology* I (Minneapolis: Fortress Press, 1991), 149. I am indebted to Sandra Hack Polaski for this lead (90).

that invites those in authority to model for the whole church a community whose leaders do not dominate for their own interests and careers but serve for the good of the whole .

As this polarization continues (with an even larger group in the middle who just don't seem to care about the issues of the right or the left), I have become convinced that we need to re-examine the "gospel" that Paul was preaching to the Galatian churches. We all need to cultivate the fruit of the Holy Spirit more than ever. This is especially true when we realize how easily both poles in our church have been buttressed with ideologies of righteousness that, I have discovered, can easily represent subtle and not-so-subtle forms of violence.

For many years I have given retreats and workshops on the all-pervasiveness of violence in society and religion, especially in the three main patriarchal and clerically controlled religions: Islam, Roman Catholicism, and Mormonism.[52] As we continue to hear some promote our faith more canonically than Christically, and promote separation that reflects the "old order" of male/female, cleric/lay, cultically clean and unclean, we need to return to Galatians and Paul's stress on the gospel before it is too late.

In a church that has some promoting a priesthood and episcopacy based on the notion of acting *in persona Christi,* which justifies separatism, we need the Spirit to remind us that the "personal Christ" resides ontologically in every baptized person. In a similar way, when many clergy consider themselves to possess a holiness that sets them apart from the laity, we need to challenge such "episcopal nomism" by reminding them not only that one of the familiar greetings of Paul in most of his letters to the members of the early churches was to greet them as the *hagioi,* the "holy ones," and that the Second Vatican Council grounded all vocations in the church in the "universal call to holiness."

This is the "gospel" that Paul spent his life "in Christ" proclaiming. This makes us want to be reminded of Paul's challenge to every member of the churches of Galatia who were not addressed according to any hierarchical rank or status like our papal and episcopal leaders today, but simply as *adelphoi*: brothers and sisters who are God's children: "But now that faith has come, we are no longer subject to a disciplinarian, for in Christ Jesus you are all children of God through faith. As many of you as were baptized into Christ have clothed yourselves with Christ. There is no longer Jew or Greek, there is no longer slave or free, there is no longer male and female; for all of you are one in Christ Jesus" (3:25-28). "This deceptively simple

---

52. For more on these patriarchal religions, see my *Repair My House,* 10-12.

listing is not haphazard," Jerome Murphy-O'Connor writes, "It covers the whole of the then known world from religious, economic, geographical, and sociological points of view."[53] In other words, the wording envisions a totally new social order that overcomes all violence in the structured divisions within the human community.

Given all the violence in, among, and around us, even in our church,[54] I find a greater need than ever to return to the gospel of the Spirit proclaimed by Paul. Hopefully it will find us becoming free of the enslaving ideologies that have overshadowed our baptismal commitment. Only the Spirit can free us from the violence that threatens to destroy us as a church, as a people, and as part of this planet. Toward that end, I have found much hope in an article written years ago by the late Edward Schillebeeckx. He stated,

> Only in the Christian confession of the Holy Spirit (pneumatology) does Christology come to its universal openness for all human beings without any discriminating undervaluing of all other religions. In the power of this gift of the Spirit, which is not bound to "the church of Christ"—although, thanks to precisely this Spirit, the highly necessary memory of the man Jesus is kept alive in word and celebration—men and women can also forgive each other and encounter "the other" in his or her otherness and affirm that other. The actual historical violence of Christianity and its Christology has its deepest roots in our communal forgetfulness of pneumatology. In it the redemption of Jesus becomes a historical and universal offer without any discrimination or violence.
>
> Only pneumatology can prevent Christology, too, from being violent. Without pneumatology Christology is false in a way that threatens human beings and is unorthodox.
>
> The actual historical violence of Christianity and its Christology is most deeply rooted in our constant forgetfulness of pneumatology: the Logos of the pneuma blows where it wills.[55]

---

53. Jerome Murphy-O'Connor, *Becoming Human Together,* 127. He writes that this passage (3:26-29) is the "most succinct expression of Paul's understanding of the nature of the Christian community" (174).

54. For a discussion of violence within the Catholic Church, using the U.S. Catholic Bishops' statement on domestic violence, see my *Repair My House,* 10. For an expanded articulation of this vis-à-vis the Roman Curia's (ab)use of its authority in forms of a command-control use of power, see Camilo Macisse, "Violence in the Church," *The Tablet,* November 22, 2002, 8-9.

55. Edward Schillebeeckx, "Religion and Violence," documentation in Wim Beuken

I now want to share the main thesis of this book: to show how cultivating the "fruit(s) of the Holy Spirit" can transform our lives into "the Christ." The five main points that will ground this book and particularly my discussion of these "fruits" are quite simple:

1. The dynamics of covenantal nomism promoted by the Teachers that undermined Paul's "gospel" proclaimed to the church(es) at Galatia has its contemporary parallel in the canonical nomism of many leaders in the institutional structure of the Catholic Church, where its male clergy is *de jure* and, too often, *de facto* separated from the laity and all women.

2. This patriarchal and clerical form of Roman Catholicism (canonical nomism) has had a significant influence in the massive hemorrhaging of baptized Catholics from participating in its organizational life. This historically derived form of monarchical church has too often eclipsed the "gospel" proclaimed by Paul. The "church" of canonical nomism would be impossible for him to imagine, just as in the same way he rejected the negative forms of "covenantal nomism."

3. Pope Francis's vision of a church that is not inner directed and self-referential (i.e., around the episcopacy and papacy) but grounded in Christ in his concern for those at the periphery is precisely the kind of church without boundaries envisioned by Paul, based on his Damascus experience. This reflects Paul's concern that the church(es) at Galatia give evidence to the world of the "fruit(s) of the (Holy) Spirit."

4. The future of the Catholic Church rests in the realization by the laity and clerics that they need to develop a mystical awareness of their baptism in Christ so as to bring about, as brothers and sisters, a new order for creation.

5. In a world where the Christian of the future will be (to quote Karl Rahner) a mystic or nothing at all, the future of Catholicism rests on the development by all members of the church of the "fruit(s) of the Spirit" in a way that will witness to a mystical/contemplative stance toward all reality.

It is my hope that those many people who are searching for a deeper experience (and expression) of the Spirit in their lives and *spirit*uality, who are tired of the works of the flesh, which represent polarization in our various religious bodies, including our Catholic Church, will find hope in this

---

and Karl-Josef Kuschel, eds., *Religion as a Source of Violence* (Concilium; London: SCM Press; Maryknoll, NY: Orbis Books, 1997), 142.

book. This hope, however, cannot be sustained without struggle. In this I am comforted with the admonition of Paul found in the last chapter of his Letter to the Galatians. I offer it as a prayer for those, especially those in the family of Catholicism, who will read this book.

> Do not be deceived; God is not mocked, for you reap whatever you sow. If you sow to your own flesh, you will reap corruption from the flesh; but if you sow to the Spirit, you will reap eternal life from the Spirit. So let us not grow weary in doing what is right, for we will reap at harvest time, if we do not give up. So then, whenever we have an opportunity, let us work for the good of all, and especially for those of the family of faith. (6:7-10)

Chapter 1

The World of the Galatian Churches and Our World Today

When I studied Paul's letters in our Capuchin-Franciscan Seminary in Wisconsin in the 1960s, I don't recall learning that only seven of them, including Galatians, were actually written by Paul.[1] Moreover, in the 1980s, in a course on Paul's letters at the Graduate Theological Union in Berkeley, I learned that most scholars now (in contrast to my 1960s impression) are proposing a much earlier date for the letter itself, possibly the late 40s or early 50s CE.[2] An even more interesting question than the date involves the origin and later identity of "the churches of Galatia" (1:2).

---

1. As noted in the Introduction, these are (in chronological order [rather than size]), 1 Thessalonians, Galatians, Philippians, 1 and 2 Corinthians, and Romans, with Philemon's dating unclear. They were written shortly before and during the 50s (the first Gospel, Mark, was not written until the early 70s). The "pastoral" letters (1 and 2 Timothy and Titus) were written long after Paul died, probably around 100. The letters whose authorship is disputed (with the majority of scholars saying they were not written by Paul) are Ephesians, Colossians, and 2 Thessalonians. Even these letters may not have been the original letters of Paul; instead the seven letters we have now may have resulted from various redactions over the decades and even the early centuries. For recent discussions regarding the development of Paul's letter collection, see Richard I. Pervo, *The Making of Paul: Constructions of the Apostle in Earliest Christianity* (Minneapolis: Fortress Press, 2010), 23-61; Stanley E. Porter, "When and How Was the Pauline Canon Compiled?," in Stanley E. Porter, ed., *The Pauline Canon* (Leiden and Boston: Brill, 2004), 95-128; Beverly Roberts Gaventa, "The Singularity of the Gospel: A Reading of Galatians," in Jouette M. Bassler, ed., *Pauline Theology* I (Minneapolis: Fortress Press, 1991), 147-59; David Trobisch, *Paul's Letter Collection* (Bolivar, MO: Quiet Waters Publications, 2001); Jerome Murphy-O'Connor, *Paul the Letter-Writer: His World, His Options, His Skills* (Collegeville, MN: Liturgical Press, 1995). I thank Lisa Marie Belz, OSU, for giving me some of these sources (http://ecommons.luc.edu, p. 80).

2. James D. G. Dunn, *The Epistle to the Galatians* (Peabody, MA: Hendrickson, 1993); J. Louis Martyn, *Galatians: A New Translation with Introduction and Commentary* (Anchor Bible; New York: Doubleday, 1998), 20 n. 20; Ronald Y. D. Fung considers Galatians the

In the middle of the third century BCE, European Celts—the Gauls of Roman times and the forerunners of Bretons, Welsh, Irish, and highland Scots—had migrated as far east as what is now central Turkey. Around 31 BCE, Rome annexed that territory into its province of Galatia.[3] The addressees of Paul's letter, whom Paul called *Galatai* (3:1; see 1:2) and whom others called *Keltoi* or *Keltai* (i.e., Celts), lived in the southern part of the province.[4]

The occasion for writing to the Galatians was a serious conflict regarding their faith, which stood at odds with the gospel that Paul had preached to them. The roots of Paul's gospel and how he understood it as a revelation from God lay in what is known as his "Damascus experience" (which will be the topic of the third chapter). But before examining the nature of the disagreement with the Galatians, we need to see the Letter to the Galatians in the context of Paul's own previous history.

First, a familiar story. Around 30 CE, in a remote province of Rome called Judea, a layman called Jesus was crucified for proclaiming and practicing what he called the "gospel of the 'kingdom of God/heaven.'" This involved a new kind of kinship-community of brothers and sisters under his "Father in heaven" (Matt. 12:46-50) rather than the gospel of the "Father of the Fatherland," Caesar and his imperial system. Jesus's gospel attracted many followers (disciples), so much so that it became a threat to key religious leaders. They were convinced that, should he continue, their authority and way of life might be undermined if not destroyed. So they colluded with representatives of Rome to have him killed as a threat to the imperial rule and its gospel of *Pax Romana*.[5]

---

first of Paul's extant letters, arguing that it may have been written as early as 48 CE, before the Jerusalem Council recorded in Acts 14. See his *The Epistle to the Galatians* (Grand Rapids: Eerdmans, 1988).

3. John Noble Wilford, "Archaeologists Find Celts in Unlikely Spot: Central Turkey," *New York Times*, December 26, 2001.

4. For more on this, see Martyn, *Galatians*, 15-16. There are different positions on the audience and time of writing of Paul's Letter to the Galatians. If it was written to people living in Northern Galatia, the hypothesis is that it was written later. It seems to me a better argument is made that it was written to people living in Southern Galatia; hence the earlier dating (49-51). Martinus C. de Boer, in *Galatians: A Commentary* (Louisville: Westminster John Knox Press, 2011), notes that Galatians could have been "the earliest known letter of Paul" (10), written in 51 CE (11).

5. I do not see much in the actual text of Galatians to suggest Paul's main opponent involved the "imperial gospel" of Caesar; his preoccupation was "the gospel" of the Teachers. My position is different from some significant exegetes such as N. T. Wright, "Gospel and Theology in Galatians" (1994), in *Pauline Perspectives: Essays on Paul, 1978–2013* (Minneapolis: Fortress Press, 2013), 79-92; and Marcus J. Borg and John Dominic Crossan, *The First Paul: Reclaiming the Radical Visionary behind the Church's Conservative Icon*

However, despite his state-sponsored torture and execution, within three days many of those disciples who had followed him now experienced this Jesus as alive: with and in them. This "good news" produced an immediate reaction: "the number of disciples kept growing" (Acts 6:1a). Such expansion of the community necessitated the creation of the diaconate to serve the Greek-speaking widows. The apostles were still so wedded to their own Jewish religious practices, connected to a biased form of "covenantal nomism," that the Greek-speaking widows were experiencing discrimination: they "were being neglected in the daily distribution of funds" (Acts 6:1b). To remedy the problem, seven men in the community were chosen to ensure a more even distribution of the necessary resources. One of these chosen to serve was Stephen.

Not long after, Stephen was brought before religious leaders , including the High Priest, on trumped-up charges. There he gave an extended, impassioned apologia for his belief in Jesus, who had been crucified by them (Acts 7:2-53). This assault on their honor led to his stoning and death, which took place in the presence of a supportive onlooker: Saul of Tarsus (Acts 7:57-60). "And Saul approved of his murder" (Acts 8:10a). The year was about 33 CE.

That same day the church in Jerusalem began to suffer violent persecution. One of the persecutors was Saul. He "tried to destroy the church; going from house to house, dragging out those who believed (in the good news of Jesus's death and resurrection) and throwing them in jail" (Acts 8:3). Nonetheless the preaching continued and the converts increased. "In the meantime Saul kept up his violent threats of murder against the followers" of Jesus (Acts 9:1a) and, in an effort to weed out those of "the Way" in the synagogues of Damascus, got permission to find them, arrest them, and return them to Jerusalem. On the way there he had an overwhelming, mystical experience (which will be discussed in the next chapter).

After this experience, often called his "conversion" (a term that is also subject to controversy!),[6] the newly baptized Paul went to Arabia (1:17) for

---

(New York: HarperOne, 2009), 93-121. For a critique of Paul as someone concerned about offering an alternative to an "imperial gospel," see Colin Miller, "The Imperial Cult in the Pauline Cities of Asia Minor and Greece," *Catholic Biblical Quarterly* 72 (2010): 314-32.

6. While questioning whether Paul's Damascus experience could be called his "conversion," James D. G. Dunn, nonetheless, uses the term through his *The New Perspective on Paul* (rev. ed.; Grand Rapids: Eerdmans, 2008). The debate, in the main, refers to the *kind* of conversion Saul experienced. The consensus is that this conversion was not from Judaism to Christianity but involved the realization that being "in Christ" involved the fulfillment of the messianic promises made to Abraham and prophets such as Jeremiah and Isaiah. Paul never formally converted *from* Judaism. For a fuller treatment of the debate,

a couple of years. But soon the word was spreading in Judea that "the one who formerly was persecuting us is now proclaiming the faith he once tried to destroy" (1:18). Three years after this (around 40 BCE), while moving between Damascus and Cilicia, the former persecutor-turned-evangelizer of "the Way" spent a fortnight in Jerusalem with Peter/Cephas (1:18).[7]

How Paul spent the next ten years after Damascus is not fully known. It seems he spent three to four years in Tarsus and Damascus (1:17-18). There he found a patron and coworker in Barnabas, who was based in Antioch and took him there for a year (44–45). Between 46 and 49 CE he embarked on his first missionary journey, which included two to three years evangelizing in the area of Galatia (48–49). Here he "first announced the gospel" (4:13); meanwhile the converts there took care of some kind of "physical infirmity" that he had suffered.

There were few Jews in Paul's Galatian churches.[8] Hence, the cultural world of the Galatians did not require Paul to spend much if any time explaining why Jesus was delivered over to the Romans by key Jewish religious leaders (his challenge to their interpretive power regarding the observance of "the works of the law" or what E. P. Sanders understood to be a violation of the correct understanding of covenantal nomism). As we have seen, covenantal nomism had not only come to describe the norms, the ritual practices, and the lifestyle of the Jews of Paul's time that they had inherited as children of Abraham and practiced in fidelity to Moses; even more so, it also had been interpreted negatively through separatist "codes of belonging" that identified one as a Jew, especially through circumcision.

Never having heard the story that the Jews considered themselves God's specially chosen children, forever set apart because of their divine calling, the Galatians eagerly embraced the gospel Paul proclaimed to them: that in Christ, they too were children of God because the Spirit of God's Son, Jesus Christ, had shared with them God's very life. This life-sharing expressed in their baptism and a life of faith was marked by love. Hearing such "good news," the Galatians welcomed Paul "as an angel of God, as Christ Jesus"

---

see Larry W. Hurtado, "Convert, Apostate or Apostle to the Nations: The 'Conversion' of Paul in Recent Scholarship," *Studies in Religion* 22.3 (1993): 280-81.

7. The chronology of Paul after the Damascus experience is based on differing statements in Acts and other Pauline texts. I am using the chronology of Joseph A. Fitzmyer, S.J., "A Life of Paul," in Raymond E. Brown, S.S., Joseph A. Fitzmyer, S.J., and Roland E. Murphy, O.Carm., *The Jerome Biblical Commentary* (Englewood Cliffs, NJ: Prentice-Hall, 1968), 215-22.

8. Martyn, *Galatians*, 16.

with good will and grace (4:14-15). Grounded in this gospel, they began to "run well" the life of discipleship (5:7). When Paul decided he could now preach the gospel elsewhere, he left Galatia assured that his message was in good hands, with good teachers in place (6:6). In due time he returned to Antioch.

The year 49 CE was a momentous year for Paul and the entire church. He had not been in Antioch long before he and Barnabas became involved in a dispute with some who were teaching that circumcision was necessary for salvation. This led the Antiochan church to send Paul and Barnabas to Jerusalem for official guidance at what became known as the Council of Jerusalem. Although "the false brothers" (1:4) insisted on circumcision, Peter finally settled the matter by declaring against obligatory circumcision for the gentile converts and any need for them to adhere to the Mosaic law except for its codes of basic morality. Paul's honor was thus vindicated, even though Peter and the other "men of repute" had said nothing about what he had already been teaching (2:6). Paul returned to Antioch. Sometime late in 49 CE, Peter visited Antioch. At first both Peter and Paul ate with Gentiles. But then "some people from James" (2:12) came and criticized Peter for eating with the gentile converts. For whatever reason(s) Peter deferred to their insistence and, in this, was joined by Barnabas: they separated themselves from table fellowship with gentile converts. At this, according to Paul,

> I opposed [Cephas] to his face, because he stood self-condemned; for until certain people came from James, he used to eat with the Gentiles. But after they came, he drew back and kept himself separate for fear of the circumcision faction. And the other Jews joined him in this hypocrisy, so that even Barnabas was led astray by their hypocrisy. But when I saw that they were not acting consistently with the truth of the gospel, I said to Cephas before them all, "If you, though a Jew (*Ioudaios*), live like a Gentile and not like a Jew (*Ioudaioi*), how can you compel the Gentiles to live like Jews (*Ioudaizein*)?" (2:11-14)

In that first-century culture, challenges to authority such as Paul's public rebuke of "Cephas" were not taken lightly. Honor was highly valued throughout the Mediterranean world. It involved one's personal or communally recognized claim to respect for one's position (including the power of influence and interpretation). Any challenge to one's honor and authority demanded some kind of corollary response to preserve one's standing. Since in Galatians Paul is telling the story, we do not know how or if Peter responded to preserve his own honor. Nonetheless, as Philip Esler notes, these dynamics continued to be played out in subsequent tensions. He also notes, however, that, for Paul, it was not only a matter of his honor that was at stake: it was his very understanding of what he meant above by "the truth of the gospel" he had received in his Damascus experience. He writes, "For Paul, in fact, the 'truth of the gospel' (2.5, 14) . . . means the freedom with which his Israelite and gentile converts can be members of the same congregation without having their 'freedom' replaced with the demands of the Mosaic law."[9]

In one of these exchanges regarding the (non)application of the Mosaic law, Barnabas sided with "the circumcision faction" (2:12-13), and his position led to a rupture not only between himself and Paul; it also resulted in Paul's alienation and separation from the church in Antioch In time, it seems, the issue also contributed to a possible break between Paul and the Jerusalem church itself.[10]

Between 49 and 52 CE, Paul left Antioch on his second missionary journey. Early on (Gal. 1:6) he heard that some unnamed Teachers[11] had come to the church(es) of Galatia and sown seeds of dissent from his gospel. These anonymous Teachers preached "a different gospel" (1:6): the newly

---

9. Philip F. Esler, *Galatians* (London: Routledge, 1998), 119.

10. Philip F. Esler, "Making and Breaking an Agreement Mediterranean Style: A New Reading of Galatians 2:1-14," *Biblical Interpretation* 3 (1995): 285-315. Esler seems to have been one of the first to set Galatians in the context of an honor/shame culture. Subsequent to him are the various contributions of Jerome Neyrey, Bruce Malina, and John Pilch.

11. As noted in the Introduction, no name is given to this group who taught "another gospel." Some refer to these outsiders as "Judaizers," such as J. Christiaan Beker, *The Triumph of God: The Essence of Paul's Thought* (trans. Loren T. Stuckenbruck; Minneapolis: Fortress Press, 1990), particularly because of Gal. 2:14. See Wayne A. Meeks, *The First Urban Christians: The Social World of the Apostle Paul* (New Haven and London: Yale University Press, 1983), 166. Frank J. Matera tends to call them "agitators" in *Galatians* (Collegeville, MN: Liturgical Press, 1992, 2007), 7ff. Others call them "enemies of Paul." Dunn calls them "missionaries." As noted earlier, I will follow the term used by Martyn, "Teachers" (18ff.). Mark D. Nanos calls them "the influencers" in *The Irony of Galatians: Paul's Letter in First-Century Context* (Minneapolis: Fortress Press, 2002). Uniting Martyn and Nanos, Robert J. Karris calls them the "Teachers/influencers," in *Galatians and Romans* (Collegeville, MN: Liturgical Press, 2005). Until recently it has been assumed that the Teachers were trying to influence the converts in Galatia to return to observance of key elements, if not all, of the Jewish law. This has been challenged by those who believe the Teachers were trying to keep the Galatians from submitting to Roman law and, thus, to be willing to be persecuted. See Alexander V. Prokhorov, "Taking the Jews out of the Equation: Galatians 6:12-17 as a Summons to Cease Evading Persecution," *Journal for the Study of the New Testament* 36.2 (2013): 172-88.

baptized must abide by practices of the "law" in their personal and communal lives, especially circumcision and various dietary practices. In Paul's mind this totally undermined the gospel he had preached: the equality of all the baptized—women and men—and the way of communal life that, together, they were called to practice. In short, their gospel, Tatha Wiley writes, "threatened the redemptive equality symbolized by baptism and made real by its performance."[12]

Having been eager to accept Paul's original gospel, many in the Galatian church(es) embraced almost as eagerly this "other gospel." For Paul their gospel demanding circumcision totally upended his own gospel. Circumcision was not just a boundary marker that gave them some kind of identity; by virtue of Jesus's crucifixion and resurrection, that old identity marked a point in the evolutionary process that was dead; it no longer gave meaning to life itself.

In an extended commentary, James D. G. Dunn summarizes brilliantly Paul's belief "why circumcision was such a retrograde step for the Galatians to take." He writes:

> [It] was not merely the step of affiliation to another group, not merely the step from one ethnic identity to another; it was also a step back into another age, another world, one in which other powers were dominant and whose authority and influence had already been superseded by Christ on the cross (4:8-10).

This is the sharpness and starkness of Paul's alternative antithesis—not just Christ and cross versus circumcision but new age versus the old age still dominated by evil, new creation versus old creation, where pride in ethnic identity cloaked a more fundamental dependence on power other than God. And this is the more fundamental theological reason why Paul so vehemently resisted the other missionaries in their attempts to have the Galatians circumcised. The issue was not just Christ and the cross, not just the reality of the Galatians' own experience of grace, Spirit, and faith, but God's own identity and mission, including his purpose for humanity as a whole.[13]

Why and how did the Galatians allow this gospel of the Teachers to seduce them?

---

12. Tatha Wiley, *Paul and the Gentile Women: Reframing Galatians* (New York/London: Continuum, 2005), 15.

13. Dunn, *New Perspective on Paul*, 329.

We saw in the Introduction that while covenantal nomism represented a way of fidelity to the law of love enshrined in the covenant, some Jews in the first century appealed to the Mosaic law (nomism) as demanding separation from other nations (2:12) in order for its adherents to become justified or righteous (2:16). Thus, Dunn raised the likelihood that such works of the law had a deeper social function (3:10), namely, being "boundary markers" separating Israel from its neighbors.[14] Consequently, this notion "played a leading role in the operation of the boundary which preserved their distinctive identity in relation to the gentiles among whom they lived."[15] This separatist gospel now stood in opposition to the law of the gospel of Christ proclaimed by Paul. Contesting understandings of the "law" (Mosaic or Christocentric) became "a critical arena in which Paul struggled to establish a positive social identity for his congregations in the context of conflict with the Israelite outgroup who were naturally determined to maintain the integrity of their ethnic boundaries."[16]

The gospel that Paul preached was based on the law of love. A "love gospel" could be somewhat nebulous in comparison with defined codes of conduct that established clear boundaries between participants and non-participants; those who belonged to the group and outsiders. A possibility such as this might have caused the Galatians to be seduced by this "other gospel" of the Teachers can be found in the "grid/group" model of Mary Douglas, the British cultural anthropologist.[17]

For Douglas, "group" addresses the dynamics of members of a group vis-à-vis authority. Generally a group is "strong" or "weak" depending on the power of the collective whole ("strong group") or the dominance of the individuals within the group ("weak group"). The term "grid" refers to the structuring of internal dynamics and relationships within a group around

---

14. Ibid., 8.

15. Esler, *Galatians*, 178.

16. Ibid.

17. There are various constructs some exegetes use to suggest a "social identity" for the Galatian churches. Philip Esler uses that of the social psychologist Henri Tajifel (Esler, *Galatians*, 40ff.). Two others using Tajifel and Esler are Atsuhiro Asano, *Community-Identity Construction in Galatians* (London: T & T Clark International, 2005; and Bernard O. Ukwuegbu, "Paraenesis, Identity-defining Norms, or Both? Galatians 5:13–6:10 in the Light of Social Identity Theory," *Catholic Biblical Quarterly* 70 (2008): 538-59. In their study of Galatians, Bruce J. Malina and John J. Pilch show their indebtedness to Esler: *Social-Science Commentary on the Letters of Paul* (Minneapolis: Fortress Press, 2006), 179. My use of Mary Douglas has been influenced by Bruce J. Malina, *The New Testament World: Insights from Cultural Anthropology* (rev. ed.; Louisville: Westminster/John Knox Press 1993).

the practice of defined laws, customs, and rituals. In a "high grid" society, following the law leads to greater societal integration; a "low grid" community does not have clearly specified patterns of behavior.[18] The interplay between outgroups and the ingroup (strong group/weak group) and interpersonal relationships within the group (high grid/low grid) determined the social identity of a people.

While both Paul and the false teachers were promoting a "strong group" that separated its members from the gentiles, who followed the way of Caesar, Paul's insistence on "faith working through love" seemed to be promoting a "strong group/low grid" model of life that was much less clear than the strict "law and order" approach toward house churches being promoted by the unnamed Teachers. Such covenantal nomism could have appealed to those in Galatia who were seeking stronger anchors in their group interactions.[19] Dunn explains:

> That the law served to *identify* the Jewish people as the people chosen by the one God for himself, and as a *boundary* to mark them off from all (other) nations, would have been a basic assumption of Jewish self-understanding. From such a sociological perspective, it also becomes self-evident that Jews (including Jewish Christians) would be particularly sensitive at the points where the boundary seemed to be threatened and consequently their own identity challenged. It is no surprise then that in Galatians 2 it is precisely in circumcision and food laws, two of the most significant boundary markers, that the larger controversy comes to focus.[20]

---

18. Adapted from Malina, *The New Testament World*, 128-29 (original edition).

19. For a more detailed investigation of social identity theory as it applies to Paul's Letter to the Galatians, see Bernard O. Ukwuegbu, *The Emergence of Christian Identity in Paul's Letter to the Galatians: A Social-Scientific Investigation into the Root Causes for the Parting of the Way between Christianity and Judaism* (Bonn: Borengässer, 2003), 76-89. For an application of the theory to Galatians, see his "Paraenesis, Identity-defining Norms, or Both?," 538-59. For other approaches using the "social identity" theory for Galatians, see Asano, *Community-Identity Construction*, and Bruce Hansen, *"All of You Are One": The Social Vision of Galatians 3.28, 1 Corinthians 12.13 and Colossians 3.11* (London/New York: T. & T. Clark, 2010).

20. Dunn, *New Perspective on Paul*, 139. Wayne A. Meeks uses basically the same rationale as to why the Teachers would be promoting the law: because it offered clear patterns for the community. "Would the abolition of the symbolic boundaries between Jew and Gentile *within* the Christian groups mean also lowering the boundaries between the Christian sect and the world?" See his *The First Urban Christians: The Social World of the Apostle Paul* (New Haven and London: Yale University Press, 1983), 97.

Being neither a psychologist nor a sociologist but a passionate evangelizer (who also wanted to preserve his honor), Paul was crystal clear: the
Galatians (he did not distinguish between those who had been seduced
and those who remained faithful) had begun their new lives in the Spirit;
now they had become seduced by the flesh; they had turned from Paul's
teaching (3:3). This challenged not only Paul's gospel but his previous labor
among them (see 4:12-15) and, ultimately, his integrity and honor.[21] He
had to respond. Unable to return in person (4:20), Paul wrote a letter that
became an impassioned appeal "to the churches of Galatia" (1:2).

Given our brief review of some key dynamics of an honor/shame culture,
it is no surprise that Paul's Letter to the Galatians begins not with a greeting but with a resounding assertion, in defense of his honor, of his divinely
ordained credentials. He has been "sent, neither by human commission nor
from human authorities, but through Jesus Christ and God the Father, who
raised him from the dead." Besides himself he names "all the members of
God's family who are with me" (1:1-2), in apparent recognition that there
are those who are against him. Among those against him are not only the
unnamed Teachers from elsewhere; they are Galatians who have been duped
by the Teachers and have exchanged the honor of being free "in Christ" for
enslavement again "under the law." As a further insult to their dignity, Paul
later will call them "foolish," not once but twice (3:1, 3). Adding to this
insult, Paul does not even recognize his audience as worthy of his gratitude.
Unlike all his other letters (1 Thess. 1:2; Phil. 1:3; 1 Cor. 1:3; 2 Cor. 1:3-11;
and Philemon 4), only this one contains no greeting with words of "thanksgiving" for his audience.[22] While such language seems to have shown deep
anger, Robert J. Karris argues, on the contrary, that "he adapted the rebuke
statement that was also common in letter writing after the greeting."[23]

Without trying to create a rhetorical outline of Paul's gospel,[24] the chart
and brief description in the few paragraphs below outline the basic themes
of the letter and highlight where Paul sets himself and his message apart
from those who have mislead the Galatian churches:

---

21. Esler, *Galatians*, 295-97.

22. For an alternative view of the rationale for the absence of a thanksgiving in Galatians, see Robert E. Van Voorst, "Why Is There No Thanksgiving Period in Galatians? An
Assessment of an Exegetical Commonplace," *Journal of Biblical Literature* 129.1 (2010):
153-72.

23. Karris, *Galatians and Romans*, 11.

24. It is also a matter of debate whether or not it is possible to structure Paul's Letter to
the Galatians. Among those who offer such, see https://epistletothegalatians.wordpress.
com/2011/03.

PAUL'S GOSPEL	THE OTHERS' GOSPEL
Preached by divine commission	Originated from questionable sources
The gospel of Jesus Christ	Stands opposed to the true gospel
Grounded in Paul's Damascus event	Grounded in the Mosaic law (*nomos*)
Inspired by the Holy Spirit	Under the rule of the *stoicheia*
Inviting justification through faith/baptism	Promising justification by law/practices
Brings about a new creation	Ensures the continuation of the old order
Results in the freedom of God's children, creates a new family under "Abba"	Adherents are condemned to the slavery of the law, which defines only one people of God
Fulfilled in love of all as neighbor	Limits "the neighbor" to Jews
Evidences the work of the Spirit	Evidences the law's inability to enliven
Life now defined by what the Spirit desires	Life continues under what the law requires
Expression of this: the fruit of the Spirit	Expression of this: the works of the flesh

Before so much as greeting the Galatians, Paul presents his credentials to establish his honor claims. Unlike those who have come to them as human emissaries with another gospel, the gospel Paul preached to them is of divine commissioning (1:11-12). Only after identifying the divine calling that legitimates him (1:1) does he acknowledge them in the short greeting "to the churches of Galatia" (1:2). Either because he knew not everyone had defected or because he wanted to use every form of persuasion, despite his anger, Paul calls the addressees *adelphoi* (brothers and sisters).

In the first-century Mediterranean world, the fact that Paul does not begin his greeting by giving honor to those in communal leadership indicates that, at least at this time in the Galatian church(es), there seems to have been no acknowledged hierarchical structures. That Paul would call the Galatians "brothers and sisters" shows that he does not define the community by a sociological construct but a theological one: because of the Spirit breathing in all, all are equal "in Christ." Moving into the heart of his argument, he wants the Galatians to know that his fidelity to the gospel of Christ has assured him of divine approval and honor, even if it may incur human rejection (see 1:10). His gospel proclaims the justifying promises of God fulfilled in Jesus Christ through faith; theirs keeps them locked in the structures of sin (2:16ff.). Paul's gospel was revealed to him en route to Damascus where a heavenly light surrounded him; their gospel was controlled by the hostile cosmic forces called the *stoicheia tou kosmou* (4:3, 9).[25] Justification would be assured for those who believed in his gospel and would be baptized; this made them a totally new creation; the false gospel of the Teachers consigned its adherents to the old practice of the law (2:15; 3:21-22) in a way that could not deliver divine justification. His gospel led to the blessing of life; theirs to the curse of death (2:19; 3:10ff.); his gospel brought its adherents the freedom of the children of God; theirs the continued yoke of slavery (5:1, 13). In the new creation free of distinctions there would be only one command: faith-working-in-love (5:6); they would continue to be defined by many laws unable to give true life.

It is important at this early juncture that we be clear about what scholars tell us today as to what "flesh" meant to Paul. Ultimately, it is not identified with anything sensate, sensual, or sexual, but that which separates. James D. G. Dunn notes that of all the various meanings of "flesh" in Paul's letters, especially in Galatians, the majority refer to that element of covenantal nomism that was linked to Jewish ethnic identity that separated itself from others (Rom. 2:28; 4:1; 9:3; 11:14; 1 Cor. 10:18; Gal. 3:3; 4:23, 29; 5:19, 24; 6:8, 12-13; Phil. 3:3-5).[26]

If they remained defined by the flesh and the control of the "law" they would be divided in their churches, doing the works of the flesh (5:17-21, 26); however, those who remained faithful would evidence faith-working-in-love through the "fruit of the Spirit" (5:22-23). In contrast to the way covenantal nomism linked to Jewish ethnocentrism meant being "in the flesh," so in Christ there is a totally transformed *ethnos*. Markus Cromhout writes that, in the Spirit rather than the flesh, "followers of Jesus are now embedded in an alternative ethnos, because Jesus himself, as the new Adam, transcends the traditional ethnic categories. This alternative *ethnos* is indeed most honourable, for it is to participate in the life of the Spirit, in the new divine (dis)order instituted by God."[27] The contrasting worldviews provided by Paul's gospel and that of his opponents could not be more stark.

---

25. Debates continue about the identity of the *stoicheia*. Paul's "world" was filled with spirits and powers of all sorts. The *stoicheia* were cosmic powers that held great power over the world; they were negative cosmic energy forces. See Clinton E. Arnold, "Returning to the Domain of the Powers: *Stoicheia* as Evil Spirits in Galatians 4:3, 9," *Novum Testamentica* 38.1 (1996): 55-76. They will be discussed in greater length in the next chapter.

26. Dunn, *New Perspective on Paul*, 129, 182, 321.

27. Markus Cromhout, "Resurrection in Paul as Both Affirmation and Challenge to the Israelite Cycle of Meaning," *Neotestamentica* 45.1 (2011): 44.

**Paul's Letter to the Galatians and
Its Applicability to Our Church Today**

It is important to realize that Paul never saw himself as separated from the Judaism that had been the environment that had nurtured him. This world of Paul, indeed the once-Pharisee Paul's whole worldview itself, was defined by what we call today Second Temple Judaism. The second great temple of the Jews was built in 515 BCE.; the Romans destroyed it after a Jewish uprising in 70 CE. "Second Temple Judaism" refers to the political and religious dynamics that engendered a way of thinking that impacted Jewish thought and practice during this period.[28]

Three key ideas undergirded the understanding, interpretation, and practice of the Torah. The first involved the belief that the Jewish nation (*ethnos*) not only was unique but was called by God to be separate from other *ethnoi* (or "gentiles") as God's *chosen* and *holy* people among all other nations. While the notion of group boundaries was as important then as now, among some groups this got interpreted in separatist ways. The second key element involved the notion of being in the final epoch of creation. This involved a belief that the end time (*eschaton*) was at hand. Consequently the people believed that there would be some kind of apocalyptic inbreaking of the final victory of God's power over the whole known world that would bring about a new cosmic order. This led to beliefs about God highly influenced by a conviction of God's final appearance that was called Second Temple Jewish *eschatology*. This eschatology was accompanied by a belief that the inauguration of this new age would be defined by an outpouring of the Spirit of God throughout the entire cosmos. The third key element involved the Jewish conviction that this new age would be *messianic*; this represented the age of the promised Messiah, or Christ. For Christians, this new age (new creation) was inaugurated by the death, resurrection, and embodiment of the historical Jesus in the members of the church(es) by baptism.

In many ways, as we move in our own lives from an overly Culture I Catholicism to reclaim a truly scriptural and mystical Culture II Catholicism (as defined earlier), one could argue that we too are in our own form of Second Temple eschatology. This is especially apropos if we take seriously what scientists are telling us about the end of this era: that we will face the

---

28. It is also important to note, as we know from the Dead Sea Scrolls, that, within Second Temple Judaism, there were different interpretations that were influenced by historical and geographic forms of (non)assimilation vis-à-vis the dominant cultures in which different groups of Jews resided.

effects of extreme climate change as the result of our own consumerism. Added to this is the increasing realization in Catholicism that a governance model of the church based on celibate clericalism has contributed much to the loss of our members[29] and the rise of the "Nones." Both of these factors invite a new understanding of the need for a new creation, centered on the cosmic Christ in the way we ground ourselves mystically with the realization that we are to be its very embodiment.

Whether we speak of the Second Temple Judaism of Paul's day or the need to "rebuild the house" of St. Francis's day or to use our imagination to bring about a new kind of way of being Catholic, the implications of all of this are wonderfully summarized by Bruce W. Longenecker:

> Paul sets his Galatian letter within an eschatological context, wherein the old world has been crucified to the believer and a new world established. The latter is a world of intimacy with God (4.4-7), in contrast to a divergent, opposing world that is dominated by evil (1.4), a world under the over-lordship of divine beings other than the true sovereign God (4.1-11).

Closely associated with the evocative concept of new creation is another important term that Paul uses frequently throughout his letters: "in Christ." The association of this term with new creation is evident from a comparison of Gal. 6:15 and 5:6:

> 6:15: For neither circumcision nor uncircumcision matters at all, but new creation.
>
> 5.6: For in Christ Jesus neither circumcision nor uncircumcision has significance.

In these two passages, Paul strikes the same eschatological tone by means of different terms. Whether Paul expresses himself by the term new creation or "in Christ," the end result is the same: circumcision has no function in defining the identity of God's eschatological people. The point to note is simply that "in Christ" and new creation are used by Paul virtually synonymously in these instances.[30]

Paul's theology was influenced by this eschatological understanding and, indeed, found its actualization in the outpouring of the Spirit of Jesus

---

29. For more on this see my *Repair My House*, esp. 1-77.

30. Bruce W. Longenecker, *The Triumph of Abraham's God: The Transformation of Identity in Galatians* (Nashville: Abingdon Press, 1998), 63.

Christ in the baptized. Thus it becomes clear that Paul never saw his theology (nor his practice of Judaism) as something that separated him from his roots. Given the eschatological lens that "undergirds the entire epistle,"[31] it might seem that Paul's whole theology (Christology, pneumatology, and ecclesiology) in Galatians has little relevance for today. On the contrary, we are moving into an entirely new epoch or "age" of the Catholic Church under the leadership of Pope Francis. A new creation is dawning.

While Pope Benedict XVI addressed the "crisis" of the church in the West, Pope Francis is speaking of a *kairos* moment for the whole church. This involves a movement away from the gospel of the Teachers of canonical nomism and the whole social and ideological apparatus that sustained it for decades (if not centuries) to a restoration of the "gospel of the kingdom of God" (or the "kindom of Trinitarian connectedness," which I have addressed elsewhere) and a new grounding in Paul's understanding of the gospel of the death, resurrection, and embodiment, in the Spirit, of the life-force of Jesus Christ in that social entity called "the church."

As we proceed to understand the relevance of Paul's Letter to the Galatians, especially how our times demand a new way of being "church," it seems that his insights are more relevant than ever. As I have already cautioned, however, we need to be careful against "reading into" the text of Paul our contemporary context. This will be critical when we consider the contextual meaning of such passages in Galatians and elsewhere that speak of the new creation revealing a reality wherein there is neither Jew nor Gentile, slave or free, female and male, (3:28).

In his analysis of the various ways Gal. 3:28 has been discussed, the African exegete G.N. Uzukwu has noted that the issues at stake are the ethnic, sexual/gender, and socio-economic implications not only for the audience of Paul's day in the context of the Roman Empire but for all generations.[32] Bernard Lategan expanded on Uzukwu's insight in *Neotestamentica*, the journal of the New Testament Society of South Africa. "It is a well-known interpretative strategy to internalize or 'spiritualize' theological principles in order to avoid their social impact," he noted, pointing to the way segregated churches have stressed a "spiritual" unity in a way that left their

---

31. Rodrigo I. Morales, *The Spirit and the Restoration of Israel: New Exodus and New Creation Motifs in Galatians* (Tübingen: Mohr Siebeck, 2010), 150.

32. G. N. Uzukwu, "The Unity of Male and Female in Christ: An Exegetical Study of Gal. 3:28c in Light of Paul's Theology of Promise" (Ph.D. diss., Leuven: Katholieke Universiteit Leuven, 2011). I was unable to get this source but was led to it by Bernard C. Lategan. See below.

"discrimination untouched." In the same way, he points to something that can easily be found among some in the Roman Catholic Church today who approach sexual and gender differences with notions of "complementarity" in ways that avoid addressing the underlying separation (through canonical nomism, I would add) between the sexes: "Likewise the pious assertion that 'in the eyes of God' men and women are equal leaves the door open to continue discriminatory practices."[33]

Paul did not seem to have been able to consciously critique the received cultural dynamics in his world that vitiated against such inclusivity. This challenge remains the task of our era. In working to bring about this new creation, are we not being faithful to Paul when we try to end social arrangements in our church and society that reinforce (often ideologically) patriarchy and other forms of sexism as well as clericalism and other kinds of power-imbalance? It helps to distinguish between what Sandra Schneiders calls "the world behind the text" (the subject matter and history that led to the composition of the text we have today), "the world of the text" (the testimony of all those whose testimony resulted in the text as we have it today), and "the world before the text," namely, the world in which we who believe in the credibility and authenticity of the text before us must hear its message for ourselves and our times.[34]

In a special way, Schneiders speaks of "ideology criticism," which not only seeks to understand "the world behind the text" and "the world of the text," but, she writes, "especially a thoroughgoing criticism of its ideology, especially in respect to the oppressive distortion of reality for the prosecution of the power agenda of the elements in society that enjoy hegemony."[35]

In an extended but very helpful paragraph that speaks of the need for ideology criticism as we consider "the world before the text," she writes:

> Ideology criticism has made us aware that the biblical text contains not only historical inaccuracies, scientific errors, mythological assumptions that are unassimilable by the modern mind, but also

---

33. Bernard C. Lategan, "Reconsidering the Origin and Function of Galatians 3:28," *Neotestamentica* 46.2 (2012): 284.

34. Sandra M. Schneiders, *The Revelatory Text: Interpreting the New Testament as Sacred Scriptures* (San Francisco: HarperSan Francisco, 1991), 157ff., esp. 167.

35. Ibid., 171. For an alternative viewpoint on power in Paul as transformative rather than an ideological justification for existing and prevailing hegemonic power, see Kathy Ehrensperger, "Speaking Greek under Rome: Paul, the Power of Language and the Language of Power," *Neotestamentica* 46.1 (2012): 9-28, esp. 23. For more on the power struggle between Paul and the Jerusalem leaders and the Teachers, see Esler, *Galatians*, and Asano, *Community-Identity Construction*, 14-15.

morally objectionable positions. Feminist criticism in particular, by exposing the patriarchal ideology, androcentric presuppositions, and sexist language and teaching of the New Testament, has raised the problem of how a sacred text that is rife with morally unacceptable material can continue to function normatively for a faith community. How is the justice-minded Christian to respond to a text that regards women as derivative and defective, that marginalizes, trivializes, and even demonizes women, that excludes women from full religious participation and legitimates male domination? Can such subject matter be appropriated by being assented to and thus allowed to structure the self-world of the reader? The answer has to be no. The hermeneutical question is how we can understand the interpretive process by which the reader identifies and repudiates the morally unacceptable subject matter of the text without repudiating the text itself and its truth claims.[36]

The task of being faithful to the truth of the text as one remains faithful to the truth of one's self, she writes, demands "transformative interpretation." By this she means that one is able to fuse in one's understanding the horizon of the text in the context of one's own horizon. This, she insists, "is essentially an enterprise within the area of spirituality, that is, of the conscious effort toward life-integration through self-transcendence toward the horizon of ultimate value."[37] I consider an example of this fusion of horizons to be the way this book seeks a real connection between Paul's challenge to the churches at Galatia vis-à-vis their seduction by covenantal nomism and the way the Roman Church itself until recently has been seduced by what I call "canonical nomism."

Because there were enough members of the Galatian communities who had been seduced by the gospel of "covenantal nomism," Paul felt compelled to write a letter to them to reclaim the gospel of life in Christ in the power of the Spirit that he had proclaimed. The fact that he did not see his own understanding of the gospel of radical inclusion of all that nonetheless still practically reinforced "the old order" does not make his insight any less truthful, especially for those who try to interpret Galatians and the other writings of Paul in the context of the church today and who do so from a quantum worldview.

This expressed need to "take back" our church by refounding it in the Spirit of Christ and the new creation that Spirit will reveal is simpatico with

---

36. Schneiders, *Revelatory Text,* 175.
37. Ibid., 174.

the thought of other theologians, including Richard R. Gaillardetz. After stating that "I am convinced that the Catholic Church has suffered from inadequate and reductive understandings of how the Holy Spirit assists bishops in their teaching," he demonstrates how the bishops have coopted the legitimate authority of the faithful:

> For much of the last one hundred and fifty years, the teaching authority of the pope and bishops has been exercised in a predominantly juridical mode, the mode of "command and obey." This juridical mode focuses narrowly on discrete, magisterial teaching acts, too easily closes off debate, suppresses disagreement and impedes the discovery of new insight on the part of the Christian faithful.[38]

Noting that the 2007 Ravenna Statement, which arose from the Catholic–Orthodox ecumenical dialogue, "insists that the authority of the bishop, as apostolic teacher, cannot be *separated from* the apostolic authority of the community for both are empowered by the same Spirit," Gaillardetz, former president of the Catholic Theological Society of America, concluded with words that I think would make Paul nod in agreement (and excitement, since we now understand, as Paul did, that the Trinity is the ultimate mode of governance in the church—something only he seemed to intuit):

> Within a developed Trinitarian framework, the language of "power" is only intelligible as a participation in the life of the Spirit at work in the church. Remove the Trinitarian framework and power is inevitably juridicized within a kind of "zero-sum" game in which some members of the church are given "power" at the expense of others. A Trinitarian theology of ecclesial power does not exclude the need for canon law and the right ordering of the life of the church, but this necessary juridical element of the life of the church will always be in service of the activity of the Spirit in the pluriform relations and practices that comprise much of what the church is.[39]

---

38. Richard R. Gaillardetz, "How Does the Holy Spirit Assist the Church in Its Teaching?," The Duquesne University Eighth Annual Holy Spirit Lecture, January 31, 2014 (Pittsburgh, PA: Duquesne University, 2014), 5. I have added the emphasis to make clear(er) my thesis that the parallel between covenantal nomism and canonical nomism involves separation.

39. Ibid., 14, 15.

With this background on the first-century understanding of "the Spirit" and Paul's stress on the Spirit in Galatians, we can now move to a deeper understanding of the function of the Holy Spirit in the life of the believer: to enable him/her to witness to a mystical life expressed through the "fruit(s) of the Spirit."

However, before doing so, it is important to refer to something Pope Francis said in his 2015 Easter homily because it wonderfully summarizes what has been articulated in this book thus far; especially the contrast between the legalism represented in the "works of the flesh" and the life of grace revealed in the "fruit of the Spirit." He said:

> In the Letter to the Galatians, Saint Paul wants to show the "fruits" manifested in the lives of those who walk in the way of the Spirit (cf. Gal. 5:22). On the one hand, he presents "the flesh," with its list of attendant vices: the works of selfish people closed to God. On the other hand, there are those who by faith allow the Spirit of God to break into their lives. In them, God's gifts blossom, summed up in nine joyful virtues which Paul calls "fruits of the Spirit." Hence his appeal, at the start and the end of the reading, as a program for life: "Walk by the Spirit" (Gal. 5:6, 25).

The world needs men and women who are not closed in on themselves, but filled with the Holy Spirit. Closing oneself off from the Holy Spirit means not only a lack of freedom; it is a sin. There are many ways one can close oneself off from the Holy Spirit: by selfishness for one's own gain; by rigid legalism—seen in the attitude of the doctors of the law to whom Jesus referred as "hypocrites"; by neglect of what Jesus taught; by living the Christian life not as service to others but in the pursuit of personal interests; and in so many other ways. The world needs the courage, hope, faith, and perseverance of Christ's followers. The world needs the fruits of the Holy Spirit: "love, joy, peace, patience, kindness, goodness, faithfulness, gentleness, self-control" (Gal. 5:22).

Chapter 2

The Holy Spirit in Paul's Story of Our Salavation History

For many years, I tried to imagine the Holy Spirit as God's energy that is the breath of life in everyone and everything. My understanding deepened in New York City on September 11, 2001. I was staying at our Capuchin Friary at St. John the Baptist Church, then on West Thirty-First Street between Seventh and Eighth Avenues. After the planes struck the World Trade Center I looked outside and saw a gorgeous blue sky. It was, in the words of a later *New York Times* piece, "the kind of crystalline blue that pilots and meteorologists call 'severe clear.'"[1] Being in the friary mid-block, I could see nothing of the devastation unless I walked to one of the avenues and looked downtown toward the dark smoke. Unable to return to Milwaukee by plane, I, like so many others, spent the next days wandering about the city paying homage at shrines that seemed to be everywhere while trying to make some sense of the events.

A couple of days later I walked outside to the same "severe clear" blue sky. Before I got to Seventh Avenue to look downtown, however, I felt my eyes drying up rapidly; my nose seemed stuffed and my mouth chalky. In only a minute or so I grasped what had happened: the wind had shifted, and I was breathing in particles from the dark smoke: now it was here, in me. I was breathing it all in: the evil and the good. It then dawned on me that this was just a microcosm of the universe. Being part of this cosmic reality, I was continually breathing in the evil and the good. It was up to me to find a way to breathe in both the good and the evil, absorb within me the evil and breathe out only the good. Rather than being part of the mindset of retaliation, this would be my way, with Paul, to overcome the evil with good (Rom. 12:21). This challenge has remained with me since.

---

1. Randy Kennedy, "The Searing Blues of the 9/11 Sky," *New York Times*, May 15, 2014, C1.

Standing outside on Thirty-first Street, I felt within my being the cosmic beings that (we will see) Paul's world called the *stoicheia*. While I will elaborate on its meaning shortly, suffice it to say (as Bruce Longenecker does) that Paul's understanding of "spirit" reflects widespread assumptions in Graeco-Roman culture. People of all sorts of religious persuasions shared the belief that the world is populated by a multitude of suprahuman powers in constant conflict with one another. Human beings could become pawns and players in the rivalry and struggles that marked out the otherworldly realm. The spirit world could envelop the concrete world, as demonic powers and mysterious forces impacted human affairs. Gods, demonic spirits, and spiritual forces were thought to be alive and well, influencing human circumstances and destiny.[2]

A strong case can be made that in our world of contemporary *stoicheia* and the unequal power dynamics they represent, the notion of "breath," "wind," or "spirit," especially the Holy Spirit, that is at the core of Paul's Letter to the Galatians, offers us a way to address the problems of our times. Indeed, in considering a passage such as Gal. 3:15 where Paul chastises as "foolish" the Galatians who have abandoned the Spirit for the law, Stephen Kerry writes that the Holy Spirit's role in the believer's life is the coterminous and confirmatory sign of authentic conversion from the "flesh" (*sarx*) to the "spirit" (*pneuma*). He notes that the passage demonstrates, for Paul, how the Holy Spirit is simply the *sine qua non* of Christian identity.[3] This insight is especially significant when we realize that elsewhere in his letters, Paul himself does not clearly distinguish between Jesus as the Christ and the power of the Holy Spirit.[4] Indeed, Christ is *the* life-giving Spirit (see 1 Cor. 15:45). The Spirit of the risen Christ is the power of God at work in the universe as well as in our lives (Rom. 15:13, 19).

Since Paul uses "Spirit" and "Christ" interchangeably, if anyone is "in Christ," it is because of the Spirit of the Christ in him or her. Even more, since that Spirit breathes Christ into each member who believes and inspires that person to be baptized into Christ's body called the church, the

---

2. Bruce W. Longenecker, "'Until Christ Is Formed in You': Superhuman Forces and Moral Character in Galatians," *Catholic Biblical Quarterly* 61 (1999): 92.

3. Stephen Kerry, "An Exegetical Analysis of Galatians 3:1-5 with Particular Reference to Pneumatological Themes That Relate to the Onset and Continuation of Christian Identity, with Respect to Law and Gospel," *Journal of Biblical and Pneumatological Research* 2 (2010): 57-86.

4. "To be 'in Christ' was also to be 'in the Spirit.' He uses these phrases interchangeably" (Marcus J. Borg and John Dominic Crossan, *The First Paul: Reclaiming the Radical Visionary behind the Church's Conservative Icon* [New York: HarperOne, 2009], 186).

church is that Spirit-fed and Spirit-led new creation of the cosmic Christ wherein all its members are called to bring about a new way of communion in the world.

Paul did not have the benefit of centuries of theological discussions regarding the unique (and common) roles of the three persons in the one Trinitarian God, as we have come to know these persons in salvation history. Consequently, in terms of their power in the lives of the believers, the various functions that we *attribute* to each (although all their functions regarding us are done in common) are not that distinguishable in Paul's letters. The ultimate goal of their functioning is the same in the lives of believers in the churches of Galatia then and in all churches throughout the world now: their/our gradual fruition and transformation (i.e., "morphing") in the power of the Spirit into the Christ of God (4:19).

Because the notion of "spirit" had varied meanings in the New Testament world, debate exists as to what "spirit" (*pneuma*) means in Paul's writings (or any of the other New Testament writings). Being a Jew, well-formed in the rabbinic and Pharisaic approach to the Jewish Scriptures, Paul envisioned "the Spirit" as God's *rûah*, breath, which gives life to everyone and everything.[5] In support of this cosmology, the Jewish Annotated New Testament notes that this "Holy Spirit" is "God's creative and enduring presence."[6] The Spirit of God is the grounding force that empowered the whole cosmos from the beginning of time.

It took over three centuries of debate to come to agreement on what "Holy Spirit" meant. Even later, the "what" that was considered to be the Holy Spirit became a "who." The divinity of the Holy Spirit (*pneuma hagion*) was dogmatically declared at the Council of Constantinople (381 CE). In subsequent writings, the Church Fathers, especially Athanasius of Alexan-

---

5. For a contrary view that does not seem acceptable to me, see John R. Levison, *Filled with the Spirit* (Grand Rapids/Cambridge: Eerdmans, 2009).

6. Gen. 1:2; 2:7; 8:1; Exod. 13:21-22; Josh. 2:16; and Ps. 51:11; see Aaron M. Gale, "Matthew," in Amy-Jill Levine and Marc Zvi Brettler, eds., *The Jewish Annotated New Testament* (New York: Oxford University Press, 2011), 4, comment on Matt. 1:18-25. Later, in referring to one of Paul's authentic letters (1 Thessalonians), David Fox Sandmel notes that the "later development of ideas about the spirit of God" found in the New Testament "may go beyond Paul's" understanding (373, comment on 1 Thess. 1:2-10). The Jewish approach to Paul is not favorable. In the last essay in this volume, "Paul in Jewish Thought," Daniel R. Langton concludes, "In contrast to the figure of Jesus, who has, in the main, been reclaimed as a good Jew of one sort or another, Paul remains an object of hostility and suspicion. While there have been a number of scholarly exceptions to this rule, one should not expect him, whose likening of the Law to 'sin' and 'death' still echo down the centuries, to enjoy a more general Jewish reclamation any time soon" (587).

dria and the three Cappadocians (Basil of Caesarea, Gregory of Nyssa, and Gregory of Nazianzus), read *into* the Pauline texts this understanding of *pneuma* and *pneuma hagion* rather than the understanding of "spirit(s)" and the "holy spirit" (including it in reference to a unique power of God) that informed Paul's worldview. Thus, in discussing the role (as well as fruit[s]) of the Holy Spirit in the Letter to the Galatians we need to be wary of "reading into" the Galatian text our contemporary theology regarding the Holy Spirit (*pneumatology*) that has evolved over more than two millennia.

Another point to consider is that Paul's worldview was highly influenced by a "flat-earth" cosmology that was expressed in the expression "ends of the earth." It was held that the "heavens" between the earth and the dome covering the earth was the dwelling place and field of battle of all spirit beings, good and bad (called at varying times either the *pneuma* or the *stoicheia*). This cosmology influenced Paul; however, he seemed to stress the negative dimension when he spoke of the *stoicheia*[7] and reserved a positive power and place to the *pneuma* he called *hagion* (i.e., the Holy Spirit).

The identity of the *stoicheia*, like so many other things in Galatians, has been the source of much controversy. Various writers interpret the *stoicheia* as located among the world rulers of darkness, the underlying power of the Torah and the domain of what Paul will call *sarx* (flesh), representing sin and death. Others see the *stoicheia* as the fundamental principle of the "shadow side" of all religions, while still more interpret them in a cosmic sense as the realm of the four "elemental" spirits of air (wind), earth, water, and fire. Whatever their differing identities and function, the *stoicheia* had one underlying impact and effect: they enslaved their adherents to their dominating and controlling power. In effect, N. T. Wright notes, they were believed to be "the tutelary deities that hold the nations in captivity."[8] In

---

7. In his *Cosmic Christology in Paul and the Pauline School: Colossians and Ephesians in the Context of Graeco-Roman Cosmology, with a New Synopsis of the Greek Texts* (Tübingen: Mohr Siebeck, 2003), George H. van Kooten writes, "In his *Letter to the Galatians*, Paul appears to share the conviction, current in the Graeco-Roman period, that the cosmos is composed of elements (στοιχεία; chap. 2.1). According to this conviction, not only is the universe composed of elements but the elements are the entities from which originate, and in which exist, all destructible and moral species too, including human beings. Inasmuch as they are composed by the intermingling of small portions from the four elements of the cosmos, it is impossible for human beings to slip out through the elements and leave the realm in which the passive and changeable elements are haunted by a destructive cosmic force. But adopting the common theory that the cosmos is made up of elements, Paul took over its negative view on the elements and man's bondage to them" (205-6).

8. N. T. Wright, *Pauline Perspectives: Essays on Paul, 1978–2013* (Minneapolis: Fortress Press, 2013), 87.

Paul's mind, when he considered what had happened to the Galatian converts, the *stoicheia* held those in bondage who had been seduced by the gospel of the Teachers.

As the above description of the realm of their power indicates, the *stoicheia* had tremendous power over the world of Paul, including both Jews and "gentiles." This worldview was not totally erased when Jews and gentiles became converts. When it came to the Jews, the *stoicheia* were always at work trying to seduce the people to forms of enslavement defined by the law; for the gentiles they took the form of gods and goddess demanding cultic worship. Thus, the heart of Paul's concern was the fear that, if the gentile converts reverted to unnecessary forms of Judaism they would again come under the power of the *stoicheia* in a way that would enslave them again.

With this cautionary background on the need to be aware of the broad cosmological, theological, and anthropological notions of the various kinds of "spirit(s)" in the world of Paul's Letter to the Galatians, aided by our own twenty-first-century quantum worldview and cosmology, we can now approach the text in its own context of Second Temple Judaism, that period between 530 BCE and 70 CE when the Second Temple existed; and, among their different interpretations of God's work in their midst, all the people generally believed in an inbreaking that would bring about some kind of Jewish restoration.

Paul's Understanding of the Spirit
Inaugurating the Apocalyptic Time

The summary of Paul's story of salvation, if not all of salvation history itself,[9] can be found in Gal. 4:4-7:

> When the fullness of time had come, God sent his Son, born of a woman, born under the law, in order to redeem those who were under the law, so that we might receive adoption as children. And because you are children, God has sent the Spirit of his Son into our hearts, crying, "Abba! Father!" So you are no longer a slave but a child, and if a child then also an heir, through God.

---

9. Another controversy regarding Paul and Galatians involves whether Paul had a "salvation history." While this will be discussed later, among those speaking in support of it are N. T. Wright and James D. G. Dunn; those arguing that Paul's stress on the *apocalyptic* was so unique that it undermines the possibility of a traditional understanding of "salvation history" are J. C. Becker, J. L. Martyn, and, to some extent, Bruce W. Longenecker.

Realizing that there is no monolithic interpretation of the Hebrew Scriptures and that most Jews in Paul's day read the Scriptures in Greek (if they were literate) and interpreted them through the lens of the prevailing Stoic cosmology, Rodrigo Morales shows that Paul was highly influenced in his understanding of the eschatological outpouring of the Spirit that defined much of Second Temple Judaism, especially various Old Testament verses[10] and others found in intertestamental literature wherein "the outpouring of the Spirit is related to a new creation that brings about a new gathering of all God's people to be part of the restoration of Israel."[11]

This restoration will inaugurate the new age; hence Paul's reference to "the fullness of time." According to Paul, God sent the Spirit of his own Son into the new embodiment of the risen Christ: the church composed of all the baptized. This embodiment by, in, and through the Spirit enables every human being who is a member of the body of Christ in every age to have the same kind of intimacy with God that the human Jesus experienced in his day. There is no enslavement to the flesh in this corporate body; there is only the kind of relationship with this God that Jesus himself had: that which enables every one of us to have the same kind of intimacy with God that enables us to call that God "Abba! Father."

While this book will not stress the dimension of mysticism that involves prayer, the fact that Paul notes that the outpouring of the Spirit in the lives of the Christian not only makes them sons and daughters of God (and, therefore, equally brothers and sisters in the household/family of God), it also evidences a unique kind of intimacy in their relationship and prayer vis-à-vis this "Abba" God that is meant to be *familiar* precisely because of its "*familiality*," that is, *familiarity*. In this sense Carolyn Osiek notes that the "preservation of the Aramaic form in a Greek-speaking tradition is noteworthy." She explains: "The simple title, *abba*, here and in Rom 8 [vv. 15-17] is not a solitary word. The use of it is meant to evoke a whole chain of associations in the readers. The form and style of prayer which they have learned from Paul and experienced in the gift of the Spirit flow from this key word." In showing how the word and meaning of *abba* summarize Jesus's teachings about life and especially our prayer life, which invites us into Jesus's own relationship with God, she concludes, "This familial form of address that is

---

10. Isa. 11:1-16; 32:15-20; 42:1-9; 43:14–44:8; 48:16; 57:14-21; 59:15b-21; 61:1-11; 63:7–64:12; Ezek. 11:14-21; 18:30-32; 36:16-38; 37:1-14; 39:21-29; Joel 3:1-5.

11. Rodrigo I. Morales, *The Spirit and the Restoration of Israel: New Exodus and New Creation Motifs in Galatians* (Tübingen: Mohr Siebeck, 2010).

so distinctive of early Christian piety is undoubtedly rooted in Jesus's own example of familiarity with God."[12]

This passage represents in its four sentences (4:4-7) that those whom God sends this same Spirit thus also are called to become adopted sons and daughters in a way that makes us brothers and sisters in one new family. This makes us heirs of everything God has promised in the past. Put in the context of the covenantal nomism that motivated Paul to write the Letter to the Galatians, the real, underlying problem for Paul was that, instead of the religion grounded in the Holy Spirit and its fruit, he found a religion of *sarx*—that is, the religion that has human motivations to it, a religion that puffs us up and divides us from one another—that was fundamentally opposed to genuine faith in Christ. Authentic faith in Christ, we will see in Chapter 12, is about justice and the kind of relationship with the Abba of Jesus as ours who demands that we treat one another as unique sons and daughters of this Abba in a way that makes us brothers and sisters.

I find it interesting that in his encyclical on the Holy Spirit, Pope John Paul II quoted this scriptural passage from Galatians (4:4-7) more than any other, concluding, "With the sending of this Spirit 'into our hearts,' there begins the fulfillment of that for which 'creation waits with eager longing,' as we read in the Letter to the Romans [8:19]."[13]

Kyu Seop Kim has shown the radicalism in its Roman context of Paul's "adoption metaphor" for our being God's sons and daughters. He explains "that this metaphor functions to stress God's unusual and extraordinary favor and love to the believers" in three main ways:

> Firstly, adopting complete strangers was rare in Roman society, and adoptees were usually chosen from among close relatives and friends' children. Secondly, adopting slaves should be distinguished from adopting freeborn children in Roman social practice and law. Thirdly, adoption in the presence of a legitimate heir was also regarded as unusual in Roman society. Therefore, it should be noted that Paul's adoption metaphor was unusual, because the metaphor refers to adopting slaves in the presence of a legitimate heir.[14]

---

12. Carolyn Osiek, R.S.C.J., *Galatians* (Dublin: Veritas Publications, 1980), 47.

13. Pope John Paul II, *Dominum et Vivificantem*, no. 14. Romans 8:19 is noted earlier in no. 14 and later in no. 39 (http://www.vatican.va).

14. Kyu Seop Kim, "Another Look at Adoption in Romans 8:15 in Light of Roman Social Practices and Legal Rules," *Biblical Theology Bulletin* 44.3 (2014): 133.

About this "fullness of time" passage, Bruce Longenecker writes, "The shift in focus from what God has done in Christ (4.4-5) to Christian sonship (4.6-7) pivots on the figure of the Spirit; just as God has sent the son (4.4), so God has sent the Spirit (4.6)." However, he notes that the Galatians passage makes it clear that it is not our own spirit but the Spirit of God united with our spirit who is crying out, and that "the state of childhood/ slavery to that of sonship is not something that can be self-performed." Furthermore, he notes that the cry of this Spirit becomes an invitation to all the baptized to articulate (if not actually experience) with the same kind of intimacy that is summarized in Jesus's own way of addressing God as his "Abba, Father."[15]

While I see in Galatians 4:4-7 a summary of Paul's salvation history, J. Louis Martyn writes in his classic (and controversial) commentary that Paul's "fullness of time" represents the inbreaking of a new "apocalyptic" era that, in effect, changes everything.[16] Because this apocalyptic invasion was so unprecedented, Martyn, along with J. Christiaan Becker[17] and, to some extent, Bruce W. Longenecker (against the position of James D. G.

---

15. Bruce W. Longenecker, *The Triumph of Abraham's God: The Transformation of Identity in Galatians* (Nashville: Abingdon Press, 1998), 61.

16. The meaning of "apocalyptic" in Paul also is the source of controversy. "Apocalyptic" can mean an *inbreaking*. This would include what (or the consequences of what) happened to Paul on the way to Damascus. It also can mean the final "return" of Jesus as it was envisioned as immanent in the early letters of Paul. There is disagreement among the exegetes as to whether Paul's version of the "fullness of time" in Galatians represents an apocalyptic moment in history, as J. Louis Martyn suggests. See his *Galatians: A New Translation with Introduction and Commentary* (Anchor Bible; New York: Doubleday, 1997), 104-5. For support, see Ernst Käsemann ,"The Beginnings of Christian Theology," in *New Testament Questions of Today* (London: SCM; Philadelphia: Fortress Press, 1969); Käsemann declared that "apocalyptic was the mother of all Christian theology," 102; Douglas A. Campbell, *The Deliverance of God: An Apocalyptic Reading of Justification in Paul* (Grand Rapids: Eerdmans, 2009). Wright, *Pauline Perspectives,* seems to support Martyn's understanding of apocalyptic (173-80), even though he considers Martyn's approach to be "seriously flawed" (191). See also Martinus C. de Boer, *Galatians: A Commentary* (Louisville: Westminster John Knox, 2011), esp. 108-9. An extended overview of the notion of "apocalyptic" can be found in Wayne A. Meeks, *The First Urban Christians: The Social World of the Apostle Paul* (New Haven and London: Yale University Press, 1983), 171-80.

17. J. Christiaan Beker, *Paul the Apostle: The Triumph of God in Life and Thought* (Philadelphia: Fortress Press, 1980); "Jewish apocalyptic forms the basis of Paul's thought. It constituted (*a*) the thought world of Paul the Pharisee and, therefore, (*b*) the fundamental grammar and context through which Paul filtered the Christ event and interpreted as the *apokalypsis tou christou* (Gal. 1:12; cf. 1:16; 2:2)." See J. Christian Beker, *The Triumph of God: The Essence of Paul's Thought* (trans. Loren T. Stuckenbruck; Minneapolis: Fortress

Dunn and N. T. Wright), says there is no longer "salvation history"; there is an entirely new creation. Thus Martyn writes, "If God's apocalyptic invasion of the cosmos in Christ creates a radically new perception of God himself, of God's Christ as a crucified criminal, of Christ's crucifixion as an incorporative event, of sin, of the law, and so on, it also creates a radically new perception of time (3:25; 4:4)."

This new perception of time has become identified with Martyn's "what time is it" question in his commentary to stress its apocalyptic, once-for-all, nature. In one of the most famous quotes regarding Paul's worldview that colored his Letter to the Galatians, Martyn writes,

> One recalls that the matter of discerning the time lies at the heart of apocalyptic. And . . . in writing to the Galatians Paul addresses the issue of time in terms clearly apocalyptic. What time is it? It is the time after the apocalypse of the faith of Christ, the time, therefore, of God's making things right by Christ's faith, the time of the presence of the Spirit of Christ, and thus the time in which the invading Spirit has decisively commended the war of liberation from the powers of the present evil age.[18]

While Paul actually narrated in the above four verses (4:4-7) the heart of the cosmic history that has now brought about a new era in creation, his grounding in the Hebrew Scriptures makes it clear that he saw in the Christ-event a never-before grasped understanding of God's original purposes for creation itself: that "in Christ" through "the Spirit" of this Christ everything in the universe is ultimately made to evolve (or be transformed) into a new creation.

While I find merit in this apocalyptic vision, I believe Paul's worldview was influenced by it but not controlled by it. For him "the fullness of time" found a flow of salvation history that was/is altered radically by creation, the incarnation wherein Jesus was "born of a woman," his gospel that led to his passion and crucifixion at the hands of Rome and his embodiment in the church of Paul's day, which continues in each of us today. Thus, in the following paragraphs I will develop from the chart below my overall understanding of salvation history in a way that is faithful to Paul's pneumatology as he understood the Hebrew Scriptures and as found in the Acts of the Apostles and Paul's authentic letters, especially Galatians.

Press, 1990), 19. Beker also notes that he is "recasting Paul's theology as a theocentric theology of hope rather than as a Christocentric salvation-history" (xiii).

18. Martyn, *Galatians,* 104.

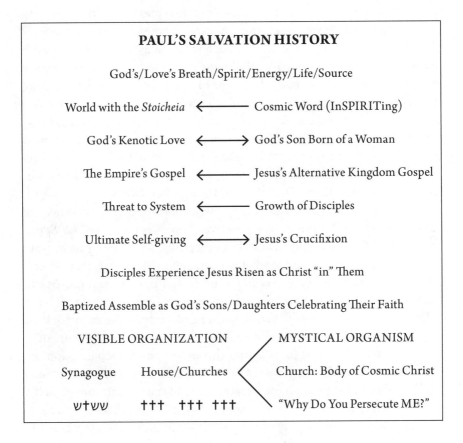

PAUL'S SALVATION HISTORY

God's/Love's Breath/Spirit/Energy/Life/Source

World with the *Stoicheia* ⟵——— Cosmic Word (InSPIRITing)

God's Kenotic Love ⟷ God's Son Born of a Woman

The Empire's Gospel ⟵——— Jesus's Alternative Kingdom Gospel

Threat to System ⟵——— Growth of Disciples

Ultimate Self-giving ⟷ Jesus's Crucifixion

Disciples Experience Jesus Risen as Christ "in" Them

Baptized Assemble as God's Sons/Daughters Celebrating Their Faith

VISIBLE ORGANIZATION   MYSTICAL ORGANISM

Synagogue   House/Churches   Church: Body of Cosmic Christ

שׁעׁtשׁ   ✝✝✝ ✝✝✝ ✝✝✝   "Why Do You Persecute ME?"

The opening lines of Divine Revelation in the Book of Genesis present us with two key images of "the spirit" expressed with quite different words as well as meanings: "In [the] beginning (*en archē*) when God created the heavens and the earth, the earth was a formless void and darkness covered the face of the deep, while a wind (*rûaḥ*) from God swept over the face of the waters" (Gen. 1:1-2). Before discussing the image of the wind, or *rûaḥ/pneuma*, we need to take a deeper look at the opening lines of Genesis to grasp the cosmic scope of the Priestly author's wording.

The Greek phrase *en archē* does not mean something that began at some specific moment in time or history. Rather, because *en archē* does not include the article "the" (as is recorded in the translation of Gen. 1:1 (and John 1:1 [as well as Colossians 1:18] where the wording also appears), "in beginning" connotes a foundational, originating, and normative underlying and overarching power of an archetypal nature. It represents a "transcending event" that is "substantive and determinative, not merely a temporal one."[19]

With this in mind, when we consider what today we call the Priestly account of creation coming from the "wind from God [that] swept over the face of the waters" (Gen. 1:2c),[20] we need to be clear as to its meaning. And, in so doing, we discover that its meaning is multiple! Scholars have debated the precise significance of *rûaḥ ĕlōhîm* in Gen. 1:2c. Some translated it as "Spirit of God," "wind from God," or even "terrible storm"; the context invites the phrase to be translated as the very "breath of God" or "God's creative force that permeates the entire universe or cosmos." In other words, using today's cosmological insights, for the believer, God's *rûaḥ* is the ultimate energy at the heart of all energy that is massed as matter. When we consider God's *rûaḥ* from this perspective, God does not "send" *his Spirit*; the Spirit of God is that which makes everything's beginning be at [the] beginning! And if this Spirit is what/who makes matter/creation, then creation is evolving to become ever-more fulfilled or transformed into Spirit. Even more so, since this Spirit of God is the love of God, all creation (for the believer) is in the process of moving to ever-greater spiritualization or love.

When we consider the earliest account of the creation of the human in Gen. 2:4b and 7 (at least in its actual chronology, even though it appears second in our Genesis text), we read that "then the Lord God formed man from the dust of the ground, and breathed into his nostrils the breath of life (*nishmat ḥayyim*), and the man became a living being." Since, in Hebrew, *rûaḥ* and *nishmat* are roughly synonymous, we find them joining in Paul's notion of *pneuma* or Spirit. *Pneuma* is the life force of everything and everyone; the *Holy* Spirit is God's being of love that enables all to be its own being. Thus, considering our first lines of the chart above, God's love has entered the world of all being through the God-given Spirit (Rom. 5:5).

This Spirit of God is the underlying spirit that enables matter to be or, as Paul wrote, "If there is a physical body, there is also a spiritual body. Thus it is written, 'The first man, Adam, became a living being'" (1 Cor. 15:14-15). The *Holy Spirit* who is at the heart of all being is the *archē*, the source, empowerer and model for all life as well as all holiness. Thus humankind,

---

19. Richard J. Dillon, "Mark 1:1-15: A 'New Evangelization'?," *Catholic Biblical Quarterly* 76 (2014): 6.

20. There are two accounts of creation in the first books of Genesis. Genesis 1:1–2:4a originated from what is called "the Priestly account." Genesis 2:4bff. is the narrative that was written earlier than the Priestly version, probably in the late seventh or sixth century BCE. The way the two stories are arranged, the last to be written comes first and the first to be written comes after.

from the beginning, is filled with the (Holy) Spirit, just as is creation. This sending of the Spirit is what makes creation be what it was, is now, and will be; this sending of the Spirit is what makes humans be, whether they were one set of parents called Adam and Eve, as Paul believed, or were from multiple parentages, as may be the actual case.[21]

Paul believed that the Spirit who hovered over the earth to bring it forth was the same Spirit that God sent upon "the woman" we call Mary to bring forth the incarnated form of his Son. Even more, Jerome Murphy-O'Connor writes, regarding the incarnation of Jesus in the "fullness of time" (4:4), that this birthing of the God-Human-One is rooted in God's original purpose in creating humans. He writes,

> God was thinking of the humanity of Christ when he formed Adam. This seems so paradoxical as to be meaningless, but once we recognize that the category of exemplar causality was furnished by the Wisdom literature (Prov 3:19; 8:22, 30), the author's mental process becomes clear. In order to create Adam, God must have had an idea of perfect humanity. For Christians, that perfect humanity was realized only in Christ. Christ, therefore, was conceived to represent the divine intent which came to historical expression in the creation of Adam.[22]

Continuing to interpret our chart of salvation history as Saul and then Paul probably envisioned it, God's *rûaḥ* or *pneuma* inspired various (male) human beings to help mold the Israelites into a people formed and/or led by humans such as Abraham, Moses, Joshua, and the judges (Num. 11:17-30; Judg. 3:10; 11:29; 13:25; 14:6-19). When Israel failed to keep its part of the covenant(s), this same "breath of God" inspired the prophets to continually call Israel back to its covenantal promises. Two great prophets[23] of the

---

21. The likelihood of humankind originating from more than one set of parents is now being seen as an evolutionary possibility. See "All about Adam: A Furious—and Political—Debate about the Origins of Mankind," *The Economist*, November 23, 2013, 37.

22. Jerome Murphy-O'Connor, OP, *Becoming Human Together: The Pastoral Anthropology of St. Paul* (Wilmington, DE: Michael Glazier, 1984), 44. The notion of exemplarism in Genesis, for St. Bonaventure, is key to understanding his notion of God's goodness that is revealed in those who image God as vestiges, images, and likenesses. This will be further discussed in our treatment of the fruit of goodness in Chapter 10.

23. How Paul was influenced in his writing about the Spirit by Old Testament prophets is covered well by James D. G. Dunn, *The New Perspective on Paul* (rev. ed.; Grand Rapids: Eerdmans, 2008), 82ff., 439-43.

exilic period[24] who were inspired by God's *rûaḥ* or *pneuma* were Ezekiel and (Second) Isaiah. Ezekiel narrated how his prophecy originated from the spirit of God that inspired him (Ezek. 3:12, 14; 8:3; 11:1; 37:14; 43:5). Centuries later, when Paul, the Jew, reflected on Ezekiel in light of what he had come to know about the "Holy Spirit" through his experience of the Christ event of resurrection, he came to understand Ezekiel's "Spirit of God" (Ezek. 36–37) as the one who would bring new life from the dry bones of his people, Israel. For Paul, the restored Israel was the church.

Paul came to believe that this eternal life had been assured for those who believe in the gospel of Jesus Christ. N. T. Wright argues that, by quoting Isa. 54:1, this "vision" of the gospel found in Second Isaiah, especially in the Servant passages, was fulfilled in Jesus.[25] Second Isaiah attributed to the Divine Breath the power that would enable Israel to be reconfigured, renewed, and reconsecrated to the Lord (Isa. 44:1-5); for Paul, this reconstituted community of Israel would be(come) the church, the new family of Abraham. This family, we will see in Chapter 12, was already present in the spirit's original promise to Abraham and his "seed" (3:15-16, 29).

Despite Israel's ups and downs in its covenantal fidelity, God's plan was that God's *rûaḥ* would bring about a human incarnation of the abiding presence in the universe of God's loving kindness through the Spirit and "the woman." Like Adam, the body of this one would be enlivened by the Spirit. (Deviating from Paul, Luke tells us of the woman, Mary, "The Holy Spirit will come upon you, and the power of the Most High will overshadow you," such that Mary gave birth to the child Jesus [Luke 1:35]. Or we can take the wording of Matthew, which states that "the child conceived in her is from the Holy Spirit" and that this child Jesus will be "'Emmanuel,' which means 'God is with us'" [Matt. 1:20]).

Next on our chart we find key parts of salvation history that were not included by Paul in his four verses (4:4-7) but became the basis for Paul's whole understanding of what he called "the gospel." Jesus proclaimed the "gospel of the kingdom of God/heaven" in a way that led to his passion, death, and resurrection (which, in turn, became experienced by Paul as "the gospel"). This gospel (of the kingdom of God/heaven) of Jesus stood in direct contrast/opposition to the imperial gospel of Caesar and Caesar's gods and spirits, which Paul believed to be part of the *stoicheia*. Jesus's fidelity to the proclamation of this gospel brought him to the cross in such a

---

24. N. T. Wright notes how many Jews of Paul's day, influenced by the mindset of Second Temple Judaism, believed that they were still in exile (*Pauline Perspectives*, 142). See his arguments under "exile" in the Index, in *Pauline Perspectives*, 618.

25. Ibid., 80-90, 302.

way that it ushered in the new, apocalyptic creation that he discovered as embodied in his living, risen body, the church. The consequent gospel proclaimed by Paul was this "good news" that the Spirit of God which enabled Jesus to be born of a woman now was the life force of each and every member of the church. In this sense, noting that both "gospels" of Jesus and Paul were grounded in the Isaiah passages (Isa. 40–55) and were a challenge to the imperial gospel,[26] N. T. Wright says that any "antithesis between the two is a false one, based on the spurious either–or that has misleadingly divided New Testament studies for many years."[27]

The link between the "gospels" of Jesus in the Synoptics and the official letters of Paul is articulated with great insight by the Capuchin pontifical preacher Raniero Cantalamessa:

> At the beginning of his ministry, Jesus went about proclaiming, "the time is fulfilled, and the kingdom of God is at hand; repent, and believe in the gospel" (Mark 1:15). What Christ meant by the expression "the kingdom of God—God's salvific initiative, his offer of salvation to all humanity—is called "the righteousness of God" by St. Paul, but it really points to the same fundamental reality. The "kingdom of God" and the "righteousness of God" are set alongside each other by Jesus himself when he says, "Seek first his kingdom and his righteousness" (Matthew 6:33). "It is [Jesus's] custom," St. Cyril wrote, "to give the name of 'the kingdom of heaven' to justification by faith, to the cleansing that is by holy baptism and the participation of the Holy Spirit."[28]

In Gal. 3:2 and 3:5 Paul makes it clear that the hearing and acceptance of the gospel by the Galatians brought about their reception of the Spirit. In one paragraph elaborating on Paul's truncated history of salvation found in a contextualized interpretation of the four verses of Gal. 4:4-7, N. T. Wright says:

---

26. As noted before, I do not find the gospel proclaimed by Paul in Galatians to be as directly or clearly opposed to the imperial gospel as does N. T. Wright. However, with him, I do find it lurking in all the New Testament writings.

27. Wright, *Pauline Perspectives*, 83.

28. Raniero Cantalamessa, OFMCap, *Remember Jesus Christ: Responding to the Challenges of Faith in Our Time* (trans. Marsha Daigle-Williamson Frederick; Frederick, MD: Word among Us Press, 2007), 46-47, quoting St. Cyril of Alexandria, *A Commentary upon the Gospel according to St. Luke*, 22, 26 (trans. R. Payne Smith (Astoria, NY: Studion Publishers, 1983), 566.

In terms of Galatians 4.1-7, the message of the Pauline gospel is this: the true god has sent his son, in fulfillment of the prophecies of scripture, to redeem his people from their bondage to false gods (described here as the *stoicheia tou kosmou* 4.3, 9); he now sends his own spirit to make his people truly what they were before only in theory and hope—his own children, heirs of his world. Equipped with this gospel, the Galatian Christians now know the true god; or rather, as Paul quickly corrects himself, they are known by him (4.9). That is, they have received the great blessing promised by Isaiah throughout chapters 40–55; the one true god has revealed himself in saving them, routing the idols of the nations in doing so. The message of good news decisively confronts the power of the spurious gods.[29]

Luke and Matthew will later make it clear that the gospel proclaimed by Jesus in the midst of the imperial gospel is one that is inspired by the Holy Spirit. Thus, in Luke, "Jesus, full of the Holy Spirit . . . was led by Spirit" into the wilderness to discern his vocation and, upon prevailing over the devil, "filled with the power of the Spirit, returned to Galilee" (Luke 4:14). When he came to Nazareth and went to the synagogue, he unrolled the scroll and found the place where Isaiah had prophesied: "The Spirit of the Lord is upon me, because he has anointed me to bring good news to the poor. He has sent me to proclaim release to the captives and recovery of sight to the blind, to let the oppressed go free, to proclaim the year of the Lord's favor" (Luke 4:18-19). That this grounding in Isaiah's vision of the new creation-informed-by-the-Spirit is the heart of the "good news" or the gospel (Isa. 61:1, 2) is also clear from the Jesus in Matthew's Gospel who refers to Isa. 61:1, 2 as the verification of his being the Messiah or the Christ (Matt. 11:2-6).[30]

When Jesus proclaimed this gospel and implemented it in his healing and restoring of broken people, he drew so many disciples that he (and his gospel) became a threat to some key Jewish religious leaders. Consequently they conspired among themselves and with the Romans to have him killed. While they believed that his crucifixion would end his influence in that remote outpost of the Roman Empire called Judea, according to Paul, it was precisely in this crucifixion that Jesus's influence now became not only personal and corporate but cosmic as well. Now Paul himself recognized

29. Wright, *Pauline Perspectives*, 85.
30. See Dunn, *New Perspective on Paul*, 249.

the need to be transformed through self-giving love as the sign of his own salvific participation in the crucifixion of Christ, which would be the model for every disciple for all time: "For through the law I died to the law, so that I might live to God. I have been crucified with Christ; and it is no longer I who live, but it is Christ who lives in me. And the life I now live in the flesh I live by faith in the Son of God, who loved me and gave himself for me. I do not nullify the grace of God; for if justification comes through the law, then Christ died for nothing (2:18-21)." There is little reason, then, to disagree with Richard Hays, who concludes, "Gal 2:20-21, with its emphasis on the union with Christ's grace-giving death, looks more and more like the hermeneutical center of the letter."[31]

This quick fleshing-out of how I understand Paul's overview of salvation history brings us to the last lines. The Spirit that brought forth the universe, the Jesus of history, now is the life force of everyone who is baptized. Having stated this, however, it is important to realize that the Spirit who makes everyone an embodiment of the Christ does so in a way that everyone is part of one body and the one body is not only the church but involves the cosmos itself. Contrary to the prevailing so-called cult of the individual in society today,[32] there is no individual enspiriting apart from the whole. This is key to understanding Paul's notion of the new creation, which comes about with the release of the Spirit of the cosmic Christ into the lives of the baptized. In this sense James D. G. Dunn writes that "this new age is characterized by the steady reclaiming of individuals for an ever closer conformity to the risen Christ. In some sense the event of Christ's passion and resurrection has to be reenacted in believers until the renewal of the new age is complete." However, he cautions, "the process cannot, almost by definition, be something merely individual or individualistic. Rather, by its very nature it is a shared experience which involves creation as well." He notes that Paul's notion of being "in Christ" and "with Christ" involves others as well as creation itself. Consequently, he concludes, "the language cannot be reduced simply to a description of baptism or of membership in the believing community. Paul's language indicates rather a quite profound

---

31. Richard B. Hays, "Crucified with Christ: A Synthesis of the Theology of 1 and 2 Thessalonians, Philemon, Philippians, and Galatians," in *Thessalonians, Philippians, Galatians, Philemon,* in Jouette M. Bassler, ed., *Pauline Theology* I (Minneapolis: Fortress Press, 1991), 242.

32. For a good demythologizing of this notion from philosophy and evolutionary theory, see the blog of John Edward Terrell, "Evolution and the Myth of the Individual," The Stone Blog, *New York Times,* November 30, 2014, http://opinionator.blogs.nytimes.com.

sense of participation with others in a great and cosmic movement of God centered on Christ and effected through his Spirit."[33]

First of all, God vindicated the gospel of Jesus that led to his death in a way that empowered the Spirit to continue his life of love in an entirely new way: in other human beings who were the living embodiment of Christ crucified. Truly in baptism God's love is poured into our lives by this same Spirit (Rom. 5:5). This embodiment was not only a new kind of ecclesiological organism; as Yung Suk Kim writes, this "body of Christ [w]as the collective participation in *Christ Crucified*."[34] If the Galatians would take on the Teachers' form of "covenantal nomism," they would become the very "disembodiment of the Christic body."[35] In order to maintain their separatism, they were avoiding embracing the scandal of the cross (5:11; 6:12), which united all of humanity. They would abandon their new cosmic identity as a community that had become one in Christ crucified, an identity born out of faith in the salvific death and resurrection that had led them to be baptized "in" Christ crucified and risen.

Jesus's disciples gathered together because of their experience of the presence and power of God's Spirit, of Jesus Christ, with*in them*. But they were not yet grounded corporately by the power of this Spirit. That would be the experience of Pentecost. Then Luke tells us, using imagery of a flat-earth cosmology, the *pneuma hagion* came "from heaven" in "a sound like the rush of a violent wind [an image conjuring the rush of the *rûah* in Gen. 1:2b] and it filled the entire house where they were sitting." This was his way of describing the mystical experience of being "filled with the Holy Spirit." Noting the unifying and cosmic dimensions of this event, Luke describes how they could now "speak in other languages, as the Spirit gave them the ability" (Acts 2:2, 4). From an evolutionary perspective, one could say that these early believers came to a consciousness of what had already begun through the Spirit or *rûah* at the beginning of creation and had been prophesied by figures such as Ezekiel and Isaiah. The disciples came to understand how the historical Jesus had allowed this Spirit to lead him and how, now and together as the communal embodiment of his presence, they were to do the same thing under the inspiration of the same Spirit.

Building on this notion that the Holy Spirit empowers all believers in a way that would fulfill the Scriptures, Peter himself referred to what had hap-

33. James D. G. Dunn, *The Theology of Paul the Apostle* (Grand Rapids: Eerdmans Publishing Co., 2006), 403-4.

34. Yung Suk Kim, *Christ's Body in Corinth: The Politics of a Metaphor* (Minneapolis: Fortress Press, 2008), 21.

35. Ibid., 54.

pened as envisioned by the prophet Joel: "In the last days it will be, God declares, that I will pour out my spirit upon all flesh, and your sons and your daughters shall prophesy, and your young men shall see visions, and your old men shall dream dreams. Even upon my slaves, both men and women, in those days I will pour out my Spirit and they shall prophesy" (Acts 2:17-18).

This passage (Acts 2:17-18) envisions a totally new anthropological and cosmological reality when the Holy Spirit breaks in: a new creation has begun in the members of the church who are filled with the Spirit in such a way that any and all previous culturally or societally structured divisions based on class and sex are a thing of the past. A new reality has begun, and the church in all its members is its revelation to the world. Each member has been given of this Spirit to be shared with and celebrated with the other members in the community.

First of all, this sharing is a sharing of faith in the evangelical message itself as the believers come to understand its being fulfilled in their very lives. This gospel is not something that is cerebral; it is mystical insofar as it is based on an understanding of the gospel that Paul envisioned as taking the believers from being defined by the law in a way that veils our consciousness or understanding but grounds us in the transforming light of the very Spirit of God that was in Jesus Christ. Paul called this "the ministry of the Spirit" that comes to us "in glory" (2 Cor. 3:8).

Referring to the glory that shone on the face of Moses upon his encounter with God, which demanded he put on a veil so that the people would not be overcome, Paul builds on the notion of the "veil." He notes that only in Christ (not in the Mosaic covenant) will the veil be "set aside" (2 Cor. 3:14). Thus whoever "turns to the Lord [will find that] the veil is removed (2 Cor. 3:16). He then articulates what I consider to be the most mystical passage in the whole Pauline corpus: "Now the Lord is the Spirit, and where the Spirit of the Lord is, there is freedom. And all of us, with unveiled faces, seeing the glory of the Lord as though reflected in a mirror, are being transformed into the same image from one degree of glory to another; for this comes from the Lord, the Spirit" (2 Cor. 3:17-18). Our transformation from glory to glory is taking place within each of us by the Spirit in a way that should make us want to move from the works of the flesh to manifest to others that the fruits of this same Spirit are operable in our lives. Contrasting this "ministry" with the inability of the law to bring about this glory, Paul moves even more deeply into his mystical understanding of how the Spirit is at work within us when he links God's original act of cosmic creation to the new creation that comes from the Spirit. Thus he emphatically declares,

And even if our gospel is veiled, it is veiled to those who are perishing. In their case the god of this world has blinded the minds of the unbelievers, to keep them from seeing the light of the gospel of the glory of Christ, who is the image of God. For we do not proclaim ourselves; we proclaim Jesus Christ as Lord and ourselves as your slaves for Jesus's sake. For it is the God who said, "Let light shine out of darkness," who has shone in our hearts to give the light of the knowledge of the glory of God in the face of Jesus Christ. (2 Cor. 4:3-6)

Faithful to his understanding of the flesh/spirit dynamic at work in our lives, Paul concludes this declaration by noting that all of this mystical transformation within us takes place in our very human bodies or, as the popular song has it, in earthen vessels: "But we have this treasure in clay jars, so that it may be made clear that this extraordinary power belongs to God and does not come from us" (2 Cor. 4:7). It is clear from this passage that Paul's anthropology, formed by his Damascus experience, assumes that, whether we know it or not, or whether we've experienced it or not, the power and process of spiritual transformation in the Spirit and "morphing" into the Christ are taking place in the believer. Because of the Spirit, then, our spirituality is ordered to mystical transformation.

Grounded in this mystical reality of the Spirit transforming us into the Christ (4:19), we are called to be ministers of this gospel in which we believe in a way that is manifest in the kind of justice within the body of Christ that gives evidence of the charisms of the Spirit that are for the building up of this body. These gifts of each to the whole Paul called the *charisms* or *charismata*; he describes their significance and function both in Rom. 12:1-3 and more extensively in 1 Corinthians 12. Indeed, all of 1 Corinthians 12 describes the various gifts and how they are to be at the service of the whole community. This is clear from its opening lines; it is also clear that these gifts are to be the normal way the Spirit enables the church to be the church of all, not just of some who have been given the function of administration: "Now there are varieties of gifts, but the same Spirit; and there are varieties of services, but the same Lord; and there are varieties of activities, but it is the same God who activates all of them in everyone. To each is given the manifestation of the Spirit for the common good" (1 Cor. 12:4-7).

According to Pope Francis, it is this very empowerment of the Spirit in all the members of the church that makes the Roman Church both "catholic" and "apostolic." Rather than using "catholic" to mean a closed group

and "apostolic" being limited to the "successors of the apostles" as separated from the rest of the church, he wrote, "the Church has been born 'out-
going', that is, missionary. It is what we express qualifying her as Apostolic.
This term reminds us that the Church—on the foundation of the Apostles
and in continuity with them—is invited to take to all men the proclamation
of the Gospel, accompanying it with the signs of the tenderness and the
power of God." He also noted, "This also stems from the Pentecost event: it
is for the Holy Spirit, in fact, to surmount every resistance, to overcome the
temptation to be closed-in on oneself, among a few elect, and considering
oneself the sole recipients of God's blessing." He concluded his reflection
on "catholic" and "apostolic" by saying,

> If a group of Christians does this—"We are the elect, only us"—
> they die in the end. They die before, in their soul, then their body
> dies, because they don't have life, they don't have the capacity to
> generate life to other people, other peoples. They are not apostolic.
> It is the Spirit that leads us to encounter our brothers, including
> those most distant in every sense, so that they can share with us the
> love, peace, and joy that the Risen Lord has left us as a gift.[36]

Unfortunately, the passage from Acts (2:1-13) that served as the basis for
Pope Francis's reflection above was not stressed in Pope John Paul II's
encyclical on the Holy Spirit in the church and the world, even though Pope
John Paul wrote eloquently in that encyclical of the Pentecost event. His
words still remain to be realized against the background of a church whose
actual government and functioning have not broken from what we have
called "canonical nomism," the result of structures that reflected more the
Constantinian dispensation rather than the economy of salvation:

> In the midst of the problems, disappointments and hopes, deser-
> tions and returns of these times of ours, the Church remains faith-
> ful to the mystery of her birth. While it is an historical fact that the
> Church came forth from the Upper Room on the day of Pentecost,
> in a certain sense one can say that she has never left it. Spiritually
> the event of Pentecost does not belong only to the past: the Church
> is always in the Upper Room that she bears in her heart. The
> Church persevered in prayer, like the Apostles together with Mary,
> the Mother of Christ, and with those who in Jerusalem were the

---

36. Pope Francis, General Audience, September 17, 2014, http://www.zenit.org.

first seed of the Christian community and who awaited in prayer
the coming of the Holy Spirit.[37]

Again, the key elements of salvation history were addressed by Paul in his
Letter to the Galatians: just as Israel reached its divine purpose with the
coming of Jesus as the Messiah (3:23-25; 4:1-7), so now, with the Spirit
enabling the baptized to embody the Christ, they can no longer be identified by any form of separation. They are no longer slaves like those still
defined by the confines of Judaism; the outpouring of the Spirit in each
and every one of them frees them from this "sin" and enables them not only
to be children of God, calling God "Abba"; they are heirs of the very life of
God in this same Spirit (4:4-7). They are children, not of the flesh and the
Mosaic covenant, but of God in the power of the Spirit (4:21-31). And if
these new family members in the church now live by this Spirit, they should
walk by this same Spirit and allow this Spirit to cultivate its fruits in them.
This is to be done by letting this Spirit direct their lives by being what Frank
J. Matera calls their "moral compass."[38]

To close this chapter—which hopefully continues to lay the foundation
for the "fruit of the Spirit" that will be developed later—I quote again from
Pope Francis. I find in his various speeches and homilies continuous intima-
tions of what science is telling us about the illusion that we are divided and
the need to develop a new consciousness about our fundamental connectedness, which is expressed throughout this book: the need to move from
all forms (personal, communal, and institutional) of closed-in canonical or
cultural "nomism" that reinforces division and separation to a new creation
that is found in a new cosmic and "catholic" body of inclusion empowered
by the Spirit who makes us members of one family wherein all of us broth-

---

37. Pope John Paul II, *Dominum et Vivificantem,* no. 66. Earlier in the encyclical on the
Holy Spirit, however, Pope John Paul II does note that the original sin of human beings
involved dynamics of separation rather than participation in the life of God. It would seem
that this "original separation" is evidenced in human separation in all forms of separation:
personal, communal, and institutional through such "isms" as clericalism, racism, sexism,
tribalism, ageism, ethnocentrism, etc. In the new creation where everyone is "in Christ"
through the empowering indwelling of the Holy Spirit, it would follow that such separation can no longer be structured into the church's dynamics. See no. 37 (http://www.
vatican.va).

38. Frank J. Matera, *God's Saving Grace: A Pauline Theology* (Grand Rapid/Cam-
bridge: Eerdmans, 2012), 167. Matera explains, "The ethics of Galatians highlights the
role of the Spirit in the moral life. In this ethic, the Spirit is the moral compass that enables
the justified to know what is pleasing to God. More importantly, the Spirit enables them
to live in a way pleasing to God."

ers and sisters can call God "Abba," "Father," because of the outpouring of this Spirit in our hearts.

In the Letter to the Galatians, Paul warned his audience to move from the works of the flesh to the fruit of the Spirit. Similarly, in one of his morning homilies in early 2015, Pope Francis began by warning about the ways so many of us can so easily become closed in on ourselves, especially when we "barricade" our selves "behind the letter of the law." He noted that those "who seek security within the law end up becoming like a man or a woman in the cell of a prison behind bars: with a security without freedom." First he noted how this self-centeredness gets expressed. He said that "being closed can turn into so many things: pride, sufficiency, to think myself better than others, also vanity." He noted, "There are mirror-men and women, who are closed in on themselves and are constantly looking at themselves. These are religious narcissists, no? But, they have a hard heart, because they are closed, they are not open. And they look to defend themselves with these walls that they have around them." In contrast to such self-centered ways, he invited his audience, as did Paul, to be open to a new way of being and living that results when we become open to the Holy Spirit: "You can do thousands of courses of catechesis, thousands of spiritual courses, thousands of yoga courses, zen and all those things. But all of that will never be capable of giving you the freedom of a son [or daughter of God]. It is only the Holy Spirit that can move your heart to say 'Father.'"[39]

This brief overview of Paul's understanding of the Spirit's role in *making* history in a way that has brought about a new social order, a new creation, brings us to describe in fuller detail the event in Paul's life that enabled him to understand God's plan of salvation outlined on the chart used in this chapter as an "apocalyptic event" that changed his life—and the lives of all who would believe: the "Damascus experience."

---

39. Pope Francis, Morning Homily, January 9, 2015, http://www.zenit.org.

Chapter 3

Saul/Paul's Damascus Experience: An Invitation to the Mystical Life

The simple thesis of this chapter can be articulated in three insights: (1) Paul's Damascus experience was a mystical experience; (2) Paul's mystical experience was of divine origin (1:12), and his insight about recognizing the risen Christ in each member of Christ's body was the heart of this experience; and finally (3) this experience was the lens through which his whole theology was developed (including his Christology, pneumatology, soteriology, and ecclesiology). Understanding Paul's Damascus experience in this way can help ground the process for contemporary readers for what Karl Rahner envisioned. In one of its various iterations he wrote, "The devout Christian of the future will either be a 'mystic,' one who has experienced something, or he will cease to be anything at all."[1]

Paul at Damascus: A Mystical Experience

The account of "the transformative event of his life"[2] that changed Saul the persecutor into Paul the evangelizer has entered our popular lexicon: a "Damascus experience." In the mind of Evelyn Underhill, it represents the "typical case" describing all mystical experiences.[3] The phrase "Damascus experience" itself gives insight into Karl Rahner's definition of a mystic as "one who has *experienced something*." But what, at its core, was this "some-

---

1. Karl Rahner, "Christian Living Formerly and Today," in *Theological Investigations* VII (trans. David Bourke; New York: Herder & Herder, 1971), 15. Also Karl Rahner, "The Spirituality of the Future," *Theological Investigation* XX (trans. Edward Quinn; London: Darton, Longman & Todd, 1981), 149.

2. Marcus J. Borg and John Dominic Crossan, *The First Paul: Reclaiming the Radical Visionary behind the Church's Conservative Icon* (New York: HarperOne, 2009), 22.

3. Evelyn Underhill, *Mysticism: A Study in the Nature and Development of Man's Spiritual Consciousness* (New York: New American Library, 1974), 178.

thing" that Paul experienced, and how did it inform Paul's subsequent theology and spirituality?[4] And, as we will see in the next chapter, why is this experience so critical for the development of a mystical theology that will have relevance for our times? Using the text from 2 Cor. 5:14, Frank J. Matera writes, "Before the Damascus Christophany, Paul knew Christ *kata sarka* [according to the flesh], by which he meant that he understood the crucified Christ from a purely human perspective." But what, we can ask with Matera, happened at Damascus that made Paul write, "But 'from now on' (*apo tou nyn*), after his call/conversion, he understood him in light of the Damascus Christophany"?[5]

Before he refers to this event in his Letter to the Galatians, Paul briefly mentions his "earlier life in Judaism." At that time he notes, "I advanced in Judaism beyond many among my people of the same age, for I was far more zealous for the traditions of my ancestors." In this capacity, as a Pharisee widely versed in the law and believing in the threat to Judaism that "the Way" of Jesus posed, he "was violently persecuting the church of God and was trying to destroy it"(1:13-14).

Before his conversion, Paul totally rejected the claims of Jesus's followers that this Jesus who was crucified had now been raised and that his resurrection was a God-given confirmation that he was not only the Messiah, or the Christ, but also the Son of God. Neil Elliott points out that Saul, as an apocalyptic-minded Pharisee living in the Roman Empire, no doubt understood the political implications of one crucified by Roman power who "now stood vindicated at the right hand of God in heaven (cf. Acts 7:55)."[6] Such claims by his followers demanded swift and decisive action lest they spread. Saul's consequent effort to squash the "Way" (the name for Christians at that time) began with his search for believers in the various house churches of Jerusalem (which, at that time, were composed primarily of Jewish converts). Thus we read, "Saul was ravaging the church by entering house after house; dragging off both men and women, he committed them to prison" (Acts 8:3). It could not be clearer: Paul repudiated the claims made by the followers of Jesus, especially that they had encountered him as alive, this One whom the Jewish religious leaders saw as undermining their teaching and who then conspired to get him crucified for challenging imperial rule.

---

4. Much of the material in this section reflects my "Reclaiming the Mystical Interpretation of the Resurrection," *National Catholic Reporter*, April 20, 2014, http://ncronline.org.

5. Frank J. Matera, *God's Saving Grace: A Pauline Theology* (Grand Rapids: Eerdmans, 2012), 28.

6. Neil Elliott, *Liberating Paul: The Justice of God and the Politics of the Apostle* (Sheffield: Sheffield Academic Press, 1995), 23.

When the numbers of believers increased beyond the house churches in Jerusalem, Saul felt the need to find those secret believers who were numbered in the synagogues of Damascus. The Acts of the Apostles describes what happened in this zeal for the law that turned him into a zealot for love:

> Meanwhile Saul, still breathing threats and murder against the disciples of the Lord, went to the high priest and asked him for letters to the synagogues at Damascus, so that if he found any who belonged to the Way, men or women, he might bring them bound to Jerusalem. Now as he was going along and approaching Damascus, suddenly a light from heaven flashed around him. He fell to the ground and heard a voice saying to him, "Saul, Saul, why do you persecute me?" He asked, "Who are you, Lord?" The reply came, "I am Jesus, whom you are persecuting." (Acts 9:1-5)[7]

The actual narrative of Paul's "Damascus experience" is not to be found in Galatians but in Paul's 1 Cor. 15:1-10 (as well as in three places in Acts 9:3; 22:6; 26:12). This was a mystical experience insofar as Saul/Paul had done nothing to cause the experience; its origin was totally divine (Gal. 1:1, 11-12). This kind of "inbreaking" is a key criterion for naming as "mystical" what Saul experienced on the way to Damascus.

It is critically important that, in 1 Corinthians, Paul identifies as "the gospel" what he hands on to the Corinthians and which he himself had received: "Now I should remind you, brothers and sisters, of the good news [gospel] that I proclaimed to you, which you in turn received, in which also you stand, through which also you are being saved, if you hold firmly to the message that I proclaimed to you—unless you have come to believe in vain" (1 Cor. 15:1-3). The apocalyptic "good news" that Paul received on the way to Damascus came to him as a personal call as well as a call to a totally new gospel. This he subsequently proclaimed was to be the basis and the core, the means and the goal of every Christian's life. Paul assumed that this gospel was meant to transform every sister and brother in the house churches of Corinth, Galatia, and everywhere else—just as it had transformed and was continuing to transform the life of Paul.

Paul summarized the core of this gospel in a few sentences, which have become the essence of Christian faith for all time:

> that Christ died for our sins in accordance with the scriptures, that he was buried, and that he was raised on the third day in accor-

---

7. Paul's " Damascus experience" of Acts 9:1-5 is narrated again in Acts 22:5-8 and 26:12-15.

dance with the scriptures, and that he appeared (*horaō*) to Cephas, then to the twelve. Then he appeared (*horaō*) to more than five hundred brothers and sisters at one time, most of whom are still alive, though some have died. Then he appeared (*horaō*) to James, then to all the apostles. Last of all, as to one untimely born, he appeared (*horaō*) also to me. For I am the least of the apostles, unfit to be called an apostle, because I persecuted the church of God. But by the grace of God I am what I am, and his grace towards me has not been in vain. (1 Cor. 15:4-10)

In quoting Paul above, I have included the Greek word for "appear." Why? Because Paul makes it clear that what happened to Peter, the twelve, and "more than five hundred brothers and sisters at one time" (without mentioning Mary Magdalene's experience), happened to him as well. These resurrection "appearances" to those who had once walked with Jesus now served as the key evidence for the "good news" that resulted from Jesus's crucifixion and death: namely, his resurrection and presence to and within the "eye witnesses" who had experienced such "appearances." But years later, after the ascension of Jesus, the same kind of "appearance" happened to Saul/Paul. How could this be? What does resurrection really mean?

Jerome Murphy-O'Connor attaches a very specific meaning to Paul's references in 1 Cor. 9:1 and 15:8: "1 Corinthians 9:2 . . . has very close parallels in Mary Magdalene's experience, 'She saw Jesus' (John 20:14), and announced it to the disciples, 'I have seen the Lord' (John 20:18). They in turn proclaim, 'We have seen the Lord' (John 20:25). The use of the verb 'to see' in immediately post-paschal contexts is well attested." He continues, "His conversion as a post-paschal apparition is confirmed by 1 Corinthians 15:8 in which he lists himself as the last of those privileged to have seen the Risen Lord."[8]

According to Martinus C. de Boer, it is "of crucial importance"[9] that Paul referred to his Damascus experience wherein he suddenly came to understand the heart of the gospel, using the noun form *apokalypsis* (1:12c) and, shortly after, its verb form, *apokalypsai* (1:15). It is the contention of this chapter (and, ultimately, the thesis of this whole book) that the apocalyptic "appearance" to Paul of Jesus risen and alive in the members of the church defines him (Paul) as a mystic, despite what many Pauline exegetes might

---

8. Jerome Murphy-O'Connor, OP, *Paul: A Critical Life* (Oxford and New York: Oxford University Press, 1996), 72.

9. Martinus C. de Boer, *Galatians: A Commentary* (Louisville: Westminster John Knox Press, 2011), 78.

contend.[10] While I admit I am no scriptural exegete, everything I have learned and experienced and discussed about spirituality makes me conclude that Paul's self-described experience of apocalyptic proportions on the way to Damascus provided for him a mystical/prophetic lens through which he developed his whole theology, be it his soteriology, pneumatology, Christology, or ecclesiology.

However, this conviction is not shared by some key Pauline experts. Along with J. Christiaan Beker,[11] the one who has articulated this position most clearly, I believe, is Richard B. Hays, who calls this approach as proffered by Albert Schweitzer and Adolf Deissman[12] "the attempt to interpret Paul's theology as an expression of his personal subjective religious experience."[13] Hays writes that "no one contests the fact that Paul underwent intense personal religious experience," which was a "nonverbal mystical experience," but he notes his doubt as to the "language with which it is apprehended and interpreted."[14] At the other end of the interpretive continuum, Daniel Boyarin writes that Paul's "universalist" theology did not develop gradually but was "complete from the first moment" of his Damascus experience and that this universalism included a rejection of any separatist form of covenantal nomism and that the various regulations and rituals *could be observed by the Jews* but need not be and that these should be able to be sacrificed if such would help ensure "the constitution of all the Peoples of the world as the new Israel."[15]

---

10. More recently, an extended argument against the claim that the relationship between Christ and the believing members of the church involves some type of "mystical participation," can be found in David A. Brondos, *Paul on the Cross: Reconstructing the Apostle's Story of Redemption* (Minneapolis: Fortress Press, 2006), 189, *passim*.

11. J. Christiaan Beker, *Paul the Apostle: The Triumph of God in Life and Thought* (Edinburgh: T & T Clark, 1980). Beker clearly states that Paul's experience "is not the theme of his theology" (6).

12. Adolf Gustav Deissmann, *Paul: A Study in Social and Religious History* (2nd ed.; New York: Doran, 1926). Deissmann noted that Paul's phrases "in Christ" (which occurs over a hundred times in the genuine letters) and "Christ in" the believer is meant vividly and mystically.

13. Richard B. Hays, *The Faith of Jesus Christ: The Narrative Substructure of Galatians 3:1–4:11* (2nd ed.; Grand Rapids: Eerdmans, 2002), 3. I will show that the experience we will be calling "mystical" involves (1) an unannounced (apocalyptic) inbreaking that (2) pervades one's whole being (3) in a way that makes one feel connected to everyone and everything, (4) which becomes the lens by which one frames one's whole subsequent worldview. Perhaps Hays and others who reject Paul's mystical experience as the basis of his subsequent theology are not familiar with the fourth point above.

14. Richard B. Hays, *Faith of Jesus*, 4.

15. Daniel Boyarin, *A Radical Jews: Paul and the Politics of Identity* (Berkeley: University of California Press, 1994), 112. I thank Sandra Hack Polaski for this lead.

Along with Frank J. Matera, who calls the Damascus experience the "generative center" of Paul's theology,[16] in my mind, nobody has made a better case for Paul's "on the road" to Damascus experience as the basis for his whole theology than Joseph A. Fitzmyer. In *Paul and His Theology: A Brief Sketch*, Fitzmyer writes, "Paul's theology was influenced most of all by his experience near Damascus and by his faith in the risen Christ as the Son of God that developed from that experience." And without noting Paul's own description of the experience in Galatians as *apocalyptic* (1:12, 16), he links that experience with what I noted in the previous chapter to be Paul's most clear articulation of what today we would call Paul's mystical theology:

> He compared that experience to God's creation of light: "For God who said, 'Let light shine out of darkness,' has shone in our hearts to give the light of the knowledge of God's glory on the face of Christ" (2 Cor 4:6). The compulsion of divine grace pressed him into the service of Christ. His response was one of vivid faith, in which he confessed with the early church that "Jesus is Lord" (1 Cor 12:3; cf. Rom 10:9; Phil 2:11). In a creative act, that experience illumined Paul's mind and gave him an insight into what a disciple later called "the mystery of Christ (Eph 3:40)."[17]

As a result of that experience, Fitzmyer writes, three things happened to impact Paul's subsequent theology: (1) Paul became aware of "the unity of divine action for the salvation of all humanity, which is manifest in both the Old and new Dispensations" in a way that made him realize the God he served before as a Pharisee and after as a missionary "was the same God";[18] (2) that "God's salvific plan" revealed in the death and resurrection of Jesus made him the Messiah/Christ in a way that freed all humanity in such a way that "the cross, which had been the stumbling block to Jews, became in his eyes the 'power and wisdom of God' (1 Cor. 1:24). Henceforth, he would understand that crucified 'Lord of glory' (1 Cor. 2:8) as his exalted Messiah"; and, finally (3) the revelation of the Risen One impressed Paul with a new vision of salvation history. Before the encounter with the Lord, Paul saw human history divided into three great periods: (1) from Adam to Moses (the period without the law); (2) from Moses to the Messiah (the period of the law); and (3) the messianic age (the period when the law

---

16. Matera, *God's Saving Grace*, 11; see 45-46, 81, 156-57, 216, 246ff.

17. Joseph A. Fitzmyer, S.J., *Paul and His Theology: A Brief Sketch* (2nd ed.; Englewood Cliffs, NJ: Prentice Hall, 1987), 30.

18. Ibid.

would be perfected or fulfilled). The experience near Damascus taught him that the messianic age had already begun and would be definitively realized with "his coming in glory, his Parousia."[19]

I maintain, with Rahner, that not only must mysticism ground the future of Christianity, but, more specifically, Paul's mystically grounded theology must be reappropriated in Catholic spirituality today. The Christian mystic is one who has experienced the mystery of Christ in a way that grounds that person in that experience in a way that makes that person come to a new consciousness of what is real in a way that drives that person to make what is now "real" that person's whole life and life-stance. In Paul's eyes, the "Christ-event" is to be transformative in one's consciousness, conscience, and concern.

The process of "transformation" should accomplish in the believer what its original Greek meaning entails: *metamorphosis.* As indicated above, Fitzmyer writes that this "mythological image was quite current in Paul's day, and he did not hesitate to borrow it and apply it to the Christ-event." Consequently, "Paul sees Christ Jesus gradually reshaping human beings 'who turn to the Lord'" with the result that "the risen Christ shines creative light anew in human lives, which transforms them." The result is found "in one of the most sublime Pauline descriptions of the Christ-event," which I believe is meant to take place in every believer, not just mystics: "All of us, with unveiled face, behold the glory of the Lord and are being transformed into a likeness of him from one degree of glory to another" (2 Cor. 3:18).[20]

Pierre Teilhard de Chardin called the new consciousness of this univocity of being "the mystical milieu." True to his evolutionary understanding of everything in the universe, he wrote, "The mystical milieu *is not a complete zone* in which beings, once they have succeeded in entering it, remain immobilized. It is a *complex* element, made up of *divinized created being.*" On the one hand, he said that we "cannot give it precisely the name of God: it is his Kingdom" and on the other hand, he concluded, "Nor can we say that it *is*: it is in the process of *becoming.*"[21]

In support of my position I find many other academic exegetes: Andrie

---

20. Ibid., 69.

21. Pierre Teilhard de Chardin, *Writings in Time of War* (trans. René Hague; New York and Evanston, IL: Harper & Row, 1968), 137.

du Toit,[22] James D. G. Dunn,[23] Tatha Wiley (who has called Paul's Damascus event "his mystical Christ experience"),[24] Marcus Borg, and Dominic Crossan. However, the one who has grounded his whole theology of Paul in Paul's Damascus experience more clearly than any other exegete is Bruce W. Longenecker. He notes how Paul's letters flow from his "apocalyptic" Damascus experience:

> Paul never claims that his gospel [i.e., his "theology"] is simply founded on the basis of stringing a few texts together into a package. Instead, he claims its source to be an "apocalyptic" revelation from God (1.15-16; cf. 1.1, 11-12), resulting in a transformation of Paul's life to such an extent that the very enterprise of scriptural interpretation has itself been reconstituted for him. Paul seems to assume that a valid reading of scripture presupposes a cruciform, Christ-like character embodied within the reader (or community of readers). . . . Paul seems to presume that his various methods of interpreting scripture are valid if only because of the embodiment of Christ in his life, invading every aspect of him including his understanding of scripture.[25]

N. T. Wright has a different perspective: While not rejecting Paul's mystical experience, he rightfully insists, "Galatians contains some of the best-known statements of what has long been seen as Paul's theology of

---

22. Andrie du Toit, "'In Christ', 'In the Spirit' and Related Prepositional Phrases: Their Relevance for a Discussion on Pauline Mysticism," in Cilliers Breytenbach and David S. du Toit, eds., *Focusing on Paul: Persuasion and Theological Design in Romans and Galatians* (Berlin: de Gruyter, 2007), 129-45.

23. James D. G. Dunn, *Jesus, Paul, and the Gospels* (Grand Rapids: Eerdmans, 2011), 130.

24. Tatha Wiley, *Paul and the Gentile Women: Reframing Galatians* (New York/London: Continuum, 2005), 36.

25. Bruce W. Longenecker, *The Triumph of Abraham's God: The Transformation of Identity in Galatians* (Nashville: Abingdon Press, 1998), 169. In restating his core thesis in the final paragraph of this book, Longenecker writes, "Paul's vision is informed by his experience and understanding of the God who transforms identity. In this way, the account of Paul's own encounter with the risen son of God (1.12-16) serves as a paradigm for the whole of Paul's theology of Christian identity in Galatians. The experience of Christ's enlivenment within Paul informs his theology of transformation and crafts his vision of corporate cruciform existence. . . . And it is in this transformed identity of God's people that Paul locates the hope for communal and societal health, the advertisement of God's sovereignty, and the embodiment of God's emerging triumph" (188).

'incorporation' or 'participation.'"[26] However, he then immediately backs off from that: "This category, perhaps misleadingly called 'mysticism' by Albert Schweitzer, is increasingly recognized as one of the central motifs, if not *the* central motif, in Paul's soteriology and perhaps his thought as a whole."[27]

I don't often disagree publicly with someone like N. T. Wright, for whom I have great respect (evidenced by the many quotations from his writings that appear in this book). However, I believe that it is far from "misleading" to call Paul's Damascus experience "mystical." It should be almost self-evident to any student of spirituality (if not theology) that (1) Paul's Damascus experience was mystical and (2) it also became the lens by which he interpreted his whole theology of what it means to be "in Christ" and to have Christ be in each and every believer who is baptized in the church.[28] In support of this position Aquiles Ernesto Martínez writes (referring to Gal. 1:22; 2:4, 17; 3:14): "The prepositional phrase ἐν Χριστῷ Ἰησοῦ [in Jesus Christ] and other parallels appear many times in the Pauline letters. In [chapter 3,] verse 26, the phrase denotes Christ as the object of the faith of the Christian. In Pauline literature this refers to the *union and mystical relationship* of the believers with Christ."[29]

In a similar vein, my fellow Capuchin Raniero Cantalamessa, the papal preacher, has written that "Christ is the heart of the message of St. Paul, even more than grace and faith," precisely because of this mystical relationship of the believers with Christ. He explains:

> For Paul, mystical union with Christ through participation in his Spirit (living "in Christ" or "in the Spirit") is the ultimate goal

---

26. N. T. Wright, *Pauline Perspectives: Essays on Paul, 1978–2013* (Minneapolis: Fortress Press, 2013), 529. Surprisingly Richard Hays himself calls "participation in Christ as the key to Pauline soteriology" but doesn't seem to see the connection between Saul/Paul's experience of this participation as flowing from the Damascus event (*Faith of Jesus*, xxix).

27. Wright, *Pauline Perspectives*, 529.

28. This position is supported by James D. G. Dunn, *The New Perspective on Paul* (rev. ed.; Grand Rapids: Eerdmans, 2008), 351-52. Dunn also notes the support of H. G. Wood, "The Conversion of Paul; Its Nature, Antecedents and Consequences," *New Testament Studies* 1 (1954-55), 276-82; P. H. Menoud, "Revelation and Tradition: The Influence of Paul's Conversion on His Theology," *Interpretation* 7 (1953): 131-41

29. Aquiles Ernesto Martínez, "Fe Cristiana, Bautismo e Identidad Social: Diálogo con Gál 3,26-29," *Revista Bíblica* 2-11, 3-4), 170 n. 16. Martínez refers to F. F. Bruce, *The Epistle to the Galatians* (Grand Rapids: Eerdmans, 1982), 184; and R. N. Longenecker, *Galatians* (Dallas: Word, 1990), 154.

of Christian life; justification by faith is only the beginning and a means of attaining it. This calls us to go beyond the incidental polemical interpretations of the Pauline message that are centered on the question of faith and works and to rediscover beneath them the genuine thought of the apostle. What he is first of all eager to affirm is not that we are justified *by faith,* but that we are justified by faith *in Christ.* It is not so much that we are justified *by grace,* but that we are justified by the grace *of Christ.*[30]

Paul's "mystical gospel" wherein he spoke of his longing, like a woman in childbirth, for Christ "*morphein/*to be morphed" (4:19) in the lives of the believers has yet to be grasped and understood. Its recognition would usher in a vision of life for our church(es) and world that could be the source of transformation and ultimate evolution into ever-greater expressions of love. This "morphing" into Christ is the unseen dynamic that is taking place in every cell of our beings as baptized members of the church, as part of Christ's living body. Consequently, our task in the world is to give birth to the Christ in ways that transform us into Christ through the power of the Spirit at work in our human bodies. Nowhere is this more powerfully described than in what I consider the most mystical of all the Pauline passages: "Now the Lord is the Spirit, and where the Spirit of the Lord is, there is freedom. And all of us, with unveiled faces, seeing the glory of the Lord as though reflected in a mirror, are being transformed into the same image from one degree of glory to another; for this comes from the Lord, the Spirit" (2 Cor. 3:17-18). Then, after having compared the Christians to Moses who had to veil his face so that the Israelites would not be able to see the glory it revealed, he makes clear that God's glory is now at work in them: "For it is the God who said, 'Let light shine out of darkness,' who has shone in our hearts to give the light of the knowledge of the glory of God in the face of Jesus Christ" (2 Cor. 4:6).

Commenting on the wider context of the passage above from 2 Corinthians, and in light of Paul's earlier reflection on his Damascus experience wherein Christ "appeared" to him, Marcus Borg and John Dominic Crossan say emphatically that such passages "indicate that Paul had mystical experiences of the risen Christ. He experienced the post-Easter Jesus as the light and glory of God, the one who enlightened and transformed him."

---

30. Raniero Cantalamessa, OFMCap, *Remember Jesus Christ: Responding to the Challenges of Faith in Our Time* (trans. Marsha Daigle-Williamson; Frederick, MD: Word among Us Press, 2007), 53.

Such an understanding of the real meaning of mysticism and its application to Paul enable them to conclude:

> Paul was not simply a mystic. More precisely, he was a *Jewish Christ mystic*. He was a *Jewish* Christ mystic because ... Paul was a Jew and in his own mind never ceased being one. He was a Jewish *Christ* mystic because the context of his mystical experiences was Jesus as risen Christ and Lord. Afterward, Paul's identity became an identity "in Christ." And as a Christ mystic, he saw his Judaism anew in the light of Jesus.[31]

When Borg and Crossan noted that Paul was a *Jewish Christ* mystic they are addressing a dimension of Paul that has not been sufficiently addressed until lately, namely, his *Jewishness*. Just as Jesus envisioned himself as *reforming* Judaism, especially to help its adherents live more in the forest of the law of love than get caught in the trees of the minutiae of the law, so Paul also envisioned a Judaism free of separatist tendencies to be grounded in that same law of love that Jesus proclaimed. At the same time, just as Jesus died trying to *reform* Judaism, the same can be said of Paul. Probably nobody has summarized as well Paul's continued fidelity to a reformed *Judaism* than Tatha Wiley. She writes,

> Paul's mystical experience motivated a shift in loyalties, a "crossing over" from Pharisaic Judaism to the messianic-eschatological Judaism of the Jesus-followers. The two Judaisms shared the religious horizon of Jewish eschatological expectations and hopes. For the pharisaic Paul, these hopes were future, as yet unrealized. For the Christ-proclaimer Paul, the event of the resurrection had initiated the time of their fulfillment.[32]

Paul's accounts of his Damascus experience make clear that his kind of mystical experience (faithful to all mystical experiences) created not only a whole new world for Paul but, even more, an entirely new worldview, a new understanding of reality itself.[33] What Saul/Paul experienced on some road

---

31. Borg and Crossan, *First Paul*, 27.

32. Wiley, *Paul and the Gentile Women*, 37. She writes (p. 38): "To speak, then, of Paul as a convert or apostate from Judaism is misleading. Paul's language, his Scriptures, his holy symbols and his institutions were and remained Jewish, and his personal reflections suggest a continuing attachment," quoting Calvin Roetzel, *Paul: The Man and the Myth* (Minneapolis: Fortress Press, 1999), 46.

33. As noted above in n. 14, it is a matter of debate whether Saul/Paul's "Damascus

somewhere between Jerusalem and Damascus over two thousand years ago had cosmic significance insofar as it ushered in a totally new cosmic reality that had claim over everyone and everything.

The "Appearance" of Jesus to Paul in the Members of Christ's Body

Despite its brevity in the canonical books, Paul's own narration represents the one and only eyewitness account of someone's experience of Jesus risen as the Christ. Paul's account of his mystical resurrection "appearance" makes it clear: the only way the historical Jesus who died on the cross is alive today is as the risen Christ, and the only way the risen Christ is "alive" today is how the Jesus of history appears in the members of his body, the church. From the words he heard in the vision on the way to Damascus, the appearance of the risen Christ, for Paul, was linked inseparably to his realization that those he was persecuting were the living embodiment of Jesus. As he was on his way to persecute *them*, he heard the following words: "I am Jesus, whom you are persecuting" (Acts 9:5; 22:9; 26:15). There is no way the Jesus of history exists any more except in those in history at any time who come to faith in Jesus Christ and are baptized. His unique embodiment lives in each and every member.

In 1 Cor. 9:1, when Paul refers to his Damascus experience of the risen Christ, he identifies it as an appearance (*horaō*). Later in 1 Cor. 15:8, it becomes clear that the appearance of the Risen One was, for Paul, the realization that Jesus was now alive in the members of his body, the church. Just as Paul experienced Christ as risen and alive in each person he was persecuting, the historical Jesus had risen in those believers as the Christ; they were "in" Christ and Christ was "in them." I believe Paul's personal account of his experience represents the key difference from the Gospel narratives of peoples' resurrection experiences, which were written decades *after* 1 Corinthians. Every one of them can be visualized by the reader because of the genre used by the four evangelists; however, it seems that the "appearance" of Jesus to Mary Magdalene, Peter, James, and the others was more like a "sighting" of Jesus in some kind of bodily form in which he is still an individual. In Paul's experience, the only bodily experience he has of Jesus is in his mystical presence in the whole body of believers who are baptized. It is hard to interpret

---

experience" can be identified so clearly as the source of his consequent Christology, ecclesiology, and pneumatology. See Dunn, *New Perspective on Paul*, esp. 353-54. Without discussing the merits of the debate, it seems to me, from Paul's recollection of the words of Jesus, that Jesus's words make the risen Jesus as "the body of Christ in his persecuted members, i.e., the church" argument quite clear.

the accounts of Jesus's resurrection as being different from the resuscitation of Lazarus except that Lazarus returned looking like himself; Jesus took on other forms, but always (except for the breaking of the bread [Luke 24:30-35]) these forms were articulated as some kind of human form.

While the Gospel narratives continue to generate articles and books trying to articulate the underlying Easter experience of those who had walked with Jesus, it is the account of the one who never met Jesus that has relevance for us *today* as members of the church. Paul's account of the "appearance" of Jesus to him invites us to retrieve his theology of the resurrection and reclaim its basis in mysticism for the church today. Once we accept the reality that, in baptism, we are incorporated into Christ and, in this incorporative and participative reality (to use N. T. Wright's terms), we are to "be Christ" in a way that moves creation into a new creation, we will find little meaning in the internecine battles of those who become separated around issues such as "canonical nomism." Once Paul had experienced Christ as equally alive and functioning in all the members of the house churches he was persecuting, that mystical experience could no longer support a structural order for those churches built upon separation; it could only be expressed in ever-greater forms of communion and incorporation. Consequently, in today's church, if we were to revive this key belief of our faith, we would be more believable to our contemporaries, who are ever more skeptical of how we have traditionally articulated our faith.

It seems to me that, if we understand the scriptural notion of "seeing" or "appearance" as a reality that is more experiential and mystical than individually physical and corporeal, the list of those Paul notes to whom Christ had "appeared" should be endless. It should include everyone of all time who believes in this Christ and joins together in that faith to become the living members of his risen body. From this understanding, the resurrection is not only something that happened long ago as recorded in the Gospels; it is also something that is to happen in every Christian for all time. As Pope Benedict XVI noted in his amazing 2006 Easter Vigil homily, this reality is to happen in each of us "through faith and Baptism."

In speaking of Easter in evolutionary and cosmic terms, he asked the perennial question but gave it a response that was very different from what any pope (to my knowledge) has ever given:

> Of what exactly does this "rising" consist? What does it mean for us, for the whole world and the whole of history? A German theologian once said ironically that the miracle of a corpse returning to life— if it really happened, which he did not actually believe—would be

ultimately irrelevant precisely because it would not concern us. In fact, if it were simply that somebody was once brought back to life, and no more than that, in what way should this concern us? But the point is that Christ's Resurrection is something more, something different. If we may borrow the language of the theory of evolution, it is the greatest "mutation," absolutely the most crucial leap into a totally new dimension that there has ever been in the long history of life and its development: a leap into a completely new order which does concern us, and concerns the whole of history.[34]

Paul's Damascus experience was a mystical one. Paul came to "see" the Jesus of history as alive in each and every woman or man whom he had persecuted in the house churches of Jerusalem and intended to persecute (if he found them) in the synagogues of Damascus. Mystical experiences can happen to anyone (including unbelievers). Paul's mystical experience, his particular way of "seeing" Christ alive in the members of the body called the "church," is possible for all who believe in this mystical understanding of the body of Christ and who enter into the experience by baptism. Stated in another way, Paul's mystical experience of the resurrection (his personal experience of faith) led him to now become incorporated into the body of Christ, the church, by baptism. He could now no longer live as once he had; now he was in Christ, Christ was in him, and this "Christ" in him included all the baptized members of the body of the Risen One.

Those Who Are "in Christ" in the Church Are the Sign of the New Creation

Who was the "I am" that Paul was persecuting? None other than those whom he had persecuted in Jerusalem and meant to persecute in Damascus. The experience made it clear: this "Jesus," whom Paul was "persecuting," was alive in those very believers who were members of his church (similar to what Matthew would later describe in 25:31-46). These individuals had now become incorporated into Christ as his living members; they participated in his very life; they were the extension in time and place of his own human body. The Jesus of history was now the community of those "in Christ," or, as Jerome Murphy-O'Connor states so succinctly of Paul, "for him, the community is Christ."[35]

---

34. Pope Benedict XVI, *Easter Vigil Homily*, April 15, 2006, http://www.vatican.va.

35. Jerome Murphy-O'Connor, OP, *Becoming Human Together: The Pastoral Anthropology of St. Paul* (Wilmington, DE: Michael Glazier, 1984), 183.

In the Damascus appearance, Saul experienced Christ *in him* making Saul/Paul aware that Christ was *in those whom he was persecuting.* Furthermore, because these others had believed in this Christ, Christ was *in them*; and *they were in Christ.* Thus Galatians very often speaks explicitly of the members of the churches being "in" (or belonging to) Christ and Christ being "in" the members of the church(es) (1:22; 2:4, 16 [2x], 17; 3:14, 26, 27 [2x], 28, 29; 5:24) and of Christ being (living/morphing) in us two times (2:20; 4:19).

This way of being in Christ and Christ being in the believers, Paul declared, was the work of the Holy Spirit. Such other related issues as the Abrahamic promise, the (ir)relevance of the Mosaic law as the basis for salvation, and the notion of justification itself, as well as the need for believers to live by the Spirit by cultivating the Spirit's fruits—in short, everything—in the subsequent letters of Paul and statements attributed to him in Acts revolve around this central reality: Christ in the believer and the believer in Christ. Paul called this "fullness of time" event when Christ "appeared" to him "the gospel." However it might be "spun," this gospel proclaimed one story: if anyone "bought this story" in faith and would be baptized into Christ by participating in a community of fellow believers, they, in their own lives, would be participants in the new cosmic order. At the core of this new cosmic order was an overturning of the rule of separation that had created structure for the Jewish community as it tried to remain faithful to the Mosaic law.

While the Synoptic Gospels tell the story of Jesus's gospel announcing the good news of the kingdom of God (or what I describe elsewhere as the rule or governance of God's Trinitarian Relatedness on earth as it is in heaven at all levels of life), it was his faithfulness to the proclamation of this gospel in the Roman world that got Jesus crucified as subversive. However, when Paul experienced Jesus no longer dead but risen in the lives of the Christians, this became *his good news.* Thus, in all his letters, paralleling the gospel of the kingdom of God proclaimed by Jesus, Paul proclaimed the working out of this gospel in the lives of those who now were to witness to that gospel in the world of every day because of the Spirit of Jesus Christ who now empowered them to do so. In this sense, Bruce Longenecker writes, "The theological thread that unites the whole of Paul's Letter to the Galatians is perhaps best summed up in the phrase 'the singularity of the gospel,'" referring to the exclusive claim of Christ upon the lives of believers, resulting in the complete transformation of their individual and corporate identity and the renunciation of all competing loyalties."[36]

---

36. Longenecker, *Galatians*, 148.

Paul's statement in Gal. 3:28 that those who are "in Christ" are "no longer Jew or Greek, slave or free, male and female" but a new creation represents his conviction that "in Christ" an apocalyptic inbreaking has erased the old categories of separation at all levels of life, including his own received Judaic law and practices, which defined holiness in terms of separation. Furthermore, when he says in two places in Galatians (5:6; 6:15) that "neither circumcision nor uncircumcision" matters it is clear that his mystical experience has demystified such heretofore significant matters of debate (and division). Does not such a conclusion speak to our contemporary battles around questions like who can and who cannot touch the sacred vessels, who can be present in the sanctuary, who can be spiritual directors for seminarians, as well as who can be ordained? All these issues reflect the "old order"; now, as Paul would write later in 2 Corinthians (5:17), "So if any one is in Christ, there is a new creation: everything old has passed away; see, everything has become new!"

If *everything* old has passed away and everything has become new by being "in Christ," this includes how we think about the passion and death of Jesus and especially how we understand and interpret his resurrection and embodiment in the lives of believers, who are the church. Thus Luke Timothy Johnson writes, "Thinking about the Resurrection in temporal terms, however, is misleading. The Resurrection is better spoken of as an existential reality; not as one event among others but as an act of God that reveals and changes the structures of existence. Paul speaks of the resurrection-life as a 'new creation' (Gal. 6:15) in which everything old has passed away and 'behold, everything is new' (2 Cor. 5:17)."[37]

It is not only how we understand the resurrection of Jesus Christ and our embodiment of this reality in our experience, but that we are to give evidence of being "in Christ" in the way we move from *everything old* that separates to bring about a new structure of existence based on inclusion and communion. This new creation is to be the personal and social identifier of every individual Christian and each and every Christian community. Thus Tatha Wiley writes,

> For Jews, the Torah marked the social boundary between the spheres of holy and unholy or, to put it in terms of purity, between pure and impure. Holiness and purity were contingent on following the way of the Torah. In a similar fashion, "being in Christ"

---

37. Luke Timothy Johnson, "History and Divinity," book review of Bart D. Ehrman, *How Jesus Became God: The Exaltation of a Jewish Preacher from Galilee* (New York: HarperCollins, 2014), in *Commonweal* 142.3 (February 6, 2015), 25.

(3:28; 5:5) was Paul's creation of a social boundary for Gentiles as God's people. The women and men who belong to this new community "define a new social reality, different from the reality of both Jews and Jewish Christians." Paul's principle for membership and salvation was the same for women and men. Their initiation through baptism was gender-neutral too.

Through Christ, the rules that mark some as persons and others as non-persons have been eliminated. The baptismal confession in Gal. 3:28 makes it clear that the old distinctions are no longer binding, and in Christ an entirely new social order must appear. Thus Wiley concludes, "The assembly restores the original equality of women and men given in Genesis 1:27."[38]

Even if this has not yet happened, the vision remains nonetheless: all ethnic, racial, and sexual divisions are to be erased; the status quo is gone. Indeed, despite being "in the United States" or any other country or "in the Catholic Church" or any other Christian community, for those who are "in Christ," a counterculture should be emerging.[39] No longer should ethnic identity be defined by actual descent; a new kind of "kinship" is established in Christ, that of sons and daughters of God through the very Spirit of Christ who creates a new family of equals: brothers and sisters. This is the new ethnicity that is not of the flesh but of the spirit. This new ethnic group is no longer to be determined by blood or any other form of descent. This new kin is now "an ethnic group [that] is constituted by people who mutually recognize each other as members of that group"[40] and who are now to be defined not by the Mosaic law but by the law of love.

Understanding Mysticism and Its Relevance
for the Christian of the Future

The turn of this century witnessed much debate arising from the writings of "the Four Horsemen of the New Atheism":[41] Richard Dawkins, Daniel Dennett, Sam Harris, and the late Christopher Hitchens. While they didn't spend much time debunking "God" as such, the "god" of the Big Three

---

38. Wiley, *Paul and the Gentile Women,* 51.

39. J. Louis Martyn, "Galatians 3:28, Faculty Appointments, and Overcoming Christological Amnesia," *Katallagete* 8.1 (1982): 41. Here I also indicate my debt to Charles H. Cosgrove, "Did Paul Value Ethnicity?," *Catholic Biblical Quarterly* 68 (2006): 268-90 (279).

40. Bruce Hansen, *"All of You Are One": The Social Vision of Galatians 3.28, 1 Corinthians 12.13 and Colossians 3.11* (London/New York: T. & T. Clark, 2010), 34.

41. For a video of their interaction, see https://www.youtube.com.

patriarchal religions (Islam, Roman Catholicism, and Mormonism) was a prime target for them because "he" looks so much like the men in charge of those religions.

While I have addressed elsewhere their key concerns as to why they reject the "god" of such religions,[42] I think that they often overstate their case. Nonetheless, one of them, Sam Harris, has intrigued me. Unlike his peers, he takes spirituality very seriously, even if he is dismissive of some mainline religions such as Catholicism. Moreover, he seems to believe deeply in the kind of mystical experiences we have discussed above, even if he believes such can be explained by neuroscience alone. Harris asserts that history has shown "a certain range of human experience [that] can be appropriately described as 'spiritual' or 'mystical'— experiences of meaningfulness, selflessness, and heightened emotion that surpass our narrow identities as 'selves' and escape our current understanding of mind and brain."[43] He notes that such "spiritual" or "mystical" experiences can be studied and analyzed. Therefore, for him, "Mysticism is a rational enterprise. . . . The mystic has recognized something about the nature of consciousness prior to thought, and this recognition is susceptible to rational discussion. The mystic has reasons for what he believes, and these reasons are empirical. The roiling mystery of the world can be analyzed with concepts (this is science), or it can be experienced free of concepts (this is mysticism)."[44]

Harris's insight holds true for me, from my own experience, my conversations with others who have claimed to have had mystical experiences, and from my research into the dynamics of mysticism. All reveal a definite pattern that can be tracked and studied. However, before I outline the four dynamics that reveal such a pattern in various people's mystical experiences, I want to begin with a personal experience that I would term "mystical."

Between 1945 and 1992 the United States tested its nuclear weapons at a site beyond the little town of Mercury, Nevada, about an hour from Las Vegas. As a doctoral student in theology in Berkeley, California, I would join the various protests outside the test site. During my first protest, we rose early in Las Vegas (the closest place for sleeping), and we got to Mercury just before the workers passed us in their buses. We stood by the roadside waving at them, giving them the peace sign. While some returned the

---

42. Michael H. Crosby, *Repair My House: Becoming a "Kindom" Catholic* (Maryknoll, NY: Orbis Books, 2012).

43. Sam Harris, *The End of Faith: Religion, Terror, and the Future of Reason* (New York: W. W. Norton, 2005).

44. Ibid., 221.

sign, others gave us only half of it; we smiled and waved anyway. After the last bus passed, taking them another sixty miles into the actual test site, the coordinators asked us to go off and reflect on what had happened.

I had never spent any time in a desert before, and was surprised to see how much green had made its way through the hard earth. As I pondered the survival skills of plants, I noticed a dainty purple flower that was at the end of some of the green plants that had survived. As I went to pick it, a voice in me said, "Don't you dare; let it be." In that moment I found myself one with it and everyone and everything in the universe. It was a kind of connection I had never known.

That experience reminds me of the great story found in Alice Walker's *The Color Purple,* where Shug tells Celie what happened when she decided to stop thinking about God as the "old white man." She begins by referring to God as "It." What transpires next sets the stage for Shug's description of her experience, one that resembles those of the greatest of mystics. Celie writes,

> It? I ast.
> Yeah. It. God ain't a he or a she, but a It.
> But what do it look like I ast.
> Don't look like nothing, she say. It ain't a picture show. It ain't something you can look at apart from anything else, including yourself...

And then comes Shug's narration of her (mystical) experience:

> She say, My first step from the old white man was trees. Then air. Then birds. Then other people. But one day when I was sitting quiet and feeling like a motherless child, which I was, it come to me: that feeling of being part of everything, not separate at all. I knew that if I cut a tree, my arm would bleed. And I laughed and I cried and I run all around the house. I knew just what it was. In fact, when it happen you can't miss it.[45]

My experience at the Nevada test site and Shug's tale reflect the same dynamics as a story told about Francis of Assisi who, in embracing a man with leprosy, discovered Christ being crucified anew in human beings whom his society had excluded. It also recalls Catherine of Genoa's trans-

---

45. Alice Walker, *The Color Purple* (New York: Washington Square Press, 1982), 178.

formative experience of being overwhelmed by a sense of her sinfulness and overtaken by a sense of God's goodness. Such inbreaking moments may also call to mind the Alcoholics Anonymous story of Bill W's famous kitchen table experience in Akron when he became free(r) of his addictions.

Having taken note of these examples, we can now consider Sam Harris's contention that such experiences may be a "matter of rational enterprise"; in other words, they follow a definite pattern that can be outlined in the dynamics of any *experience* that can be called "mystical" or "contemplative": (1) it begins with an inbreaking or apocalyptic experience such as what Paul himself described happened to him on the way to Damascus (Martyn calls it an "invasion"); (2) it overpowers one's whole being; (3) it makes one feel connected to everyone and everything. This experience provides the essential lens through which (4) one interprets all reality. In her classic work *Mysticism*, Evelyn Underhill brings together the elements of the mystical experience when she describes it as a "a sudden, intense, and joyous perception of God immanent in the universe; of the divine beauty and unutterable power and splendour of that larger life in which the individual is immersed, and of a new life to be lived by the self in correspondence with this now dominant fact of existence."[46]

To the degree that "reality" does not reflect one's mystical experience, it is an illusion, as Underhill makes clear. Paul himself articulates this new understanding when he describes the insight that came to him as a result of his Damascus experience: "In Christ Jesus neither circumcision nor uncircumcision counts for anything; the only thing that counts is faith working through love" (5:6) in all the members of the body of Christ. Even more clearly Paul interprets this new vision as a totally new creation (2 Cor. 5:17).

In his book *Waking Up: A Guide to Spirituality without Religion* (2014), Harris himself recalls his own mystical experience, which occurred on a visit to Israel. It happened on "an afternoon on the northwestern shore of the Sea of Galilee, atop the mount" where Matthew's Gospel describes Jesus preaching the Sermon on the Mount. Harris writes, "As I gazed at the surrounding hills, a feeling of peace came over me. It soon grew to a blissful stillness that silenced my thoughts. In an instant, the sense of being a separate self—an 'I' or a 'me'—vanished." While he didn't call this experience a "God-experience," merely a mystical or religious experience, what happened to him at the Sea of Galilee followed the dynamics that he outlined earlier. He wrote,

---

46. Evelyn Underhill, *Mysticism* (New York: E P Dutton, 1911, 1961), 179.

For millennia, contemplatives have known that ordinary people can divest themselves of the feeling that they call "I" and thereby relinquish the sense that they are separate from the rest of the universe. This phenomenon, which has been reported by practitioners in many spiritual traditions, is supported by a wealth of evidence—neuroscientific, philosophical, and introspective. Such experiences are "spiritual" or "mystical," for want of better words, in that they are relatively rare (unnecessarily so), significant (in that they uncover genuine facts about the world) and personally transformative. They also reveal a far deeper connection between us and the rest of the universe than is suggested by the ordinary confines of our subjectivity.[47]

Harris's insights help me recognize the futility of arguments about the resurrection, as though it were something that happened to Jesus apart from what happened to those who "saw" it or "experienced" it (or will continue to do so today). Hence I am convinced that moving from a concentration on the Gospel narratives stressing the "bodily" resurrection to a reclamation of the mystical experience of the risen Christ will help us grasp the heart of the mystery of faith.

The Challenge to Be Mystics in the Prophetic Tradition

When we look for an archetypal example of a mystical experience in the Bible, we need look no farther than that described in Isaiah 6. Evelyn Underhill, the great British writer on mysticism, has stated that the elements contained in that text constitute the core of every prophetic/mystical calling.[48] Isaiah's experience is germane to a core thesis of this book about "covenantal nomism,"[49] given that the very architecture of the Temple that

---

47. Sam Harris, *Waking Up: A Guide to Spirituality without Religion* (New York: Simon & Schuster, 2014), 81. For an interesting comment on Harris's narration by a "believer," see Frank Bruni's column "Between Godliness and Godlessness," *New York Times*, August 30, 2014.

48. Evelyn Underhill, *Mystics in the Church* (New York: Schocken Books, 1971), 32-33. Surprisingly, Underhill herself admitted that she did not seek to act on the connection between the mystical and prophetic until later in her life.

49. From my research, I agree with those who do not believe Paul ever truly "converted" from Judaism, but he did convert from "covenantal nomism." Dunn writes, "Gal. 1.13-14 certainly points us to the conclusion that Paul was converted 'from Judaism.' But the 'Judaism' of which he speaks is not the Judaism of modern historical and sociological analysis. It is the 'inside' view of first century Judaism, or rather, of a particular understanding and practice of the ancestral religion of the Jews in the first half of the first cen-

separated groups from each other was an effort to reinforce Israel's understanding of itself as "holy" and to interpret that "holiness" as separation
between what was clean and unclean; Isaiah's mystical experience shook
up that whole worldview.

Since a consequence of a mystical experience is the creation of a whole
new insight or vision of life and the world that becomes the perspective for
a whole new worldview, it is important to realize that Isaiah quite likely was
already part of the "holy" priesthood. However, his mystical experience
of *God's holiness* gave him a totally new understanding of his own priestly
unholiness as well as that of the cultic priesthood of that day. Thus, upon
his experience of the trifold holiness of God proclaimed by the seraphs (Isa.
6:3-4), he immediately proclaimed: "Woe is me! I am lost, for I am a man of
unclean lips, and I live among a people of unclean lips"; and lest anyone try
to convince him to return to what he once considered to be holy and clean,
given this mystical experience of God's holiness, he reassured himself, "yet
my eyes have seen the King, the LORD of hosts!" (Isa. 6:5). What once was
holy and clean was now unholy and unclean. This mystical grounding challenged him to proclaim it prophetically as the construct of a new kind of
holiness. It led him to hear the call to go to the people and invite them to
conversion.

If the Christian of the future must be a mystic, there is good reason to
believe that a mystical understanding of the church's identity and holiness,
ultimately grounded in baptism rather than in the dynamics of canonical
nomism or cloaked in the kind of holiness that sustains and sanctions clerical separation, will incur rejection. Still, the prophetic call for conversion
is necessary if the church is to ever return to being truly "in Christ" and a
sign of the embodiment of the risen Christ to the world in the community
of the baptized.

I sincerely believe that Paul's account of his resurrection experience will
do much to move the church into the mystical future envisioned by Rahner.
Understanding this will also honor the mythos of the Gospel writers who
tried to describe the experience of Jesus being "seen" by Cephas, Mary
Magdalene, James, and the five hundred in a way that is more believable.

Saul was transformed by his mystical experience of the risen Christ. He
insisted that his resurrection experience was equal to that of the disciples
in the Gospels who had their own experiences of "seeing" Jesus as alive in,
among, and around them. This led the convert Paul to become the mission-

---

tury CE. Indeed, it would perhaps be more accurate to speak of Pharisaic Judaism as that
from which Paul turned in his conversion" (*New Perspective on Paul*, 359-60).

ary theologian of the church's self-understanding as the extension in time and space of the Jesus of history. Now this Jesus was alive ("risen") in each and every member of the living body of Christ, in the church and throughout the cosmos.

This approach is closer to the kind of mysticism or spirituality that Harris envisions as authentic. He writes,

> There is no doubt that experiences of this sort are worth seeking, just as there is no doubt that the popular religious ideas that have grown up around them, especially in the West, are as dangerous as they are incredible. A truly rational approach to this dimension of our lives would allow us to explore the heights of our subjectivity with an open mind, while shedding the provincialism and dogmatism of our religious traditions in favor of free and rigorous inquiry.[50]

Returning to the 2006 Easter Vigil homily of Pope Benedict XVI, the pope declared that the resurrection "ushered in a new dimension of being, a new dimension of life in which, in a transformed way, matter too was integrated and through which a new world emerges." Such imagery shows the necessity for Easter people in every age to continue our own work of transformation that we might, in Christ, usher in a new created order that transcends all forms of human separation (2 Cor. 5:15-17). In this way, we ourselves will be resurrected, becoming a new creation (*kainē ktisis*) that reflects the essence and lived reality of the resurrection as revealed in Paul's account and in Benedict's remarks. This *kainē ktisis* is not something ethereal; it points to an anthropological transformation and, indeed, a cosmological one as well.[51]

There will continue to evolve in the world, beginning with us, "a new dimension of being, a new dimension of life in which, in a transformed way, matter" too will be "integrated and through which a new world emerges."

---

50. Harris, *The End of Faith*, 2004.

51. This is the thesis of a growing number of scholars. See T. Ryan Jackson, *New Creation in Paul's Letters: A Study of the Historical and Social Setting of a Pauline Concept* (Tübingen: Mohr Siebeck, 2010). Jackson interprets the new creation motif in Paul in Galatians and 2 Cor. 5:17 as both anthropological and cosmological. For a stress on its meaning as more limited to human beings (anthropology), see Moyer Hubbard, *New Creation in Paul's Letters and Thought* (Cambridge: Cambridge University Press, 2002). Hubbard also stresses the text as being more pneumatological than anthropological.

When we allow the resurrection to "reach" and "seize" us in this way, the freedom that comes from being the new creation in Christ, as Paul noted in 1 Corinthians, will be the best Easter present we will not only "receive" but can also "hand on."[52] With freedom as the "main feature of this new creation,"[53] we will have the basis for being free of the structures and dynamics of control that constitute what I have called canonical nomism and that still holds sway in the hearts and minds of many in our church today.

---

52. The core of this section has been adapted from my article on the topic in the *National Catholic Reporter*, "Reclaiming the Mystical Interpretation of the Resurrection," April 20, 2014, http://ncronline.org.

53. Gys M. H. Loubser, "Life in the Spirit as Wise Remedy for the Followers of the Flesh: Ethical Notes from Galatians," *Neotestamentica* 43.2 (2009): 356.

Chapter 4

The Fruit(s) of the Spirit: Markers of a Mystical Stance in Life

We have discussed how Paul's Damascus experience conforms to a pattern that can be called normative for a mystical experience. The Jesus followers of "the Way" whom Paul was persecuting, he now discovers, are Jesus's living embodiment; they are the "body of Christ." Christ is "in them," and they are "in Christ." The "me" that he was persecuting is "they."[1]

This mystical insight into Christ's identification *with* the very ones whom Paul is persecuting grounds his whole Christology and ecclesiology, both of which were, above all, pneumatologies. In the power/energy of the Holy Spirit, the historical Jesus is now alive in the women and men whom Paul is persecuting; those whose faith has led them to be baptized in(to) this Christ *have become* Christ's living embodiment. Because of their faith leading to their baptism, in them the Jesus of history has become the Christ of their faith. In persecuting them, Paul has been continuing the violence (to use his own image) that led to the crucifixion of Jesus. This violence must stop; it has to be transformed into love. Love in and among, for and from these members of the churches has to define the rest of Paul's life. In the power of the Holy Spirit he himself must be "morphed" into "the Christ" (4:19), a transformation that will make him the embodiment of a new created order (see 2 Cor. 5:17).

What Paul had experienced mystically, which became the foundation of his whole spirituality and theology, was what he thought should become not only the theology but especially the spirituality of his Christian converts. Thus he could urge them to imitate him as he imitated Christ (1 Cor.

---

1. A definite parallel example of the risen Christ identifying with those experiencing violence, whether through persecution in Saul/Paul's situation or the violence of hunger, thirst, inadequate health care, etc., is evident in Jesus's reference to such people in need as himself in Matt. 25:31-46.

4:16; 11:1) or, as he wrote to the Galatians, "become as I am" (4:11). But was this imitation really possible when the source of his faith was different from theirs? Was it fair for him to expect that his converts would be able to have a faith just like his, when his came from a personal experience of the risen Christ and theirs came from his testimony about it? His testimony was firsthand; theirs was handed down. To that degree it could not be as personal and convicting as his. Unfortunately, not too many authors have discussed this key difference between Paul's own conversion and that of the members of his communities. Nowhere are we told that any of them had a confirming "experience" like his on the way to Damascus. Thus their conversion and their faith might not have such a solid foundation as his. However, the fact that they were being evangelized by the one who had once been a violent persecutor of the gospel and was now its chief promoter was powerful testimony for anyone's faith!

Obviously, any assumption Paul may have had that these Galatian converts were solidly grounded in the faith would have been erased when he learned that they had fallen away so quickly from the gospel they had received. Paul's consequent detailed analysis and arguments in Galatians seemed addressed more to the Teachers than to the Galatians, who were not Jews and not steeped in the law or the promises made to Abraham (3:1-29). They would not have grasped the theological implications of the story of the male children born to Abraham by the slave woman Hagar and the (unnamed) free woman, Sarah (4:22-31). Nonetheless, Paul's question to the Galatian Christians was straightforward: Were they saved through that law or through their faith in the Spirit of Jesus Christ (2:16) living in and among them as the extension of his body in the world? As he had begun his life in the flesh and discovered the Spirit, now they, conversely, who had received the Spirit, had given themselves to the law and the flesh. They should be living the life of the Spirit by bearing witness to the Spirit's fruits in their actions and relationships rather than reverting to enslavement by the "works of the flesh" (2:15–4:32).

The challenge that faced Paul makes it clear that what we are trying to do in this book requires something else: When we try to understand what it means for us that the Christian of the future needs to be a mystic, we also must be clear(er) about what we mean by mysticism, mystical experience, mystical prayer, and the need for a mystical stance in life.

While building on Rahner and his understanding of the need to cultivate "the mystical life,"[2] I turn to the one person who, in my mind, has not only

---

2. On the applicability of the mystical dynamics for daily living, see Karl Rahner,

made the necessary distinctions but developed them as well in her classic *Mysticism*: Evelyn Underhill.[3] In one of her varied definitions of mysticism, she defines it as "the name of that organic process which involves the perfect consummation of the love of God: the achievement here and now of the important heritage of man." Linking the goal of mysticism as the dynamic that reflects the mystical experience of union with God, self and everything and everyone in the universe, Underhill also includes in her definition mystical prayer and the mystical stance insofar as she writes that mysticism "is the art of establishing his [the human's] conscious relation with the Absolute."[4] In talking about mysticism, Rahner also noted the need to include under the rubric of "mysticism" a person's mystical experiences and what I call the need for a mystical stance for the Christian of the future.[5] Because many more proficient than I have developed approaches to mystical or contemplative prayer and praying, this book will concentrate on how we can develop a mystical stance.

Someone who has outlined the main dimensions of mysticism is Pierre Teilhard de Chardin.[6] Building on some unarticulated religious experience he had early in his ministry in Egypt (1905–1908) Teilhard later said his own mystical experience came to him with the realization that through nature he was immersed in God.[7] Making the connection to his need to witness to that experience by developing a mystical stance in life, he wrote in his diary on January 26, 1918, "I see more and more that I must live and realize my mysticism—plunge myself into the divine Milieu, and develop it around me."[8]

"Experiencing the Spirit," in *The Practice of Faith: A Handbook of Contemporary Spirituality* (ed. Albert Raffelt and Karl Lehmann; New York: Crossroad, 1986), 81, *passim*.

3. Evelyn Underhill, *Mysticism: A Study in the Nature and Development of Man's Spiritual Consciousness* (New York: New American Library, 1974). I believe Underhill offers the best outline for our purposes. In choosing her approach I am aware of the work (and its limitations vis-à-vis our purposes here) of William James, *The Varieties of Religious Experiences* (New York: Collier-MacMillan, 1961); and Bernard McGinn, *The Foundations of Mysticism* (New York: Crossroad, 1991).

4. Underhill, *Mysticism*, 81.

5. Rahner, *The Practice of Faith*, 70, 84.

6. What has helped me understand more clearly the mysticism of Teilhard de Chardin is Ursula King, *Towards a New Mysticism: Teilhard de Chardin & Eastern Religions* (New York: Seabury, 1980). I am indebted to King for the references to Teilhard de Chardin in this book.

7. Pierre Teilhard de Chardin, *Writings in Time of War* (trans. René Hague; New York and Evanston, IL: Harper & Row, 1968), 28ff.

8. Teilhard de Chardin, "Journal," in King, *Towards a New Mysticism*, 48.

In arguing one of my key points about Catholicism's recent entrapment by "canonical nomism," I would ask if a key passage about "Christian mysticism" in *The Divine Milieu* can be attributed to Catholicism itself (although it certainly could be applied to many "Catholic" expressions, such as Carmelite, Franciscan, and Jesuit mysticism): "Christianity alone . . . saves . . . the essential aspiration of all mysticism: *to be united* (that is, to become the other) *while remaining oneself*." He explains,

> Christian mysticism extracts *all* that is sweetest and strongest circulating in all the human mysticisms, though without absorbing their evil or suspect elements. It shows an astonishing equilibrium between the active and the passive, between possession of the world and its renunciation, between a taste for things and an indifference to them.[9]

Because of such statements, Ursula King, who studied all the extant writings of Teilhard de Chardin, concluded that Chardin was convinced that "Christian dogma and mysticism can develop freely" and that this conviction can be found behind all his writings. Thus she writes, "Teilhard's primary concern was with such a development of Christian mysticism."[10]

Paul's "Paraenesis" Spirituality in Galatians 5:1-6:10: The Fruit(s) of the Spirit

All the authentic letters of Paul follow a basic pattern. They begin with a salutation that generally includes the sender's (Paul) or senders' names; names the recipient(s), and gives a greeting of grace and peace. Next there is some type of thanksgiving that indicates the letter's purpose, combined with a prayer for those receiving the letter. The main part of the letter, or its body, presents a theological rational or instruction that addresses problems, beliefs, and suggested practices. This is followed by a "paraenesis," an outline of ethical instructions for putting into practice the theology presented, along with an exhortation to fidelity. The body of the letter is often closed with the promise of a visit. The letter ends with a more formal closing that includes a wish of grace and peace (again), greetings to various individuals and/or groups, a "holy kiss," and some kind of doxology and blessing.

Galatians, however, differs. Given what I have thus far written, it is not

---

9. Pierre Teilhard de Chardin, *The Divine Milieu: An Essay on the Interior Life* (New York: Harper & Row, 1965), 119.

10. King, *Towards a New Mysticism*, 120.

surprising that the "thanksgiving" that usually begins a letter is missing. Rather than any thanksgiving, as we have seen, Paul moves immediately to challenging his recipients. The letter also differs in its ending (or lack thereof). It ends quite abruptly without any specific greetings to individuals or groups and merely wishes grace to all.

This unique difference in the Letter to the Galatians notwithstanding, a key element in the other letters is present here: the paraenesis, or ethical instructions, on how the members of the house churches should put into practice the theology outlined in the letter. Building on his theological arguments in 2:15–4:32, Paul moves in the final part of the letter to an exhortation that the Galatians put into practice the theology he has developed (5:1–6:10). In his encyclical on the Holy Spirit, Pope John Paul II writes about this paraenesis, especially the section that will concern us regarding the "works of the flesh" and the "fruit(s) of the Holy Spirit." "Properly understood, this is an exhortation to live in the truth, that is, according to the dictates of an upright conscience, and at the same time it is a profession of faith in the Spirit of truth as the one who gives life."[11] An "upright conscience" is not primarily based on "truths" identified with any law setting people apart; rather it is grounded in the Spirit so that one freely gives expression to that Spirit's presence in the style of one's life. Thus Paul does not articulate more norms to be practiced as a sign of the Spirit's presence in the lives of the baptized; he lists eight signs of the fruit of love (i.e., "Holy Spirit") that give evidence of this reality happening in the lives of the baptized, both personally and communally.

Furthermore, the "fruits" of the Spirit are not primarily the work of the individual or group; they are signs of the Spirit's fecundity bearing fruit in them. Thus R. Y. K. Fung notes that the phrase "fruit of the Spirit" as such "directly ascribes the power of the fructification not to the believer himself but to the Spirit, and effectively hints that the qualities enumerated are not the result of strenuous adherence to an external legal code, but the natural product ('harvest') of a life controlled and guided by the Spirit."[12]

If the Galatians were living under the power of the Spirit of truth and the Spirit of freedom, they would demonstrate their Spirit-filled lives through practices that would show that they, indeed, had moved out from under the control of the law and its enslaving works of the flesh to the freedom accorded by the "fruit(s)" of the Spirit. However, how this is to be done in

---

11. Pope John Paul II, encyclical letter, *Dominum et Vivificantem*, May 18, 1986, no. 55, http://www.vatican.va.

12. R. Y. K. Fung, *The Epistle to the Galatians* (Grand Rapids: Eerdmans, 1988), 262.

our day is a challenge. This challenge is articulated clearly by Richard B. Hays in *The Moral Vision of the New Testament*. He asks, "If the New Testament's teachings are so integrally embedded in the social and symbolic world of first-century communities, can they speak at all to us or for us." Hays believes this is possible as long as we remain faithful to the "task of hermeneutical appropriation," which, he argues, "requires an *integrative act of the imagination*." He explains that this is always the case,

> Even for those who would like to deny it: with fear and trembling we must work out a life of faithfulness to God through responsive and creative reappropriation of the New Testament in a world far removed from the world of the original writers and readers. *Thus, whenever we appeal to the authority of the New Testament, we are necessarily engaged in metaphor-making, placing our community's life imaginatively within the world articulated by the texts.*[13]

While we know the days in which we live are far removed from those of Paul, there are two key issues facing us today that were key to Paul's self-understanding of the need to become transformed into Christ through this Spirit. If we can imagine ways to address their contemporary expression, Paul's "world" will have meaning in ours. One was the power of the *stoicheias'* influence around covenantal nomism, which frustrated the power of the Spirit, and the other was his "on the road to Damascus experience," which convinced him that the historical Jesus had become embodied, through this Spirit, in the lives of the Christians and that the sign of living by this Spirit involved "walking by the Spirit" by incorporating the "fruit of the Spirit" in their lives. The consequent mystical stance that is needed in our world, with all its "spirits," will reflect lives lived under the power of this Spirit. Indeed Hays himself seems to agree with this approach when he writes that "the test that finally proves the value of our theological labors is the 'fruits test': . . . the value of our exegesis and hermeneutics will be tested by their capacity to produce persons and communities whose character is commensurate with Jesus Christ and thereby pleasing to God."[14]

It is clear to me why Paul would highlight certain virtues or practices as a way of manifesting love. Instead of the Mosaic law, the law of love was to animate the members of the community, first of all among themselves and,

---

13. Richard B. Hays, *The Moral Vision of the New Testament: Community Cross, New Creation, A Contemporary Introduction to New Testament Ethics* (San Francisco: HarperSanFrancisco, 1996), 6.

14. Ibid., 7.

corporately, toward the wider society. The first part of Paul's letter can be understood in terms of Mary Douglas's dynamics regarding "group": the Galatians had to find a way to be strong against the challenges of outsiders like the Teachers. However, they also needed to make sure they were not "tearing each other apart" internally. This demanded behavior that would strengthen their "grid," even if such behavior was not encoded in precise rules and regulations but was freely given witness to in a new creation: the implementation of the law of love in the world.

If a limited understanding of covenantal nomism defined one by blood as a member of the limited and isolated family of Jews, now, in Christ and through the power of the Spirit poured forth in the members of the house churches, a new family of brothers and sisters could bring forth beyond all limitation and isolation a wholly new self-identity: they will be a community that transcends every conceivable boundary, especially when those culturally conditioned boundaries are canonized as God's will and made to be norma-tive. This will not only make them boundary-less; they will now be Spirit-formed and bound-less in bringing about an entirely new social order. Now neither circumcision nor uncircumcision will even be considered; instead, the new creation will be grounded in the family dynamics of love.

At that time in the Mediterranean world, the "family" was equivalent to the "house(hold)." The family household was the locus of the business (i.e., the "family business"). The dynamics within each household were called its "economy." Today we would also call this the family's way of "doing busi-ness." However, as Paul envisioned it (literally "envisioned" it based on his Damascus experience), the house churches were now to be identified not by imperial and religious structures of patriarchy but, ideally,[15] as new families whose members are no longer part of the imperial family of Caesar but are members of the household of God. In this sense, Paul envisions a totally new "business" model for the future of the church: a family of equals under the one "Abba" whose Spirit they share equally by baptism. Thus Esler writes, "Paul employs imagery of family and household in this passage as a way of giving substance to the distinct identity with which he wants to characterize the members of his congregations."[16]

Unfortunately this distinct identity cannot just be defined by a "freedom from the law" (5:10) attitude; it needs something more concrete. The whole

---

15. Paul had the vision of what the "new order" was to be and believe this is the way *it should be*; however, there is no evidence that this worldview included a sense of his need to challenge his prevailing cultural order. The rationale for this has been discussed in the previous chapters.

16. Philip F. Esler, *Galatians* (London: Routledge, 1998), 218.

paraenesis of 5:1–6:10, I believe, builds to a high point with the few short sentences describing the works of the flesh (5:19-21) and the fruit of the Spirit (5:22-23). Analyzing the "works of the flesh" enumerated by Paul in 5:19-21 leads to a key realization that reinforces our approach to a restricted interpretation of covenantal nomism in its present-day canonical form. Of the various uses of the word "flesh" (*sarx*) in Paul, almost half (21) are used against the "nomists."[17] From this key realization flow two main conclusions: one *ad extra* and the other *ad intra* regarding the Galatian house churches.

Regarding the *ad extra* or "outsider" argument, Susan Elliott makes a compelling case that the first five and last two works of the flesh noted by Paul (fornication, impurity, licentiousness, idolatry, sorcery, drunkenness, and carousing) represent the popular image of the *galli* (i.e., Galatians) that they represented a way of life associated with those in Anatolia whose genitals ("flesh") were cut off. "Once they castrate themselves, they become involved in sexual excesses and in shameless and suspicious behavior, at least in the popular imagination," she notes. Then she concludes, "the first 'works of the flesh' that Paul lists evoke the behavior of the *galli* as outcomes of their action upon the flesh, and Paul intends to imply that circumcision as an action upon the flesh has these outcomes in a more generalized way."[18]

The middle eight "works of the flesh" enumerated by Paul address divisive interpersonal dynamics among the Galatian house churches (*ad intra*), dealing with their own communal conflicts and tensions (enmity, strife, jealousy, anger, rivalries, dissension, divisions, and envy). Not only was the community qua "group" in conflict with the Teachers; but in its "grid," it had its own internal conflicts that seemed to be taking a toll (5:15). In Paul's mind, as long as the members of the Galatian house churches (family based) were enslaved to the law, either that of the Anatolian Mother Goddess or of the Torah, they could expect such internal divisions. But they had another option: to live in the freedom of God's children, supporting one another by cultivating the fruit(s) of the Spirit who unites them. In their practice, they will move into what we discuss below as a new "mystical" stance in life for people who take the gospel seriously—that is, Rahner's devout Christians.

Before moving to the heart of Rahner's statement, it is critical that we examine the situation of many, if not most, *devout Christians*, or at least *devout Catholics* of the present, especially when we consider other words for

---

17. Robert Jewett, *Paul's Anthropological Terms: A Study of Their Use in Conflict Settings* (Leiden: E. J. Brill, 1971), 453.

18. Susan Elliott, *Cutting Too Close for Comfort: Paul's Letter to the Galatians in Its Anatolian Cultic Context* (London: T & T Clark International, 2003), 316.

"devout": earnest, fervent, serious, pious, dedicated, staunch, and committed. Even more so such devout Catholics (at all levels from young children to old bishops and cardinals) might be called sincere and religious. From this perspective, then, we are assuming sincerity and religiosity; however, if Rahner is correct, the reality of today's Christianity and Catholicism will not be sufficient for the future.

When we consider the Catholicism promoted by many clerics under the pontificates of John Paul II and Benedict XVI, we find a stress on morality rather than spirituality and, therefore, on rules and regulations rather than "the weightier matters of the law," justice and mercy and faith" proclaimed by Jesus (Matt. 23:23). And while "faith" might be stressed as defining a devout Catholic, even if justice and mercy received token mention, the "faith" stressed was obedience to the rules and regulations (and authority behind them) as they were articulated by the clerics. This, we have seen, contributed to what we have called canonical nomism.

The consequent morality that was canonized as "Catholic" represented obedience to the teachings of the clerics (as seen earlier in the quote from Cardinal George). Among the "devout Catholics" in the pews whose Catholicism was highly defined by the faithful acceptance and practice of what the clerics taught, the morality canonized was what has been termed "preconventional morality." Developed by Lawrence Kohlberg, Professor of Education and Psychology at Harvard in the late 1950s,[19] the notion of preconventional morality offers a way to salvation based, first of all, on reward and punishment, on doing the right thing as defined by society, and, second, on a form of "enlightened self-interest," where adherence to the laws as defined by the leaders works to the advantage of "devout Catholics" and enables them to feel a sense of belonging. I believe that this approach to morality and human development in Catholicism (as well as the counterchallenges to this approach) represents what Cardinal Joseph Ratzinger bemoaned as dynamics that keep people as "children in faith" who are defined by agreements and disagreements around doctrine.[20]

---

19. Lawrence Kohlberg, "The Development of Modes of Thinking and Choices in Years 10–16" (Ph.D. diss., Chicago: University of Chicago, 1958). After Kohlberg's approach received acclaim, Carol Gilligan published a feminist critique in her *In a Different Voice: Psychological Theory and Women's Development* (Cambridge, MA: Harvard University Press, 1982). While embracing the balance brought by Gilligan, I have chosen to remain with Kohlberg's "male" classification because of the patriarchal ideology that still colors the thinking about morality that is promoted by the male clerics in the Roman Church.

20. Cardinal Joseph Ratzinger, homily at Mass "Pro Eligendo Romano Pontifice," April 18, 2005, http://www.vatican.va.

Unfortunately, I suspect the faith of many bishops and priests who were ordained during the pontificates of Pope Benedict XVI and Pope John Paul II reflect what Lawrence Kohlberg called "conventional morality." Unlike preconventional morality, which is based on reward and punishment for (non)observance of accepted, universal codes, conventional morality stresses rewards and punishments as defined by the leaders of the group itself, that is, the clerics all the way from the Vatican to the most remote Catholic parish pulpit. This was often expressed in dynamics of blind obedience and concomitant fear of nonconformity in order to "belong." This "law and order" approach made the preservation of the male, celibate, clerical model of the church an end in itself. Consequently, at least for the leaders in the church, this "conventional morality" kept them locked into an adolescent form of (un)development that made them blind believers in a way of life that was destructive to themselves and those who followed their ways. It made them closed in on themselves and their way of life.

The "adult faith" promoted by Cardinal Ratzinger in his preconclave homily represents what Lawrence Kohlberg called "postconventional morality." Rather than being an almost exclusive concentration on observance of "truth" in the form of dogmas, truth now is seen as fidelity to those basic beliefs that constitute the core of Catholicism and all its dogmas. This gospel proclaimed by Paul to the Galatians defines that "core" as being "in Christ." This "adult faith," which is needed by everyone in the church, including the College of Cardinals, was highlighted by Cardinal Ratzinger in his preconclave homily as defined by a personal relationship with Jesus Christ:

> An "adult" faith is not a faith that follows the trends of fashion and the latest novelty; a mature adult faith is deeply rooted in friendship with Christ. It is this friendship that opens us up to all that is good and gives us a criterion by which to distinguish the true from the false, and deceit from truth.
>
> We must develop this adult faith; we must guide the flock of Christ to this faith. And it is this faith—only faith—that creates unity and is fulfilled in love.
>
> On this theme, St Paul offers us as a fundamental formula for Christian existence some beautiful words, in contrast to the continual vicissitudes of those who, like children, are tossed about by the waves: make truth in love. Truth and love coincide in Christ. To the extent that we draw close to Christ, in our own lives too,

truth and love are blended. Love without truth would be blind; truth without love would be like "a clanging cymbal" (1 Cor. 13:1).[21]

Remember that Rahner's definition of a "mystic" was one who had *experienced* something (which Cardinal Ratzinger called a "someone")! But the true mystic is not just one who has experienced *something* or someone but one who develops a spiritual life based on the desire to replicate in one's own life the reality of that which now defines that person's life. Thus, in full agreement that it will be the challenge of the church in the future to create, foster, and sustain believers who may not have had a recognized mystical experience but who share a desire to develop a mystical stance in life, I want to now consider how the fruit(s) of the Spirit can facilitate this goal.

In speaking of mysticism, we can distinguish among four kinds of contemplation: the mystical/contemplative experience itself (such as Paul's Damascus experience or Francis's leper experience); the contemplative environment (using elements of space and time to help create awareness of one's contemplative connectedness to everyone and everything); mystical/contemplative prayer; and the contemplative stance. The mystical or contemplative stance involves the practice of certain disciplines that can flow from one's mystical experience or are meant to try to replicate, as far as possible, the contemplative experience. Ideally, these are nurtured by mystical prayer. These disciplines are meant to help in one's transformation from being defined by what Paul calls the "works of the flesh" into one who manifests the "fruit(s) of the Spirit." This transformation demands another kind of flesh work: the cultivation of certain practices that will be fruitful so that the practitioner will be "morphed" into the Christ (4:19). If Christ was/is the embodiment of the new humanity, those humans who are "in Christ" must discipline themselves to reflect that embodiment. Just as Paul interprets his mystical transformation through the expression "Christ lives in me" (2:20), he sees himself as a midwife to the Galatians, a role that subjects him to "the pain of childbirth until this same Christ would be formed in them" (4:19). As Bruce Longenecker explains it, "Paul expects the formation of Christ to be evident within the social relations of Galatian Christians, and this, for Paul, is first and foremost a matter of moral character; that is, Christian transformation is to be enacted in the giving of oneself for the benefit of others (5:13; 6:2) after the manner of Christ's own selfless giving (1:4; 2:20)."[22]

---

21. Ibid.
22. Bruce W. Longenecker, "'Until Christ Is Formed in You': Suprahuman Forces and Moral Character in Galatians," *Catholic Biblical Quarterly* 61 (1999): 92.

The goal of this whole process is personal (if not social) transformation because, as James D. G. Dunn reminds us, "the Spirit is the *aparchē* (Rom. 8.23), the first fruits which signal the start of the final harvest," which is to be cultivated in the fruit of the Spirit in every believer. In wonderful imagery Dunn outlines how this *aparchē* of the Spirit in the believer is meant to be transformative. He writes,

> For Paul the Spirit is the power of God which transforms believers into the image of their Lord degree by degree (2 Cor. 3.18). The spirit is the power which, again as the prophets had hoped, enables the obedience which fulfills the law (Rom. 8.23) and bears the fruit of a transformed character (Gal. 5.22-23). The Spirit is the power which in the end will complete the lifelong process of salvation by changing our bodies of humiliation to conform them to Christ's body of glory.[23]

The Galatians' birthing of Christ, their embodiment or morphing into the Christ, would lead to a radically transformed way of life and a new identity: their life would be that of the cruciformed Christ. This life would be lived under the power of the Spirit of Christ; hence, if the believers who have been baptized live in the Spirit, so they should walk under and in the power of this same Spirit (see 5:25; 6:16). This should be done freely without any compulsion. Hence Gys M. H. Loubser writes, "A believer is and acts wisely, not by living a morally good life according to the set rules of the community, albeit Christian, but by living a cruciform life emanating from an allegiance with Christ and his love."[24]

"Walking in the Spirit" is the main theme of Paul's paraenesis, or ethical instruction, in the last major part of his Letter to the Galatians (5:1–6:10). Here we find "identity-defining norms"[25] that will characterize the contemplative/mystical stance of those who are the Spirit-led ones (*pneumatikoi*), freely reflecting a life "in Christ" rather that remaining enslaved to the demands of the law and controlled by the flesh (or *sarx*). This *sarx*, Ber-

---

23. James D. G. Dunn, *Jesus, Paul, and the Gospels* (Grand Rapids: Eerdmans, 2011), 109.

24. Gys M. H. Loubser, "Life in the Spirit as Wise Remedy for the Folly of the Flesh," *Neotestamentica* 43.2 (2009): 363.

25. Bernard O. Ukwuegbu, *The Emergence of Christian Identity in Paul's Letter to the Galatians: A Social-Scientific Investigation into the Root Causes for the Parting of the Way between Christianity and Judaism* (Bonn: Borengässer, 2003), 538-59. Ukwuegbu quotes Pseudo-Isocrates as noting that the principal function, among others, of a "paraenesis" is "to provide rules and regulations to direct the practical ethical lives of the people" (538).

nard O. Ukwuegbu writes in his very helpful reflection on the paraenesis in Gal. 5:13–6:10, "is the persistent tendency to cling to a past organizational structure at the root of group identification and ethnocentrism." A contemporary echo of this, I have intimated, is how the Roman Catholic Church, in its organizational structure and dynamics, became identified with a style that could only be defined as patriarchal and clerical.

Elsewhere I have defined spirituality in the broad sense as "the experience of some transcendent power that becomes the ultimate ground of a person's life which leads that person to translate (express) his or her experience in behaviors synchronous with that experience; ideally this takes place in solidarity with others sharing the experience and expression."[26] Urging the Galatians as a community to develop such a spirituality, Paul summarized the experiential and expressive dimensions of his pneumatology when he simply stated, "If we live by the Spirit, let us also be guided by the Spirit" (5:25). Indeed, those who have the Spirit alive in them make that Spirit live through them as they are led by the Spirit (5:18), walk by the Spirit (5:16), and are guided by the Spirit (2:25). This spirituality, grounded in and led by the Spirit and manifesting the fruit of the Spirit's love, can be called nothing else than Paul's form of mysticism. Thus, building on his conviction that the Spirit of the cosmic Christ was the energy at the heart of the universe leading to its final consummation in love, Teilhard articulated clearly the challenge to spirituality itself that faces Christians, especially its religious leaders. Rejecting the notion that mysticism is not meant to perfect the world but to remain isolated in some kind of mystical relationship with God apart from being involved in God's cares for the world, he wrote to his friend Henri de Lubac: "Nothing is, in my view, *more spiritual* that the consummation of the universe. Any spirituality pursued at the periphery of this effort is verbalism, attenuation, abstraction—the dreary piety of churches and convents."[27]

In Paul's mind, the true believer is now the "spiritual peripatetic," who is empowered to walk according to the rule of the Spirit (5:16). In commenting on the believer being one who walks (*peripatein*) in the Spirit, Hans Dieter Betz notes,

> The term expresses the view that human life is essentially a "way of life." A human being must and always does choose between ways

26. My definition of "spirituality" is an adaptation of that articulated by Sandra Schneiders. See my *Repair My House: Becoming a "Kindom" Catholic* (Maryknoll, NY: Orbis Books, 2012), 57.

27. Pierre Teilhard de Chardin, *Letter to Henri de Lubac*, quoted in King, *Towards a New Mysticism*, 135.

of life as they are presented in history and culture . . . the way of life of human beings determines the quality of their life. More than merely a matter of outward style, the way of life provides continuity, guidance, and assistance for the task of coping with the daily struggle against evil.[28]

Developing a mystical way of life begins with the desire to do so. I must make a conscious decision to turn from what Paul calls the "works of the flesh" if I am to cultivate the "fruit of the Spirit," or, as Frank Matera writes, "Living by the Spirit is not enough; one must also follow the Spirit's lead; one must make an active decision to be led by the Spirit (5:18)."[29] All authentic transformation of one's life is grounded in the desire to form one's life another way. If we are to cultivate the "fruit of the Spirit" and the *spirituality* that this entails, we must make a conscious choice to do so. In this way we begin the process of leading a spiritual life in the sense noted by Ronald Rolheiser: "Spirituality concerns what we do with desire."[30] This kind of desire inspires us to move from being defined by the works of the flesh to the manifestation of the fruit of love expressed in joy, peace, patience, kindness, goodness, gentleness, faithfulness, and self-control. This same kind of desire is what leads us to be grounded in a contemplative seeking of God in prayer even when "nothing" seems to be happening when we discipline ourselves to pray.

Once we decide we want to live mystically, developing a mystical stance is based on cultivating a mystical awareness or consciousness and living from this consciousness in whatever we subsequently do in imitation of Paul, whose "real witness" to his mystical experience(s), Evelyn Underhill writes, was in the way he labored so hard in proclaiming the gospel that led to "the trail of Christian churches by which his journeyings are marked."[31] Even when we don't experience anything at prayer, the fact that we are moving away from the "works of the flesh" to evidence the "fruit(s) of the Spirit" will be the best concrete sign of the real purpose of such prayer. When the Buddha was asked, "What have you gained from meditation?" he replied, "Nothing! However, let me tell you what I've lost: anger, anxiety, depression, insecurity, fear of old age and fear of death." To the degree we gain the

---

28. Hans Dieter Betz, *Galatians: A Commentary on Paul's Letter to the Churches in Galatia* (Philadelphia: Fortress Press, 1979), 277.

29. Frank J. Matera, Galatians (Collegeville: MN: Liturgical Press, 1992, 2007), 211.

30. Ronald Rolheiser, *The Holy Longing: The Search for Christian Spirituality* (New York: Doubleday, 1999), 7.

31. Underhill, *Mysticism,* 431.

fruit of the Spirit of love in our lives to that same degree we find we have moved away from being defined by the "works of the flesh."

I am convinced that the discipline of developing a mystical stance begins with becoming conscious or mindful or aware of one's breathing. This is not only good for daily living but is a basic discipline for cultivating a more mystical consciousness. And well it should be, for the Spirit of God, as we have seen in the previous chapter, is the "breath of God." When we practice deep breathing, we discipline ourselves to become conscious of our connectedness "in Christ," which links us to everyone and everything in the cosmos. In this way we are aware of a new creation that is evolving into ever-greater forms of communion and love. Here there is no more separation, only connectedness. In breathing in, I breathe in everyone and everything in a way that should make me an embodiment of the new creation. In breathing out, I release from myself and my control anything that may be an obstacle to the grace of the Spirit breathing in me. The practice of such breathing helps move one into a deeper consciousness of the Holy Spirit as the source of what N. T. Wright calls our "incorporation" and "participation" in the body of Christ.[32] While this consciousness or "mindfulness," a Buddhist like Thich Nhat Hanh can declare, "is very much like the Holy Spirit";[33] it is much more if it is nurtured by actually growing in mystical prayer itself.

Building on one's deep breathing and deepening mindfulness, consciousness, or awareness, one cultivates a mystical stance that eliminates obstacles to deeper union with God and others through the practice of actions (disciplines/asceticism) that are evidence of one's ever more profound transformation into cosmic love. Thus members of the Galatian church(es) must give evidence that they have moved from being under the control of the "law" by being enslaved to "the works of the flesh" to the new law of Christ in the power of the Spirit (6:2; see 5:16-18, 25; 6:8). If, in Paul's judgment, the "works of the flesh" that once defined Jewish believers are linked to the separatist dynamics involved in covenantal nomism, now a new creation defined by solidarity and support is revealed in and through the Galatian Christians, who must now cultivate, individually and communally, the "fruit(s) of the Spirit" (5:22). Like all good fruit, these need to be tended regularly; they cannot be productive unless nurtured in each person and within the right kind of communal soil. Thus Betz writes, "when the Galatians received the Spirit, they were also given the founda-

---

32. N. T. Wright, *Pauline Perspectives: Essays on Paul, 1978–2013* (Minneapolis: Fortress Press, 2013), 529-33, *passim*.

33. Thich Nhat Hanh, *Living Buddha, Living Christ* (New York: Putnam Riverhead Books, 1995), 14.

tion out of which the 'fruit' was supposed to grow. . . . In the present context of ethical exhortation we can conclude that simple possession of the 'fruit of the Spirit' cannot be what Paul means." Instead, he concludes, "the 'fruit of the Spirit' presupposes man's active involvement (cf. 5:25)."[34] William E. Brown says much the same thing: "Paul's emphasis is upon the fruit that should flourish in the believer's life. . . . The point of Paul's exhortation is that the believers now live in a new sphere of existence; therefore, they need to put the sins of the flesh behind them and live consistent with their position in Christ."[35] In effect, the "old order" of covenantal nomism reflected a distinct ethnic identity defined by "the flesh"; now the new creation is to reveal a totally new *ethic*: the "fruit(s) of the Spirit."

The old ethnic identity that set Israel apart from other nations by being a family defined by blood would now be transformed into a new family of brothers and sisters, made so because the Spirit of Jesus Christ enables them to call Israel's God their "Abba," or Father. This Spirit has now made those isolated individuals part of a communal reality of equals: brothers and sisters "in Christ." Thus Paul addresses the recipients of his writings as *adelphoi* (brothers [and sisters]) nine times in Galatians (1:11; 3:15; 4:12, 28, 31; 5:11, 13; 6:1, 18; and sixty-five times in his genuine letters); he also addresses them as God's own children (see 3:26; 4:5, 6; see 4:28, 31). This made the Galatian house churches not only families but ordered in the new creation to represent a "new way of doing business," the way of equality.

Of course, Paul did not act on his vision by speaking to the need to create communal structures and dynamics of equality. As a child of his own world with its own dominant worldview, he was likely blinded by his cultural and societal ideology of patriarchy. Nonetheless, he laid out the ideal; now it is incumbent on contemporary Christians and, in our case, Catholic Christians to implement that vision of equality.[36] For the principle involved in

---

34. Betz, *Galatians*, 286-87.

35. William E. Brown, "The New Testament Concept of the Believer's Inheritance" (Th.D. thesis., Dallas Theological Seminary, 1984), 126.

36. Kathy Ehrensperger offers a twofold approach to dealing with the ideal Paul envisioned and his limited cultural vision, which obstructed it. First of all she notes, "it is not surprising that Paul used the language of his time, nor that he used patriarchal language and imagery . . . it is impossible to escape thought and language patterns known to us. Paul is not exempt from this." Secondly, while "we should not judge Paul's use of language according to postrevolutionary categories of equality and democracy," neither can we "argue as if words have fixed connotations in and of themselves, irrespective of the construction within which they are situated. Otherwise, we are guilty of decontextualizing language." See her *That We May Be Mutually Encouraged: Feminism and the New Perspective in Pauline Studies* (New York: T & T Clark International, 2004), 159.

such a statement, I look to Marcus Borg and John Dominic Crossan, who write,

> We go into the wider matrix of Pauline theology as noted in his Letter to the Galatians. This absolutely crucial statement must be read fully, and to assist us in doing so, we set it out as follows: "As many of you as were baptized *into Christ* have clothed yourselves *with Christ*. There is no longer Jew or Greek, there is no longer slave or free, there is no longer male and female; for all of you are one *in Christ* Jesus. And if you belong *to Christ* . . ." (3:27-29).
>
> That central triad must never, ever, be cited without those framing statements containing "into" and "with Christ" and "in" and "to Christ." Quoted *without those frames*, they might correctly deny the validity of slavery, but they also incorrectly deny the validity of the difference (as distinct from the hierarchy) between women and men, and the ongoing validity of Judaism as a religion separate from Christianity.
>
> Some such declaration of equality was the heart of the radical transformation that was involved in Christian baptism.[37]

Christian baptism was to be the sign of the new community that existed without separation and distinctions, a community that would reveal the inauguration of a totally new created order on earth, one that reflected the communitarian reign of God in heaven. Thus Borg and Crossan, in commenting on Paul's statement that "neither circumcision nor uncircumcision is anything; *but a new creation is everything!*" (Gal. 6:15), conclude, "'New creation' language is not primarily about new individuals, but about a new cosmic order, a new era, a new age. This, for Paul, was what life 'in Christ,' 'in the Spirit,' 'in the body of Christ' was about."[38] Indeed, it can be argued that the dynamics of this new creation is the consequent worldview that flowed from Paul's Damascus experience.

However, a key element of the "new perspective" on Paul involves the realization that any "new life of the believer" did not involve the kind of salvation that was simply equated with having a "personal relationship with Jesus Christ." The life of each believer was saved to the degree that it was concretized in a believing community. In this sense, salvation for Paul the Jew always was about being part of a people, not being a person who was/is

37. Marcus J. Borg and John Dominic Crossan, *The First Paul: Reclaiming the Radical Visionary behind the Church's Conservative Icon* (New York: HarperOne, 2009), 110-11.
38. Ibid., 188.

saved. This movement from an individualistic notion of salvation to being part of a community is summarized clearly by Gerhard Lohfink. He notes that "what was at stake in Israel was precisely *not* a purely individual salvation that could be attained independently of the life of the people of God. In the same way salvation through Christ was bound up with the New Testament people of God" rather than some kind of "union, after the fact, of those who had already attained salvation as *individuals* through their personal union with Christ," as if they were in some "kind of fraternal society."[39] Based on the above, he concludes,

> Christian salvation, however, is something else, and takes a different path. It consists precisely in incorporation into the Church as a social body. Only in that way is it possible to participate in the history of liberation that began with Abraham. Salvation in Christ means inalienable incorporation in his "body" and life through his saving action is impossible apart from a common life with the members of this body. One can have communion with Christ only and always in communion with others.[40]

The old order, defined by conflicts, competition, and other works of the flesh, has been "nailed to the cross"; now a new family takes its place. As the most foundational sacrament of all, baptism in Christ witnessed to a new cosmic order rather than the covenantal nomism that perpetuated separation. When we consider baptism to be the sacrament that enables the church to *be* the church, anything that gets in the way of this new creation in Christ through the Spirit becomes secondary. Thus, when ordination to the priesthood and episcopacy is interpreted as something "higher" than baptism or the right to be "separate" from the baptized, we can apply Gal. 6:15 to say, "neither ordination nor not being ordained is anything"; now all that ultimately matters is that *everyone* in the church becomes "a new creation." This demands the kind of family of equals under God that Jesus describes in Matt. 12:46-50.

Just as many fruits need pruning, so the pruning demands of those who are "in Christ" a continual crucifixion (2:19) of "the flesh with its passion and desires" (5:24). Elaborating on this new communal identity, René A.

---

39. Gerhard Lohfink, *Does God Need the Church? Toward a Theology of the People of God* (trans. Linda M. Maloney; Collegeville, MN: Liturgical Press, 1999), 254. I am indebted to Bill Cavanaugh for leading me to Lohfink as a good example of contemporary soteriology.

40. Ibid., 255.

López writes, "Paul appealed to the believers' identity with Christ in Galatians 5:24 to promote the behavior indicated in verses 25-26. This contrasts with the behavior of those who are characterized by the vice list in verses 19-21."[41] If both the works of the flesh and the fruit(s) of the Spirit represent the "driving forces" of the two eras,[42] how we direct those forces will be the task of spirituality in the future. Consequently the first step in nurturing the "fruit(s) of the Spirit" will be to overcome any of the "works of the flesh" that stand in the way.

Some years ago, Ronald Rolheiser had a column in our local Catholic paper entitled "You'll Know When Yours Is a Mystically Driven Life." He argues that such a life reflects the realization of "what we need to be true to who we are" that flows from "God's kiss."[43] If our identity as images of God is what is truest about who we are, when we reveal a way of loving that is expressed in its eight manifestations according to Galatians, we (and others) will now find that ours is truly a mystically driven life.

We now turn to each of the eight, grounded in love, to suggest a way Christians of the future will become mystics through the development of a mystical awareness and the discipline of cultivating the fruit(s) of the Holy Spirit in our lives.[44] Bearing witness to these fruits in our spirituality will show that our bodies are not rejecting our "Spirit transplant."[45]

Operating on the assumption that those who, grounded in contemplative prayer,[46] cultivate the "fruit(s) of the Spirit" in their lives will be gradually transformed by this Spirit into "the Christ," I will try to suggest concrete disciplines that can be used to help the development of this "mystical stance" toward everyone and everything in the life of the believers. While there will be exceptions, the process I will use for each subsequent chapter will involve a threefold outline:

---

41. René A. López, "Paul's Vice List in Galatians 5:19-21," *Bibliotheca Sacra* 169 (January–March 2012), 62. I am indebted to Dr. López for giving me the leads to Betz and Brown.

42. Loubser, "Life in the Spirit," 360.

43. Ronald Rolheiser, "You'll Know When Yours Is a Mystically Driven Life," *Milwaukee Catholic Herald,* June 28, 2013, 10.

44. What I identify with "cultivating" the fruit of the Spirit in our lives, I believe Richard Rohr calls "ripening."

45. Borg and Crossan, *First Paul,* 207.

46. Many books are written on various approaches and practices that help one develop contemplative praying. Thus this book does not/will not develop the notion of such prayer, including the role or approach to such prayer in Paul. The purpose of this book is to show how the fruit(s) of the Spirit can be cultivated that support such prayer.

1. I believe the seed of any developed "fruit" of the Spirit originated in the "Big Bang" and is individually expressed in the uniqueness of every single being.[47] Thus, honoring the axiom "grace builds on nature," I will try to address wherever I can the evidence we have about the fruit in question from what we know of science, especially biology and neuroscience.[48]

2. Since we now know the Spirit's "fruit(s)" are signs of the life and reign of the Trinity in us, I will search the authentic Pauline corpus to find where God is identified as the source of that specific fruit. This approach is grounded in the assumption that each "fruit" of the Spirit is its own unique sign of the reign of God in a person's spirituality.

3. Using Galatians and Paul's other genuine letters, I will show what *Paul* means by the specific fruit and its role in the life of the members of the community.[49] This demands the elimination of any correlated

---

47. The Franciscan theologian Blessed John Duns Scotus called this "unique" being of every being its *haecceitas or* "thisness." This is what makes everything and everyone, in some way, its own unique image of its Divine Maker.

48. A key argument of many people involved in the faith/science debate is that neuroscience is demonstrating as fact what religion has taught as moral principles: that they are merely functions of the brain. I accept this possibility but want to demonstrate that the *cultivation* of the "fruit(s) of the spirit" offers a "value-added" dimension that can't be explained by purely scientific data. For a brief and popular summary of the recent findings of neurology and neuroscience, see Michio Kaku, "The Golden Age of Neuroscience Has Arrived," *Wall Street Journal*, August 21, 2014, A13. Despite Sam Harris's attestation (made without peer review) that all human beings' moral evaluations can be reduced to chemically specifiable brain states, I believe that the cultivation of the "fruit" of love in its eight manifestations in Galatians has yet to be demonstrated by neuroscience as simply an expression of evolved consciousness. For his argument to the contrary, see Sam Harris, *The Moral Landscape: How Science Can Determine Human Values* (New York: Free Press, 2010). There have been some fledgling attempts to make a connection between the fruit of the Spirit (instead of a specific one such as the link between kindness and oxytocin) and findings from the neurosciences. For an attempt to make some kind of connection with neurobiology, see Edward B. Davis, "The Presence of God: An Interpersonal Neurobiology Perspective" (http://www.wheaton.edu). For a seminal discussion of the link with neuroscience in general, see Derek Flood, "Neuroscience and the Mind of Christ," December 3, 2012, http://www.huffington post.com.

49. Much of the theology and spirituality regarding Paul has been influenced by the lens of the Enlightenment. This has resulted in an overstress on notions such as individual justification/salvation and personal development. The approach I will be taking is based on the realization that Paul's letters (except for Philemon) were written to individuals only insofar as they were members of communities: the house churches in which they functioned. This communitarian approach to interpreting (and applying) Paul's Letter to the

"works of the flesh" that stand as obstacles; it ends with suggested practices/disciplines to help cultivate that particular fruit.

The main underlying assumption behind the three steps above is that the members of the Galatian church and of its sister churches for all time must *choose* to stop being defined by the works of the flesh and *choose* to make conscious efforts to cultivate the Spirit's fruits. This is an ongoing process, not a once-for-all activity. Thus Paul urged his audience to continually choose to live by the Spirit. He did this because he was aware that conversion demanded daily efforts, lest one return to old ways of sin.

As with any effort at conversion, this transformation will never have effect in a person's life unless the "choice" to move from one way of living to another is conscious and deliberate.

Galatians is articulated well by Philip Esler: "The point is that Paul seeks to communicate with his audience in their capacity as obviously or demonstrably belonging to collectivities linked by some significant characteristic, above all their status in relation to God, Jesus Christ or the Spirit, but also their current geographic location, their kinship (here fictive in nature) *vis-à-vis* each other or illustrious ancestors like Abraham and Sarah and, for some of them, their ultimate place of origin in Judea (indicated by the use of *Iudaismos, Ioudaia* and *Ioudaios*). In short, Paul considers that the characteristics differentiating the persons to whom he writes should somehow be submerged in their oneness in Christ (3.28)" (Esler, *Galatians*, 38).

Chapter 5

Christ's Spirit of Love in Us: The Foundational "Fruit" of the Spirit

Hardly an area of our life remains untouched by some kind of polarization, especially in the realm of politics, the "culture wars," and religion. That would include Catholicism—indeed all the Christian denominations, which claim their foundation upon the cross of Jesus Christ, the sign of the greatest love ever shown.

Many people are seeking the magic answer that will allow individuals and groups to rise above their differences and create the kind of reconciling, loving community envisioned by Jesus and his disciple Paul. Once every now and then we are blessed with a glimpse of how some can take God's Word seriously enough to bring about reconciliation and love, even in the midst of and despite their divisions. I found a memorable example of this in the pages of *Weavings* several years ago. It serves as a wonderful contemporary instance of *agape* as described in Galatians, namely, the mandate to practice "faith working through love" (5:6).

Gerrit Scott Dawson, Marcus Atha, and E. Cary Simonton were friends from their seminary days, at each other's side "in good times and in bad," at each other's weddings, as well as with each other when family members faced crises. Their friendship deepened twice a year when they would meet to talk about their faith and struggles in theology and pastoral ministry.

While the three disagreed on many issues over the years, they always found ways to surmount those and move on. And they continued their discussions and debates. As Marcus notes, the issue of homosexuality and other issues around sexuality presented a particular challenge: "For us the scriptural issues run deep and clear. The three of us agree on how to interpret most of the basic teachings of the Scriptures as well as many of the traditions and doctrines of the church. But on the understanding (or misunderstanding) of sexuality, we have a wide breach...."[1]

---

1. Marcus Atha, in Gerrit Scott Dawson, Marcus Atha, and E. Cary Simonton, "On Our Faces Together," *Weavings* 22.2 (March/April 2007), 37.

Cary recalls how, at one gathering at a restaurant in New York, "our rau-
cous and heated argument on Amsterdam Avenue warped into debate on
other subjects as well. Sadly, the whole conversation got personal. That evening, Gerrit said in so many words, 'I guess there's no reason for me to be
here. I should just head on home.'" With that they parted and "wondered if
we would be separated forever."

Here were three Protestant ministers who proclaimed the Word of God,
and yet were unable to find in it a power greater than their theological-now-
turned-personal divide. Still, they kept trying to figure a way out of their
estrangement. Cary notes that each of them, "in our own time and way,"
came to be challenged and encouraged to rise above their alienation by
remembering the final sentences of Paul in the eighth chapter of Romans
where the word "love" is used three times:

> Who will separate us from the love of Christ? Will hardship, or dis-
> tress, or persecution, or famine, or nakedness, or peril, or sword?
> . . . No, in all these things we are more than conquerors through
> him who loved us. For I am convinced that neither death, nor life,
> nor angels, nor rulers, nor things present, nor things to come, nor
> powers, nor height, nor depth, nor anything else in all creation,
> will be able to separate us from the love of God in Christ Jesus our
> Lord. (Rom. 8:35, 37-38)

Cary concludes, "It took a few months for us to heal, to listen to one
another, and to learn from one another again, but we did get there and we
learned an important lesson. The way I read it, unity is pretty important in
the New Testament, and if love is at the heart of it, perhaps unity is not as
difficult to attain or maintain as we think. Even if it *is difficult*, it's still worth
it."[2]

Authentic covenantal nomism has a bottom line: we should feel called
to create ways of relating at every level of life that ensure the realization of
the one Great Commandment, that we remain in God's love with everyone and everything. Anything that is defined by dynamics that separate
us from that love, especially in our relationships with one another, cannot
be justified, only rationalized. This realization should convince us not only
that nothing can separate us from the love of God in Christ Jesus, but that
when these forms of separatism loom before us, we must not be overcome

---

2. Gerrit Scott Dawson, in Dawson, Atha, and Simonton, "On Our Faces Together,"
39.

by them. Rather we must work for their transformation, knowing that "in all these things we are [called to be] more than conquerors through him who loved us" first (Rom. 8:37).

Background for Charity as *the* Fruit of the Holy Spirit

To this Catholic priest, the Protestant ministers listed above represent living examples of the power of cultivating that foundational fruit of the Holy Spirit, and perhaps the only one really: love or charity and, specifically, faith working through love (5:6). Possibly because they prayed together, they could be challenged by one another, which represents one of Paul's purposes for love in our relationships. It was his prayer for the church at Philippi: "that your love may overflow more and more with knowledge and full insight to help you to determine what is best, so that in the day of Christ you may be pure and blameless, having produced the harvest of righteousness that comes through Jesus Christ for the glory and praise of God" (Phil. 1:9-11).

While the three Protestant ministers never specified exactly what created their ultimate break, it does not really matter. Why? It seems that they were sufficiently grounded in the Word of God as to take seriously its statement about "nothing" separating them from the love of God that has been revealed in Christ Jesus. That is a lesson many leaders in the Catholic Church could learn.

What a lesson for us in the Catholic Church, where we find so many excuses to justify why we can be separated! With historically developed and clerically controlled canonical nomism as the ultimate criterion for authentic Catholicism, we can see to what degree Tradition has come to eclipse the Scriptures themselves, and this happened with virtual impunity. If we have no higher power in the Catholic Church to hold us all accountable to the Holy Spirit, the spirit of the *stoicheia*, claiming to be the ultimate basis for what it means to be Catholic, will rear its ugly head just as it did in the church(es) of Galatia. It also becomes clear how opposite canonical nomism is from Paul's vision of love as the one dynamic that can break all forms of separation. In Paul's mind the only law is love; anything else is irrelevant if not idolatrous, in effect, denying the power of the Holy Spirit.

In grounding all the "fruits" of the Holy Spirit in the "fruit of the Spirit" called love, Paul will repeat in his famous "Canticle of Love" many of the same motifs as in Galatians. In fact, nine of the twenty times Paul uses "love" in 1 Corinthians can be found in chapter 13, which ends with the famous verse: "And now faith, hope, and love abide, these three; and the greatest of these is love" (1 Cor. 13:13). The centrality of love for Paul is wonderfully summarized in an insight from Walter Bo Russell, III, in his *The Flesh/ Spirit Conflict in Galatians*. While noting the singular significance of love as the chief of all the fruits of the Spirit, precisely because of its identification with the Holy Spirit, he also notes how the rest of the "fruits" of the Spirit flow from this way of love/Spirit. He writes, "Life according to the Spirit is to be characterized by ἀγάπη as the first and perhaps foremost virtue of those that should be produced in believers' lives. In a very real sense, ἀγάπη stands as the distinctive mark of the Christian life (Gal. 5:6, 13-14; Col. 3:12-14; 1 Cor. 12:31–13:13; cf. John 13:34-35). However, he immediately adds, "Paul does not just single out ἀγάπη, but refers to the nine virtues of Gal. 5:22-23a (and others like them) as a unit in v. 22b . . . and says 'against such things there is no law.'"[3]

In considering Paul's approach to living the ethical life based on the gospel, James Dunn supports a view similar to mine:

> Paul drives that distinction (faith in Christ and works of law) into an outright antithesis (2:16bc; 3:2, 5, 10-12): to regard the law (covenantal nomism) as the outworking of faith is retrogressive, a stepping back from the freedom of the children of God into immature childhood and slavery (3:23–4:11; 4:21-31). The outworking of faith has to be conceived in different terms from works of the law (circumcision, etc.): that is, in terms of the Spirit as against works of the flesh (5:16-26; 6:6-7).
>
> This, he explains, "may be conceived in terms of the law, but not the law focused in such Jewish distinctiveness as circumcision, but focused rather in love of neighbor (6:6, 13-14) as exemplified by Christ (6:1-4)."[4]

In another place Dunn notes that while Jesus's peers would have easily recognized the need to love God as a top priority, the fact that Jesus then taught that the neighbor must be loved as one's self came as "a complete surprise." Furthermore, not only did Christ exemplify love of neighbor; he taught that it must break all boundaries and forms of separation, and must even include love of enemy. This boundary-breaking love was of such a kind

---

3. Walter Bo Russell III, *The Flesh/Spirit Conflict in Galatians* (Lanham, MD/New York/Oxford: University Press of America, 1997), 164.

4. James D. G. Dunn, *The New Perspective on Paul* (rev. ed.; Grand Rapids/Cambridge: Eerdmans, 2008), 177.

that the Jewish New Testament scholar Amy-Jill Levine writes, "He may be the only person in antiquity to have given this instruction."[5]

Any motivation other than love for Christian faith, including my own Catholicism, must be suspect. Thus we must keep in mind N. T. Wright's cautionary insight when we consider our relationships in the church. He writes,

> Of course, it is fatally easy for Christians to embrace Paul's gospel as a new way of being in control of the world, a new power game, a new way of establishing one's identity as a matter of pride. To what extent this has happened and does happen in different churches and their claims is a question that cannot be ignored. But the key thing about Paul's gospel is not power, but love, the Son of God "loved me and gave himself for me" (2.20); "faith working through love" is the sign of true life (5.6); love is the first fruit of the divine Spirit, a love that leads to mutual service (5.22, 13).... God is creating in Christ a new world built on love and characterized by love. Postmodernity preaches a stern and judging law against all human pride, but those who walk by the Spirit "are not under the law" (5.18).[6]

Love has no boundaries; indeed, if it is authentic and the goal of people experiencing differences, it ultimately should have the power to break all boundaries. The unique "boundary marker" in the new law of Christ is not meant to separate Christians from one another but to become their distinguishing characteristic. If the Spirit of love is the one who unites all the members of the body of Christ together, then there is but one law and that is the law of love. Any other "law" that leads to separation must be seriously investigated as to its truth claims. Furthermore, if the proof of love is in its practice, then James Dunn's question has compelling merit. He asks,

> Is it unfair, then, to wonder whether the difference between Jewish failure to fulfill the law and Christian success in fulfilling the law is exaggerated—on the grounds, perhaps, that there *must* be a difference between the two patterns of religion, and that so far as ethics is concerned the difference can only be found in the gift

---

5. Amy-Jill Levine, "Go and Do Likewise: Lessons from the Parable of the Good Samaritan," *America*, September 29, 2014, 17.

6. N. T. Wright, *Pauline Perspectives: Essays on Paul, 1978–2013* (Minneapolis: Fortress Press, 2013), 206.

of the eschatological Spirit, and that the Spirit *must* have made a difference, otherwise the distinction/antithesis between Christianity and Judaism cannot be sustained? For unless Christians are in fact notably more loving than others, and not just loving God but loving the neighbor as themselves, one cannot help wondering where and what the difference is.[7]

Probably nowhere do we find Paul's prioritization of the practice of love among the members of his house churches more than in chapter 12 of Romans. There, while acknowledging the various gifts of all the members to be shared among all the members, he eloquently describes *how* this sharing is to take place in a way that does not "conform" with the world. Prefacing what we will be discussing with regard to Galatians about the call to become slaves of one another, these verses from Romans serve as a wonderful examen for all the members of all the churches for all times:

> I appeal to you therefore, brothers and sisters, by the mercies of God, to present your bodies as a living sacrifice, holy and acceptable to God, which is your spiritual worship. Do not be conformed to this world, but be transformed by the renewing of your minds, so that you may discern what is the will of God—what is good and acceptable and perfect. For by the grace given to me I say to everyone among you not to think of yourself more highly than you ought to think, but to think with sober judgment, each according to the measure of faith that God has assigned. For as in one body we have many members, and not all the members have the same function, so we, who are many, are one body in Christ, and individually we are members one of another. We have gifts that differ according to the grace given to us: prophecy, in proportion to faith; ministry, in ministering; the teacher, in teaching; the exhorter, in exhortation; the giver, in generosity; the leader, in diligence; the compassionate, in cheerfulness. Let love be genuine; hate what is evil, hold fast to what is good; love one another with mutual affection; outdo one another in showing honor. Do not lag in zeal, be ardent in spirit, serve the Lord. Rejoice in hope, be patient in suffering, persevere in prayer. Contribute to the needs of the saints; extend hospitality to strangers. Bless those who persecute you; bless and do not curse them. Rejoice with those who rejoice, weep with those who weep. Live in harmony with one another; do not be haughty, but associ-

---

7. Dunn, *New Perspective on Paul*, 86-87.

ate with the lowly; do not claim to be wiser than you are. Do not repay anyone evil for evil, but take thought for what is noble in the sight of all. If it is possible, so far as it depends on you, live peaceably with all. Beloved, never avenge yourselves, but leave room for the wrath of God; for it is written, "Vengeance is mine, I will repay, says the Lord." No, "if your enemies are hungry, feed them; if they are thirsty, give them something to drink; for by doing this you will heap burning coals on their heads." Do not be overcome by evil, but overcome evil with good.

How Has God Been Revealed as the God of Love?

A key thesis of this book is that, even for those who have not had a mystical experience in their lives or who have been unable to identify such an experience, the future of Christianity nonetheless demands that we develop a mystical stance toward everyone and everything in the universe. Although it is not that recognized, this notion was at the heart of all the writings of Teilhard de Chardin. Because God is love and has created everything in the cosmos to be an image of that love, and because everything in the cosmos is in the process of being Christified into that self-giving love, love was at the heart of his cosmology, his phenomenology, his spirituality, and, indeed, his whole personal and academic endeavors. God was the God of all; thus love was to be the heart of everyone and everything.

In Teilhard's eyes, this love was at the heart of Paul's writings. Teilhard waxed eloquently on this love theme in Paul, grounded in the God of All, when he wrote, "has any evolutionist pantheism, in face, ever spoken more magnificently of the All than St Paul did in the words he addressed to the first Christians?"[8] Ursula King describes the mystical basis for such a statement from Teilhard when she writes,

> Throughout his life, Teilhard was a wonderer between different worlds. His life and thought are interwoven like the parts of an immense symphony with ever new variations on a basic theme. This theme is the supreme adventure of man's ascent to the spirit, and the continuous breakthrough of God's presence in the world of matter and flesh. Teilhard's vision, like that of other seers before him, was one of consuming fire, kindled by the radiant powers of

---

8. Pierre Teilhard de Chardin, *Christianity and Evolution* (trans. René Hague; San Diego/New York/London: Harcourt, 1971), 72.

love. It was mystical vision deeply Christian in origin and orienta-
tion; yet it broke through traditional boundaries and grew into a
vision global in intent.[9]

The notion of love as the cosmic force uniting everyone and everything
is wonderfully articulated in a reflection by Henri Nouwen:

> Love unites all, whether created or uncreated. The heart of God,
> the heart of all creation, and our own hearts become one in love.
> That's what all the great mystics have been trying to tell us through
> the ages. Benedict, Francis, Hildegard of Bingen, Hadewijch of
> Brabant, Meister Eckhart, Theresa of Avila, John of the Cross, Dag
> Hammarskjold, Thomas Merton, and many others, all in their own
> ways and their own languages, have witnessed to the unifying
> power of divine love. All of them, however, spoke with a knowledge
> that came to them not through intellectual arguments but through
> contemplative prayer. The Spirit of Jesus allowed them to see the
> heart of God, the heart of the universe, and their own hearts as one.
> It is in the heart of God that we can come to the full realization of
> the unity of all that is, created and uncreated.[10]

While Nouwen does not list Paul among those "all" whom he considers
"the great mystics," we have shown that Paul is, indeed, one of the greatest
mystics of all time. Moreover, while we do not find Paul identifying God
with love so clearly and succinctly as does the author of the First Letter
of John (1 John 4:16), still the conviction that God *is* love is at the heart
of every letter he wrote. The manner in which this love of God has been
revealed to us, as articulated in the writings of Paul, is not so much linked
to creation or the incarnation but to the cross, that great act of self-giving
love whose object is every person who has ever lived. This is the love of one
whom Paul identifies as "the Son of God, who loved me and gave himself for
me" (2:20). Such self-giving, while revealed in creation and the incarnation,
is nowhere more evident for Paul than in Jesus's crucifixion. For Jerome
Murphy-O'Connor, it is "the key element" and only way to "understand"
what was involved in "Christ's death. The idea of sacrifice is introduced, not

---

9. Ursula King, *Towards a New Mysticism: Teilhard de Chardin & Eastern Religions* (New York: Seabury Press, 1980), 101.

10. Henri J. M. Nouwen, "Unity in the Heart of God," Reflection for November 16, *Bread for the Journey: A Daybook of Wisdom and Faith* (San Francisco: HarperCollins, 1997).

for itself, but in order to underline the *value* of Christ's death. It places it in the supreme category of religious values."[11]

In a wonderful summary of the meaning of love in Paul's writings, especially that love that was most powerfully expressed in the crucifixion of Jesus Christ and that now must be extended in self-giving by the members of his body toward one another and beyond, Bernard O. Ukwuegbu writes, "The love that Christ exhibited is defined further as his self-giving (2:20). Because the corporate life of the Christian community is to be the social embodiment of the self-giving and loving Christ, the fruit of the Spirit can be construed as 'dynamic extension of Christ's own character and lifestyle, the means whereby Christ is embodied and performed.'"[12]

This cruciform love of God revealed in Jesus Christ had two overriding consequences for Paul: (1) it enabled the outpouring of Christ's Spirit to penetrate the life of the believer; and (2) it empowered all the believers to embrace their own living in cruciform ways.

For Paul, the first consequence of Christ's crucifixion and resurrection was the outpouring of the Spirit that inspired Jesus of Nazareth into the lives of believers for all time. To show the absolute gratuitousness of this love, Paul wrote to the Romans: "God's love has been poured into our hearts through the Holy Spirit that has been given to us. For while we were still weak, at the right time Christ died for the ungodly. Indeed, rarely will anyone die for a righteous person—though perhaps for a good person someone might actually dare to die. But God proves his love for us in that while we still were sinners Christ died for us" (Rom. 5:5-7).

While we will discuss the implications of such love in the life of the believer later in this chapter, I do not want to proceed without showing how the above passage of Romans once brought me great healing and meaning. I found myself feeling something seriously amiss in my life regarding a certain fellow Capuchin who, among others, had been accused of sexually abusing teenage boys while he was the rector of our seminary high school.[13]

I had always thought him to be quite officious and isolated from many of us Capuchin friars in the province. However, these charges against him complicated further my relationship with him. While his actions were hor-

11. Jerome Murphy-O'Connor, OP, *Becoming Human Together: The Pastoral Anthropology of St. Paul* (Wilmington, DE: Michael Glazier, 1984), 103-4.

12. Bernard O. Ukwuegbu, "Paraenesis, Identity-defining Norms, or Both? Galatians 5:13–6:10 in the Light of Social Identity Theory," *Catholic Biblical Quarterly* 70 (2008): 550, quoting Bruce W. Longenecker, *The Triumph of Abraham's God: The Transformation of Identity in Galatians* (Nashville: Abingdon Press, 1998), 72.

13. http://content.time.com.

rendous, I was personally, relationally, and spiritually challenged, insofar as I found myself unable to forgive him. As far as I knew, he never repented of what he had done to his victims. While he later admitted to his actions, I did not know this.

I knew that reconciliation between aggrieved parties demands both repentance and forgiveness to begin the healing process. Thus the question plagued me: "How can I forgive him when he has not repented?" Before I could resolve my dilemma he died, and I was left feeling terribly guilty because I had not been present to him offering forgiveness.

Only after I read the passage from Romans did I find a way to understand why I was so plagued: I was not acting in a "godly" way toward him. Despite what *he had done*, I had not done what God has done toward every one of us "while we still were sinners" (Rom. 5:7): I had not offered him the forgiveness that is always available through that "Christ [who has] died for us."

God's love has been revealed to us in our very vulnerability and sinfulness. I am called to reveal that same way of loving toward others in their vulnerability and sinfulness. If my way of loving reflects God's unconditioned love, there can be no exceptions regarding those to whom I show it. Paul does not say Christ died for us because of anything meritorious we did but precisely "while we were yet sinners" (Rom. 5:8). Commenting on this passage, Murphy-O'Connor writes: "This rather tortuous formulation is due to an effort to insinuate that even though the decision was God's it was also Christ's. This dimension comes to clear expression in another series of texts, 'The life I now live in the flesh I live by faith in the Son of God who loved me and gave himself for me' (Gal. 2:20; cf. 1:4; 2 Cor. 8:9). Since the 'and' here is explicative, the text presents the self-giving of Christ as an expression of love."[14]

The second key consequence of the crucifixion of Jesus Christ for the life of the believer is summarized in one of the most memorable passages in Galatians: "For through the law I died to the law, so that I might live to God. I have been crucified with Christ; and it is no longer I who live, but it is Christ who lives in me. And the life I now live in the flesh I live by faith in the Son of God, who loved me and gave himself for me" (2:19-20).

When I entered the Capuchin Franciscan Order at nineteen years of age, I had a very bad self-image. I often found myself repeating the phrase, "it is no longer I who live, but it is Christ who lives in me." I wish I could have known the real meaning of this statement then. I was taking on the pas-

---

14. Murphy-O'Connor, *Becoming Human Together*, 47.

sage as a way to escape my own self-crucifixion; now I know just how key embracing the cross is for the spiritual life. Baptism itself is the reality of a life that has been crucified with Christ (2:19), not only in a sacramental way but in a way that signifies a new creation for the believer. Hence, those who belong to Christ have crucified the flesh with its passions and desires (5:24) in a way that gives evidence that the love of this Christ is now urging (see Rom. 5:5-7; 2 Cor. 5:14) them to manifest the fruit(s) of the Spirit. Thus, when Paul notes that "against such there is no law" (5:23) he is indicating that, at its core, morality is not to be defined by various norms or codes. It is to bear witness to the self-giving love of Christ on the cross, to show the world that the believer is crucified in a way that ushers in a whole new moral order grounded in love. In this sense I conclude this section with a wonderful challenge from Pope Francis: "The Christian vocation is this: to remain in the love of God, that is, to breathe, to live of that oxygen, to live of that air. Remain in the love of God."[15]

How Do We Cultivate the Spirit's Fruit of Love?

While Paul equates the "Teachers'" approach to God with the deeds of the flesh, such that its practitioners are denied entrance to God's kingdom (5:19-21), the Pauline communities manifest the fruit of the Spirit and the true fulfillment of the Mosaic law (5:22-23). Relational love of neighbor (5:14) is seen in the handling of the difficult issues of believers' sinning (6:1-15) and the sharing of material resources within and without the community (6:6-10). In both of these areas, the churches Paul planted are to live in a way appropriate for the new creation, that is, according to the standard of the Spirit rather than according to the standard of the flesh (6:12-16). This focus on love in community is the main thrust of the paraenesis of Gal. 5:13–6:10.[16]

Overcoming the "Works of the Flesh"

When we put Paul's articulation of the "fruit(s) of the Spirit," into its Galatian context, the fruits serve as a remedy for the works of the flesh. Since all of the Pauline letters except Philemon were written to communities rather than individuals, it must also be recognized that Paul's main concern was

---

15. Pope Francis, Homily, May 22, 2014, http://www.vatican.va.

16. Russell, *The Flesh/Spirit Conflict*, 147-48. Russell identifies those who see "love-in-community" as the main thrust of Gal. 5:13–6:10.

not individual spirituality but the way the house churches as entities would bear witness to the fruits of the Spirit in their corporate lives. For this reason it is not surprising that most of the "works of the flesh" highlighted by Paul in Galatians relate to group dynamics that undermine the integrity of community: enmities, strife, jealousy, anger, quarrels, dissensions, factions, and envy (5:20-21). Such ways of relating would make impossible the kind of interactions that he would later write about to the Philippians, namely, that they "be of the same mind, having the same love, being in full accord and of one mind" (Phil. 2:2).

If Paul is against a separatist form of covenantal nomism *ad extra* he cannot then have its echoes within the community itself. All those "works of the flesh" increase separation rather than reconciliation and participative community. Following any good conversion process, before one cultivates the "fruit(s) of the Spirit," the "works of the flesh" must be eradicated. As I learned as a youngster in our family garden, you must pull out the weeds before planting the seeds. The competitors must be removed in order to make the garden more productive.

There is another weed that needs to be removed that did not seem to have entered into Paul's awareness: the societal and cultural "weeds" of ethnocentrism, classism, and sexism (and any other such "ism" that reflects separatism because of unequal power dynamics) that undermined the realization of the vision of what being "clothed in Christ" truly meant and entailed for all who were baptized into Christ when he wrote, "As many of you as were baptized into Christ have clothed ourselves with Christ. There is no longer Jew or Greek, there is no longer slave or free, there is no longer male and female; for all of you are one in Christ Jesus" (3:27-28). While today we understand that many "isms" reflect unequal power relationships and, therefore, injustice, such a worldview was not Paul's. That unity could not tolerate any form of structural separatism based on unequal power dynamics among those who constitute the one body of Christ.

Paul never heard of the concept of "social sin," but he addressed its negative consequences in covenantal nomism. Indeed, to my knowledge, the first time the notion of social sin even entered into the official vocabulary of the Catholic Church came in the 1971 document of the Synod of Bishops, *Justice in the World*. At this gathering of selected bishops from around the world, those delegates representing countries outside of the Western European/North American hegemonic control of the church, especially from its center in the Vatican, made their voices heard. They were able to show that the organizational structures, dynamics, and mindset of the old ways of "being church" existed at the expense of the whole church's *being* church, especially around issues regarding justice inside and outside the church.[17] In effect, they seemed to be saying, economic and political "nomism" or patterns had become cultural nomism. These dynamics resulted in a serious separation between the "church of the North" and the "church of the South." That we still live with its consequences is evidenced in the unequal representation of the South in the decision-making and canonical apparatus of the Catholic Church. Recent appointments by Pope Francis for entrance into the College of Cardinals represent his attempt to remedy this disparity.

There is a historical reason why we have yet to achieve the kind of structures that reflect the vision of Paul in Gal. 3:27-28. The early community tried to create such structures through the exercise of the charisms, but those were gradually coopted by the wider imperial structures that undermined their realization. Gradually the new imperial way of being church was embraced by the male clerics in the church as its preferred way of governing.

The seeds (or sowing of weeds?) for this complex historical phenomenon have been described more clearly than anyone by Gerd Theissen, one of the first to articulate the impact of culture on the early Christian communities and to show how such communities gradually became seduced by the wider cultures from which they had once been alienated. He terms this form of Christian community that no longer challenged the wider societal structures as "love patriarchalism." He writes (at length),

> Faced with such radically altered social relationships, the society of late antiquity could adopt a new pattern of integration which had been developed in small religious communities within the Roman Empire—Christian love-patriarchalism. In it equality of status was extended to all—to women, to foreigners, and slaves. "For in Christ there was neither Jew nor Greek, . . . neither slave nor free, . . . neither male nor female; for you are all one in Christ Jesus" (Gal. 3:28). At the same time, however, all of this was internalized; it was true "in Christ." In the political and social realm class specific differences were essentially accepted, affirmed, even religiously legitimated. No longer was there a struggle for equal rights but instead a struggle to achieve a pattern of relationships among members of various strata which would be characterized by respect, concern, and a sense of responsibility. Thus even in the face of increasingly

---

17. Synod of Bishops, "Justice in the World" (1971), in Joseph Gremillion, *The Gospel of Peace and Justice: Catholic Social Teaching since Pope John* (Maryknoll, NY: Orbis Books, 1975), 513-29.

difficult social circumstances as the world of antiquity was coming to a close, in a period of growing social pressure, a new form of social integration was available. It held out the chance of certain humanity to those who were becoming ever more dependent while at the same time it held fast to the idea of fundamental equality of status. Constantine was able to succeed with his religious policy only because Christian love-patriarchalism, as the creative answer to radical social changes, was able to have an effect even beyond the small Christian minority.[18]

Constantine's model of governance still dominates in the church, and Constantinian dynamics govern the structures of the Roman Catholic Church rather than Trinitarian dynamics, which are the work of the Holy Spirit. And, until these human structures are eradicated, this weed will continue to choke off the word of God voiced by Paul that places all organizational models of the church at the service of his vision that all are one in Christ.

Cultivating the Fruit of the Spirit

As we begin a more detailed investigation into how we might cultivate the Spirit's fruit of love in our ecclesiastical structures and dynamics, as well as in our personal lives and relationships, we need to recall what has been discussed as the basic Pauline insight about God's love revealed in human form. The crucifixion of Jesus the Christ is the sign *sine qua non* of what God's love truly means. However, as Paul insists, Christ's crucifixion will be in vain unless it takes root in the lives of those who are baptized into Christ. This must be evident in the community as a whole, as well as in the individual lives of all its members. The Korean exegete Yung Suk Kim writes,

---

18. Gerd Theissen, *The Social Setting of Pauline Christianity: Essays on Corinth* (Philadelphia: Fortress Press, 1982), 109. As much as I would like to identify Paul with the actualization of social justice, I do resonate with the effort to do so by Marcus Borg and John Dominic Crossan: In Paul, love "is radical shorthand for what life 'in Christ' is like—life in the 'new creation,' life in the spirit, life animated by a Spirit transplant. As the primary fruit of a Spirit-filled life, love is about more than our relationships with individuals. For Paul, it had (for want of a better word) a *social* meaning as well. The social form of love for Paul was distributive justice and nonviolence, bread and peace. Paul's vision of life 'in Christ,' life in the 'new creation,' did not mean, 'Accept the imperial way of life with its oppression and violence, but practice love in your personal relationships'"; see Marcus J. Borg and John Dominic Crossan, *The First Paul: Reclaiming the Radical Visionary behind the Church's Conservative Icon* (New York: HarperOne, 2009), 204.

Belonging to this *ekklēsia* is not only something of a constitutive nature; it is meant to be a continuation of the self-sacrificing, in the members of the church, of Jesus's ultimate sacrifice of self in fidelity to the gospel of God's reign which he (Jesus) proclaimed. Thus Paul in Galatians could say that the way he was now living "in God" came about by being "crucified with Christ." Now, he said, "it is no longer I who live, but it is Christ who lives in me. And the life I now live in the flesh I live by faith in the Son of God, who loved me and gave himself for me." In other words, if Christ's crucifixion, his act of total self-giving love, were not continued in his disciples for all time, that suffering and death would be in vain. Thus Paul would conclude, "I do not nullify the grace of God; for if justification comes through the law, then Christ died for nothing" (2:19-21).[19]

If the grace of God will not be nullified and if Christ's death will not be "for nothing" and if Christ put to death on the cross the works of the flesh, the only purpose of the flesh now is to reveal the new created order of love. This brings us to discuss the three ways of love to be incorporated in our lives which Paul describes in Galatians.

For in Christ Jesus . . . the only thing that counts is faith working through love (5:6).

In Paul's understanding, faith leads to baptism. This baptism of individuals in the household church(es) and the wider church was to be expressed primarily in the members' love for one another, but not limited to the boundaries of "church"; otherwise it would be a new form of covenantal nomism. Nevertheless, charity was to begin at home in the house churches. While God's love shows no partiality (Rom. 2:11), there would be a special bond among those whose faith had led them to baptism and God. This bond is apparent in the special greeting that Paul uses to greet the members of the house churches and in his reference to them as special in God's eyes. In fact, he even calls the church(es) in Rome "God's beloved" (Rom. 1:7).

In all his letters except that to the Galatians, Paul identifies the churches and some of their various members as "beloved." He does this over twenty times. It is important to understand that Paul's use of the term "beloved" does not indicate primarily some kind of erotic love[20] or even philanthropic

---

19. Yung Suk Kim, *Christ's Body in Corinth: The Politics of a Metaphor* (Minneapolis: Fortress Press, 2008), 21.

20. A goal of mine in writing this book was to determine if the fruits of the Spirit have a clear basis in findings from neuroscience. While some studies are addressing changes in

love (allowing for certain special relationships when Paul does refer to various *individuals* as "beloved"). Rather what Paul intends by "love," especially in referring to the churches themselves, has a unique origin and meaning. We find this in Rom. 8:28.

Here Paul gets to the heart of his theology and his understanding of who are specifically God's "beloved" ones. In speaking of the Galatians, who once had been at enmity with God, Paul notes that, with their faith in Jesus Christ that has led them to baptism, now because of their "election they are beloved, for the sake of their ancestors" (Rom. 8:28). This call is universal and extends beyond any select group. In fact, Paul reminds the Romans: "the gifts and the calling of God are irrevocable" (Rom. 8:29). Paul calls them "beloved" in his greetings because they are, first of all, the beloved ones of God. This love of God for them is made known in the cross of Christ. This dynamic is further explained by James Dunn, who reminds us that "the new term is 'love' (ἀγάπη), the little used word taken over by the first Christians and made their own. It appears here no doubt because it caught another vital facet of the Christ side of the Christ/circumcision antithesis. Ἀγάπη was chosen rather than another love-word because it could express the wholly generous, sacrificial and actively outreaching concern on their behalf shown by God in Christ (2.2)." He concludes, "To stand on the Christ side of the Christ/circumcision antithesis meant a life shaped by and expressive of the same love that Christ had manifested on the cross. The love which was the basis of their acceptance by God should also be its expression."[21] Thus Paul could write to the Thessalonians: "May the Lord make you increase and abound in love for one another and for all, just as we abound in love for you" (1 Thess. 3:12).

With this understanding of the members of the house churches as God's beloved and beloved of one another, it is not surprising that Paul would stress love or charity as the foundational ethic upon which the members of the Galatian house church(es) should organize their lives. Also, as we examine how the cultivation of charity as a fruit of the Spirit enables our lives and way of life to be grounded in a more mystical stance, the three clear passages mentioning *agape* in 5:2–6:10 offer us a solid foundation as

---

the consciousness of lovers when put into certain situations, there is nothing that I have seen that addresses love as *agape* in the way Paul addresses it. We will address the role of oxytocin in the chapter on "kindness." For a popular description of neuroscience and "love," see Emily Eakin, "Looking for That Brain Wave Called Love: Humanities Experts Use M.R.I.'s to Scan the Mind for the Locus of the Finer Feelings," *New York Times*, October 28, 2000, A17, A19.

21. Dunn, *New Perspective on Paul*, 331.

well as the essential building blocks to create a visible sign of the mystical reality going on in us.

Galatians 5:6 is the foundational statement of Paul where he rejects covenantal nomism and opts for a faith that is ultimately not controlled by the law but by love. In arguing (again) why those who allow themselves to be circumcised will find that "Christ will be of no benefit to you" (5:2) and that those "who want to be justified by the law have cut ourselves off from Christ" and "have fallen away from grace" (5:4), he concludes with the text that might be considered the "hermeneutical key" not only to Galatians but to the whole Christian life;[22] it also lays the foundation for the rest of this chapter: "For in Christ Jesus neither circumcision nor uncircumcision counts for anything; the only thing that counts is faith working through love" (5:5).

Later he will say much the same thing: "May I never boast of anything except the cross of our Lord Jesus Christ, by which the world has been crucified to me, and I to the world. For neither circumcision nor uncircumcision is anything; but a new creation is everything!" (6:14-15). In the two passages mentioning "neither circumcision nor uncircumcision" as having anything any longer to do with the gospel he envisions as a result of his Damascus experience, Paul virtually equates "faith working through love" (5:5) as constituting the way of life that will reveal the baptized Christians as those who are now signifying in their relationships and dynamics that they, indeed, have become the new creation. Nothing else ultimately matters than their grounding in faith, which links them in baptism to live in love. Thus Pope Francis would say on the feast of St. John Lateran, the "Mother Church" of Catholicism:

> Today, the Church is called to be in the world a community that, rooted in Christ through Baptism, professes the faith in Him with humility and courage, while bearing witness to this in charity. Institutional elements, structures and pastoral organizations must be arranged to this fundamental purpose; to this essential aim: to give witness to faith through charity. Charity is precisely the expression of faith and faith is also the explanation and the foundation of charity![23]

Although Paul did not challenge the system of slavery, in his Letter to Philemon one gets the distinct impression that the love Philemon has

---

22. I. C. Levy, "*Fides quae per caritatem operature.* Love as the Hermeneutical Key in Medieval Galatians Commentaries," *Cistercian Studies Quarterly* 43.1 (2008): 41-61.

23. Pope Francis, Angelus Message, November 9, 2014, http://www.zenit.org.

shown to "all the saints" because of his "faith toward the Lord Jesus" (Phlm. 5, 7) is what Paul appeals to regarding Onesimus. Rather than revert to a law or command-approach regarding Philemon's slave Onesimus, Paul appeals to him "on the basis of love" to treat his slave as a "beloved brother—especially to me but how much more to you, both in the flesh and in the Lord" (Phlm. 5). To receive his former slave no longer as a slave but as a beloved brother would be, for Paul, a sign that Philemon had come to understand in his own life that the only thing that mattered to him was "faith working through love." Indeed, to receive Philemon as a beloved brother would give evidence that everything Philemon would be doing would "be done in love" (1 Cor. 16:14). Thus, without addressing head-on what we know today to be the systemic sin of slavery, Paul found a nonviolent way to promote a totally new way of undermining its dynamic: not only were all to become slaves in the way they put themselves at the service of one another, even more, all members of the community were to create one new family wherein everyone would be brother and sister to each other. This notion is echoed in Pope Francis's reflections in "No Longer Slaves, but Brothers and Sisters," which was the theme for the 48th World Day of Peace, January 1, 2015. He wrote, "Onesimus became Philemon's *brother* when he became a Christian. Conversion to Christ, the beginning of a life lived *Christian discipleship, thus constitutes a* new birth (cf. 1 Pet 1:3) which generates fraternity as the fundamental bond of family life and the basis of life in society."[24]

The whole law is summed up in a single commandment, "You shall love your neighbor as yourself" (5:14).

Another debate in discussions about Paul's writings involves what, if anything, he knew about the actual teachings of Jesus. While it would seem that he learned some things about Jesus and his teachings while in Antioch, it remains an unresolved issue. Notwithstanding this lack, James D. G. Dunn writes:

> The most striking evidence of the influence of Jesus's teachings on Paul is Paul's reference to the love command. In both Romans and Galatians he makes the same point—the same point that Jesus made! All the commands are "summed up in this word, in the command, 'You shall love your neighbour as yourself'" (Rom. 13:9).

---

24. Pope Francis, "No Longer Slaves, but Brothers and Sisters," 48th World Day of Peace Statement, January 1, 2015, http://www.zenit.org.

"The whole law is fulfilled in one word, in the well-known 'You shall love your neighbour as yourself'" (Gal. 5.14).

Dunn notes that "no other teacher known to us in Second Temple Judaism had extracted this commandment from the sequence of rulings in Lev. 19. So how was it 'well known'?" He answers his own question: "Paul can only be referring to the fact that Jesus's teaching on the love command was well known among the Christian communities. *Paul drew his attitude to the law from Jesus.* No other explanation makes such sense of the evidence available to us." Indeed, he concludes: "In short, *nowhere is the line of continuity and influence from Jesus to Paul clearer than in the love command.*"[25]

In a culture of self-fulfillment and entitlement, Gal. 5:14 might seem almost impossible to realize because of the culture's self-centeredness. That is because "love of self" has been so undermined by authority figures who have abused the "self" of innocents and by marketers who manipulate the "self" with promises of self-realization connected to some product or the latest "self-help" panacea. Thus, as we reflect on Gal. 5:14 and the call to "love our neighbor as ourselves," it might be good to hear the wisdom of Meister Eckhart, who speaks of appropriate self-love in a way that would make St. Paul proud! He writes, "If you love yourself, you love everybody else as you do yourself. As long as you love another person less than you love yourself, you will not really succeed in loving yourself, but if you love all alike, including yourself, you will love them as one person and that person is both God and humanity. Thus he is a great and righteous person who, loving himself, loves all others equally."[26]

The Old Testament text for the commandment to "love your neighbor as yourself" is found in Leviticus 19. This powerful chapter begins with the following admonition "to all the congregation of the people of Israel": "You shall be holy for I the Lord your God am holy" (Lev. 19:2). Then, after a few verses addressing right worship of God (Lev. 19:3-8), Israel is told how to structure its life as a people so that right relationships or justice will prevail (Lev. 19:9-17), evidence that Israel is keeping the basic commandment regarding its treatment of others: "you shall love your neighbor as yourself" (Lev. 19:8).

---

25. James D. G. Dunn, *Jesus, Paul, and the Gospels* (Grand Rapids: Eerdmans, 2011), 114.

26. Meister Eckhart, *Meister Eckhart: A Modern Translation* (trans. R. B. Blakney; New York: Harper & Brothers, 1941), 201.

When we take a "deeper dive" into this passage, however, we find that the passage to "love your neighbor as yourself" actually is quite unique. Indeed, James Dunn notes that Jesus's use of the passage "was a complete surprise" and that "Jesus seems to have had no precedent for doing so" because "explicit references to Lev. 19:18 are lacking in Jewish literature prior to Jesus." Dunn concludes, "Almost certainly, then, it was Jesus himself who extracted Lev. 19:18 and gave it this preeminent status within the law."[27]

Dunn also argues that Paul probably knew clearly this stress of Jesus on Lev. 19:8. Thus, in a more expansive way in his Letter to the Romans, Paul says much the same thing as in Gal. 5:14: "Owe no one anything, except to love one another; for the one who loves another has fulfilled the law. The commandments, 'You shall not commit adultery; You shall not murder; You shall not steal; You shall not covet'; and any other commandment, are summed up in this word, 'Love your neighbor as yourself.' Love does no wrong to a neighbor; therefore, love is the fulfilling of the law" (Rom. 13:8-10).

Contrary to how Paul has been interpreted in the past as rejecting the "law" altogether, the passages from Romans and Galatians show that this could not be further from the truth. However, it is true that, for Paul, the law was not to be an end in itself nor a witness to Israel's separation from its neighbors; on the contrary its end was to be a love that would include all—love for the neighbor reflecting proper self-love.

In the chapter on "kindness" as a sign of the fruit of love that reveals a mystical stance toward everyone and everything, we will show how Paul broke the ideological boundaries of his culture's notion of reciprocity, one that had been limited to one's own family and kin, to include the "other," especially the "others" who were the objects of rejection from those limited groups. Suffice it to repeat here what Dunn concludes, that Jesus's and Paul's understanding of the law was not to reject it but to fulfill its ultimate meaning in a love of neighbor that would not be exclusive: "Freed from that too narrow understanding of the law, the Jewish Christian (and Gentile) is able to recognize that the law has a continuing positive role, to be fulfilled in love of neighbor. And with the law seen to commend and confirm the right priorities, of faith in God (and his Christ) and love of neighbor, the other priorities which emphasize national distinctiveness can be seen to be false priorities, and the ritual practices involved set on one side as matters of indifference."[28]

---

27. Dunn, *Jesus, Paul, and the Gospels*, 112

28. Dunn, *New Perspective on Paul*, 140.

For you were called to freedom, brothers and sisters; only do not use your freedom as an opportunity for self-indulgence, but through love become slaves to one another (5:13).

When we consider Paul's admonition to become slaves to one another, we must recall two things: the example of Jesus Christ and the realization that Paul was not expecting anyone in the house churches at Galatia to do what others were not doing: all were called to emulate in their communal lives the example of the self-emptying love of Jesus. Paul's notion of this is best articulated in his famous canticle found in Philippians. Here Jesus's self-emptying (*kenosis* or "kenotic love/loving") is held up as the model for all disciples as a way of living in a healthy community of care. Paul writes to those who follow the way of Jesus for all time:

> If then there is any encouragement in Christ, any consolation from love, any sharing in the Spirit, any compassion and sympathy, make my joy complete: be of the same mind, having the same love, being in full accord and of one mind. Do nothing from selfish ambition or conceit, but in humility regard others as better than yourselves. Let each of you look not to your own interests, but to the interests of others.

In order to make this happen among them, he offers this time-honored advice for how everyone in the community is to become a slave of one another, all because of their love:

> Let the same mind be in you that was in Christ Jesus, who, though he was in the form of God, did not regard equality with God as something to be exploited, but emptied (*kenoō*) himself, taking the form of a slave, being born in human likeness. And being found in human form, he humbled himself and became obedient to the point of death—and death on a cross. Therefore God also highly exalted him and gave him the name that is above every name, so that at the name of Jesus every knee should bend, in heaven and on earth and under the earth, and every tongue should confess that Jesus Christ is Lord, to the glory of God the Father. (Phil. 2:1-11)

In my mind, nobody has written better on the cosmic, communal, and personal implications of living a kenotic life in our self-interested and materialistic time than the Catholic Pope Francis[29] and the Protestant Sallie

---

29. Pope Francis has outlined his call for a new way of kenotic living and loving in

McFague.[30] Both of them have shown that our consumerism is based on self-interest. The result is a globalization of indifference that has cosmic consequences that demand a new form of kenotic living. What in Paul's day was an ideal based on the model of Jesus Christ, in our Anthropocene Age, is now a call of survival itself.

When Paul wants to show how the Galatians can practice the kind of "servant love" he has in mind, he offers the example of how they gave themselves wholeheartedly to him when he lived among them. As he would have given his very life for them, so they did the same for him. Bruce Longenecker writes that "the initial behavior of the Galatian Christians towards Paul, then, was a concrete example of the moral principle stated elsewhere in Galatians: 'through love, become servants of each other' (5:13); 'bear one another's burdens' (6:2)." Longenecker explains, "These exhortations are themselves elaborations of Paul's concise remark in 5:6 that what matters is 'faith working practically (ἐνεργουμένη) in love.' In Paul's view, this posture of responsible self-giving and loving service to others which should be one of the defining marks of the Christian community enlivened by the Spirit of the Son of God—a quality manifest already in the Galatians' early reception of Paul."[31]

The only enslavement the Galatians should embrace is that freely chosen because of their mutual participation in the body of Christ. Like cells existing for the life of the other cells, each member's identity is to mirror Christ's self-giving love. Grounded in such attitudes, the community could practice again the gospel it has received. It can manifest its faith through love. We should remember that at the time Paul wrote to the church(es) in Galatia, the members of these house churches were largely composed of immediate family members and some extended kin. Thus, applying the dynamics of contemporary households to the wider community of faith can be helpful.

At great sacrifice, Paul felt compelled to preach the gospel (1:13–2:14). But any burden involved in such preaching was worth shouldering if the Galatians could be returned to that faith that works through love. Bearing

---

two main pieces of literature: *Evangelii Gaudium* and *Laudato Si*, wherein Pope Francis extends Paul's notion of being brothers and sisters in God's household to everything in creation itself.

30. While she develops the theme throughout her book, Sallie McFague devotes three of her eight chapters on kenotic living and loving in her *Blessed Are the Consumers: Climate Change and the Practice of Restraint* (Minneapolis: Fortress Press, 2013), 141-215.

31. Bruce W. Longenecker, "'Until Christ Is Formed in You': Suprahuman Forces and Moral Character in Galatians," *Catholic Biblical Quarterly* 75 (2015): 104.

one another's burdens is all the more difficult when we operate under the contemporary law of "I'll do it myself." That undermines the possibility of living in a community of "beloved" disciples. This is perhaps especially true for those of us who are not connected to one another in family or kinship groupings, where serving one another might seem a bit easier.

I discovered this one day when I was staying with friends who had a daughter who was a junior in high school. One morning their daughter, having returned from a 6:30 AM class, asked, "Daddy, would you make breakfast for me?"

"Sure, honey," her father replied without batting an eyelash or a grimace on his face: "What do you want?"

I could never have imagined myself ever asking my own religious brothers in my "house church"/friary to serve me like that (6:2), perhaps because we are much more used to practicing a misinterpretation of the later text that says "all must carry their own loads" (6:5)!

Returning from my visit, I decided I'd try to change my self-sufficient ways and begin inviting my brothers to serve me now and then. I decided to be vulnerable and acknowledge my desire for help, especially in little day-to-day matters. The next morning, my housemate Jerry was at the coffee pot in the room outside the kitchen area where I was making my breakfast. I decided to take the leap. "Jerry," I called. "Yeah," he answered. "Could you bring me a cup of coffee when you come in here?" "Sure," was his immediate answer. "How do you take it?"

The fact that I couldn't believe what I had just done and sat in awe at how Jerry had been so willing to serve told me there was still hope that Paul's advice to the house church(es) at Galatia could bear fruit in our Capuchin house church in Milwaukee!

If love never fails, then opportunities always exist for that love to be practiced by and among us and, with one another, also beyond us. Thus we can become the kind of "beloved" ones who hear, as applicable beyond our own local community, the words Paul wrote in 1 Thessalonians: "Now concerning love of the brothers and sisters, you do not need to have anyone write to you, for you yourselves have been taught by God to love one another; and indeed you do love all the brothers and sisters throughout Macedonia. But we urge you, beloved, to do so more and more" (1 Thess. 4:9-10).

Paul's statement that faith working through love is all that matters is especially true when we enter the twilight of our lives. In commenting on a familiar passage related to this idea, Dominican Mary Brian Durkin recalls a reflection in the writings of Evelyn Underhill. She writes, "When reminding retreatants that John of the Cross said, 'In the evening of life, we shall be judged on love,' Underhill emphasized the word 'evening' to reinforce once again the thought that our spiritual formation is an ongoing, lifetime process. Incomplete and unfinished, we are gradually being formed and shaped by the Divine Artist who dwells within us. Our faithful, enduring response to the Potter's chipping and chiseling will gradually enable us to seek and find the Eternal in our everyday world of duties, demands, pressures, and pleasures."[32]

"Love never ends," Paul teaches (1 Cor. 13:8). Nowhere is this insight truer than in death itself. Something happens to many people who are facing death: their priorities are reordered. I have found it in my family and among those to whom I have ministered. This insight became clear to the whole nation, however, in the days after September 11, 2001. Story after story was told and retold of people calling their loved ones knowing that they might likely die, uttering their last words in images of love. In his "Word for Word" column,[33] Scott Vealle cited news accounts from around the Northeast that featured the last words and stories of thirteen people involved. While all thirteen spoke of tenderness, eight clearly ended with farewells of love.

A man who had just begun his job at the World Trade Center a month before called his wife from the 105th floor: "Honey, something terrible is happening. I don't think I am going to make it. I love you. Take care of the children."

Kenneth Van Auken was on the 102nd floor; he called his wife, Lorie, at home. "I love you," he said, "I don't know if I'm going to get out. But I love you very much. I hope I'll see you later. Bye."

Mark Hoglan was on United Airlines Flight 93 going from Newark to San Francisco. He called his mother, saying, "We've been taken over. There are three men who say they have a bomb." Then he told her, "I love you, I love you, I love you."

Brian Sweeny was on Flight 175, that crashed into the World Trade Center's South Tower. He left a message for his wife, Julie, on their answering machine shortly before 9 AM. He said, "Hey Jules, it's Brian, I'm on a plane, and it's hijacked, and it doesn't look good. I just wanted to let you know that I love you, and I hope to see you again. If I don't please have fun in life, and live your life the best you can. Know that I love you, and no matter what, I'll see you again."

32. Mary Brian Durkin, OP, "The Wisdom of John of the Cross in the Writings of Evelyn Underhill" (http://www.evelynunderhill.org).

33. Scott Vealle, "Last Words," *New York Times*, September 16, 2001.

PBS correspondent Ray Suarez had a conversation with a woman about Moises Rivas, a chef at the famed Windows on the World restaurant at the top of the World Trade Center. He was told by the woman that Rivas just said, "I'm O.K.—don't worry. I love you no matter what. I love you. And he just hung up."

Thomas Burnett called his wife, Elena, from Flight 93, saying, "I know we're all going to die; there's three of us who are going to do something about it." Then, just before ending the call he said, "I love you, honey."

Daphne Bowers of Brooklyn got a call from her daughter Veronique at the World Trade Center. "She called me and said, 'Mommy, the building is on fire, there's smoke coming through the walls. I can't breathe.' The last thing she said was, 'I love you, Mommy, goodbye.'"

The final entry to this list came from NBC News on September 14. Jane Pauley, the NBC correspondent, talked with Lyzbeth Glick. Her husband, Jeremy Glick, was on United Flight 93. She asked, "What words from that phone call give you the most comfort now?" Lyzbeth responded, "We said, 'I love you' a thousand times, over and over and over again, and it just brought so much peace to us. . . . He said, 'I love Emmy,' who's our daughter, and to take care of her." And, then, she notes, "he said . . . 'Whatever decisions you make in your life, I need you to be happy, and I will respect any decisions that you make.' . . . I think that gives me the most comfort."

Such is unconditional love; a love that ensures that the other's freedom will always be honored. To me, that is what God's unconditional love is about and that is what we must cultivate if the fruit of this Spirit of love is to be *our* last word . . . and, too, all the words until then.

Thus, as we move on to our discussion of the way the Spirit's fruit of love is to be developed in us in a way that contributes to a mystical stance in our lives, the (somewhat dated) reflections of Evelyn Underhill still ring true:

> I do not think that St. Paul arranged his list of the Fruits of the Spirit in a casual order. They represent a progressive series from one point and that one point is Love, the living, eternal seed from which all grow. We all know that Christians are baptized "into a life summed up in love," even though we have to spend the rest of our own lives learning how to do it. Love there is the building point from which all the rest come: that tender cherishing attitude; that unlimited self-forgetfulness, generosity and kindness which is the attitude of God to all His creatures and so must be the attitude towards them which His Sprit brings forth in us. . . . And the

first-fruit of His indwelling presence, the first sign that we are on His side and He on ours, must be at least a tiny bud of this Charity breaking the hard and rigidity outline of our life.[34]

Inspired by these wonderful memorials of peoples' love, I conclude with one of my favorite prayers from Paul's writings; actually it is my favorite prayer from Paul. He writes about something that was modeled to me in the original house church of my early childhood, the house church led by my mother and father. Paul writes, "This is my prayer, that your love may overflow more and more with knowledge and full insight to help you to determine what is best, so that in the day of Christ you may be pure and blameless, having produced the harvest of righteousness that comes through Jesus Christ for the glory and praise of God" (Phil. 1:9-11).

---

34. Evelyn Underhill, in Roger L. Roberts, compiler, *The Fruits of the Spirit by Evelyn Underhill* (Wilton, CT: Morehouse-Barlow Co., 1981, 1989), 14-15.

Chapter 6

Cultivating the Joy of the Gospel to Sign the Spirit's Love in Our Lives

I want to begin this chapter with a confession of sorts. Although I admit I have been more of a "Pope Francis Catholic" than a "Pope John Paul II Catholic" or a "Pope Benedict XVI Catholic," I was surprised when Pope Francis called his first apostolic letter *The Joy of the Gospel*. I said to myself, "Why did he call it that?" What did the gospel have to do with joy?

If Pope Francis had called it *The Truth of the Gospel*, I would have expected a teaching much in the philosophical vein of Pope John Paul II: an exegesis of objective truths connected to an understanding of the gospel that must be believed if people are to consider themselves Catholic. Or, if it had come from Pope Benedict XVI, I would have anticipated an excursus as to why we need a solid foundation in "the truths of the gospel" in order to combat the "isms" of our times such as relativism, secularism, and individualism.

Even as I read (and reread) all of *Evangelii Gaudium*, I could not figure out why Pope Francis kept referring to the "joy" of the gospel. I am inspired by much of what he has written, especially about the consequences of consumerism, which creates a "culture of indifference" and the concomitant call for compassion. Yet I found myself unable to grasp the *object* (or should I say "subject") of the joy that inevitably comes from the gospel (that truly defines "the new evangelization") that his apostolic letter envisions.

It was perhaps only when I seriously studied Galatians that I began to realize what Pope Francis meant. Still, my exegetical research remained intellectual and discursive until I recalled something that had happened in my heart when I was giving an extended retreat some years ago to seventy or eighty people in Halifax, Nova Scotia.

At each conference an older sister (I reckoned her to be in her late seventies or early eighties) sat right in front of me. While the other participants had looks on their faces that ranged from interest to tiredness, her facial expression intrigued me. No matter what I said (or how long I took to say it!), she never ceased looking at me with a welcoming smile filled with joy. I could not remember ever seeing someone with such a radiant look.

In the middle of the retreat she came to the designated room for a conference. I remember nothing else from that retreat in Halifax, including anything I said and not even its theme, except what she said to me as she sat down: "Mike, I've been in religious life for sixty-two years and my whole life has been a love affair with God."

That is when the lights went on. Paul's notion of joy is intimately connected to love, a love that is not debatable philosophically (à la Pope John Paul II) or theologically (à la Pope Benedict XVI). It comes from the experience of being overpowered by the love of another; it is not of the head so much as of the heart. It knows that one is loved in a way that makes one beloved in the truest sense of the word. It is the sign of the person who, as Jesus would say in Matthew's Gospel, has "found" the mystery of the kingdom of God (Matt. 13), the one who finds the treasure that has been hidden (Matt. 13:44).

Such love has little or nothing to do with knowing about the gospel; it has everything to do with *experiencing* the gospel. It is not about "knowing" something at all; it is about finding someone. Paul's Damascus gospel came from an experience of Christ crucified and alive in the members of the church whom Paul had been persecuting. This was the cause of his joy; it was the gospel he proclaimed. Consequently, he could not believe it when he heard that the Galatians had abandoned the gospel he had shared with them. Could it be that the gospel they had received from Paul, which he had "handed on to them" (1 Cor. 15:1-9), was experienced by them in just the same way as the gospel they had received from the Teachers (1:9)? Or was Paul's way of receiving the gospel at Damascus, which brought him such joy and such zeal for it, experientially different from that of the Galatians? *Quidquid recipitur ad modum recipientis recipitur,* Thomas Aquinas taught: "whatever is received is received according to the mode of the receiver."[1] Could it be that their responses to "living" the gospel were different because their modes of receiving it were different? These differences represent the "joy" of the gospel for some but not for others.

"Joy is the most infallible sign of the presence of God," Teilhard de Chardin is reputed to have said. If this is so, its infallibility was not exactly being signified in me. This made me ask myself: why are there so many people

---

1. Thomas Aquinas, *Summa Theologiae* 1a, q. 75, a. 5; 3a, q. 5.

who are "professionals" in the Catholic Church (like me) who don't *radiate joy*, especially when many of us, like the sister on retreat in Halifax, have dedicated our whole lives to God and to living in the presence of God?

That question will be the topic of this chapter.

How Is Joy Identified with God?

It is not surprising to discover that "joy" is used only once in Paul's Letter to the Galatians and that this "joy" is limited to serving as the first characteristic in his litany of the fruits of love (5:22). Paul simply is in no joyful mood when he writes that letter; he has found nothing to rejoice about among the Galatians. He has discovered that they are "so quickly deserting the one who called [them] in the grace of Christ and are turning to a different gospel—not that there is another gospel, but there are some who are confusing [them] and want to pervert the gospel of Christ" (1:6-7). We must look, therefore, to the other authentic letters of Paul for the meaning of joy as a key characteristic in Paul's gospel of the love revealed through the death and resurrection of Jesus Christ that, by the power of the Holy Spirit, may also be found in the life of believers.

First of all, since joy is a key characteristic of love (5:22) and since God has been revealed as love, joy is the realization of the presence of the reign of God in one's life and world. In the words of the *Taitiriya Upanishad*, "Joy comes from God. Who could live and could breathe if the joy of Brahman filled not the universe? . . . for from joy, all beings have come, by joy they all live, and unto joy they all return."

I disagree here with Hans Dieter Betz, who writes in his commentary on Galatians that "'joy' (χαρά) is not clearly attributed to God or Christ, probably because of its emotional overtones, but its character as a divine gift is strongly emphasized [Rom. 14:7; 15:13, 32; 1 Cor. 7:30; 2 Cor. 1:15, 24; 2:3; Phil. 1:4, 18, 25; 2:2, 28f.; 4:1; 1 Thess. 1:6; 2:19, 20; 3:9; Phlm. 7])."[2] Of the three times Paul mentions "joy," two refer to it as something having to do with God. In a challenge to separatist forms of individual and social identity markers linked to covenantal nomism, he declares, in one of his few mentions of "the kingdom of God/heaven,"[3] that "the kingdom

---

2. Hans Dieter Betz, *Galatians: A Commentary on Paul's Letter to the Churches in Galatia* (Philadelphia: Fortress Press, 1979), 287 and 287 n. 148.

3. "Though he does not often refer to the Kingdom of God [Rom. 14:17; 1 Cor. 15:20ff.; Phil. 3:20ff.], it is clear that the meaning of the phrase [God's rule of the world through his true Israel, his true humanity] is at the heart of his thought, emerging particularly when he allows himself a glimpse of the cosmic scope of God's purposes. For Paul, as for Jesus, the salvation of the individual is set in the context of God's redefinition of Israel, his call

of God is not food and drink but righteousness and peace and joy in the Holy Spirit" (Rom. 14:17). Later, again linking joy (and the peace we will discuss in the next chapter), with the Holy Spirit, Paul offers a prayer for the Romans: "May the God of hope fill you with all joy and peace in believing, so that you may abound in hope by the power of the Holy Spirit" (15:13). Building on the role of the Holy Spirit in the life of the church, Pope John Paul II writes in his encyclical on the Holy Spirit, "The Church with her heart which embraces all human hearts implores from the Holy Spirit that happiness which only in God has its complete realization: the joy 'that no one will be able to take away' (John 16:22), the joy which is the fruit of love, and therefore of God who is love; she implores 'the righteousness, the peace and the joy of the Holy Spirit' in which, in the words of St. Paul, consists of the Kingdom of God (Gal. 5:22; Rom. 14:17)."[4]

The connection between joy and its ultimate source in and as an attribute of the Holy Spirit is clear in 1 Thessalonians. Here Paul describes the joy they experienced when they "received" the word (i.e., the gospel) as something that was "inspired by the Holy Spirit" (1 Thess. 1:7). The joy that is experienced as a fruit of the Spirit's love for us is almost automatically manifested in one's "rejoicing" in that Spirit who has made the gospel's way of salvation known to us (see Rom. 15:10).

As we have seen, in addition to that "joy" which represents the first characteristic of the love of the Spirit, Paul does develop the theme of "rejoicing," that comes with the experience of being called to inherit the promise made to Abraham and Sarah. This is highlighted in the section discussing the children born of the slave woman and of the free woman (4:21-31). The one woman represents "the present Jerusalem"; the other "woman corresponds to the Jerusalem above; she is free, and she is our mother" (4:26). Noting that the Christians are not only the children of this free woman but they are also "the children of the promise" (4:28), Paul reminds the Galatians that this has been foretold by the prophet Isaiah (54:1), who wrote, "Rejoice, you childless one, you who bear no children, burst into song and shout, you who endure no birth pains; for the children of the desolate woman are more numerous than the children of the one who is married" (4:27).

In *Recovering Paul's Mother Tongue: Language and Theology in Galatians,* Susan Eastman notes that the barren woman represents God's transfor-

---

of a worldwide family whose sins are forgiven in the blood of the new covenant"; see N. T. Wright, *Pauline Perspectives: Essays on Paul, 1978–2013* (Minneapolis: Fortress Press, 2013), 28.

4. Pope John Paul II, *Dominum et Vivificantem,* encyclical letter, May 18, 1986, no. 67, http://www.vatican.va.

mative power, which is available to all people. She notes that the transformation from desolation to joy and from the destroyed to the restored city "undergirds the movement in Paul's letter from his anxious labor pains [see 4:19] to his confidence that his converts will remain steadfast in the freedom of the gospel."[5]

The connection between Paul's proclaiming the gospel and rejoicing is especially pronounced in his Letter to the Philippians. There, despite his imprisonment, he notes that, when we are grounded in the gospel of our own Damascus experiences, no matter what, we can rejoice:

> I want you to know, beloved, that what has happened to me has actually helped to spread the gospel, so that it has become known throughout the whole imperial guard and to everyone else that my imprisonment is for Christ; and most of the brothers and sisters, having been made confident in the Lord by my imprisonment, dare to speak the word with greater boldness and without fear. Some proclaim Christ from envy and rivalry, but others from goodwill. These proclaim Christ out of love, knowing that I have been put here for the defense of the gospel; the others proclaim Christ out of selfish ambition, not sincerely but intending to increase my suffering in my imprisonment. What does it matter? Just this, that Christ is proclaimed in every way, whether out of false motives or true; and in that I rejoice. Yes, and I will continue to rejoice. (Phil. 1:12-18)

Something powerful has happened to Paul that he can proclaim "the joy of the gospel" in such a way as to rejoice even while knowing that he might never again be free to proclaim it in the way that he has previously. No matter what happens to him, he can rejoice, knowing that he has been faithful to its proclamation and that any others who do so, for whatever motives, will ultimately share in that same joy.

This deeper understanding of the joy that is connected to our experience and proclamation of "the gospel" brings us to our next section.

How Do We Cultivate the Spirit of Love through Joy in Our Lives and Relationships, Our Church, and Our World?

Some years ago Marc Almond had a popular song, "Looking for Love in All the Wrong Places." One might say the same thing about joy. Too many of

---

5. Susan Eastman, *Recovering Paul's Mother Tongue: Language and Theology in Galatians* (Grand Rapids: Eerdmans, 2007), 129.

us seem to look for it with wrong assumptions about its source and wrong expectations about where we might find it. This should not be surprising because, as Mary Michael O'Shaughnessy has pointed out, of the three great "energies" in life—the drive for love, the drive for freedom, and the drive for joy—the drive for joy is the most elusive. And yet she reminds us that we must *choose* how we direct this drive. She explains,

> Our expression of personal joy and delight reaches out expansively to self, to others, and to our *Abba*-God. Both our individual and social activities radiate our joy and gladness. Our feelings and emotional experiences of joy and delight enlarge our personal vistas, enhance our awareness of self, and energize us to reach out in joy to others. With others in our family, in our work, and in our recreation, we can radiate peace, joy, and patience. We are Gospel people of breath and depth; we are Gospel people of praise and thanksgiving. We are actively adult in our Gospel living and sharing. We carry within us and to others the Good News in our ordinary and concrete daily doings and involvements. The gift of joy and delight that we have received is freely shared with and extended to others. Our mature joy and gladness serve to generate within others joy and life-delight. We become adult Gospel bearers, not merely in speech, but in the fullness of our being, our spirit. With Mary we can sing our Magnificat, "My soul (my spirit, my being) proclaims the greatness of the Lord, and my spirit rejoices in God my Savior!" (Luke 1:46)[6]

Overcoming the "Works of the Flesh" That Repress Joy

In his own indomitable way, Pope Francis has noted that joy makes the difference between being a healthy and an unhealthy Christian. One is either a joyful person or a killjoy. Thus he said in a homily on May 22, 2014:

> Joy is the sign of a Christian. A Christian without joy is either not a Christian or he is sick. There's no other type! He is not doing well health-wise! A healthy Christian is a joyful Christian. I once said that there are Christians with faces like pickled peppers. They always have these [long] faces! Some souls are also like this, this is bad! These are not Christians. A Christian without joy is not Chris-

---

6. Mary Michael O'Shaughnessy, OP, *Feelings and Emotions in Christian Living* (New York: Alba House, 1988), 35.

tian. Joy is like the seal of a Christian. Even in pain, tribulations, even in persecutions.[7]

When I consider more deeply some key obstacles to the experience of joy I find two dominating stumbling blocks: (1) the belief that it can be achieved by means of certain practices and (2) its virtual identification with happiness.

In addressing the first false assumption about linking joy with the development of certain practices, even Mary Michael O'Shaughnessy seems to have succumbed to the belief that joy can be achieved by following an outline of practices. She uncritically repeats and elaborates on "selected strategies" suggested by M. Scott Peck, in his *The Road Less Traveled*, "for taking hold of and acting responsibly in terms of choosing to experience joy and delight in our daily living."[8] Other self-help books, such as Carolyn Hobbs's *Joy No Matter What*,[9] reflect the same equation of the achievement of joy with the development of certain practices and/or strategies.

Probably the most common problem in cultivating joy as an expression of the Spirit's fruit of love is that it is so often identified with happiness. This happens both in religion and in the wider culture. Thus we learned as children that God's plan for our lives was that we "know, love, and serve God" in this life in a way that will bring about happiness (not joy!) in the next. The assumption seemed to have been that happiness has little or nothing to do with "knowing, loving, and serving God" in this life!

A parallel residue from the collapsing of authentic joy into virtual happiness is Western culture's identification of happiness as one of the "inalienable rights," as defined, for instance, in the United States' *Declaration of Independence*. Interestingly, the link between happiness and independence is precisely why happiness will never truly be achieved, much less experienced, as joy. There was a fascinating article in the *New York Times* on this topic: "If Richer Isn't Happier, What Is?" The opening lines of the article raise a good point: "One of the most often-repeated parts of the Declaration of Independence may also be one of the least influential. People march in Washington

---

7. Pope Francis, Homily, May 22, 2014, http://www.news.va.

8. O'Shaughnessy, *Feelings and Emotions*, 23-37. No less than Pope Francis himself offered his own list of ten points suggesting what constitutes a life of happiness (July 14, 2014): 1. Live and let live; 2. Be giving of yourself to others; 3. Be kind, humble, and calm; 4. Have a healthy sense of leisure; 5. Sundays are for family time, not work; 6. Find dignified work for young people; 7. Care for creation; 8. Let go of the negative; 9. Inspire through witness, engage in dialogue; and 10. Promote peace, http://www.vox.com/2014/8/1/5955741/francis-top-10.

9. Carolyn Hobbs, *Joy No Matter What* (York Beach, ME: Conari Press, 2005).

protesting various assaults against the first two unalienable rights, life and liberty. The third, however, rarely merits mention beyond the simple recitation of the Declaration's most famous sentence." The author, David Leonhardt, points out that the third part of the triad of rights "is left to the free market."[10] Despite the fact that the nation as a whole has become far richer, data also show that, as a whole, it is not any happier. Nevertheless, the marketing of books offering the way to happiness and happiness research is big business.

A leading researcher on "the science of happiness," Martin Seligman, came to the conclusion that for most of its history psychology addressed issues that could be identified as "problems": fear and anxiety, neuroses and obsessions, delusions and paranoia. The goal of psychologists and counselors was to bring patients back from being overly influenced and controlled by these ailments. However, when Seligman became president of the American Psychological Association in 1998, he moved the association more toward "positive" psychology. He concluded that a healthier and more successful approach needed to ask, "What are the enabling conditions that make human beings flourish?"[11]

In popular parlance, the "enabling conditions that make human beings flourish" have often been expressed with the follow-up to the phrase "I would be happy (or happier) if only I . . ." Reading "Dear Abby" and her partners as well as the polls and pundits, one finds that the "ifs" promising happiness range from problems with one's partner and/or friends, one's health and/or wealth, one's work and/or salary, one's age and/or I.Q. and, oftentimes, where one lives, (especially in California). None of these conditions in themselves provide the golden answer, not even living in California. This I discovered reading the *Los Angeles Times* as far back as 1999 when health writer Shari Roan considered whether living in California made people happy, and noted that the latest body of psychological research on what makes people happy answered the question with "a resounding no."[12]

In investigating "happiness research" in terms of making money, it seems there are two main components to enable true happiness to flourish (at least in the United States where the research took place). The first mea-

---

10. David Leonhardt, "If Richer Isn't Happier, What Is?," *New York Times*, May 19, 2001, A15.

11. Martin E. P. Seligman, quoted in Claudia Wallis, "The New Science of Happiness," *Time*, January 17, 2005, A3. Seligman has brought together his research in a well-received book, *Authentic Happiness* (New York: Free Press, 2002).

12. Shari Roan, "Outlook Sunny for Those with Happy Genes," *Los Angeles Times*, February 15, 1999.

sure of happiness is called "evaluative." Behavioral economists define it as a sense that I'm making enough money to enable my life to be good and that I'm basically satisfied with my life and am progressing toward the goals for my life that I have set. The other component of happiness vis-à-vis money is called "affective." This measures positive emotions such as joy, affection, and tranquility in relationship to their negative counterparts. The research showed that, at a certain point, the affective measures did not rise after a household reached a certain annual income. However, this was not the case with the "evaluative" measure of happiness vis-à-vis money: it kept increasing. In summarizing these different findings, Andrew Blackman wrote in a special section on "Wealth Management" in the *Wall Street Journal* ("Can Money Buy Happiness?"), "When you don't have much money, a little extra can go a long way because you have more essential needs to fulfill. But as you accumulate more wealth, it becomes more difficult to keep 'buying' happiness."[13] In others words happiness, in the long run, is more identified with achieving purpose in life than profits.

Beneath all the effort to discover the secret to happiness or the steps to happiness, Paschal Bruckner points to something quite selfish. "Happiness today is not just a possibility or an option but a requirement and a duty. To fail to be happy is to fail utterly. Happiness has become a religion—one whose smiley-faced god looks down in rebuke upon everyone who hasn't yet attained the blessed state of perpetual euphoria. How has a liberating principle of the Enlightenment—the right to pursue happiness—become the unavoidable and burdensome responsibility to be happy?" Bruckner shows that even joy itself is undermined by the current cultural stress on happiness when he states, "In the U.S., morality and happiness have formed a strange pact. The result is a way of living that constantly defers genuine joy and the pain involved achieving this kind of joy in favor of a safe, steady intake of 'well-being.'"[14] An overstress on one's own well-being always undermines communal well-being because the individual self ceases to be at the service of the whole.

Cultivating Joy as a Sign of Living in the Spirit of Love

As I suggested earlier, breathing is a key practice for developing mystical awareness. A parallel discipline involves the conscious choice to cultivate

---

13. Andrew Blackman: "Can Money Buy Happiness?," Wealth Management Section, *Wall Street Journal*, November 10, 2014, R2.

14. Pascal Bruckner, *Perpetual Euphoria: On the Duty to Be Happy* (trans. Stephen Rendall; Princeton, NJ: Princeton University Press, 2011), 5, 144, *passim.*

the various characteristics of love, in this case joy. I have found the book *Awakening Joy* to be helpful to the exercise of deepening joy in my personal and communal life. An insight in this book helps now in this chapter to move from combating the obstacles to joy to ways we can cultivate this particular fruit of love in our lives. The authors write, "Awakening Joy isn't about fulfilling goals or changing particular circumstances. It's about training the mind and heart to live in a way that allows us to be truly happy with our life as it is right now. Not that we stop aspiring to grow and change in positive ways, or that we remain in harmful situations, but we begin to find the joy inside us right where we are."[15] When we cultivate such joy in our personal lives, it is bound to spill over into the lives of others, just like we experience in the presence of the joy of a child.

Probably the closest human equivalent to evangelical joy can be found in the experience of exuberance, especially the exuberance of a child. Another word for exuberance comes from Lewis Carroll. He called the way children run into the arms of their parents, skip down the street, and splash through puddles "galumphing." A "galumph" is the combination of a gallop and an "umph." Galumphers are full of the kind of hope that made Mohandas Gandhi reportedly say, "I have never met a hopeful person who was depressed or a joyful person who lost hope." Galumphers are not just happy. They find meaning and purpose in their lives because they are other oriented rather than self-centered. Indeed, they seem to have found the secret of joy itself. Galumphers are those whose joyous personalities infect the persons around them.

Kay Redfield Jamison, a professor of psychiatry at the Johns Hopkins University School of Medicine, has studied the phenomenon of exuberance. She makes the religious connection to it when she notes that "exuberance is critically related to awe, wonder and spiritual quest." She goes so far as to state, "without discovery and exploration we wither," and we find a deeper understanding of exuberance in theology that shows "where the great joy is (and great sorrow as well)."[16] She explains,

> Exuberance as applied to human nature and temperament means a copious abundance of joy and energy. It means a high-energy state, both physical and psychological. It's optimism, a passion for life that is unrestrained and irrepressible. Exuberant people have an

---

15. James Baraz and Shoshana Alexander, *Awakening Joy: 10 Steps That Will Put You on the Road to Real Happiness* (New York: Random House, 2010), 7.

16. Kay Redfield Jamison, Interview, "Feeling Joy," *AAARP Bulletin*, December, 2004, 17.

intrinsic desire to stay engaged with the world. Extroverted, talkative, their love of life is palpable and can be catching to others who aren't naturally inclined to be exuberant."[17]

In my mind, for adults, the core of that exuberance summarized by the phrase "the joy of the gospel" is a sense of being saved. That is the best understanding of "evangelical salvation." Since the root word for gospel means "salvation" from something debilitating and overpowering, which we might call sin, and for something else that is liberating and empowering, grace, it seems to me that many people don't know the "joy of the gospel" because they have not yet experienced the joy of salvation itself. Applying the military notion of being "saved" from one's enemies, we see that joy represents the difference between people going into a battle that is expected to be formidable versus those who have returned victorious from battle. Joy also encompasses those who greet the ones who have brought about this salvation, as we see in every homecoming parade of soldiers who have triumphed.

With the underlying meaning of salvation as liberation from all forms of sin—personal as well as social—I was better able to understand why Pope Francis titled his apostolic exhortation *The Joy of the Gospel*. Perhaps a few passages joined together will make this clearer, beginning with his opening sentence:

- 1. The joy of the gospel fills the hearts and lives of all who encounter Jesus. Those who accept his offer of salvation are set free from sin, sorrow, inner emptiness, and loneliness. With Christ joy is constantly born anew. In this Exhortation I wish to encourage the Christian faithful to embark upon a new chapter of evangelization marked by this joy, while pointing out new paths for the Church's journey in years to come.
- 112. The salvation which God offers us is the work of his mercy. No human efforts, however good they may be, can enable us to merit so great a gift. God, by his sheer grace, draws us to himself and makes us one with him. He sends his Spirit into our hearts to make us his children, transforming us and enabling us to respond to his love by our lives. The Church is sent by Jesus Christ as the sacrament of the salvation offered by God.
- 113. The salvation which God has wrought, and the Church joyfully proclaims, is for everyone.

17.Ibid., 16.

- 178. The Holy Spirit can be said to possess an infinite creativity, proper to the divine mind, which knows how to loosen the knots of human affairs, even the most complex and inscrutable. Evangelization is meant to cooperate with this liberating work of the Spirit. The very mystery of the Trinity reminds us that we have been created in the image of that divine communion, and so we cannot achieve fulfilment or salvation purely by our own efforts. From the heart of the Gospel we see the profound connection between evangelization and human advancement, which must necessarily find expression and develop in every work of evangelization. Accepting the first proclamation, which invites us to receive God's love and to love him in return with the very love which is his gift, brings forth in our lives and actions a primary and fundamental response: to desire, seek and protect the good of others.

- 181. We know that "evangelization would not be complete if it did not take account of the unceasing interplay of the Gospel and of man's concrete life, both personal and social." This is the principle of universality intrinsic to the Gospel, for the Father desires the salvation of every man and woman, and his saving plan consists in "gathering up all things in Christ, things in heaven and things on earth" (*Eph* 1:10). Our mandate is to "go into all the world and proclaim the good news to the whole creation" (*Mark* 16:15), for "the creation waits with eager longing for the revealing of the children of God" (*Rom* 8:19). Here, "the creation" refers to every aspect of human life; consequently, "the mission of proclaiming the good news of Jesus Christ has a universal destination. Its mandate of charity encompasses all dimensions of existence, all individuals, all areas of community life, and all peoples. Nothing human can be alien to it." True Christian hope, which seeks the eschatological kingdom, always generates history.[18]

When one reads these passages it becomes quite clear that Pope Francis's "evangelical" vision is not identified with the classic Lutheran understanding of salvation, something personal, a kind of deliverance from our sins, so

---

18. Pope Francis, apostolic exhortation, *Evangelii Gaudium*, November 24, 2013, *passim*, http://w2.vatican.va.

much as with the social and cosmic sense of salvation, that which liberates all reality, including creation itself, from the negative consequences of sin and selfishness.

This is the kind of joy and rejoicing that Paul articulates more than any other New Testament writer. Indeed, as he stated so well to the Thessalonians: "For what is our hope or joy or crown of boasting before our Lord Jesus at his coming? Is it not you? Yes, you are our glory and joy" (1 Thess. 2:19-20). Being with his "beloved" Christians is the cause of joy for Paul (Rom. 15:32), but because the gospel was the most important thing in his life, joy will always be connected for him to the embrace of that gospel by those to whom he has proclaimed it (2 Cor. 1:24; 2:3; Phil. 1:4, 25; 2:2, 29; see Phlm. 7). As he wrote to the Philippians, they whom he loved and longed for were his "joy and crown" (Phil. 4:1).

There is something more than mere happiness that shows on the faces of those who have come victorious through battle(s); they have a certain exuberance that conveys the sense that the struggle was well worth the effort and any cost involved.

Acknowledging the fact that we are all overly influenced by the "culture of the provisional" that is connected to the "if approach" to happiness, which impacts the choices we make and our consequent happiness (or joy), Pope Francis himself asks where joy is born. He asks this question in a lengthy talk with seminarians, novices, and young people, on July 9, 2013. He offered his own list of possibilities: "the things one has," such as "the latest model of the smartphone" or "extreme experiences" or "dressing more fashionably" or the "inebriation of the moment."

Rejecting those possibilities, Pope Francis notes that "true joy doesn't come from things, from having, no! It's born from the encounter, from one's relations with others." On the one hand it comes "from feeling accepted, understood, loved and from . . . hearing it said: 'You are important to me,' not necessarily in words . . . [but] from the gratuitousness of an encounter." True joy also involves that "other" who is God who has been revealed to us in Jesus Christ. Francis says,

> In calling us God says to us: "You are important to me. I love you I count on you." Jesus says this to each one of us! Joy is born from here, the joy of the moment in which Jesus looked at me. To understand and to feel this is the secret of our joy. To feel loved by God, to feel that for Him we are not numbers, but persons; and to feel that it is He who calls us. . . . And the joy of the encounter with

Him and of His call leads not to closing ourselves but to opening ourselves; it leads to service in the Church.[19]

Toward the end of his talk with the young people, Pope Francis speaks more specifically about the lack of joy in the lives of people in the various forms of priesthood and consecrated life in the church, and, pointing to its solution, he states that "at the bottom of the lack of joy" in their lives is "a problem of celibacy," which occurs when women and men in such forms of life do not bear fruit in a way that gives life to others in "pastoral maternity" because they are "spinsters" and "pastoral paternity" because they are just "bachelors" who have no bigger meaning or purpose in their lives.[20]

Conclusion: Learning from St. Francis about "True and Perfect Joy"

In the middle of his homily to those in formation, Pope Francis turns to St. Francis of Assisi and the saying attributed to him (which he really never said!): "Proclaim the gospel always, and, if necessary, use words." He explained that this "means to proclaim the Gospel with the authenticity of life, with the coherence of life." He then added that "we do what Saint Francis said: we preach the Gospel with our example, then with words! But first of all is our life in which others must be able to read the Gospel! Here too, without fear, with our defects which we try to correct, with our limitations which the Lord knows, but also with our generosity in allowing Him to act in us. With our defects, our limitations and—I add something more—with our sins."[21]

Having considered Pope Francis's reflections on true joy inviting us to show that the Spirit of joy is active in our lives, and that we are walking in this Spirit with joy-filled hearts, we conclude this chapter with St. Francis's thoughts on true and perfect joy.

This iconic story was told to Brother Leo, the confidante and secretary to St. Francis, who had gone through tremendous suffering. The Order Francis had founded with eleven others in 1209 had grown to five thousand by 1217. His vision of a group of itinerant friars "living the gospel" stood in stark contrast to the prevailing monastic or conventual form of life represented by the major religious orders of his day. After a two-year absence

---

19. Pope Francis, Address to Seminarians and Novices, Part I, July 9, 2013, http://www.zenit.org.

20. Pope Francis, Address to Seminarians and Novices, Part III, http://www.zenit.org.

21. Pope Francis, Address to Seminarians and Novices, Part II, http://www.zenit.org.

in an attempt to convert Sultan al-Malek in Egypt, Francis found that the Order had reverted to many of the very things that he had rejected. In his own way he experienced personally what Paul had learned regarding the Galatian house churches. His dream of a group of people truly living the gospel was in jeopardy if not dead.

After resigning his position as Minister General of the Order and a period of depression, he snapped out of it when he heard a passage from the gospel about faith in God alone. Sometime after that he wrote about "true joy."

> One day at Saint Mary's, Blessed Francis called Brother Leo and said: "Brother Leo, write." He responded: "Look, I'm ready!" "Write," he said, "what true joy is."
>
> "A messenger arrives and says that all the Masters of Paris have entered the order. Write: this isn't true joy! Or, that all the prelates, archbishops and bishops beyond the mountains, as well as the King of France and the King of England. Write: This isn't true joy! Again, that my brothers have gone to the nonbelievers and converted all of them to the faith; again, that I have so much grace from God that I heal the sick and perform many miracles. I tell you true joy doesn't consist in any of these things."
>
> "Then what is true joy?"
>
> "I return from Perugia and arrive here in the dead of night. It's winter time, muddy, and so cold that icicles have formed on the edges of my habit and keep striking my legs and blood flows from such wounds. Freezing, covered with mud and ice, I come to the gate and, after I've knocked and called for some time, a brother comes and asks: 'Who are you?' 'Brother Francis,' I answer. 'Go away!' he says, 'This is not a decent hour to be wandering about! You may not come in!' When I insist, he replies: 'Go away! You are simple and stupid! Don't come back to us again! There are many of us here like you—we don't need you!' I stand again at the door and say: 'For the love of God, take me in tonight!' And he replies: 'I will not! Go to the Crosiers' place and ask there!'
>
> "I tell you this: If I had patience and did not become upset, true joy, as well as true virtue and the salvation of my soul, would consist in this."[22]

---

22. St. Francis of Assisi, "True and Perfect Joy," in Regis J. Armstrong, O.F.M.Cap., J. A. Wayne Hellmann, O.F.M.Conv., and William J. Short, O.F.M., eds., *Francis of Assisi: The Saint* I (New York/London/Manila: New City Press, 1999), 166-67.

Francis was able to come to this point of *kenosis* in his life because he nurtured it in developing a mystical stance in life that was grounded in long hours of prayer. While he was quite silent about what *happened to him during* those times of prayer, it becomes evident that his self-emptying was the basis for his prayer life, his communal life, and his ministerial life. Stripped of everything (including his vision of an evangelical life modeled on the historical Jesus), Francis, the mystic, could "let go" because he had found God as his all. This was the basis of his joy.

Teilhard de Chardin came to much the same conclusion when he wrote that when one is grounded in "the basic mystical intuition" that finds all things connected through the basic "Element," the result will be joy. When we surrender ourselves to this absolute and ultimate source, he writes,

> Joy is above all the fruit of having come face to face with a universal and enduring reality to which one can refer and as it were attach those fragmentary moments of happiness that, being successive and fugitive, excite the heart without satisfying it. The mystic suffers more than other men from the tendency of created things to *crumble into dust*; instinctively and obstinantly, he searches for the stable, the unfailing, the absolute; but so long as he remains in the domain of outward appearances he meets with nothing but disappointment.[23]

In various places in Galatians, Paul talks about things mattering and not mattering; things that count and don't count—all of them in light of the gospel. For Francis, the only thing that counted was Christ and Christ crucified. Any crucifixion he might experience would count for nothing as long as "nothing" stood between him and Christ. The realization that he no longer had any obstacle to the presence of Christ and Christ's Spirit in him would be "perfect joy." This kind of "mystic joy,"[24] as Evelyn Underhill calls it, would also create the foundation for the manifestation of the fruit of the Spirit's love at work in him (and all others grounded in the same way), which is the peace that we will consider in the next chapter. Bringing together two notions of joy and peace, Evelyn Underhill wrote in her little book *The Fruits of the Spirit,*

---

23. Pierre Teilhard de Chardin, *Writings in Time of War* (trans. René Hague; New York and Evanston, IL: Harper & Row, 1968), 124.

24. Evelyn Underhill, *Mysticism: A Study in the Nature and Development of Man's Spiritual Consciousness* (New York: New American Library, 1974), 253, 439ff.

Joy and peace come into our lives then, when we mind more about God than we do about ourselves, when we realize what the things that matter really are; the spirit clears up our problems about what we want or ought to be at, simplifies us and throws us back again and again on the deep and peaceful action of God. Then, whether He speeds us up or slows us down, accepts our notions or sets them aside, gives us what we want or takes it way, gives us a useful job of work or puts us on the shelf—that serenity which is a fruit of the Sprit, a sign of God's secret support, does not fail us.[25]

25. Evelyn Underhill, in Roger L. Roberts, compiler, *The Fruits of the Spirit by Evelyn Underhill* (Wilton, CT: Morehouse-Barlow, 1981, 1989), 21.

Chapter 7

Cultivating the Peace of the Spirit's Love: A Challenge to the "Peace" of Our Empires

I begin this chapter on "peace" with an extended (but also, I hope, instructive) reflection. It has to do with an experience that helped me realize that not only does the cultivation of peace demand the effort of reconciliation but, in turn, reconciliation cannot be achieved without justice at all levels of our relationships or, as Isaiah declared centuries ago, "peace is the work of justice" (Isa. 32:17).[1]

My coursework for my education for priesthood ended in spring 1967. That summer I took a CPE (Clinical Pastoral Education) course at a prison for youth sixty miles north of Milwaukee, during which time Milwaukee experienced a "civil disturbance," or riot. My prison ministry was my first real encounter with a group of people who were not almost all white. Upon completion of this formative summer, I joined the rest of my ordination class at one of our friaries in the inner city of Milwaukee for a "pastoral" year of integration. Here again I was exposed to a reality totally different from any living situation I had ever known. I arrived at St. Francis Friary on August 28, 1967. There I heard that a rally and march for civil rights was taking place two blocks away at a Protestant church.

I think that I went to the rally and march more out of curiosity than solidarity. However, what happened to me that night proved to be transformative. The march took us over the Sixteenth Street Bridge. I'll leave it to a history book to tell this part of the saga.

---

1. This quote from Isa. 37:17 served as part of the theme of the World Day of Peace statement in 2002 of Pope John Paul II, "No Peace without Justice; No Justice without Forgiveness" (http://www.vatican.va).

The 16th Street Bridge, also known as the 16th Street Viaduct, links Milwaukee's North Side to the South Side. This bridge was considered the "Mason-Dixon Line" of Milwaukee, separating the city's white and black communities. During the 1960s, blacks resided on the city's North Side while the city's South Side was overwhelmingly occupied by whites. On Monday, August 28, 1967, close to 200 NAACP (National Association for the Advancement of Colored People) Youth Council members and supporters marched across the bridge to the South Side's Kosciuszko Park. Upon reaching the South Side, marchers were greeted by a hostile crowd of thousands of white counter-protesters. The violent crowd hurled eggs, rocks, and bottles at Youth Council members. The following night, the Youth Council marched again to the South Side. This time they were confronted by even more hecklers. Some counterdemonstrators held up signs and posters with derogatory messages on them while others continuously pelted hard objects at the young marchers.[2]

Before we crossed the Sixteenth Street Bridge, we marched down Milwaukee's "Main Street": Wisconsin Avenue. We were chanting the various songs (all new to me) that have become part and parcel of such marches then and now, especially: "What do we want? Freedom! When do we want it? Now!" As we passed one store's entrance, a group of white people were standing watching us march. Just as we passed them, one spat in the face of the person in front of me. The experience was jarring: "How," I asked myself, "can people hate those they don't even know and who are just trying to make things equal for everyone?" My next question was even more pertinent, since I knew that Milwaukee, at that time, was very Catholic: "I wonder how many of the folks standing there yelling at us and spitting are Catholics?"

In December 1967, a few months into my "pastoral year" (and after many months of walking in the daily "marches" that took place after that), I volunteered to work in the inner city where our province ministered. Our provincial asked me to go St. Elizabeth's Parish in Milwaukee "to reconcile the parish."

In the 1950s and '60s, African Americans from the South migrated to the large cities in the North looking for a better opportunity, a better future. Those who came to Milwaukee found then (and now) one of the nation's

---

2. This description of the events of that night can be found at http://collections.lib.uwm.edu.

most segregated cities. They had no place to go except where other black people lived: Milwaukee's near North Side. St. Elizabeth's had been one of the focal points, and the parish was in deep racial conflict. Now I was being asked to reconcile two communities, each of which called St. Elizabeth's "my" parish rather than "our" parish. The city's racial strife took its place in the pews of that church every Sunday.

Believing that the provincial's request represented God's will for me, I thought that my assignment to "reconcile the parish" was God's will, and that God would give me the power and knowledge to fulfill that part of God's plan for me. I accepted the posting.

In deciding, I was inspired by something I had read some years previously. My Capuchin brother, Dan Crosby, had written an article in *The Bible Today* on the role of the *shaliach*. In Hebrew the *shaliach* was an emissary or ambassador from God with plenipotentiary powers sent to reconcile divided peoples. Dan explained that *shaliach* (*presbytēs* in Greek) was the equivalent of what we now call a "priest" (i.e., *presbyteros*) in Catholicism today. Believing I was such an ambassador because I was credentialed by my provincial, I turned to Paul's Second Letter to the Corinthians (5:16-21) to guide me as I prepared for my official transfer to St. Elizabeth's Friary and Parish. I read and prayed over the passage every day between receiving the provincial's letter in January 1968 and my arrival at "St. E's" eight months later:

> From now on, therefore, we regard no one from a human point of view; even though we once knew Christ from a human point of view, we know him no longer in that way. So if anyone is in Christ, there is a new creation: everything old has passed away; see, everything has become new! All this is from God, who reconciled (καταλλάσσειν) us to himself through Christ, and has given us the ministry of reconciliation (καταλλαγή); that is, in Christ God was reconciling (καταλλάσσειν) the world to himself, not counting their trespasses against them, and entrusting the message of reconciliation (καταλλαγή) to us. So we are ambassadors (*presbeuomen*) for Christ, since God is making his appeal through us; we entreat you on behalf of Christ, be reconciled (καταλλάσσειν) to God. For our sake he made him to be sin who knew no sin, so that in him we might become the righteousness (justice [*dikaiosynē*]) of God.

In my mind, I was to bring about a new order between two previously alienated groups: the whites and the blacks; I saw myself as God's *shaliach* to St. Elizabeth's. In this thinking I was affirmed by my interpretation of the passage from 2 Corinthians (which I had come to memorize). I paid special attention to the middle lines about God giving us/me "the ministry of reconciliation; that is, in Christ God was reconciling the world to himself, not counting their transgressions against them, and entrusting the message of reconciliation to us. So we are *shaliachim* for Christ, since God is making his appeal through us" (2 Cor. 5:19-20) for reconciliation for the transgressions of the parishioners through racism and inhospitality. At least that was how I understood it.

In my first three years, one thousand white families left the parish; by the end of my first year the school enrollment had decreased from almost nine hundred to three hundred. Many parishioners signed a petition to have us Capuchins removed from pastoring the parish. I was screamed at by some of the eighth grade girls who boycotted the Eucharist at a daily Mass because I had said that if any people at the Mass had anything against anyone else, they needed to be reconciled before coming to the altar for communion. People would not talk with me, and some accused me of favoring the African Americans.

I went into a depression. After five years I asked to be transferred; I had failed miserably; instead I left with the parish more divided than before I came. What had gone wrong? What Paul wrote in 2 Corinthians could not take root at St. Elizabeth's. Rather the works of the flesh had snuffed out any possibility for peace. It was clear: "the peace of God, which surpasses all understanding" did not guard our hearts and our minds "in Christ Jesus" (Phil. 4:7); indeed, I felt, we were under the rule of the *stoicheia* (4:3, 9).

Paul's Notion of Peace in the Context of *Pax Romana*

Just as my effort to make peace at St. Elizabeth's through the ministry of reconciliation cannot be isolated from the cultural dynamics of the society and church in which I tried to do so, in a similar way we cannot understand the fuller meaning of "peace" in Paul's thought apart from the cultural context in which he proclaimed it.

Not only peace (*eirēnē*) but a whole host of words used in Paul's writings can be found in the dominant *lingua franca* of the Roman Empire. Kathy Ehrensperger notes that they "were omnipresent through the empire, even on the coins people carried around with them." She notes,

> Thus, εὐαγγέλιον [*evangelion*] alluded to the "gospel," the "good news of victory" of the imperial savior; πίστις [*pistis*] meant the

"loyalty" of the emperor, to which his subjects had to reciprocate by delivering "loyalty"; δικαιοσύνη [*dikaiosynē*] was the "justice" imposed by the emperor; and εἰρήνη [*eirēnē*] was the "peace" secured by the Roman order, imposed by Roman military conquest. The παρουσία [*parousia*] was the arrival of the king or military leader at the city gates. And the proclamation of a κύριος [*kyrios*] as lord of an οὐκουμένη [*oikoumenē*] of different nations was without doubt alluding to Roman political ideology.[3]

Paul's gospel (*euangelion*) of Christ's salvific peace was proclaimed by a Jew embedded in a worldview associated with Second Temple Judaism that existed alongside another worldview defined by Roman political domination. Consequently he was steeped in the notion of messianic peace envisioned especially in Isaiah 40-61 to such a degree that some scholars say Isa. 49:1-6 established Paul's whole apostolic agenda. The Damascus experience for Paul led him to work to bring about a new creation of peace in imperial Rome with its own evangelical notion of *Pax Romana*. However, T. Ryan Jackson writes, "Paul's gospel offered a peace and established a new world order. The peace Paul declared was based on something radically different from the imperial propaganda. For him, the new creation was based on the death and resurrection of Jesus. . . . this was a cosmological and social concept very different from imperial Roman propaganda." He adds that, given the all-pervasiveness of that Roman gospel that proclaimed "the emperor's role as savior of the world, Lord of the cosmos and guarantor of peace, concord and prosperity," it "could hardly have avoided contradiction with Paul's proclamation of Christ."[4] Thus, because of this contradiction, the cross of Rome always shadowed Jesus and his gospel. Ultimately Rome's peace would be dethroned for the peace that came through the blood of that cross.

While I do not fully support the contention that Jesus's gospel as well as the gospel proclaimed by Paul can be proven to have been intentionally "anti-imperial," there is no doubt that Paul used or alluded to imperial language, but in an inverted way that allowed him to oppose the gospel of the Roman imperial order, the "present form of this world," which is passing away (1 Cor. 7:31).[5] Consequently both biblical peace and the peace

3. Kathy Ehrensperger, *That We May Be Mutually Encouraged: Feminism and the New Perspective in Pauline Studies* (New York: T. & T. Clark International, 2004), 155-56.

4. T. Ryan Jackson, *New Creation in Paul's Letters: A Study of the Historical and Social Setting of a Pauline Concept* (Tübingen: Mohr Siebeck, 2010), 176.

5. Ehrensperger, *That We May Be Mutually Encouraged*, 154-55. Key among those

of Roman rule serve as backdrops for Paul's articulation of the peace that comes from the rule of Christ that is attendant on his resurrection from the death that was brought about by the connivance of his religion's leaders and the surrogate leaders of Roman power. In this vein Kathy Ehrensperger writes,

> I consider the political and religious dimensions [of Paul's letters] as inevitably intertwined in the message of the gospel inasmuch as this was the case in Roman society. In the context of an empire which was organized as a strictly hierarchical, autocratic structure, a structure embodied by the absolute ruler who claimed and was hailed to be "the father of the Fatherland," Saviour, Peacemaker, etc., the mere claim to call no one "father" except God, and to proclaim another Saviour or a peace other than the peace and justice of Rome was an act of resistance to the dominant and dominating imperial order.[6]

Two key images from the wider Roman and Hellenistic society that Paul used in one place are "peace" and "security" (1 Thess. 5:3). In using these two words (with the cultural images they entailed) Paul was not only challenging the twin identifiers of the *Pax Romana* of the occupying imperial power of the Galatians; he was challenging as well the Hellenistic (Greek) worldview of the "security" that comes when the ideal civic society is realized on earth. Lasting peace and security were to be found, as far as Paul was concerned, neither in the *imperium* nor the *polis*, but only in the community of believers in Jesus who had transcended their past influence of the *stoicheia* to ground their lives in their trust in "our Lord Jesus Christ" (1 Thess. 5:9-10).[7]

---

authors who have stressed the "anti-imperial" subtext of the Gospels and Paul are Richard A. Horsley, ed., *Paul and Empire: Religion and Power in Imperial Rome* (Harrisburg, PA: Trinity Press International, 1997); and Neil Elliott, *Liberating Paul: The Justice of God and the Politics of the Apostle* (Sheffield: Sheffield Academic Press, 1995).

6. Kathy Ehrensperger, *Paul and the Dynamics of Power* (New York: T & T Clark International, 2004), 10-11.

7. Joel R. White, "'Peace' and 'Security' (1 Thess 5.3): Roman Ideology and Greek Aspiration," *New Testament Studies* 60 (2014): 510. Without noting the notion of "security" I agree with the vision (at least) of what Willard M. Swartley writes in a similar vein: "In the context of this Pax Romana peace through oppression, Paul proclaims a counter-peace, a peace that repudiates domination over others, unites peoples of diverse backgrounds in the Christ-bond of peace, exhorts believers to welcome one another as brothers and sisters in Christ overcoming hierarchical societal structures marking the honor-shame culture, and commits his mission to reallocate monetary resources from the

Setting the context for Paul's letters, especially the Letter to the Galatians, in the twofold notion of the Jewish gospel of messianic peace proclaimed by Isaiah and the Roman gospel of *Pax Romana,* N. T. Wright notes, serves to help us understand the radicalness not only of Jesus's gospel of the kingdom of God but Paul's notion of the peace that comes through the death and resurrection of Jesus himself. He writes,

> *The more Jewish we make Paul's "gospel," the more it confronts directly the pretensions of the Imperial cult, and indeed all other paganisms whether "religious" or "secular."* It is because of Jewish monotheism that there can be "nothing but God." In the history of ideas, and in lexicography, derivation is important; but so should be confrontation. The all-embracing royal and religious claims of Caesar are directly challenged by the equally all-embracing claim of Israel's God.[8]

Wright argues (correctly, in my opinion) that Paul's notion of *euangelion* "is based firmly in Judaism; at the same time, and indeed precisely for this reason, it functions as the royal announcement that challenges the pagan principalities and powers. Galatians is, as it happens, an excellent example of this whole train of thought."[9]

How Is God the God of Peace?

In developing Paul's notion of the fruit of love in its various expressions, perhaps no expression deserves more contextualization than his understanding of peace. This is because Paul, a Roman citizen, traveling within the Roman Empire, was inundated by the dynamics of the patriarchal control of Roman rule that prevailed under the ethos of *Pax Romana.* Thus, one cannot read any of the authentic Pauline letters without interpreting them as, in varying degrees, offering alternatives to the imperial reign of peace defined by subjugation and violence with the rule of peace coming through

---

wealthier newly founded churches to help the poor in Jerusalem. This is Paul's alternative peace-gospel, a subversive power in the Roman Empire that promised and inaugurated a new order of society, birthing a new socioeconomic, political creation"; see his *Covenant of Peace: The Missing Peace in New Testament Theology and Ethics* (Grand Rapids: Eerdmans, 2006), 250.

8. N. T. Wright, *Pauline Perspectives: Essays on Paul, 1978–2013* (Minneapolis: Fortress Press, 2013), 83-84.

9. Ibid., 85.

the very cross that Rome used to kill the one considered subversive to that peace. This is probably evident more in Paul's Letter to the Romans than in any others in the Pauline corpus. Here it becomes clear from Paul's use of certain words that he envisions in the gospel of Jesus Christ (and his own understanding of that gospel from his Damascus experience) an alternative to the dominant social structure and ideology of Roman imperial rule. In support of this understanding, Deiter Georgi argues that

> every page of the letter contains indications that Paul has very con-
> crete and critical objections to the dominant political theology
> of the Roman Empire under the principate. By using such loaded
> terms as *euangelion* [gospel], *pistis* [faith], *dikaiosynē* [justice], *and
> eirēnē* [peace] as central concepts in Romans, he evokes their asso-
> ciations to Roman political theology. Monuments of this theology
> were familiar to his contemporaries throughout the Empire, both
> east and west.[10]

The "peace ideology" of the Roman Empire had long been a force in Roman praxis and propaganda. It achieved worldwide recognition in consequence of the peace established by Augustus. The repeated presence of *eirēnē* in Paul suggests that he is looking for critical engagement with this ideology. In Romans, the theme of peace plays a more extensive role than anywhere else in Paul (or the remainder of the New Testament): the word *eirēnē* appears ten times, the expression "to have peace" once. There are also many words of related meaning: *dikaiosynē, charis, chara, oikodomē, zōē, elpis* ("solidarity, grace, joy, constructive activity, life, hope").[11]

I believe the notion of peace is a key notion in Paul's writings; however, I am not prepared to make as generalized a statement as Willard M. Swartley, who insists, "Paul, more than any other writer in the NT canon, makes peace, peacemaking, and peace-building central to his theological reflection and moral admonition,"[12] and, later, "the notion of making peace between humans and God and between formerly alienated humans is so

---

10. Dieter Georgi, *Theocracy in Paul's Praxis and Theology* (Minneapolis: Augsburg Fortress Press, 2009), 83.

11. Ibid., 85.

12. Swartley, *Covenant of Peace*, 190. Overall I find Swartley's approach interesting but not that helpful especially because of what seems to be an agenda of finding peace to be the core of Paul's corpus. Toward this end he fails in the pursuit of rigorous biblical scholarship by acknowledging the seven letters as the authentic letters of Paul but then proceeds to widen his discussion to the other books as well, especially Ephesians and Colossians.

central to the core of Pauline doctrinal and ethical thought that it is impossible to develop a faithful construal of Pauline thought without peacemaking and/or reconciliation at the core."[13] Nonetheless, it cannot be denied that peace is key to Paul's thinking about what "life in Christ" entails. In each of the seven authentic letters of Paul, he greets the various churches in almost the same way: "Grace and peace to you." Moreover, with the exception of 1 Thess. 1:1, this "grace and peace" comes from only one source: "from God our Father and the Lord Jesus Christ."

Of the twenty-six times Paul uses the Greek word for peace (*eirēnē*), at least seventeen are treated as an attribute of God and God's reign; this is understandable because, while Paul may have used the Greek *eirēnē* for peace, his Jewish background would always lead him to interpret *eirēnē* as *shalom*. God's *shalom* has power over all other *stoicheia*, including those of Satan (Rom. 16:20). In linking peace so directly with God and God's reign, Paul is faithful to the messianic belief at his time[14] that, through the messiah, an age of peace would come upon Israel (if not the world) that would free it from all foreign control. Probably the most vivid imagery of this messianic age of peace that "surpasses all understanding" (Phil. 4:7) can be found in Isa. 11:6-10. Here are images etched into our cultural consciousness by various artistic renderings, starting in 1825, with "The Peaceable Kingdom" by Edward Hicks:

> The wolf shall live with the lamb, the leopard shall lie down with the kid, the calf and the lion and the fatling together, and a little child shall lead them. The cow and the bear shall graze, their young shall lie down together; and the lion shall eat straw like the ox. The nursing child shall play over the hole of the asp, and the weaned child shall put its hand on the adder's den. They will not hurt or destroy on all my holy mountain; for the earth will be full of the knowledge of the Lord as the waters cover the sea. On that day the root of Jesse shall stand as a signal to the peoples; the nations shall inquire of him, and his dwelling shall be glorious.

Similarly, G. K. Beale states,

> The fruit of the Spirit in Gal 5:22 and its manifestations appear to be a general allusion to Isaiah's promise that the spirit would

---

13. Ibid., 192.

14. There are some who hold to this same belief today. This is at the heart of why most Jews do not accept Jesus as the Christ.

bring about abundant fertility in the coming new age. Uppermost in mind are Isaiah's repeated prophecies (especially chap. 32 and, above all, 57) that in the new creation the Spirit would be the bearer of plentiful fruitfulness, which Isaiah often interprets to be godly attributes such as righteousness, patience, peace, joy, holiness, and trust in the Lord, traits either identical or quite similar to those in Gal 5:22-23.[15]

In his research on the two key passages from Isaiah (32:15-17 and 57:16), the primary "manifestation" of the Spirit's presence turns out to be peace. Beale writes, "these are the only passages in the OT where the spirit comes from on 'high' (ὑψηλός) *and* results in the creation of figurative or spiritual fruits in God's people. In Isaiah 32, 'righteousness,' 'peace,' and 'confidence' are produced (32:17), while 'patience' and 'peace' occur among the people in Isaiah 57 (57:15, 19)." He explains further:

> The two passages even mention "peace" twice to describe the new spiritually fertile conditions. In addition, both texts imply that "joy" will also be a characteristic of the restored nation by underscoring that "joy" will be lacking for those in an unrestored condition (cf. εὐφροσύνη in Isa 32:13 and χαίρειν in 57:21). A further link between the two Isaiah passages lies in the common idea of end-time "rest." Isa 32:18 affirms that restored Israel "will inhabit a city of peace . . . and they will rest [ἀναπαύσονται] with wealth," while Isa 57:19-20 says that, in contrast to the "peace" of God's restored people given to them by the God who "rests" in the heavenly temple (v. 15), "the unrighteous . . . will not be able to rest" (ἀναπαύσασθαι).[16]

How Do We Cultivate the Spirit's Fruit of Peace in Our Lives, Relationships, and World?

In a world and a church with so much conflict and confusion, we need to be reminded, as did Paul's listeners, that God is not a God of confusion but of peace (1 Cor. 14:33). Where God reigns, peace will be the sign. The "grace and peace" wished to the house churches comes not only from "God the Father" (Gal. 1:3; Phil. 1:2; 1 Cor. 1:3; 2 Cor. 1:2; Rom. 1:7; and Phlm.

---

15. G. K. Beale, "The Old Testament Background of Paul's Reference to 'the Fruit of the Spirit' in Galatians 5:22," *Bulletin for Biblical Research* 15.1 (2005): 1.

16. Ibid., 5-6.

3); it also comes from the one who actually brought about that peace in their households through his death and resurrection: Jesus Christ. In Paul's mind, the kingdom of God that Jesus announced and brought about was "not food and drink but righteousness and peace and joy in the Holy Spirit" (Rom. 14:17; see Rom. 15:13). Further, whoever serves Christ by displaying these manifestations of the Spirit at work in them "is acceptable to God and has human approval" (Rom. 14:18). Consequently, Paul urged the members of the Roman Church, "Let us then pursue what makes for peace and for mutual upbuilding" (Rom. 14:19).

In Paul's mind, if the members of the house churches embrace this gospel of the kingdom, they will reveal its power in their lives by how they relate to one another. Thus he writes to the house churches at Corinth: "Put things in order, listen to my appeal, agree with one another, live in peace; and the God of love and peace will be with you" (2 Cor. 13:11). When they were brought into God's reign of peace by their baptism, they were empowered to live together in that peace. The more they live in that mutual peace, the more God's peace will take over their lives personally and communally. When this happens, the house churches will be free from the works of the flesh; they will be cultivating the various expressions (including peace) of the Spirit's fruit of love. Thus Paul writes to the house churches in Rome:

> Live in harmony with one another; do not be haughty, but associ-
> ate with the lowly; do not claim to be wiser than you are. Do not
> repay anyone evil for evil, but take thought for what is noble in the
> sight of all. If it is possible, so far as it depends on you, live peace-
> ably with all. Beloved, never avenge yourselves, but leave room for
> the wrath of God; for it is written, "Vengeance is mine, I will repay,
> says the Lord." No, "if your enemies are hungry, feed them; if they
> are thirsty, give them something to drink; for by doing this you will
> heap burning coals on their heads." Do not be overcome by evil,
> but overcome evil with good. (Rom. 12:16-21)

While peace requires the commitment of all parties, there are times when that will not be achievable. Hence Paul admonishes that, insofar as peace depends on us, we must do everything we can to ensure its presence in our lives and relationships.

Overcoming the Obstacles to Peace

As we have mentioned in almost every chapter, a key purpose of this book is to understand how "the Christian of the future will be a mystic or nothing at all." While not all of us will have (or be aware that we have had) mystical experiences, we can all develop a mystical stance in life that moves us ever more closely toward that kind of union with everyone and everything that is a key characteristic of the mystical experience. Since this kind of union reflects the union called love and since the "fruit" of the Holy Spirit is love, the cultivation of the eight key manifestations of the Spirit's fruit of love (joy, peace, patience, kindness, goodness, gentleness, faithfulness, and self-control) will help us develop such a mystical stance. Conscious intention and commitment will be necessary to make this cultivation fruitful. However, like all good gardening, it is important to ensure that whatever contributes to a false consciousness be "weeded out." We will need to "cut out" whatever attitudes contribute to the justification not only of a continued separation between the "us" and the "them" but even to justifying the use of violence by the "us" against the "them."

As examples of this, I have found two sources that reflect how easily negativity and false consciousness can take over the thinking of individuals, groups, and whole societies in ways that result in violence: Ralph K. White's *Nobody Wanted War* and Edward Shils's "Authoritarianism: 'Right' and 'Left,'" in *Studies in the Scope and Method of the Authoritarian Personality*, where he describes the similarities in consciousness between the extreme ideological right and the extreme ideological left. Whenever I find myself developing similar attitudes, I try to discipline myself to eradicate such weeds from my garden of peace as soon as possible. At the same time, because I have become aware of their destructiveness, when I hear them articulated in people's conversations about issues involving potential us/them dynamics, I try to show, where possible, the futility of this approach.

Ralph K. White's attitudinal discovery helped me analyze a conflict I was engaged in that had led to a "war" with another friar.[17] At the same time it made me aware of the attitudes behind the many wars of the United States, as well as the "culture wars" inside and outside the Catholic Church. White notes that before any "final cause" that leads to an out-and-out war, there must be substrata of ideological justifications. These entail identical attitudes on the part of both "sides" toward themselves and the other(s): (1) the diabolical enemy, whereby the other represents everything that is against the good; (2) the virile self-image, whereby one's group has the resources to prevail in the conflict; (3) the moral self-image, whereby both sides believe in the righteousness of their cause and the unrighteousness

---

17. I describe this in my *Spirituality of the Beatitudes: Matthew's Vision for the Church in an Unjust World* (new rev. ed.; Maryknoll, NY: Orbis Books, 2005), 160-67.

of the other's; (4) selective inattention, whereby neither side will admit to any possible good on the part of the enemy or any possible bad on the part of themselves; (5) lack of empathy, whereby the issue is not care (despite protestations to the contrary); this is a power issue, and control rather than care is needed to prevail; and (6) overall irrational interpretation of reality, whereby those who are free of the conflict can observe this but the combatants cannot.[18]

In the case of Shils, his examples are drawn from Nazism and the Soviet style of communism, but his analysis applies to almost every instance of the various "isms" in politics, culture, and religion that are accompanied by an ideological (i.e., "faith-based") justification for the polarization. Shils outlines nine key characteristics: (1) hostility to "outgroups." You are either "for us" or "against us." To engage in dialogue with "them" is disloyalty if not outright betrayal; (2) obedience to the "ingroup"; there must be unanimity in presenting the cause; breaking with the ranks, again, is disloyalty if not treason; (3) sharp boundaries between "us" and "them"; (4) categorizing persons according to qualities that undermine the cause; (5) it is critical for the cause to realize that the world is divided between "them" and "us": the forces of evil and of good; (6) other ideas that might be of concern are actually of no concern and, therefore, repressed; (7) to call for kindness or compassion toward the "other" cannot be tolerated; it is a sign of weakness; (8) manipulation is key to the effort, especially in how we interpret our "truth" and their "lies"; (9) the above must be accepted if the goal is to be realized: a conflict-free, harmonious, peaceful world.[19]

When we examine the "works of the flesh" that undermine the fruit of the Spirit of love and its various manifestations, we need to be aware of how the elements noted by White and Shils contribute to the kind of consciousness that justifies the "enmities, strife . . . quarrels, dissensions, [and] factions" (5:20) that tear apart communities, whether these be families or ethnic groups, the rich and the poor, or Culture I and Culture II Catholics. If those attitudes are not recognized as obstacles to peace the fruits of the Spirit of love will not be able to come to harvest.

18. Ralph K. White, *Nobody Wanted War: Misperceptions in Vietnam and Other Wars* (Garden City, NY: Doubleday Anchor Books, 1970).

19. Edward Shils, "Authoritarianism: 'Right' and 'Left,'" in Richard Christie and Marie Jahoda, eds., *Studies in the Scope and Method of the Authoritarian Personality* (Glencoe, IL: Free Press, 1954), 33-34.

Cultivating Peace

Because the God of peace has called us to peace (1 Cor. 7:15) we have been given the grace to cultivate this fruit of the Spirit. We, therefore, need to pursue peace and whatever else will build up the body (Rom. 14:19). Our task involves cultivating this peace at all levels of our conflicted church and world. A primary purpose of this book is to propose a way to develop and cultivate a mystical stance toward life, beginning with making a conscious choice to do so. Paul writes to the Romans in a similar vein to his paraenesis of the flesh/Spirit in the Letter to the Galatians: ". . . those who live according to the flesh set their minds on the things of the flesh, but those who live according to the Spirit set their minds on the things of the Spirit. To set the mind on the flesh is death, but to set the mind on the Spirit is life and peace" (Rom. 8:6).

If we limit ourselves to how Paul uses *eirēnē* in Galatians, we find it only three times (1:3; 5:22; 6:16), one of them being an elaboration of this fruit of love. However, because he envisioned his interpretation of the gospel and its resulting paraenesis as implementing God's plan for every individual and house church, he calls for "peace" for all who walk in the Spirit (6:16). The God of peace is the one who sanctifies "wholly" those who believe in Christ Jesus (1 Thess. 5:23) and live lives that are reconciled with God. By making peace with God, we manifest that reconciliation in a threefold way: with ourselves, each other, and everyone and everything in a way that reveals we are part of the new creation. Because reconciliation and peace can be considered virtually synonymous,[20] when we embody this peace through the ministry of reconciliation, the peacemaker becomes a living sign of the *shalom* envisioned as the sign of the new cosmic age.

Paul describes the new cosmic age as the new creation that displaces the old order. The power of God that brought this about in Jesus's death and resurrection as the Christ has empowered all disciples to embody that same new creation in their own lives and ministry, especially through their ministry of reconciling whatever may divide human beings into man-made forms of separation, be they Jew/Gentile, slave/free, or male/female. This is

---

20. While seeing the connection between reconciliation and peace, I cannot say, with Swartley (*Covenant of Peace,* 211) that "Paul's gospel from beginning to end, is a gospel of peace and reconciliation." See also Ralph P. Martin, *Reconciliation: A Study of Paul's Theology* (Eugene, OR: Wipf & Stock, 1997), 139. Like my reaction to Swartley's stress on peace and peacemaking in Paul noted above, I do not think it can be said or implied, as seems Martin, that reconciliation can be considered broad enough to be an "umbrella" that incorporates Paul's underlying theology.

clear from 2 Cor. 5:16-21, where the "ministry of reconciliation" is directly linked to that "new creation." The old order is not just replaced, but rejected, whether that "old" order be economic (slave/free), ethnic or religious (Jew/Gentile), or sexual (woman/man). So, if anyone is "in Christ," that one has found a way to be one with everyone and everything in the realm of God's love and reconciling peace. What was God's ministry of reconciliation is now to be continued in those who are of God.

This is clarified by the way V. George Shillington describes how Paul created a "chiastic structure" of the reconciliation passage above (2 Cor. 5:17-21).[21] In a chiastic model, the first and last are connected, and the second and second to last, and so on, with a center around which everything depends. It can be outlined below:

a in Christ, there is a new creation: everything old has passed away; see, everything has become new!
  b all this is from God, who reconciled us to himself through Christ,
    c and has given us the ministry of reconciliation;
      d that is, in Christ God was reconciling the world to himself, not counting their trespasses against them, and
    c′ entrusting the message of reconciliation to us. So we are ambassadors for Christ, since God is making his appeal through us;
  b′ we entreat you on behalf of Christ, be reconciled to God.
a′ for our sake he made him to be sin who knew no sin, so that in him we might become the righteousness of God.

Grounded in this ministry of reconciliation, how do we become its ministers to ourselves and others in a way that gives evidence that we are part of this new creation of peace? We will examine this threefold ministry in the sections below.

Being Reconciled and at Peace within Ourselves

In his encyclical on the Holy Spirit, written to prepare for the third millennium, Pope John Paul II notes the desire for peace that lies in, among, and around us: "Peace too is the fruit of love: that interior peace, which weary man seeks in his inmost being; that peace besought by humanity, the human family, peoples, nations, continents, anxiously hoping to obtain it

---

21. V. George Shillington, *2 Corinthians* (Harrisonburg, VA: Herald Press, 1998), 127. I am indebted to Willard Swartley for noting this source (*Covenant of Peace*, 202-3).

in the prospect of the transition from the second to the third Christian millennium." Making the link between love and peace, he writes,

> Since the way of peace passes in the last analysis through love and seeks to create the civilization of love, the church fixes her eyes on him who is the love of the Father and the Son, and in spite of increasing dangers she does not cease to trust, she does not cease to invoke and to serve the peace of man on earth. Her trust is based on him who, being the Sprit-love, is also the Spirit of peace and does not cease to be present in our human world, on the horizon of minds and hearts, in order to "fill the universe" with love and peace.[22]

What is the source of inner peace that results in the feeling of well-being or rest that Pope John Paul II envisioned? This was a question raised by the Buddhist monk Thich Nhat Hanh, in a reflection called "Everything Depends on Your Peace." In it he writes,

> We need to find an inner peace which makes it possible for us to become one with those who suffer, and to do something to help our brothers and sisters, which is to say, ourselves. I know many young people who are aware of the real situation of the world and who are filled with compassion. They refuse to hide themselves in artificial peace, and they engage in the world in order to change the society. They know what they want, yet after a period of involvement they become discouraged. Why? It is because they lack deep, inner peace, the kind of peace they can take with them into their life of action.

Then, noting that he has recognized what he felt was authentic peace in "many, many people" who spend most of their time and effort "protecting the weak, watering the trees of love and understanding everywhere" and who come from "various religious and cultural backgrounds," he writes how he does "not know how each of them came to their inner peace, but [he has] seen it in them."[23]

From reflecting on my own life and giving retreats and workshops on Matthew's beatitudes, especially "Blessed are the peacemakers; they will

---

22. Pope John Paul II, *Dominum et Vivificantem*, encyclical letter, May 18, 1986, no. 67, http://www.vatican.va.

23. Thich Nhat Hanh, *The Sun My Heart* (Berkeley, CA: Parallax Press, 1988), 127.

be called sons [and daughters] of God" (Matt. 5:6), I think I have discovered how many people *have come* "to their inner peace." This has led me to believe there is a clear way to pursue the conditions that lead to peace in, among, and around us, as envisioned by Paul in Rom. 14:19. On the one hand, the elixir involves giving up a negative way of interacting that undermines right relationships: the need to control. On the other hand, I've discovered that the other key ingredient for coming to inner peace is accepting oneself, one's "I am" as the "very good" person that God has made one to be, equal to everyone else in the cosmic household.[24]

Besides making peace with myself by reconciling my false self with my true self (which takes a lifetime I am discovering!), I have found that another way to the secret of inner peace comes from being able to say in our hearts that we are reconciled with everyone (and everything). This demands that we realize that reconciliation always involves two necessary ingredients that are mutually symbiotic: repentance and forgiveness. On the one hand, I must make amends to everyone, as far as I know, whom I have offended; on the other hand, I must forgive everyone who has offended me. Whether or not others whom I must forgive repent or others to whom I have repented will not forgive, in the last analysis, has nothing to do with the recipe for making peace with myself. If they don't follow the recipe in their lives, it will be for them too, a flop. I just must follow the recipe for myself and leave their way of making peace to their own cookbook. Knowing that some others will do their part of repenting or forgiving to bring about reconciliation (and peace) is why, I think, Paul in his wisdom did not put the blame on them. He merely said. "If it is possible, so far as it depends on you, live peaceably with all" (Rom. 12:19). And that part of reconciliation is always possible for us!

In another of the "if" and "then" or "because of" and "thus" parallels used so often in Paul, "if" the members of the house churches would find ways to overcome their divisions, moving from being controlled by the "works of the flesh" to manifesting "the fruit of the Spirit," and becoming reconciled with each other, "then" the God of peace would rule in their hearts.

Peace as a State of Reconciliation with Others

In his *Covenant of Peace: The Missing Peace in New Testament Theology and Ethics*, Willard M. Swartley notes that Paul's innovative use of the term "the

---

24. For more on these key dynamics for personal peace, see my *Spirituality of the Beatitudes*, (Maryknoll, NY: Orbis Books, 2004), 60-61. See also my *The Paradox of Power: From Control to Compassion* (New York: Crossroad Publishing, 2008), 149-51.

God of peace" represents something much broader than a term for God; it articulates a task for all those who belong to the church of God revealed in Jesus Christ through the Holy Spirit. He consequently stresses the fact that the reconciliation of all those who are separated from God and from one another is God's fundamental objective in salvation history.

In three different places in his authentic letters, Paul urges those in the house churches he is addressing to "be at peace among [themselves]" (1 Thess. 5:13) and to find ways to "agree with one another" so that they may "live in peace" (2 Cor. 13:11). In his reflections on "Trajectories of Violence and Peace in Galatians," Jeremy Gabrielson develops the notion of Paul's notion of peace for his communities arising from their self-giving love and service to other in a way that stands in stark contrast to the wider society's approach to the "peace" arising from the conquest that results from various forms of violence. He notes, "If burden-bearing and mutual correction and forgiveness begin to fill out our understanding of the ethics of Paul's communities then alleviation of suffering and reconciliation of parties at enmity become concrete examples of peacemaking practices of the churches Paul founded." He explains,

> Paul urged his communities not to order their life according to the rule of a reciprocity of revenge, but instead implored them to order their fellowship according to the rule of a reciprocity of forgiveness. Such was one crucial aspect of the ethics of the church. If a group such as this one was to survive, its members needed unconventional "weapons" to create and sustain communal peace in a world where "peace" was normally the byproduct of violence.[25]

Because God's peace has been extended to us, we are expected to cultivate and extend the reign of that peace in our lives and relationships (Gal. 5:22). Again, what we do will be done to us. The more we live by peace and the other fruits of love, the more we experience their flowering in our own lives. This is the sense of Paul's comment to the Romans that no matter "who does good," whether Jew or Gentile," they will experience "glory and honor and peace" (Rom. 2:10).

How does the realization of God's peace in our relationships with one another *depend on* every one of us? In my mind there are two key ways: (1) making sure that such peace is, as Pope Paul VI made the motto of his

---

25. Jeremy Gabrielson, *Paul's Non-Violent Gospel: The Theological Politics of Peace in Paul's Life and Letters* (Eugene, OR: Pickwick, 2013), 116.

pontificate, "the work of justice." And (2) "making peace" in our relationships by ensuring that we are reconciled with everyone.

I believe, as Pope Paul VI so eloquently declared, that "peace is the work
of justice." This means that, without right relationships among people at all
levels, there will be no justice and, without right relationships in our families—at all levels, as Pope Francis said in his 2015 World Day of Peace Message, there will be no peace. This understanding is critical for our effort to
develop a mystical stance of peace in a world marked by injustice at so many
levels, whether it reflects the planetary crisis created by climate change or
the wealth gap created by exploitation of people and the planet. This justice
demands a nonviolent way that is neither based on "fight" nor "flight," but
an alternative form of engagement with restorative justice the goal of all
broken relationships and unjust structures.

Noting that "the way of peace is the way of justice," Robert L. Foster
shows that, in what I call a world defined by the injustice of *Pax Romana,*
the Christians were called to offer a nonviolent alternative. In elaborating
on Paul's Letter to the Romans, he writes,

> When Paul writes that the Roman Jesus communities should bless
> those who persecute (12:14), not repay evil for evil (12:17), and
> feed and give drink to the enemies (12:20), who else does Paul have
> in mind except the Roman authorities? Paul desires for the Roman
> Jesus communities, as far as possible, to live at peace with every-
> one, including the imperial persecutors (12:18). For Paul, living at
> peace is not acquiescence but rather justice. Those whom Scripture
> describes as unjust do not know the way of peace (3:17). When
> the Roman Jesus communities bless their persecutors, rejoice and
> mourn with anyone and everyone, resist repaying evil for evil but
> overcome evil with good, they persist in doing the justice required
> by the gospel.[26]

When we try to understand and implement Paul's sense of justice that
leads to peace, we must begin with the concept of justice or righteousness
(*dikaiosynē*), described by the Jesuit Scripture scholar John Donahue as
"*fidelity to the demands of a relationships.*"[27] While this notion will be devel-

---

26. Robert L. Foster, "The Justice of the Gentiles: Revisiting the Purpose of Romans,"
Catholic Biblical Quarterly 76.4 (2014): 700.

27. John R. Donahue, S.J., "Biblical Perspectives on Justice," in John C. Haughey,
S.J., ed., *The Faith That Does Justice* (New York: Paulist Press, 1977), 69. Emphasis is the
author's.

oped at greater length in Chapter 12, it's important here to see the connection between justice as "right relationships" and peace as the work of justice.

Because six centuries ago Martin Luther translated *dikaiosynē* as "righteousness" and this "righteousness" was almost exclusively linked to personal "justification," we now need to reclaim the biblical meaning and, especially, Paul's understanding of *dikaiosynē* as "fidelity to right relationships." Thus N. T. Wright argues that Paul probably intended with *dikaiosynē* both "righteousness" and "justice," equating them with each other much more than we have previously thought. He writes, "When, therefore, God's righteousness was unveiled [in the Abrahamic Covenant] the effect would be precisely that the world would receive justice, that rich, restorative, much-to-be-longed-for justice of which the Psalmists had spoken with such feeling (Pss 67.4; 82.8; and so on)."[28] He concludes,

> The gospel of the true God, then, unveils the covenant faithfulness of this God, through which the entire world receives health-giving, restorative Justice. That is the context within which . . . those who believe the gospel—who respond to the proclamation, that is, with "the obedience of faith"—are marked out by that faith, and by nothing else, as the eschatological people of God, the people whose sins have been dealt with on the cross, the people now assured of salvation/glorification.[29]

Without a fuller and more holistic approach to *dikaiosynē* as right relationships with ourselves, each other, creation, and God, there will be little *eirēnē*, or peace. This challenge is all the more necessary if we are to wean ourselves from an individualistic interpretation of Paul's letter (i.e., what does this mean to *me?*) and realize that his audience was made up not merely of individuals in themselves but only of individuals who were were part of house churches. This makes the question of interpretation today, "What does this mean to *us?*"

With the exception of his letter to the Thessalonians, all of Paul's authentic letters begin with a greeting of "grace and peace from God our Father" to the members of the house churches. "Father" here does not have the characteristics of domination such as does Caesar, the "Father of the Fatherland" (*Pater patriae*); rather this is the Loving Patron whose patronage extends to everyone in the household of faith as well as to creation itself.[30] This is

---

28. Wright, *Pauline Perspectives*, 179.
29. Ibid., 180.
30. For much more on this idea see my *House of Disciples: Church, Economics and*

the God of every household, whose love extends to all equally making all "brothers" and "sisters" in a way that prescinds existing cultural dynamics of inequality and oppression.

Reconciliation with All as the Sign of the New Creation

In Gal. 3:27-29 we glimpse the new creation of the peaceable "kindom" of equals that Paul envisioned for the church. This alternative model of peace based on right relationships or justice stood in sharp contrast to peace predicated on domination. As Borg and Crossan explain Paul's understanding of this peace, "justice means distributive and not retributive justice (punishment). There will only be peace on earth, Paul claims, when all members of God's world-home receive a fair and equitable share of its bounty, when all members of God's family have enough." Then they immediately caution us: "Do not confuse, he might have added, peace with lull."[31]

Considering what has been explored in the section above and as I bring this chapter to a conclusion, it will be good to note something that happened to me only recently. This concerns the apocalyptic or eschatological sense of the new creation that Paul envisioned as breaking into the cosmos with the death and resurrection of Jesus in the members of the house churches themselves. Now let us return to the story that began this chapter. In Romans, Paul talks about those who have "not known . . . the way of peace" (Rom. 3:17) while in 1 Thessalonians, we have seen earlier, he shows his apocalyptic side when he cautions his audience to be vigilant in contrast to those who say, "There is peace and security" (1 Thess. 5:3).

While Paul's critique of those in the Thessalonian community who were saying "peace and security" came from his belief, at that early time in his writing career, that Jesus Christ was going to return in the *parousia*, the admonition still holds today. When the dream of "peace and security" lulls us from working continually to bring about a new social order of reconciliation and justice in a way that will bring about the "peaceable kingdom," we ourselves can incur Paul's critique.

Having addressed my failure to bring about reconciliation at St. Elizabeth's, I did not reflect that much about my ministry of "reconciliation" and its meaning in my life. However, once I started probing the core of Gala-

---

Justice in Matthew's Gospel (Eugene, OR: Wipf & Stock, 2004), as well as most of my recent books. For a list of these see http://www.michaelcrosby.net.

31. Marcus Borg and John Dominic Crossan, *The First Paul: Reclaiming the Radical Visionary behind the Church's Conservative Icon* (New York: HarperOne, 2009).

tians, two passages suddenly gave me a totally new insight. These are places where Paul talks about neither circumcision nor uncircumcision mattering. In the first he writes, "For in Christ Jesus neither circumcision nor uncircumcision counts for anything; the only thing that counts is faith working through love" (5:6). Later the theme appears again when he declares, "For neither circumcision nor uncircumcision is anything; but a new creation is everything" (6:15).

If we are "in Christ Jesus," no moral law or canonical nomism should "count for anything"; the need to preserve the organic unity of the members together trumps any other "code" of belonging. Furthermore, by juxtaposing the texts of 5:6 and 6:15, it becomes clear that the only thing that *ultimately should matter in the church* is that all of us remain "in Christ Jesus" in a way that reveals an entirely new creation and that reflects that messianic vision of *shalom* prophesied by Isaiah and inaugurated by Jesus in his proclamation of the kingdom of God that was to bring peace to every household.

In my mind, the only way we can get to the *heart* of what Paul means by being "in Christ" and being part of the new creation that goes beyond all existing human categories, is by revisiting Paul's own account of his resurrection/mystical experience and how the Risen One was revealed to him on his way to Damascus (1 Cor. 15:1-9). While I developed this at length in Chapter 3, I think it is critical to understand "resurrection" as a whole new creation with consideration of the manner in which the Christ is embodied. Paul makes it clear that, like those who had walked with Jesus to whom Jesus appeared (*horaō*) as "the Christ," Paul experienced this appearance, as internal, *within himself,* as the embodiment of the historical Jesus in those baptized into Christ in the church. This church is not only the embodiment of the historical Jesus; it is the new creation in whom the Christ now lives, moves, and has being (see Acts 17:28). Therefore any divisions within the church represent a contradiction of its mystical foundation. That old order is gone; all must be new.

The need to go beyond any ritual that is divisive and undermines being "in Christ Jesus" and the urgency to evolve into "a new creation" became apparent to me in an amazing way when I returned to the passage on reconciliation that guided me as I prepared to minister at St. Elizabeth's parish that first eight months of 1968.

Even though it has been almost fifty years since I was nourished by that passage on reconciliation, I now find myself returning to that same passage but with a stress on something I missed altogether back then. Moreover, I am now no longer drawn to an interpretation that would legitimize me as a *shaliach* of God through the ministry of reconciliation. I have discovered that the ministry of reconciliation is the first fruit of something much more important: the ushering in of a wholly new creation (of *shalom/eirēnē*) in the world. Building on Paul's insight repeated twice in Galatians about neither circumcision nor uncircumcision mattering (5:6) but a "new creation is everything" (6:15), I have now moved to a much deeper understanding of what Paul means by "reconciliation." Now the polarizing concepts of "circumcision" and "uncircumcision" and their equivalents in every other form of polarization (slave/free, male/female, Jew/Gentile) are simply passé; for all those who are truly "in Christ," there is an entirely new way of being, and the dynamics of that reality are described in 2 Cor. 5:17: "So if anyone is in Christ, there is a new creation: everything old has passed away; see, everything has become new!"

In the past I have approached contemporary issues through the lens of such dualistic thought, such as male/female dynamics of sexism, slave/free elements in classism, and Jew/Gentile in ethnocentrism, racism, and tribalism. And I did so from an either/or "old order" way of thinking. But the consciousness or mindset that made me do so came from an "old order"; I was not being "in Christ." If I am "in Christ" and we are "in Christ," this old-order thinking is gone. We are saved from this old order of division; not only are we empowered in the Spirit of Christ to reveal salvation in how we work toward that justice and peace, which brings with it the "integrity of creation"; we do so in a way that itself ushers in an entirely new creation.

No longer may our consciousness reflect any form of polarization, dualism, or irreconciliation; nor should we think with either/or and neither/nor categories; we have to creatively develop entirely new categories with our common life in the body of Christ as the underlying principle. In this body there may be various functions, but none of these should be interpreted as over/under or better/worse than any other, lest the unity of the body be fractured (Rom. 12:3-8). Whatever the function in the church, be it that of apostles or prophets, teachers or healers, there is to be no further hierarchy that imposes separation; any hierarchy is to serve the wholeness of the body (1 Cor. 12:1-31) in a way that reveals that all are oriented to the ultimate fruit of the Spirit: love (1 Cor. 13:1-13).

When love defines the body, when love is all that ultimately matters, any category based on the old order, like being cleric or lay, woman or man, gay or straight, or any other classification secondary to being "in Christ," should no longer "matter." Any contemporary form of canonical nomism in the Roman Church or any other form of religiously sanctioned separation (and, therefore, violence in our politics, economics and culture) must no longer matter. Then we can come to an entirely new consciousness that reflects a mystical stance toward everyone, and everything brings about a new creation and shows that we are "in Christ Jesus."

I can think of no better way to end this chapter on the Spirit's fruit of love that is expressed in peace in, among, and through us into our world than a key part of Paul's concluding chapter of his Letter to the Philippians:

> Rejoice in the Lord always; again I will say, Rejoice. Let your gentleness be known to everyone. The Lord is near. Do not worry about anything, but in everything by prayer and supplication with thanksgiving, let your requests be made known to God. And the peace of God, which surpasses all understanding, will guard your hearts and your minds in Christ Jesus. Finally, beloved, whatever is true, whatever is honorable, whatever is just, whatever is pure, whatever is pleasing, whatever is commendable, if there is any excellence and if there is anything worthy of praise, think about these things. Keep on doing the things that you have learned and received and heard and seen in me, and the God of peace will be with you. (Phil. 4:4-9)

Chapter 8

Cultivating Patience as a Sign of the Spirit's Love in Our Busy World

Among the expressions of the fruit of the Spirit of love, the one that most challenges me is patience. It is definitely not my strong suit; in fact, too often it has been my Achilles' heel. I've learned, often the hard way, that if I am to be effective in my relationships with others and truly collaborate with them, I am going to have to address my impatience in a special way.

All of us have a basic "self" or personality. Personality profiles help us understand our true selves in ways that can help us discover those qualities that impede healthy interactions and relationships with others. Over the years I have taken a few personality profile assessments (the Enneagram, Myers Briggs, DiSC, and StrengthsFinder). Several things seem constant: I operate more from my head than my heart or gut; I am highly intuitive; and I have a need to achieve. I'm also a Type-A person who is a multitasker.

When it comes to applying what I have learned from these personality profiles, I discover that patience does not come easily to my personality type. I think people who are more "intuitive" than "sensing" on such profiles have trouble with patience. They can see the end product (or believe they can see the end product) and have little tolerance for the steps other people need to take to get there. That is one of the reasons why I do not like meetings; I suggest a solution to a problem, and people keep talking as though they did not hear me; they need to work it out according to their own personality types.

When I was a child, I had trouble speaking clearly; I could not pronounce "I," "L," and "R."[1] And I inverted my "ST" to "TS." This necessitated speech therapy. I still recall the third day of first grade, when I was six years old. My

---

1. While writing this book I discovered that I have had company in not being able to say, among some letters, my "R's": see Sumathi Reddy, "Say 'R' Right: New Tool for Children with Speech Errors," *Wall Street Journal*, October 21, 2014, D1, D4.

mother had already called me a few times to get up and come downstairs for breakfast. When I didn't appear downstairs, she came to my room. I was sitting dejectedly on the side of the bed.

"What's the matter, Michael," she asked?

"Ah'm not going to schoo no mo," I declared.

"Why not," she asked?

"Hea A've been going to schoo two ho days and A don't know how to wead or wite."

I don't know how I would have reacted at that time in my young life had I been one of the children in the control group that was created to test the benefits of cultivating patience, which was demonstrated by the well-known Stanford University marshmallow experiment (which really was undertaken to measure self-control). These were studies geared to determine the immediate and long-term effects of delayed gratification. In the late 1960s, Stanford psychologist Walter Mischel and his colleagues at Stanford created an experiment to measure self-control at the Bing Nursery School there in what has become one of the best-known psychological experiments of all time. Children between four and six were gathered together in a bare room and given a choice between one marshmallow that could be eaten immediately or two marshmallows if they waited fifteen minutes. The study showed that, while some ate the marshmallow right away, most concocted all sorts of quite humorous efforts at patience (the real purpose of the study) to get their two marshmallows. Of these, a third of the whole group deferred gratification long enough to get their second marshmallow.

Mischel later published a paper on the same subjects who now had become adults. The 2006 paper showed that the longer the children delayed immediate gratification and showed patience (albeit often impatiently!) the better they did in their adult lives. They had higher SAT scores, higher GPAs at the end of college, and made more money after college. They also had lower body mass indexes. All this was summarized in Mischel's 2014 book *The Marshmallow Test: Mastering Self-Control*.[2]

While Mischel identified systems in the brain that nurtured self-control, it is clear that impatience does seem to be more inherent in certain personalities than others. Nonetheless, it is something that can be developed and, therefore, can become a learned habit. It can also be unlearned by the practice of deep breathing and patience. Patience can be cultivated, but this cultivation, like that of any good fruit, demands a desire for the change,

---

2. Walter Mischel, *The Marshmallow Test: Mastering Self-Control* (New York: Little, Brown, 2014).

a consistent practice, and the realization that what has been learned over time (impatience) will also take time to unlearn.

To this day I still want to be among the first or last in line, whether it is a food line or a queue at an airport. But when I am stuck in the middle, my patience "mantra" gets good use!

Saint Augustine of Hippo is supposed to have said that "patience is the companion of wisdom." Maybe that is why the only little "wisdom saying" I have kept with me from my novitiate, after I had lived my first score of years, was one from Father Raymond, the Trappist writer. "Patience," it said at the top of the holy card. And then, "A Life's Work Takes a Life's Time."

As we will see, patience has a lot to do with time. Because God has all the time in the world, God has all the patience in the world with us, especially when we mess up.

How Is the Patience of God Revealed?

Biblical Greek has two main words for "patience." *Hypomenō* means "to endure or stand firm," especially in face of trials and tribulations (Rom. 12:12; 2 Cor. 1:6). *Makrothymeō*, one of the eight manifestations of love in Galatians (5:22), is also found a handful of times in Paul's other authentic letters (Rom. 2:4; 9:22; 1 Cor. 13:4 [in Paul's Canticle of Love]; 2 Cor. 6:6; and 1 Thess. 5:14). The best way I have come to understand its meaning is to divide *makrothymeō* into its two component parts: *makro* (meaning "long or extended") and *thymia* or *thymos* (meaning "temper"). So *makro* + *thymia/thymos* means "to be long tempered or forebearing."

Before discussing *makrothymeō* in God and in God's way of dealing with us, especially when we do wrong and compromise our relationship with God, I think it best if we consider how *thymia/themos* itself is an attribute of God.

The Scriptures have various words for anger, but in the Greek two are dominant: *thymia/themos* and *orgē*. *Thymia/themos* and *orgē* can be used interchangeably, but *orgē* often is connected to God's wrath. Because God is seen as a personal force in the Scriptures, *thymia* (often translated as anger, rage, or wrath) is attributed to God in ways that can be more complex than can be dealt with here.

In the second chapter of Romans we find kindness—the fruit of love—mentioned in a passage dominated by the idea that Christians are to judge others as God judges; God's judging is to be our way of judging. Paul writes, "in passing judgment (*krinōn*) on another you condemn yourself, because you, the judge (*krineis*), are doing (*krinōn*) the very same things. You say,

'We know that God's judgment (*krima*) on those who do such things is in accordance with truth.' Do you imagine, whoever you are, that when you judge (*krinōn*) those who do such things and yet do them yourself, you will escape the judgment (*krima*) of God? Or do you despise the riches of his kindness and forbearance and patience (*makrothymeō*)" (Rom. 2:1-4).

It should be quite clear from the many uses of the words for "judgment" that God's patience (and impatience or anger) is connected to God's judgment, and that God's judgment involves God's justice. John L. McKenzie noted in his comments on "anger" that "the anger of God in the NT also must be conceived in a wider context." Then, referring to the passage above he writes,

> For Paul it is a corollary of His justice (Rm 2:4-5), which is displayed in the day of wrath; without anger God could not judge the world (Rm 3:5). It is hardly necessary to add that the theme of love and mercy in the OT is the background of the theme of anger, and the relationship of the themes is best and most simply stated in the affirmation that it is Jesus who saves us from the anger (Rm 5:9; 1 Th 1:10). For were there no anger, there would be no need of deliverance.[3]

The second time *makrothymeō* is used in Romans also involves God's judgment. Paul wants to show that God's plan includes all people, but, given God's unique history with Israel, Paul describes how God's patience has tempered God's justified anger at Israel's resistance to the divine plan. He asks, "What if God, desiring to show his wrath (*orgē*) and to make known his power, has endured with much patience (*makrothymeō*) the objects of wrath (*orgē*) that are made for destruction; and what if he has done so in order to make known the riches of his glory for the objects of mercy, which he has prepared beforehand for glory— including us whom he has called, not from the Jews only but also from the Gentiles?" (Rom. 9:22-24).

In effect, given Israel's promises to God about keeping the covenant, God could be justified in exercising wrath against it for its many violations, but God exercises divine patience to give it almost unlimited chances to change its ways. "God, says St. Paul, is a God of patience," Evelyn Underhill wrote in her short reflections on "The Fruits of the Spirit." She explains, "He works in tranquility and tranquility seldom goes into partnership with speed. God breaks few records but He always arrives at

---

3. John L. McKenzie, S.J., "Anger," *Dictionary of the Bible* (Milwaukee: Bruce Publishing, 1965), 34.

the end. One of the best things we can do for souls is to wait, and one of the worst things is to force the issue. God lets the plant grow at its own pace. That is why He can bring forth supernatural beauty in and through imperfect instruments."[4] This model of God's patience revealed in our lives invites us to reveal it to others, especially when we judge.

How Do We Cultivate the Spirit's Fruit
of Patience in Our Lives, Relationships, and World?

In discussing the notion of Paul's understanding of (im)patience, it is important to contextualize it in light of the passion that accompanied his Second Temple apocalyptic worldview. When Galatians was written, Paul fully expected that Jesus Christ was about to return. This led to what J. Christiaan Beker calls the "dialectic of patience and impatience in Paul's apostolic life," which reflected the same assumptions found in all "apocalyptic sects."[5] Beker concludes, "There is, then, a passion in Paul, but it is the passion of sobriety; and there is impatience in Paul, but it is the patience tempered by the patience of preparing the world for its coming glory, which the Christ-event has already inaugurated."[6]

Jeremy Gabrielson makes a fine contribution to our reflection on *makrothymia as* patience, especially in the face of opposition. He reminds us that since the motif of suffering and persecution runs throughout Galatians, the main figurative use of βάρος for "suffering" bears on Paul's usage here. In this respect, the fruit of the Spirit that Paul calls *patience* (μακροθυμία) might profitably be identified as one of the founding disciplines of the community that comes to know suffering acutely.[7]

When we live in such a fast-paced society, patience or long-suffering seems almost anachronistic. Yet, surprisingly, it is the glue that holds society together.

In 2003, M. J. Ryan published a fascinating (and wise) book entitled *The Power of Patience*. Since we have identified the Holy Spirit with the "power" of God, we also might do our own interpretation of "patience" as evidence that the power of the Holy Spirit is being cultivated in our lives. With that connection, Ryan notes that patience is needed in individuals as well as society.

---

4. Evelyn Underhill, in Roger L. Roberts, compiler, *The Fruits of the Spirit by Evelyn Underhill* (Wilton, CT: Morehouse-Barlow Co., 1981, 1989), 25-26.

5. J. Christiaan Beker, *The Triumph of God: The Essence of Paul's Thought* (trans. Loren T. Stuckenbruck; Minneapolis: Fortress Press, 1990), 35.

6. Ibid., 36.

7. Jeremy Gabrielson, *Paul's Non-Violent Gospel: The Theological Politics of Peace in Paul's Life and Letters* (Eugene, OR: Pickwick Publications, 2013), 115.

Because "love is patient" (1 Cor. 13:4), it can be said that patience is the first fruit of loving. Thus Ryan writes, "Patience helps us be more loving toward others, more at ease with the circumstances of our lives, and more able to get what we want. It constantly rewards us with the fruits of maturity and wisdom: healthier relationships, higher-quality work, and peace of mind."[8] For a Type-A personality like me, she makes sense when she argues that in a society that thinks many things can be accomplished by sheer "will power," often the best recipe is "wait power." Consequently, patience becomes the glue that holds society together, and, as such, it constitutes the essence of "diplomacy and civility, lawfulness and civil order." She concludes, "Without it, people can't work together and society can't function at all."[9] Such insights led me to use patience for reflection during Lent one year.

Before we consider the obstacles to patience (especially impatience and anger) and how to grow in love so that we become increasingly more patient, it is good to look at the many stories and parables told by Jesus that reveal the patience of God as a sign of God's kingdom. We will also consider how Jesus patiently embraced even the suffering of the cross in order to reveal his love. In this way, Christopher P. Vogt writes in his *Patience, Compassion, Hope, and the Christian Art of Dying Well,*

> Jesus Christ serves as a model for Christians in his exercise of patience not in the sense that he embraced suffering and pain and even death for its own sake, but rather in his willingness to endure these things for the sake of love of God and humanity (i.e., out of a recognition of himself as being in relationship with both). His example also, by contrast, illuminates the shape of impatience. Impatience is to regard suffering (whether understood in the sense of interconnectedness or of the endurance of pain and sorrow) as a hindrance to human flourishing and something to be avoided at all costs.[10]

Overcome the Obstacles to Patience

In Galatians Paul refers to one of the works of the flesh as *thymoi* (5:20). Its varied translations are instructive: "fits of rage," "outbursts of anger,"

---

8. M. J. Ryan, *The Power of Patience: How to Slow the Rush and Enjoy More Happiness, Success, and Peace of Mind Every Day* (New York: Broadway Books, 2003), 9-10.

9. Ibid., 59.

10. Christopher P. Vogt, *Patience, Compassion, Hope, and the Christian Art of Dying Well* (Lanham, MD: Rowman & Littlefield, 2004), 75.

"fits of anger," "wrath(s)," or, as in the translation used for this book, the New Revised Standard Version of the Bible, *thymoi* is simply translated as "anger."

It is good to be aware of the factors that usually generate anger in our lives. Invariably, returning to the connection between patience and judgment, anger involves the visceral reaction one makes to something that has "gone wrong" or to someone having been "wronged" or to someone(s) doing wrong in a way that results in some form of injustice to others. Thus, as I noted in my book *The Paradox of Power: Moving from Control to Compassion*, anger results from a sense of being hurt unjustly or not being given one's just due.

Each Tuesday in the *Wall Street Journal*, a column entitled "Bonds: On Relationships" offers insight into the dynamics of human interaction. The October 16, 2012, edition carried an article entitled "Big Explosions, Small Reasons: Study Explains Why Social Rule Breakers Spark Angry Outbursts." After a catalog of seemingly meaningless incidents that elicited outrage on the part of allegedly aggrieved victims (finding a pickle on a hamburger when it was not to be there; being asked to silence the noisy tapping on a smartphone in "the quiet car" of a commuter train), the question was asked, "Why do adults throw tantrums over seemingly trivial provocations?" The answer seems to be that basic societal rules around justice and fairness are involved.

The author of the *Wall Street Journal* article pointed to the work of researchers in the psychology and neuroscience departments at Duke University that shows that we generally live by "social exchange rules." These rules tell us, "We're not supposed to be rude or inconsiderate; we are supposed to be polite, fair, honest and caring. Don't cut in line. Drive safely. Clean up after yourself." When these rules are violated, we sense that successful human interactions are at stake.[11]

In the Duke study, Dr. Mark Leary asked two hundred people in romantic relationships to think of something their partner did that was annoying or upsetting to them, even though they knew it was fairly inconsequential. He found that, regardless of gender or personality, everyone could name something that drove them over the edge, although people who were more "rule bound" tended to be more upset. Social exchange rule violations had a 30 percent greater effect on the magnitude of a person's anger than the amount of tangible harm the person felt had been done, he concluded. In an

---

11. Elizabeth Bernstein, "Big Explosions, Small Reasons," *Wall Street Journal*, October 16, 2012, D1.

earlier study, he found that, a third of the time, people who overreacted to a small annoyance said it was the last straw in a string of events.[12]

Once we realize that our anger often involves issues of perceived injustice, we can choose how to express it: in rage or revenge or in passion and zeal to right the wrong. In addressing the injustice among and around us, however, it is critical to the health of a group (marriage, family, community, and team) that we find a patient way to do it. Pope Francis has written (reflecting on the compassionate father who waits patiently for the return of the prodigal son) that God is "the only who can truly be called 'the Good Father'" and is the example that one should follow. He explained,

> How much dignity can be found in that father who waits at the door of the house, waiting for his son to return. Fathers must be patient; many times there is nothing else that can be done but to wait. Pray and wait with patience, sweetness, magnanimity and mercy. A good father *knows how to wait and knows how to forgive,* from the depths of his heart. Certainly, he knows how to correct with firmness: he is not a weak father, complacent, sentimental. A father who *knows how to correct without degrading* is the same as one who knows how to protect tirelessly.[13]

Such words apply to us all!

Cultivating Patience

We remember that when Paul refers to *makrothymia,* or patience (as well as everything connected to the fruit[s] of the Spirit), he does so within his Second Temple Judaism's apocalyptic worldview that the end of the world was at hand. Impatience would do little to speed that day. What was needed was a mystical stance of waiting in joyful hope for that day; this demanded patience then as well as now. The New Revised Standard Version brings these ideas together when it quotes Paul's insight: "if we wait in hope for what we do not see, we wait for it with patience."[14] In this sense, Edward Allen offers a good insight when he writes,

> When Paul talks about patience (*makrothymia*) as one of the fruits of the Spirit he means something quite different from quietly wait-

---

12. Ibid., referring to Mark Lear's Duke Study, D2.

13. Pope Francis, General Audience, February 4, 2015, http://www.zenit.org.

14. The actual word for "patience" in this text is not *makrothymia*; it is Paul's other word for patience, *hypomonē.* Besides Rom. 8:25, this Greek is used in Rom. 2:7; 12:12; 2 Cor. 1:6; 12:12

ing when you would rather get on with it. He means that the Spirit will inspire in us persistence and centeredness. Patient people persist in doing what is good and right until they accomplish what they intend to accomplish. In order to do that, patient people are focused. They cannot be pulled away from their central convictions and goals.[15]

Throughout this book I have stressed the importance of awareness of breath to the development of a mystical stance in life. Nowhere, one could argue, is this kind of breathing more necessary than in cultivating patience.

In a very helpful chapter in her book *The Power of Patience*, Meg Ryan notes how consciousness or mindfulness in our breathing can make a huge difference in our lives and relationships. She writes,

> Breathing with awareness also helps us tune in to our bodies and notice what is going on internally. Patience and impatience are not just ideas in our minds, but also sensations in our bodies. We each have our own words for those sensations. To me, patience is a feeling of calm groundedness, a rooted, expansive feeling of wellbeing, while impatience is a jittery, flustered, off-balance sensation.
>
> When we become aware of the sensation of impatience in our bodies, we can use our breath to come back to patience by slowing the inhales and exhales a bit. This signals our nervous system to begin the relaxation response. In as little as a minute, our shoulders relax, muscles loosen, blood pressure drops, and our heart beats a bit slower. From this physically calmer place, we are able to respond more effectively because we have access to all of our emotional and mental resources.[16]

A *Wall Street Journal* article from 2015 offered four points about proper breathing: (1) Slow, deep breathing can trigger a relaxation response in the body that slows the heart and reduces stress. (2) Breathing through the nose filters the air and provides better oxygen uptake. The exhale, which slows the heart rate, should be longer than the inhale. (3) Keep your shoulders as relaxed as possible. The neck and shoulder muscles shouldn't be part of the

---

15. Edward Allen, "The Meaning of Patience," January 24, 2010, http://spectrum magazine.org.

16. Ryan, *Power of Patience*, 143.

breathing process. And (4), take a bigger breath by forcing your abdomen to expand. As the diaphragm extends, it pushes your ribs out.[17]

The Buddhist monk Thich Nhat Hanh connects the need to breathe in and out with connecting to God through the energy of the Holy Spirit; this makes great sense to me as I try to practice mindful breathing and contemplative awareness, not only when I (try to) pray but in my daily life. He believes "all of us also have the seed of the Holy Spirit in us, the capacity of healing, transforming, and loving. When we touch that seed, we are able to touch God the Father and God the Son." He also explains why "touching deeply is an important practice." Again this requires that we breathe in a manner that generates mindfulness. He writes,

> We touch with our hands, our eyes, our ears, and also with our mindfulness. The first practice I learned as a novice monk was to breathe in and out consciously, to touch each breath with my mindfulness, identifying the in-breath as in-breath and the out-breath as out-breath. When you practice this way, your mind and body come into alignment, your wandering thoughts come to a stop, and you are at your best. Mindfulness is the substance of a Buddha.[18]

It is important to discuss at this point the role of patience in prayer itself. One well-known Buddhist teaching is that "the greatest prayer is patience."[19] In my own life, I have found that my daily attempts to pray in silence have often been followed by a lot of impatience at my efforts. Because this book is not an attempt to develop a Pauline form of mystical prayer but a mystical stance (which many consider to be a more authentic sign of living mystically than any kind of mystical prayer), suffice it to say that I have found the absolute need to approach praying with a combination of patience and *kenosis,* especially regarding any (anticipated) results. As long as the *seeking* of a contemplative form of praying is established regarding time and space, the *asking* grounds the request of God to be faithful to the process; whether or not we are *finding* that we are praying contemplatively is secondary, at least to me.

---

17. Sumathi Reddy, "Breathe Better: Doctors Try Using the Most Basic Medicine," *Wall Street Journal,* January 27, 2015, D1.

18. Thich Nhat Hanh, *Living Buddha, Living Christ* (New York: G. P. Putnam's Son/ Riverhead Books, 1995), 15.

19. For a fascinating discussion of the authenticity of this saying, see *Fake Buddha Quotes,* http://www.fakebuddhaquotes.com.

When "nothing" happens at prayer, I remember the consoling words of Thomas Merton, who wrote, "Prayer and love are really learned in the hour when prayer has become impossible, and your heart turns to stone."[20] Regarding the dark night of the soul, he writes,

> During the dark night . . . anxiety is felt in prayer, often acutely. This is necessary because this spiritual night marks the transfer of the full, free control of our inner life into the hands of a superior power. This means too that the time of darkness is, in reality, a time of hazard and difficult options.
>
> If we set out into this darkness, we have to meet these inexorable forces. We will have to face fears and doubts . . . and, at this moment, precisely, all spiritual lights is darkened, all values lose their shape and reality and we remain, so speak, in the void.[21]

However, this "void" can be filled productively if I approach it with patience and the "joyful hope" for that time when the darkness will be turned to light. This makes me realize that the importance of "time" connected to (im)patience cannot be overestimated. Our impatience is often expressed in the face of waiting, delays, arrivals (and departures), slowness (and "too-fastness"). Similarly, it is expressed in the context of "place" as well. Thus someone or something is "out of place" or is "not present" (here/place) when expected (now/time).

In dealing with place and time dynamics with regard to (im)patience, I have found that a quantum approach to being in the "now" that senses my underlying connectedness is more helpful than a mechanistic approach based on absence. I learned this the hard way when I made my thirty-day retreat.

On a thirty-day retreat, following the *Spiritual Exercises* as outlined by St. Ignatius and his followers, the retreatant is urged to meet with a spiritual director each day, preferably at the same time. When I made my retreat a few years ago, the time set for me by my director was 10:00 AM. However, she was invariably late. I had *endured* this in the meaning of *hypomenō* above, but my *makrothymeō* was wearing thin.

One day in the "third week" of the four-week retreat she was particularly late. I paced back and forth in growing anger, judging her lateness quite harshly: "The province is putting up $3,000 for me to make this retreat

---

20. Thomas Merton, *New Seeds of Contemplation* (New York: New Directions, 1961), 221.

21. Thomas Merton, *Contemplative Prayer* (New York: Herder & Herder, 1969), 96.

and I am not getting my money's worth." And then the judgment: "I would never do this so consistently to anyone."

But then an insight came, fifteen minutes after her expected arrival, just as she appeared at her door. As long as I was expecting her to be in her office (place) at 10:00 (time) with me, rather than experiencing God where I was (place) in her absence (time), I remained impatient. But patience came when I realized everything I truly wanted had to do with "finding God in everything," and one of those "everythings" was her absence both from her place and at that proscribed time. It was liberating as well as instructive for my future. In my impatience I had come to mindfulness: the ability to enter deeply into the reality of the present moment. In my own way I discovered the wisdom of what Gerald Jampolsky has written: "How simple it is to see that all the worry in the world cannot control the future. How simple it is to see that we can only be happy now. And that there will never be a time when it is not now."[22]

When I sat down, now at peace rather than controlled by my impatience, she apologized for being late. "No apologies needed," I said sincerely. "I discovered something very important in your delay. I was frustrated because you were not here at 10:00, but I discovered a new meaning to what St. Ignatius said: 'I found God *in* your absence,' and that's what a retreat like this is all about." "Now" is always the sacrament of the present moment.

Living or entering into the "sacrament of the present moment" is at the heart of the work of many great spiritual writers. The eighteenth-century Jesuit Pierre de Caussade, in his classic *The Sacrament of the Present Moment,* expressed this notion well. When we give ourselves over to God in each moment, we are living the "sacrament of the present moment." To live in that moment and to be abandoned to the God found in that moment is the essence of holiness. This insight was further developed and practiced by mystics like Brother Lawrence[23] and St. Thérèse of Lisieux, who wrote, "If I did not simply live from one moment to the next, it would be impossible for me to keep my patience. I can see only the present, I forget the past, and I take good care not to think about the future."[24]

Continuing with the link between patience and time, we come to another of the handful of places where Paul uses the word *makrothymia.*

22. Gerald Jampolsky, *Goodbye to Guilt: Releasing Fear through Forgiveness* (2009).

23. Brother Lawrence, *The Practice of the Presence of God* (trans. Robert J. Edmondson; Orleans, MA: Paraclete Books, 1995).

24. St. Thérèse of Lisieux, *The Story of a Soul: The Autobiography of Saint Thérèse of Lisieux,* trans. John Clarke, O.C.D. (Washington, DC: ICS Publications, 2005).

Here it becomes the "acceptable time" that enables one to put up with all forms of suffering and inconvenience:

> See, now is the acceptable time; see, now is the day of salvation! We are putting no obstacle in anyone's way, so that no fault may be found with our ministry, but as servants of God we have commended ourselves in every way: through great endurance, in afflictions, hardships, calamities, beatings, imprisonments, riots, labors, sleepless nights, hunger; by purity, knowledge, patience (*makrothymia*), kindness, holiness of spirit, genuine love, truthful speech, and the power of God; with the weapons of righteousness for the right hand and for the left; in honor and dishonor, in ill repute and good repute. We are treated as impostors, and yet are true; as unknown, and yet are well known; as dying, and see—we are alive; as punished, and yet not killed; as sorrowful, yet always rejoicing; as poor, yet making many rich; as having nothing, and yet possessing everything. (2 Cor. 6:2-10)

As indicated in the passage above from 2 Corinthians, patience is often the product that emerges from the cauldron of various forms of suffering: physical, personal, and organizational. Perhaps that is why, in addition to meaning "even tempered," *makrothymia* in Galatians has often been translated as "long-suffering." Maybe this is an even better translation, if we think of God's patience with us, especially when we contribute to God's suffering by making other people suffer our unfairness and injustice.

Paul compared his own suffering to that of a mother "in the pain of childbirth until Christ is formed in you" (4:19). We also find some of the best descriptions of this kind of patience borne of suffering in the writings of Julian of Norwich. She was an English anchoress/mystic who lived around 1342–1416. In a near-death experienced around 1373, when she was around thirty years old, she had sixteen mystical experiences (which she called "showings," or *appearances*) that took place over a two-day period. Her description of these, in her *Revelations of Divine Love*, is said to be the first published book in the English language written by a woman. Some of her key teachings help me understand the notion of patience as a manifestation of the Spirit of love unlike any others: (1) because God is love there can be no wrath in God as humans understand wrath; and (2) because God (and Jesus Christ) is a mother, the suffering a mother endures in childbirth and in feeding and nurturing her children also brings forth patience.

Julian writes, "For I saw no wrath except on man's side, and he forgives that in us, for wrath is nothing else but a perversity and an opposition to peace and to love."[25] Given our contention that there is but one "fruit" of the Holy Spirit, and that being love, it follows that Julian would not find God's wrath to be that as understood by humans; any wrath of God would have to be a manifestation of God's love, of God's passion for justice (right relations with all), and peace. Such thinking reflects very much what a learned scriptural scholar would say as well. Thus, Johannes Horst, in his entry on *makrothymia* in the *Theological Dictionary of the New Testament*, writes that while Paul's understanding of "God's long-suffering is related to His wrath" (Rom. 2:4; 9:22), "God's patience does not overlook anything. It simply sees further than man. It has the end in view. It has the true insight which knows best. It is not swayed by human emotions. The fact that divine *makrothymia* stands alongside God's *orgē* means that this is freed from anthropomorphic misunderstanding."[26]

Identifying God and Jesus as a *mother*, whose long-suffering with us children evokes patience, Julian found in Jesus's suffering of his passion an example of a mother's patience during childbirth. Just as the mother brings forth a new creation, so has Jesus's passion and death given birth to an entirely new creation that will take place in all those who allow God's love to enter the world through them. Thus, she writes that she

> saw that God rewarded man for the patience which he has in awaiting God's will and his time, and that man has patience to endure throughout the span of his life, because he does not know when the time for him to die will come. This is very profitable, because if he knew when that would be, he would set a limit to his patience. Then, too, it is God's will that so long as the soul is in the body it should seem to a man that he is always on the point of being taken. For all this life and this longing we have here is only an instant of time, and when we are suddenly taken into bliss out of pain, then pain will be nothing.[27]

Having come to this realization, she then understood that all this suffering and patience that we bear is reflective of what is core to God.

---

25. Julian of Norwich, *Showings* (Classics of Western Spirituality; trans. and intro. Edmund Colledge, O.S.A., and James Walsh, S.J. (New York/Ramsey/Toronto: Paulist Press, 1978), 14th Rev., 48th chapter, 262.

26. J. Horst, "Μακροθυμία," in Gerhard Kittel, ed., *Theological Dictionary of the New Testament* (ed. and trans. Geoffrey W. Bromiley; Grand Rapids: Eerdmans, 1967), 382.

27. Julian of Norwich, *Showings*, 15th Rev., 64th chapter, 306.

Very meekly our Lord showed what patience he had in his cruel Passion, and also the joy and delight that he has in that Passion, because of love. And he showed me this as an example of how we ought gladly and easily to bear our pains, for that is very pleasing to him and an endless profit to us. And the reason why we are oppressed by them is because of our ignorance of love. Though the three persons of the blessed Trinity be all alike in the self, the soul received most understanding of love. Yes, and he wants us in all things to have our contemplation and our delight in love. And it is about this knowledge that we are most blind, for some of us believe that God is almighty and may do everything, and that he is all wisdom and can do everything, but that he is all love and wishes to do everything, there we fail. And it is this ignorance which most hinders God's lovers, as I see it. . . . [28]

Some years ago I was asked to give some talks over the course of a year at a parish in the Midwest. Little did I know that I would meet there a woman whose life embodied what Julian of Norwich experienced. I would like to end this chapter with her story as she told it to me.

Each time I came to the parish, she sat in the same chair for my lectures. I found her to be strikingly good looking; yet, the first three times that I came for my quarterly talks, her face showed some kind of deep suffering. But all this changed into a kind of radiance the fourth time. Because this was so noticeable, I sought her out. That led to a narration of the glow that comes from the Spirit when we are grounded in love that brings forth patience in a profound way.

She explained that just before she came to my first talk, her husband of thirty-three years announced he was leaving her for a "younger" woman. It came as a total surprise and was devastating. Then, just before the second talk, she discovered that their only daughter, now twenty-seven, with whom she had begun to develop the kind of relationship that moves from being mother/daughter to friend/friend in a way that might somewhat ease the loss of her husband, had begun exhibiting strange behavior. This led to a diagnosis of the daughter as schizophrenic. Now this loss meant a reversion of the dream she had had: she would now have to take care of her as a child, rather than be with her as an adult friend. Finally, just before my third visit, she lost her job as a dental assistant because her boss had retired and did

---

28. Ibid., 16th Rev., 73rd chapter, 323.

not leave the business to anyone. This meant the potential loss of her livelihood and the home in which she lived. She felt totally alone; everything of importance to her, it seemed, had been taken away from her.

"One day, when I thought I couldn't take it anymore, something in me said, 'Drive away.' So I got into my car and began to drive. I kept driving west. Finally I found myself at the Grand Canyon just at sunset. It is one of the most beautiful sights anyone can ever see. However," she said, with a deep smile of utter awareness coming to her face, "as I was standing there looking at the canyons etched out over centuries, overwhelmed with what had happened to me, I heard the words that changed everything around in a way that gave me meaning for the rest of my life: 'We are made beautiful by what is taken away.'"

In that experience at the Grand Canyon, the woman found, in her suffering and loss, her own version of the famous words that came to Julian of Norwich: "Jesus in this Vision informed me of all that is needful to me, answered by this word and said: It behooved that there should be sin; but all shall be well, and all shall be well, and all manner of thing shall be well."[29]

---

29. Ibid., 13th Rev., 27th chapter, 224.

Chapter 9

Cultivating Kindness as a Sign of the Spirit's Love That Makes Us Kin

When I began to write this chapter, I was aware that I did not have a good example to introduce the themes I planned to address. Providentially, however, I found myself part of the story of a person who is not just a good example of "kindness" but a *kind of sacrament of kindness*; a wonderful model for this manifestation of the fruit of love. But first some background:

As I mentioned in my introduction to the chapter on *peace*, I have been involved in the ministry of socially responsible investing ever since I left St. Elizabeth's parish in Milwaukee. This ministry involves efforts to bring Catholic institutions into the Interfaith Center on Corporate Responsibility (ICCR), which began as an effort of the major Protestant denominations to use their investments to end apartheid in South Africa. Since the late 1960s and early '70s, ICCR has expanded to address a score of issues, ranging from human rights and health concerns to energy and the environment. Since 1980, I led the effort to address the health hazards of smoking.

In the 1990s I was noticed for my anti-tobacco work by a married couple, Stanley and Susan Rosenblatt, both lawyers, in Miami. When no other lawyers would take on the plight of flight attendants who had to breathe in other peoples' tobacco smoke, they took on the issue and sued the major tobacco companies. Their efforts led to the only instance (to my knowledge) of the tobacco companies settling a suit without contest. The resulting 1997 settlement of $350 million was put into an organization to research the dynamics and consequences of secondhand smoke (SHS), the Flight Attendants Medical Research Institute (FAMRI). This would be overseen by the Rosenblatts, one other lawyer, and five flight attendants. Under these "trustees," there is a medical board and a lay board. I was asked to chair the lay board.

When one of the original flight attendant trustees died as a result of SHS, another former flight attendant, Kathleen Cheney, took her place. She was already suffering seriously from various cancers connected to SHS, but, with the support of her husband, Kevin, she joined the trustees. Sadly, she died in 2014. A memorial service was planned for Miami on Sunday, September 21, 2014. I was asked to give one of her eulogies. In effect, the material below reflects what I said spontaneously and from my heart.

That morning I went outside the Westin Hotel where FAMRI had accommodated some of us. Almost immediately a young employee asked me, "How may I be of assistance to you?" I replied, jokingly, I don't need any assistance from you but I appreciate your kindness." He had approached me with a smile and, when he got close enough to me, I noticed that the name-plate on his uniform read "Eduardo." But what was below it caught my eye. It read, "My Passion?" "Films."

I'd like to suggest that Kathie's passion was *kindness* in the fullest meaning of the word. When I looked around at the memorial at some of those in attendance whom I know personally, I saw Jews, Christians of different kinds (including Catholics), Buddhists, unbelievers, and at least one avowed atheist, who would go unnamed. (This generated laughs because everyone knew who she was).

When we look at the word for "kindness," in Hebrew it is *ḥesed*; in Greek for the Christians it is *chrēstotēs,* and for the Buddhists it involves *metta* and the prayer of loving kindness. However, for believers and nonbelievers alike, neuroscientists tell us that kindness is in all of us: it's called oxytocin. Oxytocin was originally identified as the chemical or hormone released in a mother at childbirth and for breastfeeding; its purpose is to make it easier for the mother to give birth and release her milk. That is why we say "the milk of human kindness."

I told the assembly that, because I am writing on kindness, I brought along from Milwaukee a book by Janet Martin Soskice called *The Kindness of God: Metaphor, Gender, and Religious Language.*[1] In it I noticed a strong connection among three words, "kindness," "kind," and "kin." When I looked at Kathie's life, I discovered that she had brought together those three words in a remarkable way. She practiced "kindness" to her own kin, like all of you here; but she also broke down barriers dealing with those who were not "her kind" in a way that extended her "kin" beyond her immediate family. In the process she made "family" not only with all of us but with people all around the world, as well as future generations who will not have to suffer the consequences of secondhand smoke.

---

1. Janet Martin Soskice, *The Kindness of God: Metaphor, Gender, and Religious Language* (Oxford: Oxford University Press, 2007).

Janet Martin Soskice writes in *The Kindness of God*, "In Middle English the words 'kind' and 'kin' were the same—to say that Christ is 'our kinde Lord' is not to say that Christ is tender and gentle, although that may be implied, but to say that he is kin—our kind."[2] Kathie tried to follow the example of Jesus who, though being God, became "our kind." Furthermore, because she was baptized "in Christ," as a member of Christ's living body, she became "our kind." This meant that she made kin or family with each one of us in *our own* way, not her own way. That's true *incarnation*. Every one of us felt she was our "kind" of friend.

When I considered Kathie's life, I saw that she had been that *kind* of person: for every one of us. It started with her own blood family and then extended to Kevin. With Kevin, she brought Patrick into our world and joined Kevin in treating Tom [Kevin's son by a previous relationship] as her own son, making him her "kin." As I listened to her family, friends, and neighbors, it became evident that, beyond all the people at the memorial service, she made "kin" with all sorts of other people too. How many times had I heard people say things like: "she always had a kind word to say about everyone; I never heard an unkind word about anyone coming from her mouth"?

That might have been good enough for most of us, but not for Kathie. And so I consider her a kind of "quantum Catholic." Quantum theory tells us that we are no longer defined by space-and-time categories like here and now but by relationships. I think that Kathie broke those space-and-time categories in a marvelous way. First she broke boundaries around space, expanding her kindness to make kin with some of the most abandoned people. This took her to work in India with Mother Teresa to welcome into families children who had been abandoned. No space boundaries there.

Through her anti-tobacco work, especially in using her own suffering caused by secondhand smoke, she was a pioneer in the state of Georgia in helping it move toward smoke-free workplaces. This effort continued when she joined the FAMRI Board of Trustees. There she found a way to ensure that future generations will not have to suffer as she did because of its work addressing the nature of and consequences of the hazards of secondhand smoke. Despite being very seriously ill, she joined the effort to make sure there would be a healthy family or "kin" in the future. I remember with a smile what happened at our FAMRI meeting in May.

Kathie was very, very sick. She couldn't talk because the cancer had affected her trachea. The doctor had warned her that she should only be with her family. Well, the doctor did not know that Kathie's definition of

---

2. Ibid., 5.

family was not the same as his. Everyone at the FAMRI meeting in Miami last May was "kin" to her, her "kind." The FAMRI family, as we called it, was just one more part of her kin and kind. We were her "Kinde."

Perhaps because of what Kathie experienced working as a flight attendant and seeing people like her, who never smoked but suffered from its effects, she expanded her kindness to break down barriers, to make other victims of tobacco, first in Georgia and then through FAMRI, her kin. In the fullest meaning of the original Middle English, her kindness made them kin, her Kinde. But Kathie's efforts at kinship were not only toward victims of her kind who suffered the results of tobacco; they extended to people who suffered half a world away. She went to India to work with Mother Teresa. Now her kindness had become universal. And that is what made her for me what we Catholics call a sacrament. For us, the definition of a sacrament is "an external sign of an interior reality that gives grace."

In her external life, Kathie kept expanding her kindness to make kin of everyone; all became her "kind." In that she became for me an external sign of an internal reality: the *ḥesed*, the *chrēstotēs*, and the loving kindness of the Buddhist *metta* I try to say every day: "May I/we/he/she/it/they be safe from inner and outer danger; may I/we/he/she/it/they be sound and peaceful of mind; may I/we/he/she/it/they be strong in spirit and body; may I/we/he/she/it/they spend life being kind." In this, for those of us who believe, she witnessed to the kindness of God that has made God our Kinde, our kin. And, in the process, we who received her kindness received grace. In her graceful way of being God's loving kindness in ever-widening circles, we, who knew her, have all been inspired to continue to make everyone and everything "our Kinde" so that one day we'll realize that this kindness that makes us kin with all is what life asks of us all.

In going beyond her own family to make "kin" of people around the world, she broke the category of space that limits so many of us; in extending her care and kindness to generations after us through her work in Georgia and FAMRI, she broke the boundaries of time. When our lives break those two great boundaries of space and time, that reflects what we know from quantum theory that reality is all about: universal connectedness and oneness. For me, a Catholic priest, she represents my dream of being and becoming a truly "quantum" Catholic: a sacrament of God's care in every place and for all time.

How Is the Kindness of God Revealed?

We saw in the introduction to this chapter that the Greek words *chrēstos* and *chrēstotēs*, Paul's words for the fruit of love that is "kindness," are derived from the Hebrew word *ḥesed*. Indeed, one of the most popular translations of *ḥesed* is "loving kindness." *Chrēstos* and *chrēstotēs* are used only seven times in the authentic Pauline letters, and these in only four places (Rom. 2:4 [2x]; 11:22 [3x]; and in the litanies of 2 Cor. 6 and Gal. 5:22). An eighth use, *chrēsteuomai*, is found in Paul's Canticle of Love, wherein he describes a love that is patient and kind (1 Cor. 13:4).

In order to understand how Paul used the various forms of *chrēstotēs* we need to look at their appearance in his Letter to the Romans, since five of the eight uses of the word appear there. First, in chastising the house churches for the mean things they were saying about one another, he asks cynically how they can continue to do such things: "Or do you despise the riches of God's kindness (*chrēstotēs*) and forbearance and patience? Do you not realize that God's kindness (*chrēstos*) is meant to lead you to repentance?" (Rom. 2:4). Here we have another example of how what we have received freely from God (in this case, God's kindness while we were in our sins) demands a response. It demands that we repent of our own sins and extend loving kindness to others in their sins. Indeed, we must extend *chrēstotēs* to others if we are to reveal that God's kindness has "taken" effect in our own lives. God's kindness is meant to heal us of our unkindness, God's mercy from our unmercy.

This need to transmit to others what we have received (i.e., *chrēstotēs*) is articulated more starkly later in Romans. In commenting on how the "wild shoot" that they were has been grafted on to the vine and some of the other branches have been cut off, Paul warns the Romans not to become proud of heart and righteous: "Note then the kindness (*chrēstotēs*) and the severity of God: severity towards those who have fallen, but God's kindness (*chrēstotēs*) towards you, provided you continue in his kindness (*chrēstotēs*); otherwise you also will be cut off" (Rom. 11:22). While God will never be separated from us ("cut off"), our lack of kindness will have the effect of cutting us off from God.

The assumption that Paul seems to be making is that *chrēstotēs* reflects more the idea of God's wrath because of our lack of mercy, which is expected to be reciprocated, rather than the original connotation of *ḥesed*.

A fuller understanding of *chrēstotēs* emerges when we probe the original biblical notion of *ḥesed*. There we find something that seems almost alien to Paul's use of *chrēstotēs* above, that seems to imply a *quid pro quo* or legalistic approach to kindness (what we have received from God must be shared with others or we are in trouble). However, a deeper examination of the second part of the passage in Rom. 2:4 reveals Paul's explanation of why we continue to fail to show to others the kindness God has shown us: we *presume upon that kindness*. We know God is not like us in our transactions with one another and is always ready with kindness when we need it. Too often we take that dimension of God's kindness for granted; indeed, it has been enshrined in the "Catholic imagination" since our youth: no matter what we do, if we repent, God is always ready to take us back. We may be unfaithful and unkind, but God never is.

When *hesed* is used as a reference to God in the Old Testament, it almost always refers in some way to the original covenant God made to Israel through Abraham and, later, with Moses. In one of the deepest insights into *hesed* I have ever read,[3] Pope John Paul II once wrote that there was something about God's covenant with Israel that went beyond any possible interpretation of it in terms of a basic juridical document (a contract or treaty made between or among humans). Thus, noting the strictly legal dimension of the covenant God made with Israel, the pope writes, "On God's part, this covenant was a gift and a grace for Israel. Nevertheless, since, in harmony with the covenant entered into, God had made a commitment to respect it, *hesed* also acquired in a certain sense a legal content. The juridical commitment on God's part ceased to oblige whenever Israel broke the covenant and did not respect its conditions." However, as Pope John Paul II immediately makes clear, this is where God's *hesed* in relationship to Israel's infidelity is not the kind of being "cut off" about which Paul seems to warn; rather it becomes a sign of the eternal fidelity of God that God will never cut off any of God's people, even if those people choose to separate themselves from their covenantal promises. The pope writes, "But precisely at this point, *hesed,* in ceasing to be a juridical obligation, revealed its deeper aspect: it showed itself as what it was at the beginning, that is, as love that gives, love more powerful than betrayal, grace stronger than sin." He continues to make clear what happens when the kindness (as *chrēstotēs,* which reflects biblical *hesed*) we are discussing in this chapter is seen in its deepest meaning: *as the fruit of God's Spirit that is love.* Pope John Paul II concludes, "Israel, although burdened with guilt for having broken the covenant, cannot lay claim to God's *hesed* on the basis of (legal) justice; yet it can and must go on hoping and trusting to obtain it, since the God of the covenant is really 'responsible for his love.' The fruits of this love are forgiveness and restoration to grace, the reestablishment of the interior covenant."[4]

---

3. I am indebted for this lead to my brother, Dan Crosby, OFMCap. For more on mercy, see the audiocassette series by Fr. Dan Crosby, OFMCap., *Mercy, the Heart of Faith, the Reason for Hope* (Washington, DC: Now You Know Media, 2014).

4. Pope John Paul II, *Dives in Misericordia (Rich in Mercy)*, November 30, 1980, n. 52, http://w2.vatican.va.

Building on the theme of God's forbearance over against our sinfulness, Konrad Weiss writes that the kindness of God (*chrēston tou theou*) represents God's "gracious restraint in face of the sins of His people."[5] In other words, instead of recrimination or, at least, irreconciliation, which would be legally justified, God will never be separated from us, *no matter what we do*. It is this *going beyond one's expected obligation* because of unconditional love that helps me best understand the power of the Spirit that is expressed in loving kindness, and also how critical it is for our world that more and more people cultivate this fruit of the Spirit's love.

How Do We Cultivate the Spirit's Fruit of Kindness in Our Lives, Relationships, and World?

According to Paul, God's kindness toward us is to be reciprocated in the way we manifest kindness to all God's people, especially in the household of faith (Rom. 15:14; 2 Cor. 6:6). Said in another way, kindness must "begin at home," but it must not end there; it must be extended to everyone. A problem with some ways that covenantal nomism had come to be interpreted wrongly was that it limited God's *universal agapē* in the form of *chrēstotēs* to the members of the House of Israel exclusively; this could not be the way for those guided by the Holy Spirit to reach beyond their groups and even beyond their built-in nature in order to be available to those in need. Indeed the universality of kindness without boundaries makes *chrēstotēs* something much more than what we mentioned earlier, the substance neuroscientists call oxytocin.

Oxytocin was first identified as the reproductive peptide hormone that is released in pregnant women to help them control contractions during labor and childbirth. Sometimes a synthetic version (called pitocin) is injected to induce labor. As fitting the theme of this chapter, it also has been called "the milk of human kindness" because it is connected to breast feeding. Here it is expressed in the calm and centered focus of women toward their babies while breastfeeding. Women have told me that when their baby cries to be fed, their breasts tingle and release milk (the "let-down reflex") in anticipation of feeding the child. In other words, something in these women is naturally triggered in response to the needs of this "other."

When I first heard about oxytocin and its identification with birthing and breast feeding, I must admit I was somewhat envious of women. Then

---

5. Konrad Weiss, "*Chrēstotēs*," in Gerhard Friedrich, ed., *Theological Dictionary of the New Testament* (trans. and ed. Geoffrey W. Bromiley; Grand Rapids: Eerdmans, 1974), 9:490.

I learned that it also applies, in varying degrees, to any manifestation of physical kindness. It made me understand why I get a warm glow when I celebrate Mass and see a parent (most often a father) holding a child. That glow resembles the feeling of being touched, as in a hug or massage, a gentle caress of the cheek or (so they say) even sex. When one experiences such forms of touch, oxytocin is released in the brain to encourage reciprocation by extending care to others, even strangers.[6]

Oxytocin has also been linked to "care for the other" or "altruism." Moreover, biologists will tell you it is necessary for the survival of the human species. As such, it represents the willingness of an organism to sacrifice itself so that the species will survive. And when an organism sacrifices its life to save another, it helps perpetuate the species by the sharing of its life. In this sense, oxytocin is a kind of "molecule of morality."

More than 2,000 years ago, Hillel the Elder (whose end of life coincided with the beginning of the life of Jesus) is said to have coined the saying that expresses the core of what can be called balanced reciprocity, or the Golden Rule: "That which is hateful to you, do not do to your fellow. That is the whole Torah; the rest is the explanation; go and learn." However, according to economist Paul J. Zak, the Golden Rule is written in our very genes. Zak writes that "oxytocin orchestrates the kind of generous and caring behavior that every culture endorses as the right way to live—the cooperative, benign, pro-social way of living that every culture on the planet describes as 'moral.' The Golden Rule is a lesson that the body already knows, and when we get it right, we feel the rewards immediately." However, in an article on oxytocin in the "Review" section of the *Wall Street Journal*, he adds,

> This isn't to say that oxytocin always makes us good or generous or trusting. In our rough-and-tumble world, an unwavering response of openness and loving kindness would be like going around with a "kick me" sign on your back. Instead, the moral molecule works like a gyroscope, helping us to maintain our balance between behavior based on trust and behavior based on wariness and distrust. In this way oxytocin helps us to navigate between the social benefits of

---

6. This lasts as long as these "strangers" do not represent our actual or perceived "enemies" (as will be discussed in the subsequent paragraphs). For a good, popular summary of studies done on the impact of oxytocin that extends to such strangers, see Natalie Angier, "The Biology behind the Milk of Human Kindness," *New York Times*, Science Section, November 24, 2009, D2.

openness—which are considerable—and the reasonable caution that we need to avoid being taken for a ride.[7]

When oxytocin is administered to both women and men, they tend to show greater empathy and a willingness to sacrifice themselves on behalf of others. However, data also indicate that this empathy (or "kindness" in a secular sense) is most often limited to "one's own" or one's "kin" or "kind." Indeed, such data show that when oxytocin is administered in controlled settings, people not only actually *refuse* kindness toward those not of their own "kind"; the oxytocin often reveals a genuine lack of kindness and even malice toward those not of one's "kin" or "kind."

In a 2010 paper, Carolyn Declerck and colleagues at the University of Antwerp detailed the results of oxytocin's effects on participants who played an economic game. If they had met each other before the game they tended to be cooperative. However, if they had not met beforehand they were less cooperative. In other words, the "trust molecule" called oxytocin had definite limits.[8] In a parallel study of Dutch participants done in 2011, Carsten De Dreu and colleagues at the University of Amsterdam posed a moral question to the participants: Should they push someone under a runaway trolley car in order to save five other people? The hypothetical victim was given a typical Dutch name or a name from one of two groups that often evoke prejudice among some Dutch citizens, namely, Germans or Arabs. In the control condition, the person's name didn't affect the decision. But when oxytocin was administered, the subjects preferred to throw Helmut or Abdul under the train, as opposed to Luuk or Maarten. The conclusion: while oxytocin seems to promote xenophobia,[9] what Paul calls *chrēstotēs* makes Helmut and Abdul members of the family whose boundaries are not defined by separatist notions like ethnicity, tribalism, gender, or any other exclusive grouping.

Oxytocin is not just limited in terms of one's own "kind"; it is limited in time as well. Data shows that it is active in the brain for about thirty minutes after it has been released or injected. This restricted benefit of oxytocin to kin, "kind," Kinde, and chronology invites us to look beyond a purely neurological interpretation of oxytocin to a much more expansive meaning.

---

7. Paul J. Zak, "The Trust Molecule," *Wall Street Journal*, April 28-29, 2012, C2.

8. Robert M. Sapolsky, "Peace, Love, and Oxytocin," *Los Angeles Times*, December 4, 2011.

9. Robert M. Sapolsky, Mind & Matter Column, "A 'Love Hormone' with a Nasty Little Secret," *Wall Street Journal*, June 27, 2014, http://online.wsj.com.

Overcoming the Obstacles to Kindness

In the section above I noted how kindness in the form of oxytocin is built into our very bones or nature. However, when people cannot naturally produce oxytocin, they also are more likely not to show empathy and often fall into such various anti-social personalities as psychopaths and other borderline types.

Another hormone stands virtually opposite to oxytocin and, when dominant in a person's life, can actually undermine the ability to function: testosterone. Testosterone is secreted in a woman's ovaries and a man's testicles; however the secretion is in much higher levels in males, thus its popular association with "alpha males." If it dominates in a relationship, instead of care there will be control. However, when men move into deeper care of others, especially in a sexual way, their testosterone levels decrease. Interestingly, the reverse happens in women. Thus oxytocin and testosterone are hormones that increase and decrease in the sexes in varying ways; the more balanced the testosterone levels are in both women and men, the deeper the care or release of oxytocin there seems to be.

Given this background, it is understandable why so many works of the flesh are associated with what today would be considered increases in and release of testosterone in ways that do not reflect care and kindness but, more often, control and even malice. That is why Paul urged the Corinthians to model their lives on his own: "We are putting no obstacle in anyone's way, so that no fault may be found with our ministry . . . by purity, knowledge, patience, kindness, holiness of spirit, genuine love, truthful speech, and the power of God" (2 Cor. 6:3, 6-7).

Some time ago I read about a very subtle obstacle to genuine loving kindness that can even further undermine conflicted relationships. Unfortunately, I have experienced it and, alas, probably even shown it to others. It has been demonstrated that people experiencing lingering guilt do so depending on how those affected by it respond. Tamara Ferguson, at Utah State University, reported on data that showed that, when confronted directly with a protest such as "That's not fair" or "Do you know what you've done?" or less directly but clearly through tone of voice, the guilt subsides more quickly. However, when the supposed victim responds with apparent kindness, with statements such as "It's all right, I forgive you. . . . It's not your fault. . . . You don't need to make it up to me," the guilt lingers. Thus there seems to be a real basis for the phrase "killing with kindness!"[10]

---

10. Anonymous, "To Forgive Is Divine . . . If You're Trying to Inflict Guilt: But Study

One way we create pain in others regarding their "character flaws" (to use an expression familiar in the Twelve-Step Program) is how we characterize them with our judgments that do not reflect loving kindness. Instead, all too often we invite the *cri de coeur* of Gerard Manley Hopkins, "O why are we so haggard at the heart, so care-coiled, care-killed."[11]

I recall how deeply hurt (in my ego) I became when I was discussing my confusion with some housemates as to whether I was an "8" or a "1" on the Enneagram. In my province we have a friar who has become quite proficient in giving talks on the Enneagram and, without my awareness (and against a key tenet of the Enneagram), had categorized me in a group of friars. One of them was involved in the conversation where I had expressed my dilemma. "You're not an '8'; you're not a '1,'" he said. "You're a '3.'" "What's a '3'?" I asked. "You're a peacock," he declared, much to his own and the others' delight.

However, in the same community, we had another friar who practiced loving kindness in a way that was redemptive and not punitive. I experienced this redemptive loving kindness in the form of his correction of me when I had said something that was true (like the above) but without kindness to another friar who was visiting our house. The next morning, the friar who had observed my way of challenging the other friar said to me: "Mike, do you think you were kind to Friar "John" last night when you said that?" His way of loving kindness exposed my lack of it.

Cultivating Kindness to Make Those Not "Our Kind" Our Kin

Romans 12:14-22 outlines a whole litany of how one should practice kindness in the face of opposition: Do not curse (Rom. 12:14); do not repay evil for evil (Rom. 12:17); do not avenge yourselves (Rom. 12:19); do not be overcome by evil but overcome evil with good (Rom. 12:21); and, finally the passage that shows *chrēstotēs* to be much more than oxytocin, "if your enemies are hungry, feed them; if they are thirsty, give them something to drink; for by doing this you will heap burning coals on their heads" (Rom. 12:20).

Heaping this kind of burning coals on the head of one's opponents is hardly a form of reciprocating evil for evil; rather it reflects the kind of

---

also Suggests Killing with 'Kindness' Can Damage Personal Relationships," *Dallas Morning News*, August 16, 1998, 5A.

11. Gerard Manley Hopkins, "The Leaden Echo and the Golden Echo," in *Gerard Manley Hopkins: Poems and Prose* (ed. W. H. Gardner; Harmondsworth, Middlesex, England: Penguin Books, 1963), 54.

"third way" opposed to "fight" or "flight" that Walter Wink has noted to be so critical to the Christian message. Or, as Toews writes, "the exhortation to act kindly is clear. Responding to evil with hospitality and kindness has a positive effect—it unsettles the enemy. The final counter-action uses the imagery of Christian standing in the middle of a battle with the evil of the present age. Do not respond to the power of evil by using the means of evil, hostility or retaliation but with the power of good."[12]

Paul's understanding of how the members of the house churches were to relate to one another and, indeed, everyone, was simply to "continue in God's kindness/*chrēstotēs*" (Rom. 11:22). However, because of this, the kindness of a Christian could never be merely equated with what we read on bumper stickers: "Practice random acts of kindness." The kindness of a Christian is to reveal the kindness of God, which extends to everyone, including our enemies, with no conditions.

Henri Nouwen has written about kindness in a way that shows how essential it is to being human. He explains, "When we say, 'She is a kind person' or 'He surely was kind to me,' we express a very warm feeling." Nouwen probably didn't know it, but here he was simply describing the release of oxytocin that comes when someone shows us care. However, he immediately adds, "In our competitive and often violent world, kindness is not the most frequent response. But when we encounter it we know that we are blessed." Having said this, Nouwen asks a question that is at the heart of this section of this chapter: "Is it possible to grow in kindness, to become a kind person? Yes, but it requires discipline. To be kind means to treat another person as your 'kin,' your intimate relative. We say, 'We are kin' or 'He is next of kin.' To be kind is to reach out to another as being of 'kindred' spirit." But he continues, "Here is the great challenge: All people, whatever their color, religion, or sex, belong to humankind and are called to be kind to one another, treating one another as brothers and sisters. There is hardly a day in our lives in which we are not called to this."[13] Blessed (Mother) Teresa of Calcutta is said to have urged, "Be kind! Be the loving expression of God's kindness: kindness in your eyes, kindness in your face, kindness in your smile, kindness in your warm greetings. I believe that the way in which an act of kindness is done is as important as the action itself."

12. John E. Toews, *Romans* (Scottdale, PA: Herald Press, 2004), 312. I am indebted to Willard M. Swartley for this source (*Covenant of Peace: The Missing Peace in New Testament Theology and Ethics* [Grand Rapids: Eerdmans, 2006], 238-39).

13. Henri J. M. Nouwen, "Becoming Kind" (February 4), *Bread for the Journey: A Daybook of Wisdom and Faith* (San Francisco: HarperSanFrancisco, 1977), no pagination.

Echoing the approach we have taken throughout this book, based on the cultivation of the various manifestations of love in a mystical stance toward life, loving kindness is first cultivated through the practice of what the Buddhists call the *metta* of loving kindness. In fact, Khenpo Tsewang Dongyal Rinpoche, who founded in 1988 a Buddhist Center in New York (Padmasambhava) has said, "The whole Buddhist teaching is based on loving kindness toward yourself and all beings and in the *Vajrayana* teaching that is the heart of the [*metta*] practice."[14] This understanding has led me to develop my own *metta*, which I often recite, with the result that I feel more connected to everyone and everything in the universe. Depending on whom I am thinking about (myself, other persons, events, and things close to me or supposedly far away), I use the following as my mantra of care:

May I (s/he, they, it) be safe from inner and outer danger.
May I (s/he, they, it) be sound and peaceful in mind.
May I (s/he, they, it) be strong in body and spirit.
May I (s/he, they, it) spend my life by being kind.

As we try to cooperate with the Holy Spirit in developing "loving kindness" in our personal, communal, and organizational lives, I believe it important to recall how *chrēstotēs* was expressed in the first-century world of Paul and the Galatians, so that we can apply its wisdom to our lives as we try to have an impact on our twenty-first-century world.

In the first-century Mediteranean world, wealth was usually determined by inheritance within families. Thus, household economics was grounded in kinship. Kinship formed the foundation for the wider polity. Economic functions such as production and consumption, planting and sowing, hiring and firing were determined ultimately by kinship (belonging or family) and political (power or honor) considerations, rather than the "market" or "economic" factors of today. According to Karl Polanyi, economies at that time (and until the end of feudalism in Western Europe) were organized around three poles: redistribution, reciprocity, and house holding. Sometimes, as in the first-century world of Paul, all three were combined and legitimized by religion, whose dynamics were embedded throughout.[15]

---

14. Khenpo Tsewang Dongyal Rinpoche, interviewed in "Joy and Loving Kindness: An Interview with Khenpo Tsewant Dongyal Rinpoche," in *Fellowship in Prayer* 46.5 (October 1995), 5.

15. Karl Polanyi, *The Great Transformation: The Political and Economic Origins of Our Time* (Boston: Beacon, 1958), 47ff.

The first-century world considered all resources limited in a kind of zero-sum way. Only so many resources were available to the people claiming them or desiring them. Distribution, as well as redistribution, represented the collection, storage, and reallocation of goods and services determined by some center (usually some form of government or temple). Taxes and rents often constituted the main form of redistribution.

Reciprocity involved a kind of implicit, nonlegal, contractual obligation between ranked people and was enforceable by codes of honor and shame. According to Marshall Sahlins, there were essentially three types of reciprocity:[16] (1) negative reciprocity—doing to others what you would *not* have them do to you (hostility and warfare toward nonkind or enemies); (2) balanced reciprocity—*quid pro quo* exchanges; and (3) general reciprocity—the giving or sharing of gifts and various resources (especially to household members) without expecting return. The levels of kindness followed a clear and cultural trajectory. The more closely one was related to household, family, and kin, the more likely general reciprocity would characterize social interactions; the farther away, negative reciprocity would be the norm. To think of any other kind of ordering would be out of the question.

The moral claims of individual A or group A paralleled the moral obligations of individual B or group B. Only if these claims were violated through injustice, especially exploitation on the part of the dominant group, would challenges to the system's order be justified. Otherwise the basic order would stay in place. Stephen Charles Mott points to the power of religion as legitimator or deligitimator of the social system when he writes, "Any system of stratification requires a system of belief to explain, justify, and propagate the inequalities and persuade people to accept as legitimate the fact of their inequality. In a traditional society religion provides the ideological basis for status in the system. When this base is removed the whole system is shaken."[17]

The third form of reciprocity, house holding, grounded relationships of (re)distribution into general reciprocity for all. Within the traditional first-century economy, household members interacted with one another with regard to resources and in such a way that the wider community was able to function.

---

16. Marshall D. Sahlins, "On the Sociology of Primitive Exchange," in Michael Banton, ed., *The Relevance of Models for Social Anthropology* (London: Tavistock, 1963), 145-49. For more on the various kinds of reciprocity, see T. F. Carney, *The Shape of the Past: Models and Antiquity* (Lawrence, KS: Coronado Press, 1975), 166ff.

17. Stephen Charles Mott, "The Use of the Bible in Social Ethics II; The Use of the New Testament: Part I," *Transformation* 1 (1984): 25.

Based on his Damascus experience, Paul discovered that the God he had now come to believe in was the God of all and that God's loving kindness or *chrēstotēs* was to become a manifestation of the fruit of the Spirit's love in the house churches that he had evangelized. This became especially clear when he was urging the Galatians to move from an approach to life based on a separatist understanding of covenantal nomism to an approach that would reflect the Damascus experience of the general reciprocity of servant love (discussed in Chapter 5) and would reveal God's unique self-giving love, which demanded nothing in return.

Unfortunately, while Paul envisioned a new creation of general reciprocity for all God's children, his own households of faith still perpetuated the cultural dynamics that undermined the possibility of that ever happening. Consequently we cannot "read into" Paul what Paul was unable consciously to understand. Thus, whether the reciprocity was general, balanced, or negative, it all could only be understood through the lens of the patriarchal and patronage culture of his day, the dynamics of which kept Paul from realizing that their patterns actually undermined the fulfillment of the pneumatological vision that guided his whole Christology and ecclesiology and that must guide our reflections as well. In this sense, I find helpful the insight of Borg and Crossan regarding the concept of "house" or *oikia/oikos* (which I have called elsewhere "the assumed primary metaphor" vis-à-vis the house churches in the New Testament world). They write,

> Paul's vision for the world is a transcendental projection of his vision of home and family. That is the only other model he has to work with. He does not work from universal human rights or democratic social privileges. He is thinking of the householder, who in a patriarchal society is usually the father, so we can with full integrity replace the gendered word "father" with the ungendered world "householder" or even "homemaker." . . . For Paul, the Householder of the earth-house, the Homemaker of the world-home, is God, and all people are God's dependents and God's children. God as Householder is the One who has responsibility and charge for the home's extended family.[18]

---

18. Marcus J. Borg and John Dominic Crossan, *The First Paul: Reclaiming the Radical Visionary behind the Church's Conservative Icon* (New York: HarperOne, 2009), 114. For a fine development of the meaning of various familial terms in Galatians and how they all were articulated by Paul from an uncritiqued patriarchal worldview, see Jeremy Punt, "He Is Heavy . . . He's My Brother: Unravelling Fraternity in Paul (Galatians)," *Neotestamentica* 46.1 (2012): 153-71.

From this perspective of God as universal householder, the followers of Jesus Christ must deal with one another as members of the same household or family. Thus, clearly Paul's understanding of the new creation went beyond his world's categories of circumcision and uncircumcision as the delineators of belonging to the Christian community, so that, if anyone was "in Christ," there could no longer be negative reciprocity (for sure) nor even balanced reciprocity; the only kind of "faith working through love" required a new kind of family where everyone would be servant of everyone else, no matter what those "others" had done to separate themselves from that love.

General reciprocity, then, represented the kind of *ḥesed* cited above by Pope John Paul II; it was to be given, *despite* the others' works of the flesh. This manifestation of the Spirit's love was to be extended to everyone, beginning with those in the household, the family, of faith itself, but not ending there (see 5:10).

Paul's Mystical Understanding of the Eucharist

Building on what we noted in Chapter 4 about the dynamics of a mystical experience, including a sense of being one with everyone and everything, it's not surprising to find echoes of Paul's Damascus experience in his understanding of the Eucharist: both involved his realization that they were the embodiment of the risen Christ in each member of the community. Thus, there could be no divisions in either expression of this risen body. Consequently, it is understandable why he was as adamant about failures to demonstrate this mystical reality in his First Letter to the Corinthians as he was about the dynamics in the Galatian churches that represent the divisions associated with the works of the flesh (5:16-21).

It is evident from the opening chapter of 1 Corinthians that the members of the house churches there were divided around exclusivist and competing claims regarding their social identity based on their human founders (Paul, Cephas, Apollo) (1 Cor. 1:10-13). In Paul's mind was this just another form of separatism that he railed against with the covenantal nomism of the Teachers' efforts to promote their gospel among the Galatians?

As the letter develops, he identifies still other divisive dynamics in and among the members of the various house churches—especially when they came together to break bread. These factions were based along class lines with the result that at these "Eucharists" some were being sated and others were going hungry (1 Cor. 11:17-34). This reality was undermining what he understood from his Damascus experience to be a violation of their participation in the body of Christ. Consequently, because they assembled to celebrate themselves as the Eucharistic body of Christ but were divided, they were sinning against this body. If they were celebrating the Eucharist they had to be grounded in communion if this was to be ritualized in Communion. Not only this; if there were any among them who were out of communion with another in any way, those divisions and factions had to be reconciled. There could be no sinful brokenness among the members of the house churches when they broke the bread.

I was blessed with my own mystical understanding of this mystical meaning of the Eucharist in an experience in 1973; it has been indelibly etched in my approach to the Eucharist every time I am part of its celebration.

I was at a summer live-in course studying Spanish with around twenty other students and teachers. One of the students was a semiretired nun, whom I'll call "Mary Agnes"; she had come to the course with her own brokenness and pain as a result of serious divisions in her community. Besides this, once at the program, she was feeling more and more broken because she was not able to learn Spanish the way she had hoped; she was finding it increasingly difficult to remember the words and grammar.

Each morning all of us would gather for the Eucharist, sitting in a circle. We would share our reflections on the readings of the day during the Word Service and then move into the Eucharist Service, passing the consecrated host among us, receiving together. After a few weeks of increasing frustration, during our faith-sharing Mary Agnes poured out her pent-up pain, then broke down in tears and left the gathering. She didn't return.

At the time the Eucharistic bread was passed around, my eyes were opened: I recognized Mary Agnes—in her brokenness—in the breaking of the bread. Immediately I also found in the broken bread the farmer with whom I talked as I walked on the road, studying my Spanish vocabulary. The area was experiencing a drought, and he was deeply in debt; he was anxious that he would lose his family's farm. However, my awareness of who it was in that Eucharistic body of Christ did not stop there: at the same time I found millions of people from the Sahelian area of East Africa in their brokenness because of the drought they were experiencing; I was receiving them; they were part of me; they could not be separated from my care. This led to an immediate experience of the whole earth in its brokenness becoming part of me. It was then that I recognized the Christ in each and every part, especially in the brokenness in each and every member. And if I was going to say "Amen," I had to receive them as part of my body.

They were my body; they were my blood. I was in them; they were in me. We were one. I might not be able to do anything about their pain, but my kindness and care had to be extended to them or I would be violating them as members of the Eucharistic body. Not only that, even if they were not baptized members of that body, they were in the Eucharist as members of the cosmic body of the Word-Enfleshed as the Christ. I had to be in communion with the whole universe.

If 1 Cor. 13:4 had shown that love is kind, that love had to be extended to everyone, without distinctions about "kind," in ways that would ensure they were all "kin," even more, Paul would remind the Galatians that faith working through love had to be expressed in ways that would "work for the good of all, and especially for those of the [Eucharistic] family of faith" (6:10).

Conclusion

The *chrēstotēs* that is faithful to God's *hesed* has no boundaries. If a mother or father willingly gets up in the middle of the night to meet the needs of her/his crying child, our practice of *chrēstotēs* is premised on the conviction that we are all God's children and members of God's household and that this kind of care must be extended, at least ideally (if not practically), toward everyone, especially those, as Paul says, in the household of faith. I got a sense of this in the new year's reflection of Fred Cavaiani, a former classmate of mine who left our Capuchin order to get married but who still is very much part of the brotherhood.

In his always-inspiring "The Counselor's Corner," which runs every other week in a Southeast Michigan newspaper, Fred wrote a column entitled "The New Year Begins with One Simple Resolution," which is a great way to cultivate loving kindness. "I would suggest that, as we begin the new year, we make just one simple resolution to be renewed every morning. If this resolution is made it will change the world into a much happier planet. The resolution is simply this: Every morning or evening make a determination that this coming day you will be kind and loving to everyone no matter how someone else treats you."[19]

When Fred invites us to "be kind and loving to everyone no matter how someone else treats you," I believe he is getting to the heart of how the Jews understood/understand *hesed* and what Paul meant by *chrēstotēs*: no matter what the other does, even if they are our "enemies," *chrēstotēs* demands that we practice toward them God's unconditional care. This is clear from

---

19. Fred Cavaiani, The Counselor's Corner, "The New Year Begins with One Simple Resolution," *Legal News,* January 6, 2015.

Rom. 2:4: "Do you not realize that God's kindness (*chrēstos*) is meant to lead you to repentance?"

The assumption behind Paul's challenge to the Romans is that Christian repentance occurs within the ongoing, unconditional kindness of an understanding God who is always awaiting our conversion from sin. Thus, if the members of the house churches were to "continue in God's kindness (Rom. 11:22), a key sign that this is happening would be their way of responding to other members of the house churches (and, indeed, all people) who have sinned. In my mind, this is the best way to understand (and apply to oneself) Paul's challenge to the Romans: "Do you not realize that God's kindness (*chrēstos*) is meant to lead you to repentance" (Rom. 2:4). Continuing in God's kindness (Rom. 11:22) demands that we show that same *chrēstotēs* to others in their sin, if we truly want to lead them to repentance.

In my experience, it is precisely in those moments of being "caught" in my sin and failing, and even my mistakes and missteps, by someone who has shown me *chrēstotēs*, precisely in those embarrassing situations, that I have been given a glimpse of God. The "angels of kindness" in my life have served as my liberators and saviors. Indeed, I believe that *chrēstotēs* represents the godly way of relating to others through good works that saves them (liberates/frees them) from all those times they "miss the mark" or sin.

The connection of "acts of kindness" with "good works" brings us to our next chapter.

Chapter 10

Cultivating Goodness as a Sign of Love's Generosity That We Are to Image

Most of the time these days, I wear two hats. Seventy percent of my time is spent preaching retreats and reflections and writing on contemporary spirituality (such as this book). The other 30 percent is spent promoting "corporate social responsibility" with the investments of my province and also my Order. In this capacity I also am executive director of SGI/CRI, the Seventh Generation Interfaith Coalition for Responsible Investment. I represent it at the Interfaith Center on Corporate Responsibility (ICCR) in New York. ICCR is a coalition of over two hundred Protestant, Jewish, and Catholic institutional investors (like my province and Order) who want to be sure we are not only doing well with our investments but *doing good.*

Goodness (*agathosynē*) or *doing good* is the fifth sign of living in the love of the Spirit and has been translated as "generosity." Given the Jewish background of both Jesus and Paul, it was not sufficient just to "do good" to those in the household of faith; rather, as shown in the previous chapter, goodness and kindness had to go beyond all boundaries, especially toward those people who are most marginalized and impoverished. Furthermore, as we will see in this chapter, *not* acting in the face of the structures that create or sustain unjust boundaries makes one an *evildoer.* But more of that later. Here I want to continue my reflections on "doing good" in corporate America, where the evils of human rights violations and inequality too often continue unabated.

For years I have been concerned about wealth, income, and the wage gap. During the writing of this book, it seemed my clippings from the *Wall Street Journal, The Economist, Bloomberg's BusinessWeek,* and the business pages of the *New York Times* included many articles addressing the subject.[1] Almost

---

1. Typical of these news items were articles noting the warning of Janet L. Yellen, the Federal Reserve chairwoman; see Pedro Nicolaci da Costa, "Yellen Decries Widening Wealth Disparity," *Wall Street Journal,* October 18-19, 2014, A2; and Binyamin Appel-

simultaneously, reports were issued highlighting the consequence of stag-
nant wages on the flat earnings of most retail corporations.[2] Then a report
appeared in the *Harvard Business Review,* pointing out that the pay gap
between CEOs and workers was even greater than most Americans realize.[3] All this was clear enough, but, I wondered, what can be done about it?

Before long I found an answer. An article by an auxiliary bishop, Robert W. McElroy (now bishop of San Diego), appeared at almost the same
time in *America,* entitled "Market Assumptions." In it McElroy refers to
Pope Francis's concern, expressed in *Evangelii Gaudium,* about structural
issues of poverty and inequality. He begins the article by referring to "a
tweet read around the world this past April [2014 when] Pope Francis told
over 10 million online followers, in nine different languages, 'Inequality
is the root of social evil.'" McElroy then concludes, "The pope's diagnosis
did not go over well with many American Catholics, who criticized the
statement as being radical, simplistic and confusing." He writes, "But that
Francis' teaching on the scandal of economic inequality in our world has
inspired a decidedly mixed response has not deterred the pope from speaking on this theme, one very close to his heart, repeatedly and forcefully."
In fact, Francis's tweet simply reflected what he had taught earlier in his
apostolic exhortation *The Joy of the Gospel* (No. 202):

> The need to resolve the structural causes of poverty cannot be
> delayed. . . . As long as the problems of the poor are not radically
> resolved by rejecting the absolute autonomy of markets and finan-
> cial speculation and by attacking the structural causes of inequal-
> ity, no solution will be found for the world's problems, or, for that
> matter, to any problems. Inequality is the root of social ills."[4]

I decided to do something. In my capacity as director of SGI/CRI I took
the articles noted above to my regular fall meetings, which are meant primarily to determine what shareholder resolutions we will file with the various companies in our portfolios. I suggested that we file a resolution with

baum, "Yellen Issues a Warning on the Risks of Rising Inequality," *New York Times,* October 18, 2014, B1.

2. Brendan V. Duke and Ike Lee, "Retailer Revelations: Why America's Struggling
Middle Class Has Businesses Scared," October 2014 (Washington, DC: American Prog-
ress); also Rick Romell, "Low-Wage Jobs Grew Fastest in Wisconsin since 2000, New
Study Shows," *Milwaukee Journal Sentinel,* October 28, 2014.

3. Roberto A. Ferdman, "The Pay Gap between CEOs and Workers Is Much Worse
than You Realize," Wonkblog, *Washington Post,* September 25, 2014.

4. Robert W. McElroy, "Market Assumptions," *America,* November 3, 2014, 14-18.

those retail companies who have indicated that their own weak returns are influenced by workers' flat wages. So I sculpted a shareholder resolution that would address the inequality of the top executive wages vis-à-vis the average worker. Part of the resolution addressed the average top CEO pay ($12,259,000) compared to the average worker. In the United States the gap was 354 times (well beyond that of second-place Switzerland, which had a gap of 148 times).[5]

While I decided to do the ratios for companies like Kohl's and Walmart, McDonalds and Wendy's, there was another company on my radar because of a recent double-page ad it had placed in the *New York Times*: Whole Foods Market. Under the banner "Values Matter," it used the image of *ripeness,* which spoke to me of the thesis of this book: cultivating the fruit of love into ripeness:

> We're hungrier for them than we ever realized. / We want to know where things come from. / We care what happens to them along the way.
>
> We want to trust our sources. / We want to have the information to make meaningful choices about what we decide to buy and support. / We want people, and animals, and the places our food comes from to be treated fairly.
>
> The time is ripe.
>
> We are part of a growing consciousness that's bigger than food— one that champions what's good, and the greater good, too.
>
> Where value is inseparable from values.[6]

Probably the combination of wanting to do something to address the issue of inequality and being struck by the Whole Foods claim to being "part of a growing consciousness that's bigger than food—one that champions what's good, and the greater good, too"—while writing this chapter on "what's good[ness]," made me decide to see if Whole Foods was, in fact, involved in efforts to show that the average workers were "treated fairly," as the add purported.

I began my investigation cynically, only to be immediately chastised by the data. Indeed, Whole Foods Market, where the average worker makes about $15.00 an hour with health benefits, was markedly different from

---

5. Ferdman, "Pay Gap."

6. Ad for Whole Foods Market, "Values Matter," *New York Times*, October 22, 2014, A14-A15.

the average U.S.-based company on our SGI/CRI list for potential filing of shareholder resolutions.[7] CNN Money reported,

> Whole Foods co-CEO Walter Robb may not make as much as some of his fellow corporate chiefs. But that's all right with him. After all, there are benefits to keeping his pay tied to that of his workers.
>
> "I can look a team member in the eye and say I'm doing exactly what you're doing," Robb, a co-CEO of the grocery giant, recently told *Fortune*, referencing a company policy that caps executive pay at 19 times the average employee's salary. Though the policy only caps salary and not total compensation, Robb's total pay package was a relatively low $1.2 million in 2012, according to *Business-week*.[8]

I decided we did not need to file a shareholder resolution with Whole Foods Market; instead we needed to compliment them.

Unfortunately, the example of the CEO at Whole Foods Market points to someone who has *done good* in the midst of an evildoing structure of injustice. Thus, while "market forces" may justify the 354-times pay disparity in the average company, an understanding of Pauline goodness demands something more challenging. This is all the more necessary when one considers an additional piece of information from the perspective of the biblical adage "To those who have, more will be given while from those who have not, even that will be taken." The *Chronicle of Philanthropy* released a study at the same time as the articles cited above (September 29, 2014) indicating that the share of income donated to charity by Americans who earned $200,000 or more decreased by 4.6 percent between 2006 and 2012. Those earning less than $100,000 gave 4.5 percent more of their income to charity.[9]

Some renderings of the "fruits of the Spirit," such as *The Catechism of the Catholic Church*,[10] add "generosity" to "goodness" (*agathos*) to create a list

---

7. Our effort received quite a bit of press, including a front-page story in the *Milwaukee Journal Sentinel*; see Rick Romell, "Retailers Urged to Raise Wages, Close Pay Gap: Activist Pushes to Get Issue on Annual Meeting Agendas" (http://www.jsonline.com), November 24, 2014. See also the *National Catholic Reporter*, November 26, 2014, http://ncronline.org.

8. See http://www.huffingtonpost.com.

9. Jess Bidgood, "Study Finds Shifts in Charitable Giving after Recession," *New York Times*, October 5, 2014.

10. "The *Fruits* of the Spirit," *Catechism of the Catholic Church*, 1832 (Washington, DC: United States Catholic Conference, 1994), 451.

of twelve "fruits." From the data above, it seems those who are most generous are those who have the fewest "goods!" Arguably it might be helpful to return to Jerome's twelve "fruits of the Spirit" just so that we might learn again the power of generosity in our lives and relationships as a sign of how God's goodness is being manifest in and through us!

How God's Goodness Is to Be Reflected in Those Who Have Been Made "Good" and Who Are to "Do Good"

Nowhere but in Paul's Letter to the Romans do we find so developed a notion of God's goodness and its implication for our moral lives of "doing good" and "avoiding evil."[11] At the very beginning of the epistle (Rom. 1:18-32) Paul identifies God as the source of good while noting that those who truly grasp the nature of God, especially as revealed in nature, can only do good.

In her reflections on Paul's notion of God's goodness, Dorothea Bertschmann identifies it as a manifestation of God's faithful, abundant, universal love, even in face of absolute human sinfulness. While not denying the reality of God's wrath in the face of human sinfulness, she writes that it is because of God's love that "God seeks to win back bad people for goodness, not to condemn them. This approach is 'asymmetric' because in it God's response to evil is goodness."[12] Having stressed this point she goes on to discuss God's *wrath* as well:

> While God's reaction to all-pervasive sinfulness is God's present and future *wrath*, denoting God's passionate and deeply involved stance towards evil, the emotional force behind God's salvific action is *love*. Paul uses the term sparsely but very effectively in [Rom] 5.5, 8 and [Rom] 8.35, 37, 39. Love is what motivated God and what becomes part of the innermost existence of the believers through the spirit. ([Rom] 5.5). God's love precedes human response to reaching out to weak and hostile people ([Rom] 5.6, 8).[13]

On August 19, 1866, while on a retreat, Sister Therese Couderc, now St. Thérèse Couderc, the founder of the Sisters of the Cenacle, wrote a let-

---

11. Dorothea H. Bertschmann writes: "We find 'good' and 'bad' as a pair in Romans 2.9-10; 9.11; 12.9, 17, 21; 13.3a; 13.3b and 4b; 14.20; 16.19; and in especially high frequency in Romans 7.12-21"; see Bertschmann, "The Good, the Bad and the State—Rom 13.1-7 and the Dynamic of Love," *New Testament Studies* 60 (2014): 236.

12. Ibid., 239.

13. Ibid., 240.

ter to her superior that has come to be called her "Vision of Goodness." Referring to "the Good God," she recalled in a somewhat lengthy passage elements of what we have termed a mystical experience, where her sense of being connected to God and everything around her was tied to the reality of "goodness" itself. She writes,

> I had, a few days ago, an insight which consoled me very much. It was during my thanksgiving, when I was making a few reflections upon the goodness of God, and how could one not think of this at such a time, of the infinite goodness, uncreated goodness, the source of all goodness! And without this there would be no goodness whatsoever, whether in humans or in other creatures. I was extremely touched by these reflections when I saw written as in letters of gold this word *Goodness,* which I repeated for a long time with an indescribable sweetness. I beheld it, I say, written upon all creatures, animate and inanimate, rational or not, all bore this name of goodness. I saw it even upon the chair that served as a *prie-dieu.* I understood then that all these creatures have of good and all the services and assistance that we receive from each of them is a benefit which we owe to the goodness of our God who has communicated to them something of His infinite goodness so that we may meet it in everything and everywhere. Yet all that I am here describing is nothing; if I could but tell you something of what I experienced in that moment, what a joy it would be, but it is impossible to describe it: that which is divine cannot be described. Only I am no longer surprised that the saints were enraptured at the sight of the goodness of which so many souls know so little; this impression stayed with me several days, during which I could find no pleasure in anything save only in what I had seen and experienced. Please, my very Reverend Mother, thank this divine Goodness for me and beg Him that I may no longer be so unworthy, for I find myself no better.[14]

Another saint who was "enraptured at the sight of the goodness of which so many souls know so little" was St. Bonaventure. Indeed it might be

---

14. Thérèse Couderc, "Vision of Goodness," Letter to Mother de Larochénegly, August 10, 1866, *Anthology of Congregation Documents* (Chicago: Congregation of Our Lady of the Retreat in the Cenacle, 1985), 178. I am grateful to Sr. Barbara Ehrier for sharing this with me during a retreat I gave on "The Fruit of the Spirit," which she attended in 2014.

said that the idea of God's goodness is central to his theology because for him God is a triune community of love, and love is the highest good; God is supreme goodness and the "fountain of fullness" of that love which is expressed in such a creative goodness that human beings are made in its image and called to reflect that divine goodness.

His understanding of God as supreme goodness led Bonaventure to posit this same diffusing goodness as manifest in creation itself. He writes, "For the diffusion in time in creation is no more than a center or point in relation to the immensity of the divine goodness." In this diffusion of one's self there is communicated "to the other" one's "entire substance and nature."[15]

Pope Francis has said, "The goodness of God does not have limits and does not discriminate against anyone."[16] In a similar way Richard Rohr has written, "The goodness of God fills all the gaps of the universe, without discrimination or preference. God is the gratuity of absolutely everything. The space in between everything is not space at all but Spirit. God is the "'goodness glue' that holds the dark and light of things together."[17]

In commenting on God's supreme goodness as a manifestation of God's triune self-giving love, Ilia Delio writes that "we can say that God's *being* is the embodiment of the self-diffusive good. Being is embodied love—and agapic love which possesses nothing for itself but rather gives itself entirely and completely to the other just as the Father eternally diffuses his entire good to the Son and Spirit." Moreover, this self-diffusing goodness and love do not stop here. Delio adds, "Agapic love is the foundation of all created reality." Indeed, "we can say that creation is truly loved into being" and that "the consummation of the human person and of all created reality is not participation in absolute being but in absolute good or love."[18]

The idea that God's goodness is revealed in everyone and everything can be found in the first chapter of Genesis. When God has finished creation with humankind made in the image of God, God finds that *everything* God made is "very good" (Gen. 1:31). Because God is love, the only driving force for creation and everything in it is love. However, when God looks at everything that God has made, because of love, and finds it "very good,"

---

15. St. Bonaventure, "The Soul's Journey into God" 6.2, in *Bonaventure*, trans. Ewert Cousins (New York/Ramsey/Toronto: Paulist Press, 1978), 103.

16. Pope Francis, Address, St. Peter's Square, October 12, 2014, http://en.radio vaticana.va.

17. Richard Rohr, *Immortal Diamond: The Search for Our True Self* (San Francisco: Jossey-Bass, 2013), xix-xx.

18. Ilia Delio, OSF, *Crucified Love: Bonaventure's Mysticism of the Crucified Christ* (Quincy, IL: Franciscan Press, 1998), 75.

then everything in creation is good not because of anything it has done but because of everything that God has done. We are made in the image of God's divine goodness, and, as such, our vocation is to reveal that goodness in the way we "do good."

However, when we examine more deeply the second story of creation in Genesis (starting in Gen. 2:4b), we find that the divine goodness, which constitutes the ground of our being and which we are to image, has been compromised by the choices we make that involve the tree of knowledge and the doing of "good and evil" (Gen. 2:9, 17; 3:5, 22). When we embrace the ways of evil that undermine the divine goodness we find ourselves outside the garden of God's love to the degree we freely separate ourselves from that divine goodness and live in sin.

The word "goodness," which Paul understood as a fruit of the Spirit's love, is *agathōsynē* (5:22). *Agathōsynē* is used only one other time in the genuine Pauline letters, in a passage where Paul speaks of his confidence that the brothers and sisters in the church(es) of Rome are "full of goodness, filled with all knowledge, and able to instruct one another" (Rom. 15:14). Because they are images of the God who is good, the Christians are not called only to be full of God; they are called to reflect God's goodness in their care for others. This care cannot be exclusive in the way of the covenant nomists; it must extend to all. In the words of Pope Francis (who is offering an alternative to canonical nomism), "The goodness of God has no bounds and does not discriminate against anyone . . . no one has the right to feel privileged or to claim an exclusive right. All of this induces us to break the habit of conveniently placing ourselves at the centre, as did the High Priests and the Pharisees."[19]

To understand more fully the universality of what Paul meant by goodness, we will consider two others words for "good" that Paul uses, more or less interchangeably: *agathos* and *kalos*.[20] Indeed, I believe that unless we

---

19. Pope Francis, "No One Is Excluded," Angelus Reflection, October 12, 2014, *L'Osservatore Romano* 47.42, October 17, 2014.

20. A clear place in the Gospels that links *agathos* and *kalos* together has much to do with the theme of this book dealing with the "fruit" of the Spirit. This is found in Matt. 7:17-19: "every good [*agathos*] tree bears good [*kalos*] fruit, but the bad tree bears bad fruit. A good [*agathos*] tree cannot bear bad fruit, nor can a bad tree bear good [*kalos*] fruit. Every tree that does not bear good [*kalos*] fruit is cut down and thrown into the fire." For further discussion on the connection between *agathos* and *kalos* as "good" having different objects, see James R. Harrison, *Paul's Language of Grace in Its Graeco-Roman Context* (Tübingen: Mohr Siebeck, 2003), 314-21.

link *agathos* and *kalos,* it will be difficult, if not impossible, to understand what Paul in Galatians means by that fruit of love which he calls *agathōsynē.*

In Rom. 2:6 Paul connects the "good," "God," "heaven," and "eternal life" when he warns that on the day of judgment we will be judged by our good deeds. A few verses later he attributes "glory and honor and peace for everyone who does good, the Jew first and also the Greek," concluding that "God shows no partiality" (Rom. 2:10). In other words, the doing of good is the ultimate judgment that will determine our standing with God, no matter who we are (at least according to Matt. 25:31-46). If God is good, those who "do good" are being godly, and this is the ultimate justification. At the same time, in one of the most hopeful passages in the whole Pauline corpus, we are the ones who "know that all things work together for good (*agathos*) for those who love God, who are called according to his purpose" (Rom. 8:28). It is this love, in which we are called, that grounds our very being even before we have done or do *anything,* whether it is good (*agathos*) or bad (Rom. 9:11). This call invites us to a life of doing good in a way that is other than that of the "world." Thus, in another one of Paul's classic lines, we are warned: "Do not be conformed to this world, but be transformed by the renewing of your minds, so that you may discern what is the will of God—what is good (*agathos*) and acceptable and perfect" (Rom. 12:2).

In Rom. 5:7 Paul talks about a "good" (*agathos*) person in a commonly understood manner today: one who *does good* in a way that makes him or her *good.* Outside of Romans, Paul uses *agathos* once in 2 Corinthians (5:10), in a passage where he talks about being judged "for what has been done in the body, whether good or evil," and twice in his Letter to Philemon, where he refers to "the good we may do for Christ" (6) and urges Philemon to do a "good deed" (*agathos*) toward his slave Onesimus voluntarily (14).

Addressing Obstacles to Goodness

In *Mysticism,* Evelyn Underhill notes that when people are "awakened" by some kind of mystical experience that gives them a new understanding of what reality truly entails (i.e., universal connectedness), they realize they also must "get rid of all those elements of normal experience which are not in harmony with [that] reality: of illusion, evil, imperfection of every kind."[21] Consequently, because God is all-good and since mystical union involves

---

21. Evelyn Underhill, *Mysticism: A Study in the Nature and Development of Man's Spiritual Consciousness* (New York: New American Library, 1974), 198.

the process of being transformed into God's goodness, she concludes that "the self must be purged of all that stands between it and goodness" itself.[22]

While he addresses more evident forms of "doing evil," Paul was also concerned about a more sinister form of "doing evil" vis-à-vis his churches. Pope Francis calls one of its contemporary manifestations the "globalization of indifference": how we close our eyes to evils like consumerism and ecological degradation. "The only thing necessary for the triumph of evil is that good men do nothing" may be the most popular quote of all time (with questionable attribution). However, it is biblically sound. In the Jewish mind, which linked injustice with evil, to do nothing in the face of injustice was "doing evil": thus evil triumphs when good people do nothing to remedy it. This becomes all the more so in situations of systemic injustice.

As we read in the Synoptics and in Paul, the mandate to do good was basic to the commandments, and this "good" must be extended in ever-widening circles. However, in the struggle between good and evil, there were and are many nuances. Doing good involved actions that were constructive of community, fruitful living (as in the "fruit of the Spirit"), works of justice that showed an embrace of God's will. Not to be doing such, especially in the face of evildoers and evildoing, identified the one indifferent to the presence of evil as an evildoer. Thus the Romans were "to be wise in what is good (*agathos*) and guileless in what is evil" (Rom. 16:19).

Convinced that good cannot come from evildoing (Rom. 3:8), Paul addresses a key element of "doing good" in Romans. He refers to dynamics that operate in the community, either among the members or with their critics. It seems that, even though nothing is "unclean," because of creation making all things "good" and also because, in the Lord Jesus Christ, nothing is unclean, it is clear that, for those who think something is unclean, even that which is clean becomes unclean. Hence, Paul urged the Romans not to let such people attribute to them ill will, even though they actually were doing something clean or good, so that good might not be spoken of as evil (Rom. 14:16). The fact that this is even mentioned indicates the strong possibility that there were serious disagreements in ideology. After all, a key ingredient in polarization is attributing evil or, at least, ill will, as a motivation of those who do good.

This identification of good actions with evil intent gets played out in another good/evil scenario that is one of the most famous in the Pauline literature; in this passage (Rom. 7:11-25), the word *agathos* is used four times, while its "sister," *kalos*, is used three times, in ways that parallel each other.

---

22. Ibid., 199.

For sin, seizing an opportunity in the commandment, deceived me and through it killed me. So the law is holy, and the commandment is holy and just and good (*agathē*).

Did what is good (*agathon*), then, bring death to me? By no means! It was sin, working death in me through what is good (*agathou*), in order that sin might be shown to be sin, and through the commandment might become sinful beyond measure.

For we know that the law is spiritual; but I am of the flesh, sold into slavery under sin. I do not understand my own actions. For I do not do what I want, but I do the very thing I hate. Now if I do what I do not want, I agree that the law is good (*kalos*). But in fact it is no longer I that do it, but sin that dwells within me. (Rom. 7:11-17)

If we are honest with ourselves, Paul's words here serve as a narration of the struggle between the good of the Spirit and the works of the flesh that play out in the lives of each of us. I know it is so in my life both in how I am tempted by "the flesh" to fill up the hole in my heart that tells me I am "not *good enough*"[23] and in how I too often get caught in a key "work of the flesh" noted by Paul and stressed so much by Pope Francis, gossip. While Paul specifically may not have listed it among his "works of the flesh," he did find it in his house churches (6:19-21). In a similar way, I find that gossip about others represents the main obstacle to my contribution to communal life in the Spirit. Consequently, given my ways (subtle and not so subtle) of gossiping, I too can say with Paul, "I do not do what I want, but I do the very thing I hate."

Pope Francis has equated the destructive role of gossiping in our communities and relationships with the planting of bombs. In a homily addressed to the Vatican security forces on September 27, 2014, he said, "There are bombs in here, very dangerous bombs in here." "Please, keep your eyes open, because in the darkness of so many wicked lives, the enemy has sown weeds." He explained, "The worst bomb inside the Vatican is gossip," which "threatens the life of the church and the life of [the Vatican] every day," because it "sows destruction" and "destroys the lives of others."

As I read this, I found myself indicted by the pope when I realized how I have been one of those who also has sown the destructive seeds of gossip. But, I am not alone: it consoled me (a bit) to read that he also said that "the

---

23. For more on this dynamic, see Michael H. Crosby, *The Dysfunctional Church: Addiction and Codependency in the Family of Catholicism* (Eugene, OR: Wipf & Stock, 2011), 147-73.

pope is not immune to this temptation." It's a danger "for me, too," because "the devil gives you that yearning." As a concrete way to "crack down on backstabbing," the pope urged the security people to stop whoever might be doing the gossiping by saying, "Please sir, please ma'am, please father, please sister, please your Excellency, please your Eminence, please Holy Father, don't gossip; that's not allowed here."[24]

Being aware of the subtle ways the works of the flesh undermine our desire to do good is critical for our spiritual journey. At the same time we can be encouraged by Walter Grundmann, who in his entry on *agathos* in the *Theological Dictionary of the New Testament*, states that nothing can be considered "good" or any action can be defined as "good" apart from its connectedness to the only one who *is* good. Thus our consolation comes from realizing that our desire to do good, even when it is undermined by the works of the flesh, is what the good God sees and judges as what is ultimately the good in us and the good we do. Building on Jesus's statement that God alone is good (Mark 10:18; Matt. 19:17; Luke 18:19), Grundmann writes that the "two statements, 1) that God alone and no other is *agathos* and 2) that the μέλλοντα ἀγαθά are the only real *agatha* because in them sin and death are done away, give us the insight that strictly speaking there is nothing in this world that deserves the predicate *agathon*, and that there is no one who has the predicate *agathos*." Having made this point, he moves to the second section of the famous Pauline passage above by noting something that may not be cosmologically grounded but is faithful to the religious and ethical message of Jesus Christ: "This insight is complete by the statement of Paul which deals a mortal blow to every other humanistic or religious conception of life": [25]

> For I know that nothing good (*agathon*) dwells within me, that is, in my flesh. I can will what is right, but I cannot do it. For I do not do the good (*kalon*) I want, but the evil I do not want is what I do. Now if I do what I do not want, it is no longer I that do it, but sin that dwells within me.
>
> So I find it to be a law that when I want to do what is good (*kalon*), evil lies close at hand. For I delight in the law of God in my inmost self, but I see in my members another law at war with the law of my mind, making me captive to the law of sin that dwells in my mem-

---

24. Pope Francis, Homily, September 27, 2014, http://www.catholicnews.com.

25. Walter Grundmann, "ἀγαθός," in Gerhard Kittel, ed., *Theological Dictionary of the New Testament* (trans. and ed. Geoffrey W. Bromiley; Grand Rapids: Eerdmans, 1964), 1:16.

bers. Wretched man that I am! Who will rescue me from this body
of death? Thanks be to God through Jesus Christ our Lord!

So then, with my mind I am a slave to the law of God, but with
my flesh I am a slave to the law of sin. (Rom. 7:18-22)

Reading this passage, as well as others such as Rom. 13:8-10 and Gal.
5:14, one would be wrong to say that Paul rejected the law itself; indeed
all these passages show the law itself to be a revelation of the good and, as
Charles Cosgrove writes, "a witness to his gospel (Rom 3:21)."[26] Rather, it
is when the evil of separation from others becomes justified as the law that
Paul minced no words of challenge; this was the evil he rejected as false
covenantal nomism. No wonder the early house churches prayed in their
Eucharistic prayers the same thing we pray today: "deliver us from evil!"

Before finishing this section, I think it is important to reiterate a caveat
about "doing good" that has been raised by Pope Francis. In a speech discussing the "shadow side" of both liberals and conservatives, he spoke of
"the temptation to a destructive tendency to goodness [i.e., *buonismo*], that
in the name of a deceptive mercy binds the wounds without first curing
them and treating them; that treats the symptoms and not the causes and
the roots. It is the temptation of the "do-gooders," of the fearful, and also of
the so-called progressives and liberals.[27]

Cultivating Doing Good

A key purpose of this book is to offer suggestions for how, as we evolve into
greater forms of cosmic love, we might be helped in our disciplines to do so
through the cultivation of the signs of that love revealed in "the fruit of the
Spirit" (of love). A key manifestation of this love is revealed in how we practice "goodness" in our lives and relationships. Indeed, some might argue
that "goodness" is *the key* in this effort because, as we have seen above, that

---

26. Charles H. Cosgrove, "Did Paul Value Ethnicity?," *Catholic Biblical Quarterly* 68
(2006): 289.

27. Pope Francis, Closing Speech at the 2014 Synod on the Family (http://en.radio
vaticana.va). In the same speech he also addressed the opposite temptation, that is "a
temptation to hostile inflexibility [rigidity], that is, wanting to close oneself within the
written word [the letter], and not allowing oneself to be surprised by God, by the God of
surprises [the spirit]; within the law, within the certitude of what we know and not of what
we still need to learn and to achieve. From the time of Christ, it is the temptation of the
zealous, of the scrupulous, of the solicitous and of the so-called—today—'traditionalists'
and also of the intellectuals."

God who *is love* made humankind to image that love, which Genesis equates with the "doing" of what is "very good" (Gen. 1:26-27).

This became very clear to me while I was writing this chapter in a couple of daily readings from the Scriptures. The first reading for the Mass of the day on November 6, 2014, came from Paul's Letter to the Philippians. According to the "official" translation for the Mass, it concluded that whatever "gains" Paul may have as one who was defined by "the flesh" (expressed, for him, in circumcision) "these I have come to consider a loss because of Christ. More than that, I even consider everything as a loss because of *the supreme good of knowing Christ Jesus my Lord*" (Phil. 3:7-8a; my emphasis).

While it is true that the actual Greek that Paul uses for the *supreme* "good," *hyperechōn*, has for its root neither *agathos* nor *kalos*, nevertheless, its meaning as "eminent," "superior," and "sublime" makes "supreme good" a correct translation. However, as Paul notes, this supreme good has as its object one thing and one thing only: "knowing (*gnōseōs*) Christ Jesus [as] my Lord." The word for "knowing" (*gnōseōs*) that Paul uses here is not the "knowing" that comes from observation of something but the "knowing" that comes from an experience of someone, in this case, Paul's mystical union with Christ at Damascus with its implications for this life and the next. This understanding is reinforced two lines later when he writes: "I want to know (*ginōskō*) Christ and the power of his resurrection and the sharing of his sufferings by becoming like him in his death, if somehow I may attain the resurrection from the dead" (Phil. 3:10-11).

In the same sense and spirit, centuries later, St. Francis of Assisi would echo Paul's insight into seeking and desiring knowledge of the "supreme good" when he wrote in his Earlier Rule (1221) to his brothers, "Let us desire nothing else, let us want nothing else, let nothing else please us and cause us delight except our Creator, Redeemer and Savior, the only true God, Who is the fullness of good, all good, every good, the true good, *Who alone is good.*"[28]

In one of the most beloved passages in the Bible, there is a link between goodness and the kindness discussed in the previous chapter. In a text that has brought much consolation to people who are dying (as I found with my own brother), we read in Psalm 23 that the Lord, who is our shepherd, is the one who promises that goodness and kindness shall follow us all the days of our lives and that we are chosen to "dwell in the house of the Lord" our

---

28. St. Francis of Assisi, "The Earlier Rule," 23.9, in Regis J. Armstrong, O.F.M.Cap., J. A. Wayne Hellmann, O.F.M.Conv., and William J. Short, O.F.M., eds., *Francis of Assisi: Early Documents*, vol. 1 (New York: New City Press, 1999), 85.

whole life long (Ps. 23:6). In another link between the objects of our goodness and those who are to be the recipients of our kindness, so that there will be general reciprocity for all, we hear Pope Francis warn us: "It is not enough to love those who love us. It is not enough to do good to those who do good to us in return. To change the world for the better is it necessary to do good to those who are not able to do the same for us, as our Father did for us in giving us Jesus? How much have we paid for our redemption? Nothing. It was all free. Doing good without expecting anything in return—that is what our Father did for us and what we too must do."[29] What a contrast this approach reveals to the self-interested ways in which so many "do good" today![30]

Another insight from the daily scriptural readings during the writing of this chapter came to me while I was teaching in Berkeley at the School of Applied Theology sabbatical program in November 2014.

I was staying with my Capuchin brothers of the Western Capuchin Province. At the morning's Mass, the Responsorial Psalm was Ps. 34:8. It speaks of the invitation to "taste and see the goodness" of our God. As I listened to the psalm I came to realize that ours is a "journey" into God's goodness. This involves an inner dimension (how we pray) and an outer dimension (how we live). I then recalled St. Bonaventure's classic reflection, *The Soul's Journey into God,* that begins with the senses, such as tasting and seeing, and ends in contemplation. I also recalled a piece by Philip Chard I had read in the *Milwaukee Journal Sentinel* on how we can move from a consciousness of reality mediated through our senses to the highest form of consciousness, that experience of contemplation where we know ourselves connected to everyone and everything.

When I returned from California, I sought out the Chard article and also opened Bonaventure's *The Soul's Journey into God.* While I realized there was not a perfect correlation between the two approaches, I was amazed at the similarities in the processes that Chard the therapist talks about with regard to consciousness and the way Bonaventure the theologian describes the levels of prayer. I parallel their processes in the chart below in the hope that it might serve as a helpful guide for our "journey" into mystical trans-

---

29. Pope Francis, General Audience, St. Peter's Square, September 10, 2014, http://w2.vatican.va.

30. Ian McGuban has shown that data continually reveal that self-interest is at the bottom of most charitable giving; see "Bucket Racket: What Science Can Tell Us about the Strange Reasons We Give to Charity," *New York Times Magazine*, November 16, 2014, 34-36.

formation, especially when we "imagine that human awareness consists of levels of inner experience."[31]

	Philip Chard's "Deep Probe Inward Dissolves Sense of Self"	St. Bonaventure's *The Soul's Journey into God"*
1	Sensation: Being aware of what we are experiencing through our senses and feelings	Sensation: Contemplating the emanations of God in the "vestiges of God" in the sensate world"
2	Visualization: Allowing mental images to arise without trying to control them	Imagination: Contemplating God's Trinitarian image stamped on our natural powers
3	Intuition: Serious meditators and mystics go there: which is the realm of "illuminating insights"	Reason: Contemplating God in the embrace of our journey from purgation to illumination to unification ("perfection")
4	Transition: Here one's sense of self (the ego) starts to evaporate. Mystics develop this "in hopes of growing closer to God"	Understanding: Realizing that all being (all good) is part of one being and this being is grounded in the "being" of God as good.
5	Transformation: "Mystics call it a timeless state of pure being in which the feeling of separation ('me' as distinct from everything else) dissolves, replaced by an experience of complete oneness with the creation, God, one's higher power, etc."	Intelligence: Consciousness that "the good itself is the principal foundation for contemplating the emanations. See, then, and observe that the highest good . . . is said to be self-diffusive, therefore the highest good must be most self-diffusive
7		Ecstasy: This spiritual and mystical experience finds the intellect at rest and "our affection passes over entirely into God"

The connection (in English) between the kindness we discussed in the last chapter and the goodness we are trying to understand in this chapter is evident in the NRSV translation of *agathos* in 1 Thessalonians as "kindly." In it Paul also posits the grounding of this kindness in the Thessalonians' "faith and love." Indicating that he may not have written his letters in one sitting (or, at least, he wrote them over an extended time), Paul writes, "Timothy has just now come to us from you, and has brought us the good news of

---

31. Philip Chard, "Deep Probe Inward Dissolves Sense of Self," Out of My Mind Column, *Milwaukee Journal Sentinel*, March 15, 2014, 2F.

your faith and love. He has told us also that you always remember us kindly and long to see us—just as we long to see you" (1 Thess. 3:6).

One final dimension of "doing good" is critical for our reflection here, that is, "being zealous for the good." In this case, more often than not, the Greek word for "good" is not *agathos* but *kalos*. In his "Misdirected Emulation and Paradoxical Zeal: Paul's Redefinition of 'The Good' as Object of ζῆλος [Zeal] in Galatians 4:12-20," Benjamin Lappenga makes two main points about Paul's use of the term "zeal." First, his zeal for the good (evidenced before his conversion in his persecution of the believers) was redirected to the proclamation of the gospel, thus exposing the "zeal" sought by the Teachers as merely elevating themselves (4:17). Second, Paul invites his readers to *emulate him* in his willingness to be crucified for the sake of the cross as his new definition of "the good" for those who would be zealous Christ-followers.[32] Lappenga elaborates on both notions in his own helpful translation of Gal. 4:17-18 when he speaks of the ones we have called "the Teachers":

> Let's talk about zeal for a moment. They are "zealous" for you—but what they have in mind is not "good"! They want to exclude you so that you will bring them fame by making them objects of your emulation. What is good, as I have just reminded you, is to be zealous for what you yourselves have shown that "the good" really is— so do this always, not just when I am present with you.[33]

When we examine the first of the two usages in Paul about "zeal," which links it with "doing good," we see that, as in our own day when some philanthropists "do good" but want to make sure their names go on a plaque or on a building, "the good" for Paul was not that practiced in the Roman world. Jeremy Gabrielson tells us that, in the Roman world where people continually engaged in efforts at honor and challenges to honor, "the performance of 'the good' became a weapon deployed in self-interest to accumulate honor at the expense of all other competitors" in a way that "reinforced the systemic violence that characterized so many social engagements in the Roman world." In contrast to this, he writes,

> Paul, on the other hand, continued to attempt to persuade his churches to perform "the good," but categorically opposed the

---

32. B. J. Lappenga, "Misdirected Emulation and Paradoxical Zeal: Paul's Redefinition of 'the Good' as Object of ζῆλος in Galatians 4:12-20," *Journal of Biblical Literature* 131.4 (2012): 775-96.

33. Ibid., 782.

"lure of honor" and its implicit endorsement of the systemic violence of the empire. Doing "the good" was for Paul a mark of the community of faith and was motivated not by the opportunity for increased honor . . . but by imitation of or participation in the undignified, cruciform Christ.[34]

Our investigation of understanding what Paul meant by *zeal for the good* can also be helped by understanding how being zealous for the law had a deep foundation in Second Temple Judaism.[35] According to James D. G. Dunn, this zeal "was marked by three features in particular": (1) at the sight of Jews who disregarded the law, especially regarding the separateness from others practiced by covenantal nomism; (2) toward Jews and non-Jews when it was perceived that Israel's boundaries were being breached and (3) "regularly *involved violence and bloodshed,* as necessitated (in the view of the zealots) by the severity of the danger to Israel's exclusive set-apartness to and holiness before God."[36]

When Paul refers to the way he "was violently persecuting the church of God and was trying to destroy it" (1:13), he notes that this represented the period in his life when he had "advanced in Judaism beyond many among [his] people of the same age" and "was far more zealous for the traditions of [his] ancestors" (1:14). There are three striking features of "zeal" as noted in this first part of Paul's Letter to the Galatians, and all of them refer in some way to his zeal, which once led him to do violence against the early Christians. As Dunn notes,

First, in each case the zeal was an unconditional commitment to maintain Israel's distinctiveness, to prevent the purity of its covenant set-apartness to God from being adulterated or defiled, to defend its religious and national boundaries. Second, a readiness to do this by force; in each case it is the thoroughgoing commitment expressed precisely in the slaughtering of those who threatened Israel's distinctive covenant status which merited the description "zeal" or "zealot." And third, the fact that this zeal was directed not only against Gentiles who threatened Israel's boundaries, but

---

34. Jeremy Gabrielson, *Paul's Non-Violent Gospel: The Theological Politics of Peace in Paul's Life and Letters* (Eugene, OR: Pickwick Publications, 2013), 136.

35. "Second Temple Judaism" is the term that characterizes the period between the end of the Babylonian Exile (530 BCE) and the destruction of Jerusalem, including the Temple (70–72 CE).

36. James D. G. Dunn, *Jesus, Paul, and the Gospels* (Grand Rapids: Eerdmans, 2011), 152.

against fellow Jews too. It need hardly be said that this must be what Paul had in mind when he speaks of himself as a "zealot" and of his "zeal" manifested in persecution of the Church (Gal. 1.13-14; Phil. 3.6).

The second aspect of the kind of zeal that Paul promoted was his invitation to the Galatians to be zealous in the way that they emulated *his* zeal. However, it would be more correct to nuance this kind of emulation by adding with Beverly Gaventa, what the Galatians are to imitate is not Paul's life per se but rather "Paul's single-minded response to the gospel that was revealed to him."[37] That zeal became manifest in his life; that same zeal for the good is the invitation to us all. When we are motivated by this zeal for the good, the divine goodness becomes gradually more evident in our lives. This realization became clear to me when I heard someone say of another, "She seems to exude God's goodness." Whether it be charity, joy, peace, patience, goodness, kindness, gentleness, faithfulness, or self-control, when we practice it enough through developing its part in the mystical life, we will begin to exude it; we will be on the way to transformation into the goodness, etc., of the Christ.

As I conclude this chapter, I'd like to narrate an incident in my family's life that revealed to me how the two understandings of "zeal" (for the good and in emulation) are expressed.

In 1984 my brother Pat called me after having been on a cruise for a week, telling me that, instead of gaining weight, he had lost fifteen pounds. It was clear that he had a serious health problem. Indeed, he had just visited his doctor in Shreveport, who had told him that he thought it was cancer. On Holy Thursday evening, Pat called again with the bad news: he had cancer of the esophagus and did not expect to live to see his two sons, Craig and Kevin, grow up.

When I arrived in Shreveport, I went immediately to the hospital. That evening when I was alone with him, after having celebrated the Sacrament of the Sick with him and the family, he asked, "Why me, Mike? I'm a good guy." "You know, Pat, that's what I've heard ever since the word got out about your cancer: why Pat? He's such a good guy." And then I decided to do a little evangelizing, a task that is not always easy to do with one's own family members. But I plowed ahead. "But Pat," I said, "one of our saints, St. Bonaventure, said there are four kinds of goodness that we can

---

37. Beverly Roberts Gaventa, "Galatians 1 and 2: Autobiography as Paradigm," *Novum Testamentum* 28 (1986): 322. I am indebted to Lappenga, "Misdirected Emulation" (p. 793), for this source.

show.[38] The first kind is good people who don't consciously sin anymore; the second group is people who don't consciously sin and do good to those around them. The third kind is good people who don't consciously sin, do good to those around them, and have zeal to live in union with God. But the fourth kind is good people who don't really sin any more, do good to those around them, have a zeal for God, but also a zeal to do good for others beyond their immediate circle. Why don't you think about that as we ask God for healing?"

The next morning, before he went for his operation, we had a few more moments together. And it was in those moments that I heard someone committed to emulate the vision of Saint Bonaventure. "I've been thinking, Mike, about what you said about that saint. I'm not consciously sinning, and you know I'd do anything for Carol [his wife], Craig, and Kevin and for you, Dan, and Jerry [the other brothers]. But I haven't done the third and fourth kind of doing good. If I get out of this thing and live, I know I've got to get closer to God and do more good for other people."

The operation was successful, and Pat lived another sixteen years. Whether he was faithful to his sickbed commitment to be zealous for God and do good beyond the family, only God will be the judge.

Upon his conversion, Paul realized that Christian morality is not ultimately about following rules and regulations (which often reinforce a kind of separatist "nomism") but about being ethically responsible for the common good. This is evident in his letters, including the Letter to the Galatians. Thus, in writing to this community, when Paul talks about "doing good," the goal of that doing good is the common good. Realizing the need to apply that goal to the church for all time, Gys M. H. Loubser envisions communities of all times discerning how that "doing good" will take place. He writes that "Christian communities are called to contextualize their ethics for the situation in which they find themselves. To *do good* (Gal. 6:10) to all people could be interpreted differently in different communities. In the household of faith it would have a very specific Christian slant, but Paul refrains from detail. For this reason it might be wise practice to Christianize maxims for the community in which it is operative in order to do good in that community's perception. However, this cannot be done without discernment"[39]

---

38. I think that my attribution of the four levels of goodness to Bonaventure is more of an urban legend. I was unable to find a source in his writings for this.

39. Gys M. H. Loubser, "Life in the Spirit as Wise Remedy for the Folly of the Flesh: Ethical Notes from Galatians," *Neotestamenica* 43.2 (2009): 367.

If Whole Foods can publicly declare that it realizes "the time is ripe" for it to be part "of a growing consciousness that's bigger than food—one that champions what's good, and the greater good, too," then those who claim to be followers of Christ can do no less. Indeed that doing good should make them willing to emulate Christ by laying down their lives for the sake of the common good.

As we end this chapter, perhaps Paul's prayerful admonition to the Galatians might inspire us to embrace the kind of goodness that has been the subject of this chapter, so that our goodness will bear the fruit of love:

> Do not be deceived; God is not mocked, for you reap whatever you sow. If you sow to your own flesh, you will reap corruption from the flesh; but if you sow to the Spirit, you will reap eternal life from the Spirit. So let us not grow weary in doing what is right, for we will reap at harvest time, if we do not give up. So then, whenever we have an opportunity, let us work for the good of all, and especially for those of the family of faith. (6:7-10)

Indeed, as Pope Francis has said so succinctly, in an image that fits the theme of this chapter on the spirit of love expressed in "goodness" or "doing good": "the final word written about our lives will be, 'He was a good person. He sowed good seed.'"[40]

---

40. Pope Francis, Speech to Vatican Security Force, September 30, 2014, http://ncr online.org.

Chapter 11

Cultivating Gentleness as a Sign of the Spirit's Love in a Violent World

If ever the word "gentle" fit a human being, it fit Ernie Larkin. Though he must have been at least 6'3" and large framed, I would say that *gentleness* was his key characteristic, from his voice to his gait to his way of listening to anyone who approached him. I came to know the Carmelite Ernest (Ernie) Larkin during the eighteen years I taught a two-week summer course on the "Eight Beatitudes of Matthew's Jesus" at Notre Dame University, where he was also a frequent workshop speaker.

Years later, I met him again in Tempe, Arizona. For health reasons, Ernie had left his teaching position at Catholic University of America in 1971 to reside permanently in Phoenix. In 1972 he cofounded the Kino Institute, a school for adult religious education for clergy, religious, and laity. While there, Ernie became a founding member of the Carmelite Forum, which explored many of the forms of mysticism and mystical stances that I have tried to address in this book, but from a Carmelite perspective. After retirement, he continued to teach courses on prayer and spirituality at the Kino Institute and at the Cornerstone Center for Christian Meditation in Phoenix, where he also served as spiritual director. He also worked on weekends doing what priests call "help-outs" or "supply."

I had been asked to lead parish retreats on two different occasions at Holy Spirit parish in Tempe. However, in order to influence the people to come to the "parish mission," it was expected that I preach at all the parish Masses on the preceding weekend. Before one of the Masses at which Ernie was to preside and I was to preach, the pastor entered the sacristy where Ernie was in quiet prayer. "Ernie," the pastor said, "I don't know how many times I've told the people not to leave after communion, but they don't listen to me. I want you to tell them that they are not to leave Mass until it is over, after the last song."

I could feel the tension in Ernie over what the pastor expected of him. I wondered how this "gentle giant" would respond. After what seemed to be the proverbial "eternity of silence," Ernie simply said, "Frank, I just can't do it; that's not my way of doing things."

How do *we do things*: how do we relate? Even more so, how do we relate when we face conflict or, more so yet, when we feel we must correct someone with whom we disagree?

All relationships, whether in physics, biology, spirituality, or in the Trinity itself, involve power. The pastor had power and Ernie had power. That was never in question. The issue was how the pastor wanted Ernie to use the "bully pulpit" (if we can call it that in this case); something inside Ernie actually rebelled at using his power in that way.

When we consider gentleness in Paul's writing and its appearance especially in Galatians, and more specifically as a fruit of the Spirit's love, it will be important to realize that gentleness (*praütēs*) has to do with how people use power, especially the use of power to influence people's thinking, feelings, and acting.

Understanding Power in the Pauline Corpus: Violence or Nonviolence; Care or Control

Before considering *gentleness* in Paul (which will be interpreted as nonviolence in the use of power, especially by the house church leaders) it will be important to understand power itself in Paul, both in his letters and in the way he used it to lead the community. Because of the manner in which some have interpreted Paul ideologically in an effort to legitimize their own ways of control and domination, abuse, and oppression, Kathy Ehrensperger writes, "we need to make a careful analysis of his letters and focus on these power issues if we want to move beyond the failure to address these [unfortunate] aspects of Christian tradition."[1]

In this chapter we will consider power as the grace or *charis* of God that turned upside down the power dynamics of the Romans, the gentiles, and the Jews, especially vis-à-vis any forms of violence. Before doing so, however, since we have already seen that the Spirit is "the power of God" (1 Cor. 1:24) at work in us and our world and that love itself is the greatest power in the world, we shall define what we mean by power itself and, in particular, how Paul used the power of *his* "bully pulpit" to try to effect change in the Galatian (and other) house churches.

---

1. Kathy Ehrensperger, *Paul and the Dynamics of Power: Communication and Interaction in the Early Christ-Movement* (New York: T & T Clark International, 2009), 201.

In her *Paul and the Dynamics of Power: Communication and Interaction in the Early Christ-Movement*, Ehrensperger writes, "Power issues in the Pauline letters are all-pervasive" and "are not restricted to the occurrence of explicit power terminology" but also involve "'the network of power', that is, with aspects of group dynamics within the early Christ-movement in the context of Judaism under the conditions of empire."[2] At the same time she acknowledges what has been noted throughout this book: "the Pauline discourse of power is not uniform. Depending on the perspective chosen, different aspects of the Pauline claim to, and exercise of, power are highlighted—all of which have had a major influence in the course of the history of interpretation."[3]

Traditionally most classic discussions of power interpret it in one of three main ways: power over, power to, or power with. Rather than using a definition of "power" from a dictionary, most exegetes writing on it in Paul's letters approach power from the definitions or descriptions of classical social theorists, especially Max Weber, Michel Foucault, and Hannah Arendt. For Weber, "Power means every chance within a social relationship to assert one's will even against opposition."[4] Michel Foucault did not agree with Weber's assumption that power invariably involved imposition and subordination. Instead, while noting its positive dimensions, Foucault saw power as something dangerous because of how easily it can turn into domination.[5] Even though Foucault stated that power was technically neutral, insofar as it could be a positive or a negative force, he, like Weber, saw the social impact of power in a sense of "power over" in the command-and-control dynamics of domination. For this reason, someone like Riane Eisler would consider the whole male-controlled Western world as defined by negative power and domination.[6]

Hannah Arendt developed a more nuanced understanding of power, akin to the approach I will use in this chapter, which stresses its presence and force in all relationships. This social dimension led her to define power

2. Ibid., 12.

3. Ibid., 2.

4. Max Weber, *The Theory of Social and Economic Organizations* (ed. Talcott Parsons; trans. A. M. Henderson; New York: Oxford, 1947), 152.

5. For a key summary of his many writings on the subject, see Michel Foucault, "Truth and Power," in *Power/Knowledge: Selected Interviews and Other Writings, 1972–1977* (ed. Colin Gordon; New York: Pantheon, 1980).

6. A fine interpretation of the male domination system vs. the woman's collaborative model is found in Riane Eisler's classic on the subject, *The Chalice and the Blade: Our History, Our Future* (New York: HarperCollins, 1988).

as "the human ability not just to act but to act in concert."[7] However, I don't think power (at least in its fullest sense) can be limited to humans; it is the stuff of all that is. I find this insight valid whether we consider power in science—from quantum theory, neuroscience, and cosmology—or power in humans' interactions with one another in communities of all sorts or in the organizational dynamics found in economic, political, and religious structures.

Among more recent scholars who have written on power in the Pauline corpus are Bengt Holmberg, Sandra Hack Polaski, and the aforementioned Kathy Ehrensperger. In his book *Paul and Power: The Structure of Authority in the Primitive Church as Reflected in the Pauline Epistles,* Holmberg uses Weber as an interpretive lens for understanding the dynamics of the house churches and their various leaders.[8] While Polaski seems more influenced by Foucault, Ehrensperger appears to shows deference to Arendt. However, neither offers a clear definition of power that might underpin their reflections. Nonetheless, the approach they take to power in Paul's understanding of his calling and in his consequent letters is most helpful. Recognizing that no approach to power in Paul will go unchallenged, Ehrensperger points to the all-pervasiveness of power when she notes, "Whatever conceptions of power we are dealing with, and in whatever way we are engaging in such a project—it cannot but be shaped by contexts and relations which are influenced by power."[9]

About twenty-five years ago, during a time when I discovered that I had been quite dominating and even manipulative in many of my relationships, I decided to study power in a serious way. This led me to read the authors mentioned above, but I always came away rejecting their approaches. Gradually, as I summarized my thoughts, I wrote *The Paradox of Power: From Control to Compassion,* in which I offered my own definition of power based on a dictionary definition as "the ability to influence."[10] This is somewhat identified with the Pauline concept as outlined in Michael J. Gorman's *Cruciformity: Paul's Narrative Spirituality of the Cross.* While Gorman unfortunately seems to equate control with influence (while I show power as the ability to influence that can come from and be expressed through care [positive power] or control [negative power]), his understanding does

---

7. Hannah Arendt, *On Violence* (San Diego: Harcourt Brace, 1970), 44.

8. Bengt Holmberg, *Paul and Power: The Structure of Authority in the Primitive Church as Reflected in the Pauline Epistles* (Philadelphia: Fortress Press, 1978).

9. Ehrensperger, *Paul and the Dynamics of Power,* 19.

10. Michael H. Crosby, *The Paradox of Power: From Control to Compassion* (New York: Crossroad, 2008), 24.

not differ from mine when he defines power as the "ability to exercise significant control or influence, either for good or for ill, over people and/or history."[11]

Beginning our approach to gentleness with a discussion of power might seem to be out of order, but it becomes quite understandable, if not indispensable, when we apply the idea of power as "the ability to influence" to the very reason that provoked Paul's angry Letter to the Galatians. At issue was which gospel was going to influence the Galatians: that which Paul proclaimed or that of the unnamed ones we have called "the Teachers." Both had power in those house churches insofar as both evidently had significant influence. Consequently, we might consider Paul's Letter to the Galatians as a high-stakes power play around influence in an honor/shame culture with the main "influencers" being Paul and the other Teachers. However, even in the rhetoric we use to name those anonymous influential forces who came with "another gospel" that countered Paul's, we must realize that the very interpretation of the conflict that ensued involved (and involves to this day) language that can mask deep layers of control and violence. Consequently, Jeremy Gabrielson in his book on nonviolence in Paul reminds us,

> It is important to flag a critical issue at the outset: from the moment one identifies the other "influencers" as Paul's opponents or as "agitators," as advocates of "another gospel," the effort to describe them is decisively based on Paul's rhetorical point of view, and does not necessarily reflect or correspond to the historical influencers' self-understanding, which is exceedingly difficult to reconstruct anyway.[12]

Returning to my definition of power as "the [my, your, his, her, their, as well as Paul's and the Teachers'] ability to influence," I find it to be at the core of and applicable to relationships at every level of life then and now: intrapersonal, interpersonal, institutional, and infrastructural. At the same time, I find, as I write this chapter, that the reference in my 2008 title to the *"Paradox" of Power* is especially important, given this book's insistence

---

11. Michael J. Gorman, *Cruciformity: Paul's Narrative Spirituality of the Cross* (Grand Rapids: Eerdmans, 2001), 298.

12. Jeremy Gabrielson, *Paul's Non-Violent Gospel: The Theological Politics of Peace in Paul's Life and Letters* (Eugene, OR: Pickwick Publications, 2013), 80. Gabrielson notes in n. 3 that his use of the term "influences" for Paul's opponents comes from Mark D. Nanos, *Irony of Galatians: Paul's Letter in First-Century Context* (Minneapolis: Fortress, 2002).

on the need for a mystical stance to address the power of today's Teachers who have promoted for decades a form of canonical nomism in the Catholic Church.

Power becomes "paradoxical," especially in organizations, when the very attitudes and stances of care that contributed to people becoming leaders turn into command-and-control dynamics once they rise to positions of authority. This was the paradox of power that Paul was challenging regarding what he considered to be an abuse of covenantal nomism, especially in his Letter to the Galatians and those to the Corinthian house churches. Unfortunately, the paradox of power continues today, from the Vatican offices to the diocesan chancery office to the parish itself. Here the inherited cultural patterns of domination and control can, in some leaders, easily eclipse the earlier manifestations of care that may have brought them to their positions of authority in the church. Pope Francis spoke of this in his December 23, 2014, challenge to the members of the Roman Curia when he described as one of the "sicknesses" that can overcome church officials "closed circles where belonging to a little group becomes more important than . . . belonging to the Body and, in some situations, to Christ himself." He noted that "this sickness begins always with good intentions but with the passing of time enslaves the members, becoming 'a cancer' that threatens the harmony of the Body."[13]

Pauline Nonviolent Power in the Shadow of the Violence of Imperial Power

Later in this chapter, I will argue that Paul's concept of gentleness can best be interpreted as nonviolence. While I find it a strong theme, I will not approach it as universally present in the manner of Jeremy Gabrielson, who notes that the "weight of evidence" is such that it "suggests that 'the historical' Jesus and his immediate followers practiced nonviolent peacemaking,"[14] or of Douglas Harink, who writes that, while "Paul does not make an explicit call to nonviolence in Galatians, as he does elsewhere (Rom 12:14-21), nonviolent witness to the universal lordship of Jesus Christ is everywhere implicit in Galatians."[15] However, I, along with an increasing number of Pauline scholars, do agree on one element of power in Paul's writings

---

13. Pope Francis, Address to Roman Curia, December 23, 2014, http://www.zenit.org.

14. Gabrielson, *Paul's Non-Violent Gospel,* 17.

15. Douglas Harink, *Paul among the Postliberals: Pauline Theology beyond Christendom and Modernity* (New York: Brazos Press, 2003), 102.

that stands as the shadow behind everything else: namely, the all-pervasive power of the imperial rule of Rome, which dominated every facet of life in the house-church audiences of Paul, including the Galatians. This has already been discussed to some degree in Chapter 8. There we saw that all of Paul's letters, including Galatians, are written with an understanding of the cultural context of Roman imperial power and its gospel vis-à-vis the gospel proclaimed by Jesus and experienced and promoted by Paul. Whether or not it can be proven that Paul's letters are a direct, frontal attack on the power of Rome vis-à-vis the power of the newly created order in the risen Christ will remain a debatable point; yet the question asked by Neil Elliott cannot be dismissed: "Given the enormity of suffering inflicted on Paul's own people by the Romans in the first century, shouldn't we expect to find that the political violence of Rome played some role in his thought?"[16] In a similar way, Brigitte Kahl writes,

> Read before the Great Altar of Pergamon and in the scriptural code of Exodus and Deuteronomy, Galatians emerges as a passionate plea to resist the idolatrous lure of imperial religion and social ordering. The six chapters [of Galatians] spiral in several movements around the basic juxtaposition of God versus idols, and the clash of two different self/other-constructs that are implied. The entire letter is the "coded" theological manifesto of the nations under Roman rule pledging allegiance to the one God who is other than Caesar; this "semi-hidden transcript" contradicting and resisting the dominant order is embodied in a new horizontal and international community practice of mutual support.[17]

Kathy Ehrensperger presupposes throughout her approach to Paul and the dynamics of power that "the imperial context had a significant impact on the dynamics of power to which the Pauline letters bear witness."[18] In an explanation that echoes my concern above about the need for a contemporary understanding and application of what Paul was trying to address in the church of his day, she explains her approach in much the same way.

---

16. Neil Elliott, *Liberating Paul: The Justice of God and the Politics of the Apostle* (Maryknoll, NY: Orbis Books, 1994), 88. Elliott consequently "argue[s] that Paul recognized the depths of political terror in the violence of the crucifixion, and saw specifically this violence overcome in Christ's resurrection" (89).

17. Brigitte Kahl, *Galatians Re-Imagined: Reading with the Eyes of the Vanquished* (Minneapolis: Fortress Press, 2010), 287.

18. Ehrensperger, *Paul and the Dynamics of Power,* 11.

This study does not seek to extract an ethics of power from the Pauline letters; or to develop a contemporary ethics of power in light of the Pauline letters. Rather it seeks to listen into the conversation of early Christ-followers, trying to hear what they say about, and how they deal with, issues of power within their movement, embedded in the Scriptures and informed by traditions about Christ. This listening is informed by contemporary issues of power which are a matter of concern in churches and societies today. It is driven by the hope that aspects of the early Christ-followers' conversation, without providing direct guidance, may stimulate and illuminate contemporary conversations and thus contribute to the finding of ways to negotiate the dynamics of power in contemporary churches and societies so that they contribute to the life and well-being of all their members.[19]

Paul's Experience and Understanding of God's Power as God's Gift of Grace to All

A key difference in the gospel accounts of the life of Jesus Christ and Paul's account of the life of Jesus Christ in him involves their different concepts of power. While the gospels use words for power such as *dynamis* and *exousia* (which are also used in Paul's authentic letters thirty-six times and seventeen times, respectively), Paul's rendering of power is invariably *charis* (which is not used at all in Mark and in Matthew). This has led Polaski to write in her *Paul and the Discourse of Power*, "On the whole, however, Paul's use of the specific terms δύναμις and ἐχουσία does not greatly advance interpreters' understanding of the larger *discourse* of power that underlies the Pauline texts."[20] Consequently, to understand Paul's theological understanding (and use) of power, one must investigate Paul's notion of *charis,* or grace, because Paul believed his whole vocation called him in grace to be its minister (1:15).

Polaski writes that "the theological concept of grace, as developed from the Pauline texts, is closely related to notions of power."[21] Furthermore,

---

19. Ibid., 13.

20. Sandra Hack Polaski, *Paul and the Discourse of Power* (Sheffield: Sheffield Academic Press, 1999), 104.

21. Polaski, *Paul and the Discourse of Power*, 106. She adds that "interpreters have noted that the grace of God, which always remains God's act, is for Paul a fitting way to express God's power as well" and that, in considering Paul's use of power, his "language of 'grace' functions as a signal to attend to the power relations that underlie the text" (107).

she writes: "'Grace', χάρις, is frequently used by theologians of the New Testament as shorthand for Paul's entire theological project." Indeed, she notes: "In a classic study, James Moffatt summarizes, 'his good news may be described as a message or proclamation announcing that all is of grace, and grace is for all.'"[22] In effect, for us, God's power is the power of grace; indeed, we might say that God's power is shorthand for God's grace, especially if we allow it to work in us in our powerlessness. This is clear from Paul's own understanding of a revelation he says he received from God when he heard the following words: "My grace is sufficient for you, for power is made perfect in weakness" (2 Cor. 12:9).

One of the best-known greetings of Paul to his house churches speaks of the "grace and peace" from God that was extended by God to all the baptized. However, God's *charis* is not something that is limited to certain individuals alone. It is never private but always public. God's graciousness has been extended to everyone through the death, resurrection, and embodiment in those open to this *charis* of Jesus Christ. As such it is not only public; it is cosmic, insofar as it is through God's gracious activity in the faithful obedience of Jesus to the proclamation of the gospel that God's gracious reign of love has become universally available to all believers. This new creation involves an entirely new way of understanding and expressing power. Rather than the Roman notion of *charis*, which involved a hierarchical structure of patrons doling out their *charisms* or gifts or benefactions in ways that ensured control of the higher benefactor over the lower to preserve structures of domination and dependency, Paul's vision of *charis* was something extended equally to all without commands or demands. Rather than being limited to a few who exercise it through domination, now this *charis* of God's saving act in Jesus Christ finds all who embrace it not only filled with that *charis* but actually empowered to work with one another through their individual *charismata* or gifts of grace to make of themselves that one body of Christ that Paul experienced on the way to Damascus. That includes all the baptized, especially those being marginalized and violated. In the words of J. Christiaan Beker (whose work on Paul places a great stress on Paul's Damascus experience as apocalyptic),

> [Grace] marks a new epoch and a new dominion of power that is antithetical to that of the power of sin. . . . In the light of this apoca-

---

22. Polaski, *Paul and the Discourse of Power,* 105-6, quoting James Moffat, *Grace in the New Testament* (London: Hodder & Stoughton, 1931), 131.

lyptic meaning of grace, the debate about Paul's view of grace in the history of Western doctrine must be taken out of its privatistic moorings and placed in its original setting, where it refers both to a cosmic power and to the domain of our life in Christ.[23]

In speaking about power from the perspective of God's grace or *charis*, one sees that this must be the grounding for all forms of authority in the church. All discussions about leadership and power involve the exercise of authority, and all authority, including apostolic authority, is given and ordained by God to serve the whole. Thus, Paul realized that his own power could not be exercised in isolation from the power given to each and every baptized member of each and every house church in the cosmos. In a church in which many had come to believe that God's grace was totally dependent on the mediation of a certain group to the wider whole, Polaski writes that Paul's theology is a theology of that "grace given to the community by God [which is] given directly to each and every one, unmediated by *anyone* except Jesus Christ." She adds, "Paul uses the language of grace to describe this act of salvation and to stress its free availability, even as he uses the very same terms to reserve his unique place in God's plan."[24]

In this sense, while pointing out that the Paul who wrote that "grace [was] given to me" (Rom. 12:3) also wrote in the same vein and in the same place that God's "grace [was] given to us" (Rom. 12:6), Polaski writes that Paul never viewed himself as "the singular conduit of divine power. Thus Paul cannot simply impose his wishes and beliefs on powerless others. He must negotiate a position of power with others who, having received grace, have power from God on their own."[25] However, even here, this power from God is never because of anything they have done "on their own"; it is always and only because of God's graciousness that it comes to any person, and no person can claim it as his or her own because this grace is meant for the community rather than any individual.

Given Paul's understanding of grace as a gift of God shared in different ways in the community, it is surprising how power in the Catholic Church became so identified with the leadership group apart from the rest of the members of the church. However, if power as "the ability to influence" is

---

23. J. Christiaan Beker, *Paul the Apostle: The Triumph of God in Life and Thought* (Philadelphia: Fortress Press, 1980), 265. I am indebted to Polaski for this source.

24. Polaski, *Paul and the Discourse of Power,* 123.

25. Ibid., 115.

understood by the leaders in the church to be "power over" rather than "power with," it will follow that power in the Catholic Church, at least in its organizational structures, will result in an imbalance of power. Consequently, there will be a perceived need to reinforce that power through self-serving laws and a protectiveness of those leaders from challenge. Pope Francis has commented that "our defensiveness is evident when we are entrenched within our ideas and our own strengths," saying that

> These defensive mechanisms prevent us from truly understanding other people and from opening ourselves to a sincere dialogue with them. But the Church, flowing from Pentecost, is given the fire of the Holy Spirit, which does not so much fill the mind with ideas, but enflames the heart; she is moved by the breath of the Spirit which does not transmit a power, but rather an ability to serve in love, a language which everyone is able to understand.

Pope Francis added that, when the power in the church is grounded in the power of the Holy Spirit who "brings forth *different charisms* in the church, there will be authentic diversity and multiplicity," which bring about true "unity, which is not the same as uniformity." However, he pointed out that when power is abused, the very things we try to achieve become undermined. "When we try to create diversity, but are closed within our own particular and exclusive ways of seeing things, we create division. When we try to create unity through our own human designs, we end up with uniformity and homogenization." This invites us to "let ourselves be led by the Spirit." When this happens such "richness, variety and diversity will never create conflict, because the Spirit spurs us to experience variety in the communion of the Church."[26]

The variety of gifts in the church will not create divisions under inspired leadership; however, left to its own power, uninspired leadership will easily move from care to control, and authority in the church will exercise its power as violence rather than nonviolence and gentleness. In the process, to paraphrase Cardinal Newman's famous definition of the gentleman as the one who does not create pain, there will be injury and suffering in the body of Christ such that great harm will be done to all. The result will be a compromise in the proclamation of the gospel itself. This was Paul's greatest fear with covenantal nomism; it should be our greatest fear with canonical nomism as well.

---

26. Pope Francis, Homily, Cathedral of the Holy Spirit, Istanbul, November 29, 2014, http://www.zenit.org.

Christ's Gentleness: Model for Our Own

The Greek word for "gentleness," *praütēs*, is found only four times in the whole Pauline corpus. Besides being sixth in Galatians' list of the "fruit of the Spirit" of love and "quite the overlooked 'virtue' from Paul's lists,"[27] we find it again in 6:1, when he urges the Galatians to restore to the church "in a spirit of gentleness" any member who has been found to have transgressed. What Ernie Larkin was resisting in Phoenix was the command given by the pastor for him to correct the people in a way that he did not see as gentle. In this he seems to have been in good company, not only with Paul but with Jesus himself. For instance, C. H. Dodd has pointed out how the passage in Paul's Letter to the Galatians about correcting members of the community with gentleness reflects in a striking way Jesus's teaching in Matthew 18 on fraternal correction of communal transgressions.[28] Commenting on this insight, Gabrielson concludes, "Similarly, Paul writes to the Galatians that if a person is detected in a transgression, the spiritual among the Galatians ought to *restore*... the person gently."[29]

The other two mentions of *praütēs* in the Pauline corpus are addressed to house churches in Corinth (1 Cor. 4:21; 2 Cor. 10:1). All of the references deal with relationships between Paul and the house churches or among the members of the house churches. Similarly, all involve dynamics of power.

Some in the early churches seem to have had a tendency to identify themselves according to their founders or leaders, such as Apollos, Peter, or even Paul himself (1 Cor. 1:10-17). In challenging this human grounding of the church, Paul urged them to return to their true foundation in Christ. In this admonition he noted that his power as "the ability to influence" could be negative (control) or positive (care): "What would you prefer: Am I to come to you with a stick, or with love in a spirit of gentleness" (1 Cor. 4:21)?

This reference invites us to reflect on how Paul used his power (i.e., influence) in writing letters like those to the Galatians and the Corinthians: did they originate from his need to control, command, and coerce? Or were they grounded in care, concern, and compassion?[30] Polaski sees

---

27. Gabrielson, *Paul's Non-Violent Gospel*, 118.

28. C. H. Dodd, *Gospel and Law: The Relation of Faith and Ethics in Early Christianity* (Cambridge: Cambridge University Press, 1957), 64-83.

29. Gabrielson, *Paul's Non-Violent Gospel*, 111.

30. Ehrensperger's triad of positive power is "communicative, transforming and empowering" (*Paul and the Dynamics of Power*, 14).

some "power over" dynamics at work in how Paul sculpted his letters in ways that brooked no opposition and demanded unquestioning obedience. Some other scholars interpret Paul as preoccupied with maintaining his apostolic authority over against the other apostles in an almost obsessive way. However, most exegetes see his use of power vis-à-vis his own standing in the community as representing "an advocate of an alternative discourse of power, a discourse of transformation" with a higher goal than self-aggrandizement. This was "transformation to mutual empowerment in Christ."[31] Furthermore, upon deeper examination of Paul's writings themselves, it becomes quite clear that (as Jeremy Gabrielson writes) "gentleness was not only Paul's personal 'style' in ministry, but he believed it to be incumbent upon all disciples (and apostles) to behave in a way that expressed the meekness and gentleness of Christ rather than demonstrating one's enslavement to the appetite of the flesh for outbursts of anger."[32]

In the other usage of *praütēs* to the Corinthian house churches, Paul speaks of "the meekness (*praütēs*) and gentleness (*epieikeia*) of Christ" (2 Cor. 10:1).[33] Since Paul never met Jesus before his death, how could he speak of "the meekness (*praütēs*) and gentleness (*epieikeia*) of Christ"? Most authors believe he first learned more deeply about the historical Jesus in the years immediately following his Damascus experience and before any of the gospels were committed to writing. However, Ehrensperger asserts that "even without many explicit references to the teachings of Jesus," various references "resonate with the gospel traditions. . . ." A particular reference involves one of the three times that Matthew's Gospel, unique in its use of *praüs* among the other Gospels, refers to Jesus's gentleness as the model for relating among the members of the house churches. She writes,

> Paul's stress on gentleness and humility not only of Christ as in
> 2 Cor. 10.1 but also on these as attitudes through which Christ-
> followers should relate to each other (as in Gal. 6.1; 5.23; 1 Cor.
> 4.21) resonates with traditions such as "take my yoke upon you,
> and learn from me; for I am gentle and lowly in heart, and you will
> find rest for your souls," in Mt. 11.29.[34]

---

31. Kathy Ehrensperger, "Speaking Greek under Rome: Paul, the Power of Language and the Language of Power," *Neotestamentica* 46.1 (2012): 26.

32. Gabrielson, *Paul's Non-Violent Gospel*, 121.

33. Paradoxically, instead of "gentleness" being *praütēs*, as in the other three Pauline usages, it is *epieikeia* (which is translated in canon law as *epikeia*, the ability to overlook an infraction of the law because of a human predicament).

34. Ehrensperger, *Paul and the Dynamics of Power*, 112.

While I saw in Ernie Larkin a way of using his power in the pulpit with gentleness, I also find it helpful to translate *praüs* as "nonviolent" in our effort to develop, like Ernie, a contemplative/mystical stance in life toward others. This is especially important when some traditional translations have rendered *praüs* as "meekness."

While meekness is praised as nonviolence in the *Acts of Judas Thomas*,[35] the contemporary understanding of "meek" meaning "nonviolent" in Scripture gained ascendancy when the German equivalent of the English *Good News for Modern Man* (*Einheitsübersetzung*) translated the blessedness of the *praütēs* as "Blessed are those who do not employ violence."[36]

Before moving into the ideas of violence and nonviolence, harshness and gentleness in Paul, and their application to our lives today as individuals, groups, and members of the institutional church (especially those of us who are Roman Catholics), it will be good, as we did above with *power*, to define what we mean by "violence."

In my own writing and speaking, building on my definition of power as "the ability to influence," I define violence as "any power or force that inflicts injury." In this sense we can speak of everything from natural disasters to domestic and child abuse to environmental degradation as "violent." However, because a key purpose of this book is to suggest a way the Catholic Church in its organizational structure and socialization can move beyond what I consider to be some of its own leaders' religiously sanctioned violence through an entrenched canonical nomism, I have chosen here to use (and adapt) the U.S. bishops' own definition of violence, albeit this will be an adaptation of the violence they have defined as "domestic violence."

In their revised 2002 statement "When I Call for Help: A Pastoral Response to Women," the U.S. Catholic bishops state, "Domestic violence is any kind of behavior that a person uses to control an intimate partner

---

35. For more on the *Acts of Judas Thomas* 9.82-87, see Mary R. D'Angelo, "Blessed the One Who Reads and Those Who Hear: The Beatitudes in Their Biblical Contexts," in *New Perspectives on the Beatitudes* (ed. Frank Eigo; Villanova, PA: Villanova University Press, 1995), 68. For a more recent translation of *praüs* as "nonviolence," see H. Benedict Gree, C.R., *Matthew, Poet of the Beatitudes* (Journal for the Study of the New Testament Supplement Series 203; Sheffield: Sheffield Academic Press, 2001), 187-88.

36. G. F. Hauck and S. Schulz, "*Praüs*," in Gerhard Kittel and Gerhard Friedrich, eds. *Theological Dictionary of the New Testament,* vol. 6 (trans. Geoffrey W. Bromiley; Grand Rapids: Eerdmans, 1981), 647-51. I first was led to this insight reading Gottfried Vanoni, "Shalom and the Bible," *Theology Digest* 41 (1994): 120; and Norbert Lohfink, "The Appeasement of the Messiah: Thoughts on Ps. 37 and the Third Beatitude," *Theology Digest* 44 (1997): 234ff.

through fear and intimidation."[37] However, because they begin their statement by maintaining "as clearly and strongly as we can that violence against women, inside or outside the home, is *never* justified," and then make the sweeping statement that "violence in any form—physical, sexual, psychological, or verbal—is sinful,"[38] it seems that one can apply the underlying elements of this definition to assert that the use of violence *anywhere* in any way can *never* be justified. This would expand the forms of violence to groups and institutions, especially where there are unequal power relationships that result in sexism and racism, ethnocentrism and tribalism, as well as clericalism and elitism, such that one group with "power over" dominates another, especially when that power is legitimized by canon law. Thus this kind of canonical nomism represents its own form of religiously sanctioned violence.

As support for this position, one need only recall the years of the pontificates of popes John Paul II and Benedict XVI (1978–2013). During this thirty-five-year period, anyone in the church in any official capacity who criticized any form of its canonical nomism (from publicly disagreeing with its position on women's ordination to discussing who was to clean the sacred vessels after Mass) did so in fear of retaliation. The sweeping extent of the emotional violence of this curialization of the Roman Church was outlined in a courageous 2002 article by Camilo Macisse, who served as president of the Union of Superiors General between 1994 and 2000 in his capacity as superior general of the Discalced Carmelites.[39] By extended definition then, the hierarchical realities of that period represented a use of power that could be called violent, insofar as it was not only grounded in "control" but because it was able to be sustained (and canonized) "through fear and intimidation." Indeed it was not until the 2014 Synod on the Family that this dynamic of violence and control in the Roman Church was undermined when Pope Francis urged the participants not to be afraid of being frank or of saying what they really thought.[40]

---

37. U.S. Catholic Bishops, "When I Cry for Help: A Pastoral Response to Domestic Violence against Women," An Overview of Domestic Violence, November 12, 2002, http://www.nccbuscc.org.

38. Ibid., Introduction.

39. Camilo Marcisse, "Violence in the Church," *The Tablet* 257, November 22, 2002, 809. This was an abridged version of his earlier article in *Testimonio* (from the Chilean conference of Religious), November 15, 2002, http://archive.thetablet.co.uk.

40. Elise Harris, "Be Frank, Humble—Pope Francis Tells Bishops at Synod's Launch," Catholic News Service, October 6, 2014, http://www.catholicnewsagency.com.

Did Paul's Damascus Experience Transform His Violence to Nonviolence and Gentleness?

In quite a sweeping declaration, Richard Hays writes, "There is not a syllable in the Pauline letters that can be cited in support of Christians employing violence."[41] If this is true, we need to address two key questions: (1) how can one interpret Paul's apparent employment or use of violent language and imagery when speaking of his opponents or patterns of behavior in the house churches with which he disagreed (violently?); (2) how do we address his apparent silence on the systemic violence against certain groups in Roman society, especially women and slaves?

As we consider the first point above, I think that it is important to realize that no discussion of violence or nonviolence, anger and gentleness in Paul's letters, especially Galatians, can take place apart from that experience that colored everything in Paul's whole life: what happened on the way to Damascus.

The accounts in Acts of the transformation of power in the man who had "violently persecuted" the members of the early church and embraced the very instrument of state-sponsored violence (i.e., Rome's cross) in a way that promoted a new creation defined by nonviolence and even gentleness provide one of religion's most fascinating stories. We find it discussed in the first chapter of Galatians in Paul's own words. He writes, "You have heard, no doubt, of my earlier life in Judaism. I was violently persecuting the church of God and was trying to destroy it. I advanced in Judaism beyond many among my people of the same age, for I was far more zealous for the traditions of my ancestors" (1:13-14). Here he connects four critical words: persecution, violence, zeal, and Judaism. But what was this Judaism? It seems it was the unique brand of covenantal nomism we have discussed, especially in light of Paul's own words about having "advanced in Judaism beyond many among my people" (1:18). Quite possibly his own later zealous rejection of exclusive forms of covenantal nomism was a reaction to the very zeal with which he had promoted it to the point of persecuting any Jews who deviated from its separatist tendencies. A few verses later in Galatians, he adds that he had achieved such notoriety by persecuting the early churches and their members that his violent ways of persecution had been embedded in their memories. Now, with his conversion they still remem-

---

41. Richard Hays, *The Moral Vision of the New Testament* (San Francisco: Harper San Francisco, 1996), 238. For more on this, see Willard M. Swartley, *Covenant of Peace: The Mission Peace in New Testament Theology and Ethics* (Grand Rapids: Eerdmans, 2006), 331.

bered him with these words: "The one who formerly was persecuting us is now proclaiming the faith he once tried to destroy" (1:18).

Later Paul would write that, because his zealotry had led him to persecute the church, he did not deserve to be called an apostle (1 Cor. 15:9). However, in that same passage he refers to the mystical experience that called him to proclaim the Christ, whose followers he had once persecuted. More and more scholars who are probing Paul's concern about covenantal nomism and his persecution of the church have reached the (now majority) conclusion that Paul never rejected his Judaism, his faith in the God of Abraham and Sarah, nor even the law itself. What he rejected, and with vehemence, was the way some promoted observance of the law in a violent way to reinforce a separatist kind of covenantal nomism that involved dynamics of control rather than care. In one of the best articulations of what Paul's conversion entailed in this regard, Derek Flood has written,

> Paul's great sin, as he came to see it, had been participation in what he understood as religiously justified acts of violence motivated by religious zeal. Paul did not see himself as converting from one religion to another. Paul continued to regard himself as a Jew. His conversion was a conversion away from the religiously justified violence he had formally [sic] embraced. It was not a rejection of his faith; it was recognition that his former embrace of violence in God's name was not in fact an act of faithfulness, but a grave sin. Before his conversion, Paul had read his Bible and concluded that he should commit violence in God's name. After his encounter with Christ on the road to Damascus, Paul completely reassessed how to understand scripture, leading him to a radically different understanding.[42]

If we remain faithful to our definition of "violence" from the U.S. Catholic bishops as any control of another through fear and intimidation, it becomes quite clear that something happened to Paul in his Damascus experience that was transformative and that became life-changing at all levels. That this can be stated so clearly simply flows from the point made in Chapter 3 regarding the worldview attendant upon any mystical experience: it becomes the "reality" from which one's whole subsequent life is perceived and directed.

---

42. Derek Flood, "The Way of Peace and Grace," January, 2012, *Sojourners* blog (http://sojo.net).

When Saul, the violent persecutor, heard the words "Why are you persecuting me?," two things happened. First he came to believe in the one whose "gospel of the kingdom of God" had been such a threat to the religious and political forces that they joined together to have him killed on the cross. The cross was Rome's instrument of ultimate violence against all those whom it perceived to be a threat. So the experience on the road to Damascus made Paul realize that the Crucified One was now alive, risen in his members. This led to the second point: he came to a mystical understanding that each of the individual members of the house churches in Jerusalem, whom he had thrown into prison, and each of the individual secret believers he would find in the synagogues in Damascus now embodied the crucifixion of Christ-being-persecuted. How else would one understand the "me" whom he was persecuting? Consequently, grounded in this mystical experience, he had to free himself of all forms of "violent persecution" if he was going to be "in Christ"; otherwise any form of violence would be crucifying Christ all over, only now in his members. If the crucifixion of Christ was a sign of the powers and principalities triumphing, to do violence to the members of the body would be to declare that Christ had died on the cross in vain.[43]

Jeremy Gabrielson has written, "After his transformational encounter with the risen Jesus, Paul became a herald of the gospel of Jesus, a message that included at its core a commitment to eschewing the inherently violent politics of the present evil age."[44]

While one can assume that Paul's conversion experience included a radical transformation, it can still be asked if this transformation included a parallel movement away from a violent promotion of his former religious beliefs to a nonviolent promotion of his new understanding of the gospel. Even if he stopped the physical violence in the name of the God of his religious understanding (which was echoed in the understanding of the early community who had heard about this), one cannot avoid addressing the possible images of verbal violence that seem to shout out for attention. After

---

43. Ehrensperger writes in her *Paul and the Dynamics of Power*: "His emphasis on the cross (1 Cor. 1.18-24), read in the context of the Scriptures, which emphasize repeatedly that special attention is owed to those in a weaker position in the community (and society), is further indication that an exercise of power as domination, not to mention force or violence, is virtually inconceivable in the realm of Christ. No member of the movement is exempt from these parameters. The anti-domination dimension of the gospel is the overarching umbrella under which all the social interactions including those of authority and leadership stand. It would be contrary to the gospel to claim authority and leadership according to patterns of domination and control, or any kind of absolute power" (186).

44. Gabrielson, *Paul's Non-Violent Gospel*, 10.

all, the U.S. bishops have named "verbal" violence as one of those forms of violence that not only cannot be justified but is actually sinful. One cannot easily dismiss what Jeremy Gabrielson notes as those "certain points in the Pauline letters [that] are regarded by many interpreters as language which occupies the border between physical violence and verbal violence."[45] How does one justify Paul's anger against the Teachers (or "Influencers") that led to the writing of the letter and colors everything in it? And how among all the statements would one not conclude that the clearest example of his language bordering on "physical violence and verbal violence" is his wish that physical violence would come upon those Teachers in the passage that says, "I wish those who unsettle you would castrate themselves" (5:12)! And, in the same vein, is it not a form of verbal violence to call people "stupid" (*anoētoi*) not just once but twice (3:1, 3)?[46]

To all these questions about the accusation that Paul's writing, especially in Galatians, reflects verbal violence, I would say in response, "Look not only at Paul's words but at what impelled him to write them the way he did." Just as one can justify Jesus's anger and physical violence in the temple regarding the money-changers (and exploiting the poor), so it seems clear from the context of Paul's own words that he saw in these Teachers people who were undermining the very integrity of the gospel he had proclaimed; salvation was at stake. If there is to be any accusation of verbal violence on Paul's part, it would have to interpreted that this form of "justified violence," to use the U.S. bishops' reference, was not only "justified" but "free from sin."

In this vein, in considering the Letter to the Galatians, Polaski writes, "Paul's task in this epistle, then, is to renegotiate power relations so as to re-establish his authority."[47] We must look at the epistle itself to understand how Paul used his power in the community, how he related to his audience, and whether or not he did so out of control or care, violence or nonviolence, wrath or gentleness.

Paul first establishes his own authority by the *apocalypse* that came at Damascus and then his equality with the other apostles in the community. His visit to the churches in Jerusalem and Antioch established the fact that he saw their leaders as his equals, and they reciprocated. Even if there was a primacy of authority among them, their basic equality did not depend on any specific differentiation of roles among them, but upon the fact that

---

45. Ibid., 3.

46. For an application of the term to our contemporary life (before Pope Francis) see my "Does Paul's Adjective for the Galatian Church Apply Today?," *National Catholic Reporter*, January 5, 2013, http://ncronline.org.

47. Polaski, *Paul and the Discourse of Power*, 75.

they all had the same task: to proclaim the gospel. Building on this under-standing and realizing that the power that Paul attacks in the Letter to the Galatians is that of the Teachers, it becomes very clear that Paul's use of power throughout the letter is one of persuasion rather than domination. Thus Polaski writes,

> Paul's approach to his Galatian congregation is primarily one of appeal, not of command. He uses every persuasive tool at his dis-posal: he cajoles, he chides, he praises, he reasons, he uses sarcasm. He cannot afford to underestimate the allure of his opponents' arguments. The Galatians retain the power to choose their alle-giances, as well as the power to change their minds. Paul may rail against them for doing so, call them foolish and tell them that they have made the wrong decision, but he cannot prevent them.[48]

Another quality in Paul's use of power in his letters, especially Galatians, is how he uses familial terms in contrast to the absolute and dominant authority model (command/control) of the family system that prevailed at that time. He uses the whole letter not to make threats but nonviolently and gently trying to persuade with his arguments, as would any concerned teacher (see 6:6). And in one of the most tender passages in the whole Pau-line corpus he writes to them about his mother-like anguish of being in childbirth until Christ would be formed in them (4:19).

As we consider such a mother image in Paul (who actually uses mater-nal images more than paternal ones), we find that Paul, more than any other writer in the New Testament, uses the word *adelphoi* to articulate the brother/sisterhood that contrasts with the patriarchal dynamics of the empire and should characterize the new community of those led by the Spirit who can call the head of their new household "Abba." It is hardly in imitation of the Roman or Jewish structures when the members of the house/family/churches are addressed in "the αδελφ-lemma" form "a total of nine times (Gal. 1:11; 3:15; 4:12, 28, 31; 5:11, 13; 6:1, 18), and twice more (Gal. 1:2, 19) for fictive and biological kinship, respectively."[49] Reider Aasgaard has stressed the fact that *no other* author, even outside the first-century world, used metaphorical sibling language to the extent and with the variety that Paul did in his letters. [50]

---

48. Ibid., 101.

49. J. Punt, "Pauline Brotherhood, Gender and Slaves: Fragile Fraternity in Gala-tians," *Neotestamentica* 47.1 (2013): 157 n. 19.

50. Reider Aasgaard, "'Role Ethics' in Paul: The Significance of the Sibling Role for Paul's Ethical Thinking," *New Testament Studies* 48.4 (2002): 517.

Bringing together the nonviolent images above, where Paul refers to himself as a teacher and an anxious mother, Ehrensperger writes:

> It is interesting to note that Paul does not hesitate to use maternal and paternal language alongside each. In a society primarily structured according to the dominating power of the father/*pater*, maternal and nurturing imagery does not provide the strongest support for establishing dominating power over rebellious "children"! Thus rather than being indications for dominating power or even force which Paul wishes to exercise over his communities, the father and mother images with which Paul refers to his relationship with his communities might rather resonate with an educational discourse in his letters.[51]

Regarding Paul's reference to himself as a teacher and anxious mother, in our discussion of possible violence in Paul (at least in his Letter to the Galatians), how do we interpret Paul's own words about how, in that honor/shame culture with its ranked order, he publicly opposes "to his face" the acknowledged head of the family of families (i.e., the house churches): the one he calls Cephas (2:11). How? Again, Paul's own clear words reflect none of the verbal violence or the challenge/riposte dynamics typical of the first-century patriarchal world. An unbiased analysis of his rhetoric shows that there is no *mano-a-mano* style to his questioning: only a clear question (rather than a query) about a critical matter affecting not only the church at Antioch but potentially also the entire church of the future. He simply (and, I believe, nonviolently [gently?] but firmly) says to Cephas before them all, "If you, though a Jew, live like a Gentile and not like a Jew, how can you compel the Gentiles to live like Jews?" (2:14).

I think that this way of Paul's speaking to Peter has an echo in his challenge to the Corinthian community in 2 Cor. 10:1-6 that they choose how he should come to them: in harshness and boldness or with the gentleness and forbearance of Christ (2 Cor. 10:1). Pointing out that Paul refers here "to a quality that Matthew's Jesus applies to himself, especially as those qualities relate to the manner in which Jesus exercises authority: 'Take my yoke upon and learn from me, because I am meek and gentle in heart,'" Gabrielson continues that, while "Matthew does not divorce this 'gentle'

---

51. Ehrensperger, *Paul and the Dynamics of Power*, 128. Later she notes, "I think it is more significant that the immediate as well as the wider context of the 'father' metaphor resonates as much with a teaching and learning discourse as with a foundational discourse" (129).

portrait of Jesus from a dose of rather more severe rhetoric (see Matt 11:2)," then "neither does Paul. Paul virtually begs the Corinthians to respond to his appeal in such a way that he needn't be 'bold' when he visits them again."[52]

Further evidence against interpreting Paul as violent, at least in his authoritative approach and rhetorical style, comes from Paul's invitation to "imitate me as I imitate Christ" (1 Cor. 11:1; see Gal. 4:12).[53] Imitation represents a high form of honor in our day as well as Paul's, and the word "imitation" (*mimesis*) itself is used by Paul with an echo of our definition of power as "the ability to influence." In this sense, the whole thesis behind Elizabeth Castelli's book, *Imitating Paul*, is that "the notion of mimesis functions in Paul's letters as a strategy of power."[54] However, when Paul invites his audience to imitate him it is because both he and they know he is trying to imitate Christ. Thus, if mimesis is a form of power, it is clear that Paul knew that his approach to power had to be grounded in Christ's use of power. If he had learned that the yoke of Christ was meek and gentle, he had to model that same kind of gentleness in his exercise of authority in the communities he addressed in his various letters. Ehrensperger writes,

> Thus if Paul, as well as all other apostles and leaders of the move-
> ment, did not embody the message they proclaimed with their
> entire lives, the message could not be trustworthy. Only apostles
> who were willing to "take up the cross" and risk their own lives for
> the sake of life; who were willing to be πραΰς [*praüs*] and ταπεινός
> [humble] (2 Cor. 10.1) . . . accepted the risk of being beaten up and
> humiliated in their male honour (2 Cor. 11.23-25); in the context of
> a society which was dominated by cultural values and social codes
> which advocated aggressive, competitive and dominating behavior
> of men in an all-pervasive quest and defence of honour, could be
> trustworthy messengers of the gospel of the kingdom of God.[55]

Ehrensperger's comments bring us to the second point about violence in Paul's writings: How can we can address the fact that, while Paul articu-

---

52. Gabrielson, *Paul's Non-Violent Gospel*, 119.

53. "It is beyond dispute that for an analysis of the dynamics of power in the Pauline letters the notion of imitation is an important one which needs to be imitated" (Ehrensperger, *Paul and the Dynamics of Power*, 138).

54. Elizabeth Castelli, *Imitating Paul: A Discourse of Power* (Louisville: Westminster/John Knox, 1991), 15. I am indebted to Sandra Hack Polaski for leading me to this quotation (*Paul and the Discourse of Power*, 14).

55. Ehrensperger, *Paul and the Dynamics of Power*, 115.

lated a new creation that seemingly involved the breakdown of all kinds of socially and culturally imposed distinctions, he did little or nothing to promote the dynamics that would ensure that these boundary-breaking social relationships would replace the discriminatory and dominating power relationships in his communities? It is quite clear that Paul was able to find ways to rise above the Jew/Gentile alienation and that he might have found a way within the social dynamics of slavery to have (at least) a fellow-Christian treat his slave as an equal. Why, we can ask, didn't Paul challenge the system of slavery itself and socially structured sexism as he did the sinful power dynamics he associated with wrong interpretations of covenantal nomism? When we consider the famous passage in Gal. 3:28 about the new creation where there is neither Jew nor Gentile, people who are enslaved or free or categories such as women and men, it is quite clear that the concrete challenge of covenantal nomism, which stressed separation of Jew from Gentile, was interpreted by Paul as the underlying threat to his understanding of the gospel. Why was it that Paul was not able to see as countergospel the same separatism applied to the categories of slave/free and male/female?

Ehrensperger writes that the "appreciation and acceptance of people under the presupposition of their difference, as Jews and people from the nations/gentiles, was a non-negotiable dimension of the gospel, and Paul and the Pauline circle passionately advocated this with whatever power of persuasion they had at their disposal from whatever side it was called into question."[56] However, if this religious (quite secondary) difference was "a non-negotiable dimension of the gospel," how could it be that the division between class (slave/free) and, even more, sex (male/female) did not elicit the same kind of passion in Paul? The fact that Paul never critiqued the social structures supporting slavery and sexism have contributed to centuries of violence against people who were commercially enslaved and others who remain, to this day, under the domination of male control at all levels of life—from the domestic household to the household of faith itself.

Building on the same understanding of power that has been used in this chapter, Ehrensperger offers an approach that is instructive insofar as it cannot be isolated from the overall vision of Paul of a community of equals, in theory if not in practice, and, moreover serves as a challenge to anyone who would speak about Paul's virtual silence on the matter of structured inequality in power relationships in the church as a form of consent to them. She writes,

---

56. Ibid., 193.

To conclude from the ambiguous attitude concerning gender issues, and the non-challenging statement in relation to the institution of slavery in the Pauline letters, that Paul advocated an exercise of power and the establishment of structures within the Christ-movement which promoted domination, means to ignore the far more frequent indications of challenges to structures and attitudes of domination, challenges to the all-pervasive system of domination in the form of empire. The undeniable fact that in the course of history such stances have been advocated, claiming support from statements in the Pauline letters, provides no evidence that Paul and the Pauline circle advocate them. It is rather evidence that points to the choices of the interpreters to read certain statements, or the absence of others as proof in support of claims to power and authority in a dominating and thus oppressive way. It is not texts which have oppressive effects, but interpretations which are used to substantiate certain stances at the expense of others.[57]

Overcoming Violence and the Need to Control: Cultivating Gentleness and Nonviolence for a Productive Life

Bruce Longenecker is convinced that Paul's whole aim was to persuade his audience to a transformation of their individual, group, and corporate identities. The movement from violence to nonviolence and from ways of correcting based in gentleness instead of harshness is representative of that transformation. He offers a reflection that might be considered a summary of what I have tried to outline above: "In Paul's mind transformation by the Spirit results in a dramatic inversion of lifestyle." He adds that a sign of that "inversion of lifestyle" in the Christian is the way "the fruit of the Spirit in 5:22-23 becomes further amplified in 6:1-10. The character of 'gentleness' (πραΰτης) listed in 5.23 becomes the basis for Christian discipline and accountability in 6.1, where transgressors are to be dealt with 'in a spirit of gentleness' (πραΰτητος) rather than in an attitude of haughty contempt (cf. 5.15, 26)."[58] For his part, Rodrigo Morales writes that, since "the vast majority of Paul's references to πνεῦμα refer to the Spirit of God," it follows that "as people of the spirit, the Galatians should not fall into the works of the flesh, accusing or mocking a brother or sister who falls into sin. Rather,

---

57. Ibid., 195.
58. Bruce W. Longenecker, *The Triumph of Abraham's God: The Transformation of Identity in Galatians* (Nashville: Abingdon Press, 1998), 77.

in the spirit of gentleness they ought to restore the person, knowing that they themselves are equally capable of falling into sin."[59]

In my own life, I have found that any transformation of my life and relationships has involved an ongoing process and that, at least for me, much of this "change of heart" has been linked to the need to move from a way of power defined by control (and its abuse and violence) to care (and its nonviolence and gentleness). Thus, after a long time, when I thought I might be ready, I took Pax Christi's "Vow of Nonviolence." This was only after I had done the necessary work of trying to free myself from anything conscious that would be construed as violence because taking the "Vow of Nonviolence" implies a serious commitment to overcoming its obstacles. This has been the approach throughout this book: overcoming the obstacles to the manifestations of the fruit of love in our lives demands a serious conscious effort.

One of the six commitments involved in the "vow" involves a refusal "to retaliate in the face of provocation and violence"[60] as a way of modeling one's life on that of Jesus, especially as he taught his way of discipleship in the Sermon on the Mount. Even if he never met the physical Jesus, Paul knew that the gospel he proclaimed had to be practiced through nonviolence in a key way: nonretaliation. In discussing how Paul addressed nonretaliation in his letters, Jeremy Gabrielson writes,

> Vengeance, cursing, litigating, and tallying up evils received are all related to the theme of retaliation; all of these activities are off-limits in Paul's letters. Likewise, positive responses that Paul advises as alternative to retaliation are doing good, blessing, conciliating, forgiving, and loving. Not only are these various actions and prohibitions part of Paul's paraenetic material, these themes appear in a variety of other genres: Paul's descriptions of his own behavior in trying circumstances, the hymn extolling love; and the "virtue" and "vice" lists of Galatians.[61]

---

59. Rodrigo I. Morales, *The Spirit and the Restoration of Israel: New Exodus and New Creation Motifs in Galatians* (Tübingen: Mohr Siebeck, 2010), 160.

60. The six commitments include: striving for peace within myself and seeking to be a peacemaker in my daily life; accepting suffering rather than inflicting it; refusing to retaliate in the face of provocation and violence; persevering in nonviolence of tongue and heart; living conscientiously and simply so that I do not deprive others of the means to live; and actively resisting evil and working nonviolently to abolish war and the causes of war from my own heart and from the face of the earth. For more on the Vow of Nonviolence, contact Pax Christi USA (http://paxchristiusa.org).

61. Gabrielson, *Paul's Non-Violent Gospel*, 58.

Some years ago I copied a short piece called "Endangered Virtues" from *The Tablet* magazine. As we build on the previous fruitful manifestations of love and move to *faithfulness* and *self-control*, we can be accompanied by the wonderful insight about gentleness (as well as each "fruit of the Spirit") offered by the author, David Goodall:

> Gentleness in its Christian sense is a complex concept. It tempers and informs conduct more than it initiates it. It does not preclude anger in a just cause, but restrains and modifies it. Notions of compassion, forgiveness, generosity, attention to truth, and above all kindness are included in it: indeed each "fruit of the Spirt" partakes to some degree of all the others, although each has its own emphasis. Together they add up to that single quality of holiness of which Hilaire Belloc wrote that to encounter it in another human being is to be confronted with the sixth and most conclusive proof of the existence of God.[62]

---

62. David Goodall, "Gentleness," *The Tablet*, April 15, 2000, 512.

Chapter 12

Cultivating Faith and Working through the Love That Does Justice

In a conversation I had with a bishop some years ago, he bemoaned the fact that his priests did not respect his authority, quoting the Scripture passage calling for them to show him "obedient faith." When I suggested that this is not what Paul meant by "the obedience of faith," he was quite surprised; he had come to believe that those in his diocese had an obligation in faith to obey him without question. It seems he had not read Jerome Murphy-O'Connor's *Becoming Human Together: The Pastoral Anthropology of St. Paul.* There, the late Dominican writes, "Christians know themselves to be no longer bound by the Mosaic law with which Paul was so concerned. This can blind us to the fact that his basic principle remains valid with respect to any law. To give blind obedience to any authoritative directive is to place oneself in a state of inauthenticity, because to do so is to surrender one's freedom in an endeavor to escape responsibility."[1]

Returning to the bishop's conviction that, because he was shepherd of his flock, the priests and people in his diocese should practice blind obedience to him, I think that this bishop would have been even more surprised—as was I myself a few years later—to learn that another word for "faithful obedience" is *justice.*[2]

When I give talks on faith, I often distinguish three levels of faith, which we can apply to the three key stages in life: childhood, adolescence, and adulthood. *Childhood faith* is learning about practices associated with religion that are to be observed; this represents faith received from others; it often involves learning religion's rules, regulations, and rituals. The scho-

---

1. Jerome Murphy-O'Connor, *Becoming Human Together: The Pastoral Anthropology of St. Paul* (Wilmington, DE: Michael Glazier, 1984), 119.
2. Robert L. Foster, "The Justice of the Gentiles: Revisiting the Purpose of Romans," *Catholic Biblical Quarterly* 76.4 (2014): 696.

lastic theologians believed that, if people understood the rules, they then could be clear about how to translate them into moral living. Obedience is defined by observance of this way of living. *Adolescent faith* involves embracing what others say about someone or something and expressing this "received teaching" through various practices; this interprets faith as the data coming from the testimony of another or others, especially the leaders of the group to which one belongs. Here obedience is defined by acceptance of the authoritative teaching of the leaders and even non-authoritative decisions such as those by the bishop described above. *Adult faith* represents a way of knowing someone in whom another can believe and trust; it is personal faith. The obedience involved here involves fidelity to the demands connected with maintaining the relationship itself.

Child-grounded faith stresses observance; adolescent faith stresses belonging; adult faith stresses a personal relationship of trust that leads to a commitment. It is only at this level, I believe, that one can begin to move toward an authoritative "obedience of faith," which Paul identifies with living out the gospel imperatives (Rom. 1:5; 16:26; see 16:19). In the end, however, whatever the object of obedience that is required, all responses must be reflective of the faith of Jesus to the mission of proclaiming the gospel that led him to the cross. This obedience of faith of Jesus Christ is meant to be(come) our model. James D. G. Dunn elaborates,

> Jesus Christ is the one human being who embodies radical obe-dience by remaining faithful to God, to the painful end. For that reason, his fidelity overcomes Adam's rebellion, and he constitutes in himself a new, faithful humanity: "For just as by the one man's disobedience the many were made sinners, so by the one man's obedience the many will be made righteous" (Rom 5:19). Second, and equally important, this death of Jesus is mysteriously also a gracious act of God. As Paul formulates it in Rom 5:8, "*God* proves his love for us in that while we still were sinners *Christ* died for us."[3]

Returning to the opening paragraphs of this chapter, it should be clear now that while the creed, catechism, and canonical faith have their place in the life of the believer, only when that faith has been internalized in a way that the faithful person's spirituality is modeled on the loving faithfulness to the gospel of Jesus Christ—expressed in a cruciform life of the Chris-tian—will that "faith" become the fruit of love in the way it is worked out.

---

3. Richard B. Hays, *The Faith of Jesus Christ: The Narrative Substructure of Galatians 3:1–4:11* (2nd ed.; Grand Rapids: Eerdmans, 2002), xxx.

This notion was summarized in a tweet (2014) from Pope Francis: "Love is the measure of faith."

Bruce Longenecker states clearly that faith working through love encapsulates "Paul's theology of union with Christ whereby Christians are incorporated into Christ." He writes,

> Whereas Paul can speak of being crucified with the crucified one, of dying with the one who died in order to live with the one who lives, and of Christian "sonship" arising out of participation in the "sonship" of Jesus, so he can talk of Christian participation in the faithfulness (πίστις) of Jesus through their own faith (πίστις)—a faith occasioned and inspired by the coming of Christ's faithfulness. If God's in-breaking into the world has emerged from the faithfulness of Christ and resulted in the establishment of a new world, so Christian faith in the Faithful One is the means of participation in that eschatological event, in anticipation of its future culmination.[4]

Both before and during his papacy, Benedict XVI often spoke about what he called "the crisis of faith in the Church of the West." The signs of this crisis were most evident in the lack of participation of baptized Catholics in Europe, Australia, New Zealand, Canada, and the United States. For Pope Benedict XVI, building on the insights of Pope John Paul II, the blame for this crisis was often placed on Catholics' embrace of the culture of secularism, relativism, and individualism, where there were no objective truths to ground one's faith. Some are convinced that it was his elaboration of this in his conclave homily in 2005 that led to him being elected pope the following day.

When he first began identifying the "crisis of faith in the Church of the West" with the individual Catholic's relativism, I wrote him suggesting that the crisis of faith went deeper than just those in the pews. It was paralleled by another crisis even more systemic and institutionalized: the crisis occurring in the organizational model of the church itself. For me, any challenge regarding the relativism and secularism among the people could not be addressed without an equal effort to transform the increasingly irrelevant human-made, culturally conditioned structures of the church itself.

The model of the church and the mores of many church leaders under Popes John Paul II and Benedict XVI—from the Curia to the chancery and

4. Bruce W. Longenecker, *The Triumph of Abraham's God: The Transformation of Identity in Galatians* (Nashville: Abingdon Press, 1998), 106.

the episcopacy to the local parish—often received their meaning and support around what we have called canonical nomism. Faith became identified with fidelity to the norms defined by the clerics; many clerics assumed such norms could never be questioned; anyone doing so lived in fear. For people like me, who disagreed with this understanding of the church, which seemed overly identified with its hierarchical leaders,[5] to do so publicly meant possible silencing or disassociation if it was considered by church leaders that such ways were not their ways.

As noted throughout this book, when we examine Paul's Letter to the Galatians, we find significant parallels regarding the struggle he faced with those Jews who stressed covenantal nomism in ways that emphasized an exclusivistic separation of one group in the church from others around them, resulting in a closed system. This dynamic reflects remarks made in his own preconclave reflection by Cardinal Jorge Bergoglio. It is commonly assumed (without clear data, given the secrecy around papal elections), that his insights had some influence impacting his subsequent election as Pope Francis. Almost immediately after his election, Francis's actions (from his daily homilies to his naming of people to leadership positions in the Vatican and throughout dioceses in the world) raised the concerns of some of those episcopal leaders who had come to virtually identify themselves as "the church" in a way that reflected what we have called canonical nomism. This tension between ecclesiologies came to a head in the pope's December 23, 2014, speech to the Roman Curia. Here he addressed contemporary forms of canonical nomism as a disease that threatened the church itself and demanded transformation.

The extent of and seriousness of this polarization was discussed by Gerard O'Connell, *America* magazine's correspondent in Rome, in an article entitled "Call to Conversion," with a subtitle "Francis' Call Has Clearly Disturbed Some Cardinals and Bishops":

> Pope Francis is calling everyone in the church to conversion, especially cardinals, bishops and priests. He is doing so first by example and then by words. And he is disturbing not a few in the process....
>
> While Francis' call has energized and inspired many in the church, and indeed far beyond its boundaries, it has clearly disturbed some cardinals and a number of bishops in such countries

---

5. Michael H. Crosby, *Repair My House: Becoming a "Kindom" Catholic* (Maryknoll, NY: Orbis Books, 2012); Michael H. Crosby, *Rethinking Celibacy; Reclaiming the Church* (Eugene, OR: Wipf & Stock, 2003).

as Italy, Poland and the United States, as well as in the Roman Curia [i.e., "the church of the West"].

The pope's call and insistence that this is the time (*kairos*) for mercy makes some uncomfortable, because they feel the substantive truth of Catholic faith is being contradicted, or is in danger of that, by the course he is steering. Their discomfort arises from a perception that the new pathway abandons some authentic articles of faith. This is especially the case when his call for conversion is a call "to concentrate on the essentials, on what is most beautiful, most grand, most appealing, and at the same time most necessary," and "not to be obsessed with the disjointed transmission of a multitude of doctrines to be insistently imposed" (*The Joy of the Gospel*, No. 35).

As we have seen in the way of the meeting of the Synod of Bishops, some are disturbed by the shift in ecclesial culture from one of clarity, ideas and logic to one of induction and real life as the foundation or theological reflection and pastoral practice—a discomfort that arises from a shift in first principles and theological method.

Francis' call also disturbs those pastors and lay intellectuals who feel that the Catholics who have tried to live the clear standards of the catechism are being placed second to those on the periphery of faith. The Argentine priest-theologian Carlos Galli calls this "the elder brother syndrome." Francis' call to conversion is hard for them; especially if they see no need for conversion....

Francis' denunciation of clericalism and careerism in the church, and his call to abandon such ways has upset not a few bishops and priests; they lament that the hierarchical order and rules for success that have prevailed in recent decades are being jettisoned.... His call to conversion is first and foremost a call for a change in attitudes among cardinals, bishops and priests. It is a call to be humble, welcoming, open, nonjudgmental and merciful. It is a call to reach out to those who are on the peripheries of life and society and to promote a culture of encounter and inclusion, not one of confrontation and exclusion.[6]

One would have to be quite delusional not to find clear parallels with the gospel of the Galatians' false Teachers, which Paul was challenging in

---

6. Gerard O'Connell, "Call to Conversion," *America*, December 8-15, 2014, 26.

light of his Damascus experience. Here the Christ was not separated or "more" identified with one group (i.e., the male leaders) vis-à-vis any other; all shared in the Spirit, and, especially, those who had been marginalized in the past by false expressions of covenantal nomism had to be brought into the community from which they had been excluded in the name of "faith."

Building on this challenge (whose outcome, I believe, may have lasting impact on the Roman Catholic Church for generations to come), the following reflections will address what arguably might be considered the two main points of contention among Pauline scholars. However, I will not address them exegetically but with regard to their implications for our spirituality and, especially, how they bear on the cultivation of a more mystical stance in life. The two points debated by the scholars involve (1) whether *pistis Iesou Christou* should be interpreted as the "faith of Jesus Christ" or "faith in Jesus Christ"; and (2) what we mean today by justification[7] by faith. However, while acknowledging the state of the debate, my main concern is to show what these notions mean in the life of the believer today, especially the believer committed to live mystically as well as prophetically in the promotion of the "faith that does justice."

Did Jesus Have Faith or Was He Faithful?

In the introduction to this book, I wrote that virtually everything in Paul's Letter to the Galatians has been the subject of controversy. Nowhere is this statement more apropos than when we consider a key passage in Galatians 2:16, 20, and 3:22-23 (as well as Rom. 3:22, 26 and Phil. 3:9). Here Paul talks about the "faith of [Jesus] Christ" (πίστις [Ἰησοῦ] Χριστοῦ / *pistis [Iesou] Christou*). The question that continually gets raised (and has never been definitively resolved), depends on whether and how the phrase *pistis Christou* should be translated: as the "faith *of* [Jesus] Christ" or as one's "faith *in* [Jesus] Christ."

The main proponents of each position have been among my most significant dialogue partners throughout this book. James D. G. Dunn argues for the "faith in Christ" position, while Richard B. Hays argues for the "faithfulness of Christ" understanding.[8] It seems to me Hays has the compelling arguments on his side, especially if one can translate πίστις/*pistis* not only as "faith" but as "faithfulness." This becomes more persuasive when we

---

7. For a summary review of discussions around *justification*, see Stephen Westerholm, *Justification Reconsidered: Rethinking a Pauline Theme* (Grand Rapids: Eerdmans, 2013).

8. Much of the recent debate between Dunn and Hays has been brought together in Hays, *The Faith of Jesus Christ.*

consider "faithfulness" as the translation of that fruit of the love of Jesus Christ's very Spirit that is the subject of this chapter. I find the best summary of the debate and the argument for "the faith[fullness] of Jesus Christ" sculpted in the brief remarks of Bruce Longenecker:

> On the one hand, it is possible to read the phrase to mean that Christ is the object of πίστις ("faith"), in which case Χριστοῦ is (usually identified as) an objective genitive ("in Christ"), rendering the phrase to mean "faith in Christ." On this reading, the πίστις is that of human believers who acknowledge and commit themselves to Christ. On the other hand, it is possible to read the phrase to mean that Christ exemplified πίστις ("faithfulness") within his own life, in which Χριστοῦ is (usually identified as) a subjective genitive ("of Christ").[9]

In examining the reason for the passion, crucifixion, and resulting death of Jesus, it cannot be disputed that all this happened because of his faithfulness. His faithfulness to proclaiming the gospel of the kingdom of God, or, as I have shown elsewhere,[10] the rule and governance on earth as it is in heaven of triune relatedness at all levels of life, was subversive enough both to the covenantal nomism of some religious leaders and to the local leaders pledged to preserve the reign of Caesar that he suffered the consequences of that subversion: death on a cross. However, precisely in this faithfulness to the gospel that took him to that cross, Paul realized that true salvation has come to us: not through any law nor through any empire but in the death and resurrection of Jesus that enabled the Spirit of that one to enspirit all who had/have faith in him in a way that led to their baptism as members of the church.

In supporting the translation "faith of Jesus Christ," an examination of Paul's authentic letters, including Galatians, makes it clear that the faith of Jesus Christ is what has justified us, not our faith in Jesus Christ. This faith of Jesus Christ has been manifest in his fidelity to the gospel that led him to his passion and death. This "obedience of faith" resulted in Jesus fulfilling the covenantal promise made to Abraham and his seed.

Because Paul saw Jesus as the revelation of God's love in the world, any understanding of the "faithfulness of Jesus Christ" cannot be divorced from its context revealed throughout the history of the Jews, namely, the faithfulness of God. This is clear from the four "books" that constitute N. T.

---

9. Longenecker, *Triumph of Abraham's God*, 95.

10. Crosby, *Repair My House*, 79-121.

Wright's monumental *Paul and the Faithfulness of God.*[11] In these he makes it clear that the Pharisee Paul's notion of God's *pistis* cannot be separated from the worldview of Second Temple Judaism. This, he writes, is clear for three reasons (all of which some others challenge!):

> First, there is every indication that the kind of Jew who became a Pharisee was implicitly aware of living in *a continuous story going back to Abraham, perhaps even to Adam, and on to the great coming day,* and of being called to be an actor within that drama, to play a particular part in bringing the story forward into its final, decisive moment.
>
> Second, there is every indication that Pharisees, like other Jews of the period, did not expect that decisive moment to involve the collapse or disappearance of the universe of space, time and matter. It would involve, rather, the transformation, redemption and renewal of that universe.
>
> Third, there is every indication that Pharisees, like many other Jews of the period, saw their own time within this narrative as one of *continuing exile* awaiting the final promised rescue.[12]

Jesus's Faithfulness: Model for the Disciples' Justification and Righteousness

Faith is key to understanding Paul's whole theology, and nowhere is that faith developed in Galatians more than in the third chapter. Indeed thirteen of its twenty-nine verses address faith and its role in our salvation. While the divine origin of this faithfulness is the faithfulness of God,[13] the human origin of our salvation is not through observing the law of Moses but because of faith, beginning with the faith of Abraham. Thus Robert Karris writes, "Abraham is the father of faith, not of circumcision, for he believed and was declared righteous before he or his descendant was even circumcised." As a result, he concludes, "Consequently, those who have faith [the gentiles] are blessed along with Abraham who had faith (3:9)."[14]

---

11. N. T. Wright, *Paul and the Faithfulness of God,* Book I (Parts 1 and 2) and II (Parts 3 and 4) (Minneapolis: Fortress Press, 2013).

12. Wright, *Paul and the Faithfulness of God,* Book 1, Part 1, 113-14.

13. This is the whole thesis of Wright in his *Paul and the Faithfulness of God.* Throughout he notes that, while Paul remained a Jew, he came to a new understanding of Judaism in light of his faith in Jesus Christ and the Spirit he experienced.

14. Robert J. Karris, *Galatians and Romans* (Collegeville, MN: Liturgical Press, 2005), 20.

Because Abraham believed, the "promise" or "blessing" was given to him and his *offspring* (in Greek, *sperma*). "Offspring" is used five times in Galatians (3:16 [four times], 29). In Paul's eyes, because of Jesus's faith, this offspring (not "offsprings") was found in those whose faith convinced them that this Jesus was the Christ who had become embodied in them. Consequently the blessing given to Abraham continues in his "offspring" of every generation whose belief in Christ finds them "in Christ" in a way that makes them "heirs according to the promise" (3:29). Frank Matera summarizes this salvation history that began in Abraham and continues in us through the Spirit of Christ when he writes,

> Paul insists that God's covenant promises to Abraham (that all the nations would be blessed in him) had a singular descendant (*sperma*) in view—the Christ. Consequently, those who have been incorporated into Christ are Abraham's descendants because they have been incorporated into Abraham's singular descendant, the Christ. There is no need for those who are in Christ to be circumcised. Paul argues that the Galatians have already been justified, because of what God accomplished in Christ's saving death and resurrection, pointing out that the empirical proof of their justification is their dynamic experience of the Spirit. They need not do the works of the law in order to be justified because they are already justified. They now live in the realm of the Spirit, and if they allow the Spirit to lead and guide them, they will fulfill the law through the love commandment.[15]

In this way faith is not only grounded in the fruit of love, but it also works through love. Love thus is the seed and flower of the faith of Jesus's disciples for all time.

Paul returns to his excursus on the faith of Abraham in 3:1-29 by offering in 4:21–5:1 his interpretation of the "allegory" of Hagar and Sarah, two of the wives known to have been married to Abraham. However, in this Letter to the Galatians, Paul sets the context for his argument by referencing the "god(s)" who controlled the religious imagination of his converts even before his own visit to them and the subsequent visit to them of the Teachers with their own gospel. This seems clear when he refers to them being formerly "enslaved to beings that by nature are not gods" (4:8). These were the *stoicheia* noted in 4:3 and 9.

---

15. Frank J. Matera, *New Testament Theology: Exploring Diversity and Unity* (Louisville: Westminster John Knox Press, 2007), 153.

Susan Elliott sagely reminds us that before the Galatian *men* converted to the gospel Paul preached and then converted to the gospel that the Teachers promoted, many Galatian men practiced some form of castration to evidence their dedication as *galli,* or "sacred slaves," to the "Anatolian Mountain Mother of the Gods," who went by different names in different parts of the area. Such castration sealed their participation in the worship of the Galatian mother goddess. This "guardian goddess" was the protector of Galatia (Anatolia).[16] This background could help us understand what led Paul to identify Hagar with a mountain and the law of slavery that had once bound them to the Mountain Mother of the Gods.

When Paul tries to explain his stress on the new family that finally has resulted in God's promise to Abraham and *his seed* (4:4-7), the offspring he describes thus descend not from Hagar but from the unnamed but clearly assumed Sarah. The slave Hagar's unnamed son is connected with a mountain (4:24) that continues the enslavement, while the freed offspring, Isaac, is not connected with a mountain. Sarah is "our mother" (4:26). Paul's contrast between Sarah representing freedom and Hagar slavery, Elliott says, is critical because "the inheritance of a position in the family structure is what is at issue."[17] Building on Elliott, Tatha Wiley highlights this crucial difference: "In Greco-Roman law, the mother's slave status determines the status of the child. Paul's point is implied: If you choose the *slave woman* as your *mother,* you will inherit her *slave status.*"[18]

In all the interpretations of Paul's discussion of circumcision in Galatians, most exegetes concentrate on its Jewish context. However, given the above, it cannot be forgotten that most, if not all, of the men in Paul's audience were not Jewish converts but the "Galli" who converted from the dominant gods of central Anatolia, where castration was part of the worship of the Mother of the Gods. Elliott writes,

> Gal. 4.21–5.1 poses the choice before the Galatian Gentile audience in graphic imagery drawn from their own context in central Anatolia. As Paul presents it, the choice for circumcision would

16. Susan M. Elliott, *Cutting Too Close for Comfort: Paul's Letter to the Galatians in Its Anatolian Cultic Context* (London: T & T Clark International, 2003), 94-126.

17. Susan M. Elliott, "Choose Your Mother, Choose Your Master: Galatians 4:21–5:1 in the Shadow of the Anatolian Mother of the Gods," *Journal of Biblical Literature* 118.4 (1999): 661. See also ibid., 666 n. 19.

18. Tatha Wiley, *Paul and the Gentile Women: Reframing Galatians* (New York: Continuum, 2005), 69. I am indebted to Wiley for giving me the lead to Elliott. And, in turn, I am indebted to Sandra Schneiders for giving me the lead to Wiley!

take them back into a world dominated by the Mother of the Gods, a world ruled by a pathetic παιδίσκη, whether in the form of the Mountain Mother or in the form of the Law. Circumcision would enslave them in that world. If they remain uncircumcised, they will instead continue to be sons and heirs.[19]

The whole argument underlying Paul's Letter to the Galatians, in his attempt to undermine the covenantal nomists, who stressed an elitist understanding of Israel's destiny, is that because of Christ's faithfulness, salvation is God's freely given gift to all people, Jew and Gentile alike. This is the core of Paul's argument in Gal. 3:1–4:11 about whether the source of our salvation is in the law or in faith in Jesus Christ. Indeed, Richard B. Hays writes, the whole "argument of Gal 3:1–4:11 finds its point of coherence in the story of the Messiah who lives by faith."[20]

The background to Hays's sentence above involves what has become, arguably, the most important passage in Paul's Letter to the Galatians. It has been rendered in different ways at different times—most often, "the just person lives by faith" (3:11b). This text involves three key Pauline words: justice, life, and faith. "Consequently," Dunn writes,

> Gal 3:11b should be translated "the righteous one shall live (= be justified) by faith." But the *meaning* of this statement is substantially identical to the affirmation that "the one who is righteous [= justified] by faith shall live." If there is any material distinction to be found between these statements, it lies in a realm of theological nuances far subtler than Paul could have imagined. In either case, the phrase ἐκ πίστεως specifies the manner in which ὁ δίκαιος shall find life (be justified).[21]

To strive for the historical Jesus's fidelity to the gospel of God's reign is the task of every baptized Christian. In other words, the faithfulness of Jesus Christ is to be modeled in the faithfulness of every Christian because fidelity for both the Jesus of history and us in every period of history remains the same. For our part as disciples, the proclamation of the gospel demands that our salvation depends on how we share in this faithfulness of Christ through grace in a way that finds us in faithful communion with one

---

19. Elliott, *Cutting Too Close for Comfort*, 286.
20. Hays, *The Faith of Christ*, 207.
21. Ibid., 134.

another. Hays summarizes this notion of our need to be "caught up into the story of Jesus Christ" when he eloquently writes,

> In a mysterious way, Jesus has enacted our destiny, and those who are in Christ are shaped by the pattern of his self-giving death. He is the proto-type of redeemed humanity. Thus for Paul, "the faithfulness of Jesus Christ" has an incorporative character. That is why Paul says, "I have been crucified with Christ, and it is no longer I who live, but it is Christ who lives in me. And the life I now life in the flesh I live by the faithfulness of the Son of God, who loved me and gave himself for me" (Gal. 2:19-20). Jesus is not merely a good moral example; rather, his story transforms and absorbs the world. The old world has been crucified and new creation has broken in through Jesus's death and resurrection (Gal. 6:14-15).[22]

Since faithfulness is the core of believing, believing without fidelity to the truth and practice of the belief is a contradiction. The righteousness and justice that come to us from this faithfulness bring about in us and in our world through us a new understanding of what it means to be in right relationships. Thus Bruce Longenecker writes that Christ's own faithfulness becomes the reason for our own:

> This is a dramatic redefinition of right relationship with God centred on Christ and his faithfulness, in contrast to Paul's own nomistic observance . . . a new order of "power-existence" (3.10) has come into being through Christ which can be said to arise out of a faithfulness (Christ's own) that qualitatively surpasses all other expressions of faithfulness. In fact, with Christ's faithfulness in view, Paul looks back with hindsight upon his own blamelessness in the law and sees it to be as worthwhile as excrement. To be in Christ is to have his (and only his) faithfulness as the mark of one's own identity before God.[23]

The challenge facing every Christian and, within Christianity, for every Catholic is the need to manifest that kind of faithfulness to God and the person of Jesus Christ as his disciples in a way that does not discount our

---

22. Ibid., xxix. Hays calls this incorporative character "participation," particularly in "Gal 3:15-29, in which 'participation in Christ' is the "controlling soteriological motif. In short, I would contend that the interpretation proposed here offers the most satisfactory way of reading Paul's argument as a coherent piece of thinking" (206).

23. Longenecker, *Triumph of Abraham's God*, 99.

Catholic tradition and its core teachings. This kind of faithfulness is critical when faith has been often identified with uncritical fidelity in the form of submission of mind and heart to what the leaders have taught. Given what we've developed in this book and chapter thus far, this need to incorporate and embody the faithfulness of Jesus in our lives represents a perennial challenge. This is true of all of us, but especially true for those who have found their identity as Catholics in those nomistic practices that we have identified as canonical nomism today.

Struggles around the Meaning of the *Dikaiosynē* That Comes from Faith

Having discussed the meaning of *pistis* as faithfulness, we now can move to address what perhaps represents the greatest challenge of this whole book: Paul's interpretation of *dikaiosynē*. Here he had come to a faith (*pistis*) in Jesus Christ that resulted in his mystically grounded faith that demanded justice (*dikaiosynē*). In this sense, Richard Hays writes, "Paul's understanding of the πίστις of Jesus is integrally related to his understanding of δικαιοσύνη."[24] For some it comes as a surprise that this has little or anything to do with Paul or authentic Pauline scholarship; rather it has to do with what history has done to the notion of *dikaiosynē*. Just the realization that it can be translated as "justification" as well as "righteousness" should make it clear why this is so to any historian of Christianity. The basis for this challenge is articulated clearly and succinctly by Alister McGrath:

> The *doctrine* of justification has come to develop a meaning quite independent of its biblical origins, and concerns *the means by which man's relationship to God is established*. The church has chosen to subsume its discussion of the reconciliation of man to God under the aegis of justification, thereby giving the concept an emphasis quite absent from the New Testament. The "doctrine of justification" has come to bear a meaning within dogmatic theology which is quite independent of its Pauline origins.

Given this warning, we can now move to examine justice (*dikaiosynē*) from the world within which Paul discussed it, not the interpretive world of Luther and the Reformation nor the reaction to Luther that came from Catholicism and the Counter-reformation, both of which were guilty of

---

24. Hays, *The Faith of Jesus Christ*, xxix.

overindividualizing the notion to the detriment of their Christian communities.[25] However this is easier envisioned than accomplished, especially
when we consider what N. T. Wright calls "the cluster of words and phrases
which, in many biblical contexts, help to hold in place the notion of 'righteousness,' particularly 'God's righteousness.'"[26] This leads him to the following caution in an extended but clarifying passage:

> The biblical terms for various attributes of the divine character and
> activity overlap considerably, and we would be wrong to play them
> off against one another. We have mentioned the divine "righteous-
> ness" (*tsedaqah/dikaiosynē*); but we often find, in the same passages,
> "judgment" or "justice" (*mishpat/krisis*); truth/truthfulness (*emu-
> nah/alētheia*); steadfast love (*raham* or *hesed/eleos*); and, in slightly
> different mode, "salvation" (*teshu'ah/sōtēria*). Both in Hebrew
> and in the LXX [Greek Septuagint] these seem to intertwine; all
> together are ways of speaking of the character and even identity
> of the one God, but with the different attributes called up for the
> particular nuances required. Thus, we can say that this God's "sal-
> vation" is his rescue-operation; his "steadfast love" is that because
> of which he will woo his people back again, forgiving their previous
> wrongs; his "truth" (which can also be expressed as "trustworthi-
> ness" *pistis*) is that because of which he will say what he means and
> do what he says; his "justice" is the characteristic because of which
> Israel will know that it can rely on him to do what is right; and,
> above all, his "righteousness" is his *faithfulness to his previous com-
> mitments*, particularly of course the covenant.[27]

Michael J. Gorman notes that, in both Hebrew and Greek, "the terms
justification, justice, and righteousness are all related to the same root (*dik*).
In each language, this root word is part of at least three interrelated lexi-
cal clusters from Paul's Jewish environment: the language of divine and
human virtue, the language of covenant, and the language of apocalyptic
judgment." However, he notes (in a passage that every reader must take to
heart) that, while this triad applies to God, it applies equally to those who
are to lead godly lives:

25. Alister McGrath, *Iustitia Dei: A History of the Christian Doctrine of Justification
from 1500 to the Present Day*, vol. 1 (Cambridge: Cambridge University Press, 1986), 2-3.
26. Wright, *Paul and the Faithfulness of God*, Book II, Part III, 795-96.
27. Ibid., 96.

In biblical theology, God is a righteous and just God who has created a people from whom corresponding righteousness and justice are expected. The righteous character of God is supposed to
be embodied in the righteous character of the people, expressed
in such ways as care for the widow and the orphan. Those who are
truly righteous will be acquitted and vindicated on the day of judgment.[28]

Paul proclaimed unabashedly, "I am not ashamed of the gospel, since it is
the power of God for salvation, to all who believe, Jew first but also Gentile.
For the righteousness of God is being revealed in it from faith to faith." It
has been a source of debate for centuries as to what this means. Even more
debated is the next sentence, one of the most quoted lines in the whole Pauline corpus: "He who is righteous by faith shall live" (Rom. 1:16-17).

However, because of the way *dikaiosynē* has been translated linguistically
and interpreted culturally and religiously, rather than giving justice (no pun
intended) to its historical context, we have experienced significant misun-
derstandings that have kept us blinded to what Paul, who always remained
faithful to his Jewish roots, most likely meant by the notion. This challenge
has been reinforced in the way the traditional Lutheran interpretation and
its counterinterpretation in Catholicism have skewed our understanding.
Without revisiting the traditional arguments, I here will only discuss the
challenges facing us around two interpretations of *dikaiosynē*. One comes
when it is interpreted as "justice" or "justification," and the other when it is
translated as "righteousness."

Notwithstanding our need to be aware of this history, as we move into a
discussion of the various meanings, I find it helpful to begin our excursus by
accepting what seems to be a generally understood meaning of *dikaiosynē*
that involves the way we are faithful to God, ourselves, and others. Building on this understanding, I find very helpful the definition put forward by
my former Scripture teacher, John R. Donahue. Simply put, justice means
"fidelity to the demands of a relationship."[29]

By setting Paul's gospel of God's faithfulness and righteousness toward
us within its Judaic context, it becomes clear that *dikaiosynē* has more applicability communally than individually and is more challenging relationally

---

28. Michael J. Gorman, *Cruciformity: Paul's Narrative Spirituality of the Cross* (Grand
Rapids: Eerdmans, 2001), 162.

29. John R. Donahue, S.J., "Biblical Perspectives on Justice," in *The Faith That Does
Justice* (ed. John W. Haughey, S.J.; New York: Paulist Press, 1977), 69 (emphasis in original).

than legally. Indeed, as J. Christiaan Beker insists, "The center of Paul's thought is misunderstood when it is located in individual justification or in the equation of redemption with individual heavenly bliss or in a sectarian and elitist ecclesiology that defines itself simply *over against* the world." This understanding not only must color our interpretation of Paul's meaning of "justification" but how it applies to Christians of every day. Thus he writes,

> The universal scope of God's coming reign necessitates a radical conception of the church *for* the world. Christians are only "in Christ" when they become partners in God's cosmic redemptive plan for his world. Since the human being is placed within the power structures of the world, there is a profound solidarity and interdependence not only between all people in the world, but also between our "inner world," our "social world," and our "ecological world."[30]

As we move more deeply into our understanding of how God's covenantal faithfulness is to be replicated by our own, Kathy Ehrensperger notes (in ways that recall what we said about the connection among God's faithfulness, mercy, and kindness in Chapter 9),

> The term encompasses the obligations of someone who is part of a relationship. Scholars have not yet fully thought through the consequences of this understanding for the theological explication of "justification by faith." God's righteousness is his faithfulness to this chosen people. God is righteous; he is faithful in a relationship he once entered, and faithful despite the unfaithfulness of his people.[31]

Even though God's faithfulness continues, despite the times we are unfaithful to our part of the covenant, nonetheless the invitation remains. Given the covenant, our faithfulness is to be manifest in our love of God, our neighbor, and ourselves. It is not surprising that, in her little book of reflections on *The Fruits of the Spirit*, Evelyn Underhill spends more time elaborating on "faithfulness" than anything else. For her, "Faithfulness

---

30. J. Christiaan Beker, *The Triumph of God: The Essence of Paul's Thought* (trans. Loren T. Stuckenbruck; Minneapolis: Fortress Press, 1990), xiv.

31. Kathy Ehrensperger, *That We May Be Mutually Encouraged: Feminism and the New Perspective in Pauline Studies* (New York: T & T Clark International, 2004), 150.

is consecration in overalls."[32] In her homespun way she writes (reflecting some of the daily patterns of her times),

> The fruits of the Spirit get less and less showy as we go on. Faithfulness means continuing quietly with the job we have been given, in the situation where we have been placed; not yielding to the restless desire for change. It means tending the lamp quietly for God without wondering how much longer it has to go on. Steady, unsensational driving, taking good care of the car. A lot of the road to heaven has to be taken at thirty miles per hour. It means keeping everything in your charge in good order for love's sake. . . . If your life is really part of the apparatus of the Spirit, that is the sort of life it must be.[33]

Dikaiosynē Understood as Justification

A key part of Paul's Letter to the Galatians revolves around his expanded discussion of justification and whether this justification comes through the law identified with the Moses or the faith of Abraham. Indeed 55 of the 148 verses of Galatians (3:6–5:1), over one-third, ultimately address Paul's understanding of what "justification by faith" in the law of Moses or the law of Christ entails.

When we translate *dikaiosynē* as "justification," we need to be clear about the notion. And today's notion is very different from that of Martin Luther. Probably the best contemporary explanation of justification itself I have read comes from Marcus Barth. He writes, "Justification is a social event. It ties human to human together. Justification by works would segregate people because each person would select his/her own arbitrary criterion of good works. Justification by grace, however, brings people together in reconciliation, even those of alien background, like the Jews and Gentiles."[34] Made just by God we seek to be just with all in the way God has made us just: that is, to be in right relationship. From this one can conclude that the believer's faith that is expressed in the practice of justice in a way that manifests itself as "working through love" is the core of Paul's theology.

---

32. Evelyn Underhill, in Roger L. Roberts, compiler, *The Fruits of the Spirit by Evelyn Underhill* (Wilton, CT: Morehouse-Barlow Company, 1981, 1989), 27.

33. Ibid., 28.

34. Marcus Barth, "Jews and Gentiles: The Social Character of Justification in Paul" (trans. Norman Adams), *Journal of Ecumenical Studies* 5 (1968): 241.

Despite Barth's remarks about justification, there remains confusion about how to translate *dikaiosynē*. This occurs when justice and being right(eous) become almost synonymous, as in the writing of such a recognized Pauline scholar as N. T. Wright. This is evident when he writes that, theologically, "justification is not the means whereby it becomes possible to declare someone in the right. It is simply the declaration itself. It is not how someone becomes a Christian, but simply the declaration that someone is a Christian." And, for Wright, the Christian of all times is the one who embraces the gospel as a way of life. This is so, he writes, because,

> with the Gospel of Jesus Christ a dramatic new turn has been taken. God's verdict has been brought forward into the present. Even now God declares that certain people are in the right. Even though the declaration concerns sinners, it is itself righteous, because of two things: grace and faith. We can therefore expand our definition as follows: justification is not only God's declaration on the last day that certain people are in the right: It is also his declaration in the present that, because of the death and resurrection of Jesus Christ, the person who believes the Gospel is in the right.[35]

This person is the Christian of Paul's day as well as ours who embraces the gospel of the kingdom of God that led Jesus to his passion and death and the equally important gospel of Paul that proclaimed that this Jesus who was crucified is now alive in the lives of all believers. Given this understanding, the Joint Declaration on the Doctrine of Justification between the Catholics and Lutherans declared,

> We confess together that persons are justified by faith in the gospel "apart from works prescribed by the law" (Rom. 3:28). Christ has fulfilled the law and by his death and resurrection has overcome it as a way to salvation. We also confess that God's commandments retain their validity for the justified and that Christ has by his teaching and example expressed God's will which is a standard for the conduct of the justified also.[36]

As we move to end our brief consideration of *dikaiosynē* as justification, I think that N. T. Wright summarizes it best when he directly connects

---

35. N. T. Wright, *Pauline Perspectives: Essays on Paul, 1978–2013* (Minneapolis: Fortress Press, 2013), 22-23.

36. Lutheran World Federation and the Catholic Church, Joint Declaration on the Doctrine of Justification, 4.5.31 (http://www.vatican.va).

dikaiosynē with our faith in the Jesus Christ of the gospel and the practice of his/its message. He writes, "Here, then, is the watch spring of justification. It is God's declaration, in the present, that those who believe the Gospel are in the right, are members of the covenant family."[37] Expanding the link between justification and the covenant, Gorman offers three points that help our understanding of the meaning of justification. "Justification, then, may be described," he writes, "as (1) right relations with God (covenant) issuing in (2) right (even 'godly') relations with others (virtue) and (3) acquittal on the day of judgment (vindication). In other words, justification, righteousness, and their related terms in English refer to *covenant faithfulness with respect to God and neighbor,* and *ultimate divine approval.*"[38]

The covenant made with Abraham and his offspring centuries ago, according to Paul, is meant to continue today in the members of the church who believe and, in this belief, lead virtuous lives in such a way that they reveal their justification by continuing to proclaim that gospel to the world, and this will bring them ultimate vindication on the day of judgment. This faith is grounded not in any kind of law that results in separation and exclusivism but in that law of love that unites and creates ever-wider forms of community. Pope Francis stressed the joy that comes from such faith that is grounded in love in contrast to those religious leaders who stressed covenantal nomism in a way that actually found them "without faith." Thus he said in 2015, "Our father Abraham was able to rejoice because he had faith: he was made just in faith. These lost their faith. They were doctors of the law, but without faith! But more so: they lost the law! Because the center of the law is love, love for God and for neighbor."[39]

Dikaiosynē Understood as Righteousness

In his *The Spirit and the Restoration of Israel: New Exodus and New Creation Motifs in Galatians,* Rodrigo Morales makes a clear argument that the Spirit about which Paul talked at length in Galatians was inseparable from righteousness and that both notions were at the heart of the eschatology of Second Temple Judaism, which colored Paul's thought about the dynamics that would characterize the new creation. The sign of the Spirit's inbreaking, Morales notes, would be identified with "the expectation of

---

37. Wright, *Pauline Perspectives,* 23.

38. Gorman, *Cruciformity,* 163.

39. Pope Francis, "The Joy of the Gospel Is the Touchstone of One's Faith," March 26, 2015, http://www.zenit.org.

'righteousness.'"[40] Just as our vision of the end of the world envisions a heaven where "all is made right," so this vision was to be realized on earth in those who claimed to be followers of the Righteous One and guarantor of their salvation.

One of the core points raised in this book has shown how the Teachers with whom Paul contended believed that righteousness, or justification, could only come through obedience in a way that was linked to observance of the law. This was also linked to an aberration of authentic covenantal nomism, which demanded separation from "outsiders" by those who justified their actions with an ideology of "righteousness" that made them the uniquely chosen and blessed community. They did not ground their blessing, Philip Esler notes, where it belonged: in "faith in the crucified Christ as the source of that life and the experience of the Spirit as the primary content of that blessing."[41] Indeed, this "righteousness" stood in marked contrast to authentic Hebrew "righteousness," which, James D. G. Dunn insists, "refers to the *meeting of obligations* which arise out of a relationship." Consequently God's righteousness "refers to *God's enactment of the obligation he had accepted in so creating the world and in so choosing Israel to be his people.*[42] For his part Ernst Käsemann insists that, for Paul, the "righteousness of God" means not only God's gift in Christ to the church, but also God's sovereign claim as creator over the world.[43] Given such cosmic interpretations, it is most disappointing to realize how it got translated in the kind of elitist and separatist covenantal nomism that made some in Israel (as well as Paul's opponents in Christianity) *righteous*. However, their righteousness was based not on a faith that made them just but a sense of their superiority in the eyes of God.

Until now I have showed that this tendency has found its echoes in canonical nomism, which has virtually identified *dikaiosynē* with a sense of "righteousness" as privileged identity. This has contributed to much tension and conflict and separation and polarization in the Catholic Church. However, this "ideology of righteousness" is reinforced by the culture itself, or at least by contemporary U.S. culture.

---

40. Rodrigo I. Morales, *The Spirit and the Restoration of Israel: New Exodus and New Creation Motifs in Galatians* (Tübingen: Mohr Siebeck, 2010), 133.

41. Philip F. Esler, *Galatians* (London: Routledge, 1998), 176.

42. James D. G. Dunn, *Jesus, Paul, and the Gospels* (Grand Rapids: Eerdmans, 2011), 155.

43. Ernst Käsemann, *New Testament Questions of Today* (trans. W. T. Montague; Philadelphia: Fortress Press, 1969), 178-82. I am indebted to J. Christiaan Beker for this lead (*The Triumph of God*, 21).

In 2012, Jonathan Haidt published what I consider one of the seminal books that have influenced my thinking, *The Righteous Mind: Why Good People Are Divided by Politics and Religion*, in which he argued that "human nature is not just intrinsically moral; it's also intrinsically moralistic, critical, and judgmental." While noting that its roots in the Scriptures reveal *dikaiosynē* (he uses the Hebrew word *tzedek*) as "an attribute of God and of God's judgment of people," he also says that the word is used "to describe people who [think they] act in accordance with God's wishes." While such justice is linked to what God desires regarding making right our relationships as is at the heart of what we mean by *dikaiosynē*, what Haidt has shown is that, when "righteousness and judgmentalism" are linked, we move into the arena of polarization. Thus he writes,

> I want to show you that an obsession with righteousness (leading inevitably to self-righteousness) is the normal human condition. It is a feature of our evolutionary design, not a bug or error that crept into minds that would otherwise be objective and rational.
>
> Our righteous minds made it possible for human beings—but no other animals—to produce large cooperative groups, tribes, and nations without the glue of kinship. But at the same time, our righteous minds guarantee that our cooperative groups will always be cursed by moralistic strife.[44]

I believe Haidt's insight can be adapted in a way that might help us understand why it will be very hard for many who have a mindset supportive of canonical nomism to move to the kind of observance of justice as "faith working through love" of which Galatians speaks and which Pope Francis has been promoting.

Haidt is in sync with what neuroscientists and evolutionary psychologists are telling us about the way our moral stances have evolved—how they are grounded not so much by actual reasoning (which we think to be the case) but by our emotions.[45] Consequently our reasoning is actually suffused with emotion (or what researchers often call "affect"). Thus our positive or negative feelings about people, things, and ideas arise much more

---

44. Jonathan Haidt, *The Righteous Mind: Why Good People Are Divided by Politics and Religion* (New York: Pantheon Books, 2012), xiii.

45. See Daniel Kahneman, *Thinking, Fast and Slow* (New York: Farrar, Straus & Giroux, 2011). Kahneman argues that the mind incorporates two systems: (1) an intuitive "system one," which makes many decisions automatically, and (2) a calculating but lazy "system two," which rationalizes system one's ideas and sometimes overrules them in a way that prizes emotional intelligence over rational intelligence.

rapidly than our conscious thoughts. We react emotionally by "disliking" or "liking" something (a person's figure, a statement, a stance) in a way that interprets that as "bad" or "good" and makes us rationalize that this must be "wrong" or "right." When we become convinced, in this way, that something is "wrong" or "right," Haidt shows us, moralization and *righteousness* are necessary corollaries and consequences.

I have adapted a chart made by Haidt to help me understand the process underlying all our so-called rationality in moral reasoning in a way that makes us polarized and *righteously* so, whether in religions such as Catholicism or between left and right in politics. Our moral judgments (regarding "good" and "bad") are grounded in emotional reactions identified with the heart ("like" and "dislike") as well as in the reasoning that is identified with the head, which determines whether something is "right" or "wrong"; however, neuroscience shows us that reasoning is secondary to the emotions; the head is servant of the heart.

A consequence of such emotionally grounded rationality impacts how we look at data regarding our deeply held beliefs (including whether such beliefs have scientific grounding).[46] In turn, someone such as Dan Kahan, professor of law and psychology at Yale, has shown that this leads to our sense of belonging to groups that are defined by such opposing cultural values as those noted by George Lakoff and Jonathan Haidt in the next chapter. Kahan classifies individuals, based on their cultural values, as "individualists" or "communitarians" and as either "hierarchical" or "egalitarian." To show the difference in worldviews his 2011 research demonstrated that, while 88 percent of "egalitarian communitarians" accepted the scientific data only 23 percent of "hierarchical individualists" did so.[47]

---

46. For a popular overview of this phenomenon, see Chris Mooney, "The Science of Why We Don't Believe Science," *Mother Jones*, April 18, 2011, http://www.motherjones.com.

47. For more on Dan Kahan's research, see Nancy Huynh, "Cultural Cognition and Scientific Consensus," *Yale Scientific Magazine* 88.1 (2011). For a more recent piece on Kahan's research, see Brendan Nyhan, "When Beliefs and Facts Collide," *New York Times*, July 6, 2014. For more on the phenomenon, see Margaret Heffernan, *Willful Blindness: Why We Ignore the Obvious at Our Peril* (New York: Walker Publishing Company, 2011).

I believe that, when so many American Catholics have developed a mindset of "hierarchical individualism," to convert to the kind of egalitarian communitarian model envisioned, at least theoretically, by Paul will be very difficult. However, this transition is critical for the future of Roman Catholicism, especially in the United States.

The Challenge of Interpreting Dikaiosynē as [Doing] Justice

As suggested above, the meaning of *dikaiosynē* has not had an easy history. This is especially true when we consider how elements of the traditional Lutheran understanding of the term have been overly identified with the notion of personal salvation through faith alone. This invites us to move from placing too much stress on individual righteousness, so we can emphasize "fidelity to the demands of relationships" among and beyond our churches themselves. This demands social justice.

It was not until 1971, when the episcopal leadership of the Roman Catholic Church began to move significantly from being composed almost exclusively of white males from the dominant economic powers to including those nonwhite bishops of the South, that the notion of social justice became interpreted in a way that challenged the privilege of those white males and the dominant cultures where they lived. Thus, in the 1971 Synod of Bishops discussion "Justice in the World," the bishops stated that they had "been able to perceive the serious injustices which are building around the world of men a network of domination, oppression and abuses which stifle freedom and which keep the greater part of humanity from sharing in the building up and enjoyment of a more just and more fraternal world."[48]

Faithful to the prophetic dimension of every authentic mystic, they described more fully what they meant by social injustice:

> We see in the world a set of injustices which constitute the nucleus of today's problems and whose solution requires the undertaking of tasks and functions in every sector of society, and even on the level of the global society towards which we are speeding in this last quarter of the twentieth century. Therefore we must be prepared to take on new functions and new duties in every sector of human activity and especially in the sector of world society, if justice is really to be put into practice. Our action is to be directed

48. 1971 Synod of Bishops, *Justice in the World*, 3, in Joseph Gremillion, *The Gospel of Peace and Justice: Catholic Social Teaching since Pope John* (Maryknoll, NY: Orbis Books, 1976), 514.

above all at those men and nations which because of various forms of oppression and because of the present character of our society are silent, indeed, voiceless, victims of injustice [i.e., migrants, refugees, those deprived of religious freedom and the right to life].[49]

Philip Esler notes that the stress of viewing biblical justice ensuring right relationships that bring about a "social identity" made the bishops realize that they themselves needed to be converted to its purposes. The promotion of what Esler calls a "social identity" around justice that is grounded in a "self-sacrificing and life-giving Christ" at all levels is critical today. He writes,

> Given the rampant secularism and the development of multicultural societies in the West, the inequality of wealth within and among nations, the pace of technological change, the scope of environmental degradation, and the profusion of long-established religious and new religious movements, the critical question of who we, as Christians, actually are has never been more pressing.[50]

Esler's notion of "rampant secularism," as well as the other forms of what I believe represent elements of the apocalypticism of our Anthropocene Age, is something that has great application to a core argument of this book, namely, Rahner's statement that "the devout Christian of the future will be a mystic—one who has experienced something—or nothing at all." This became clear to me while I was finishing this chapter and book. In another one of his very helpful columns, "Building Better Secularists: Moral Struggle without God," David Brooks pointed to the data showing the rising numbers of atheists, agnostics, and persons without religious affiliation that have been accompanied by a more robust form of secularism. However, he noted that, despite the increasing articulations promoting the benefits of a secular life that follows the Golden Rule in ways that evidence empathy and consideration of others, "I can't avoid the conclusion that the secular writers are so eager to make the case for their creed, they are minimizing the struggle required to live by it." Such struggles, he implies, can be found in religions that "arouse the higher emotions [and] exalt the passions in pursuit of moral action." In two beautiful paragraphs he notes what I have tried show as the way Paul found to take the best of Judaism and link it with his gospel of Jesus Christ and the Christian com-

---

49. Synod of Bishops, *Justice in the World*, 20 (518).
50. Esler, *Galatians*, 177.

munity that evolved from his death, resurrection, and embodiment in the members of the church:

> Christianity doesn't rely just on a mild feeling like empathy; it puts agape at the center of life, a fervent and selfless sacrificial love. Judaism doesn't just value community; it values a covenantal community infused with sacred bonds and chosenness that make the heart strings vibrate. Religions don't just ask believers to respect others; rather each soul is worthy of the highest dignity because it radiates divine light.
>
> The only secularism that can really arouse moral motivation and impel action is an enchanted secularism, one that puts emotional relations first and autonomy second. I suspect that over the next years secularism will change its face and become hotter and more consuming, less content with mere benevolence, and more responsive to the spiritual urge in each of us, the drive for purity, self-transcendence and sanctification.[51]

If this sanctification comes from faith and if this faith is grounded in self-giving love, the challenge to be mystics-in-action becomes all the more clear.

The Collection: Paul's Solidarity Effort to Bring about Justice

A key problem facing people in the wealthy nations involves the issue of disparity of income between companies' top executives and the average worker. This issue involves concerns and challenges about wealth and income gaps that go back all the way to Paul's own communities. It seems to have been a consequence not only of his Jewish sense of justice but also a concrete carryover of the commitment he made to James, Cephas, and John when he, Barnabas, and Titus met with them in Jerusalem to "remember the poor" (2:10).

Commenting on this passage, Carolyn Osiek notes that while most "scholars agree that 'the poor' are the Christians of Judaea for whom Paul organized at least one and possibly two collections of money from most of the Churches of the Diaspora that he had founded (see Rom. 15:25-27; 1 Cor. 16:1-4; 2 Cor. 8, 9; Acts 11:28-30)," she also notes that there "is less

---

51. David Brooks, "Building Better Secularists," *New York Times*, February 3, 2015, A21.

agreement on whether the expression 'the poor' indicates genuine economic need on the part of those in Jerusalem."[52]

While Paul found concern for the poor to be foundational to the gospel he proclaimed, as Larry Hurtado has written, the collection Paul promoted to take care of those who were poor in the Jerusalem church(es) has not received the recognition it deserves as being an ongoing concern of Paul himself:

> One of the most important projects of the Apostle Paul has often been neglected in scholarly treatments of him and his mission: Paul spent several years and considerable effort in organizing a financial collection to offer to the Jerusalem church. Indeed, in a surprising number of scholarly studies one can't even find a single reference to this project. The Jerusalem collection is referred to in several of Paul's letters: Galatians 2:10; 1 Corinthians 16:1-4; the entirety of 2 Corinthians 8–9; and, in the final days before setting off to carry the collection to Jerusalem, in Romans 15:25-33. This surely indicates that it was not a passing thought for him, but occupied him quite seriously.[53]

While Hurtado notes the theory that Paul's concern about helping out the church in Jerusalem might not have been altruistic (instead, he shows how some think it might have been a "bribe" to win favor), an examination of the rationale he offered in his letters appears to me that, in his mind, the collection he envisioned involved a justice between these communities (i.e., right relationships) that actually demanded this form of wealth/income redistribution. However, rather than concentrate on the reordering of the monies, Paul was more concerned about the equalization and reordering of the very lives of the people involved. By sharing their resources the Christian communities were giving a sign of their self-sacrificing, which made them servants, if not slaves, of total strangers: those "others" who constituted the house churches, especially in Jerusalem.

---

52. Carolyn Osiek, R.S.C.J., *Galatians* (Dublin: Veritas Publications 1980), 22. Osiek argues that the expression in 2:10 regarding "the poor" is such that it "functions not so much as an economic but rather as a theological title of spiritual privilege, as indeed it often does in the biblical tradition. In other words it says less about their economic status than about their position of honor among Christians from other communities" (23). This argument seems to belie why the collection would involve monies if it had no economic basis.

53. Larry R. Hurtado, "The Jerusalem Collection: A Polite Bribe?," Larry Hurtado's Blog, August 13, 2013, https://larryhurtado.wordpress.com.

When Paul talked about the sharing of resources in the community, he often did so under the umbrella of the sharing of gifts (*charismata*) as the normal outflow of God's generous *charis* freely bestowed on all. Thus in Romans Paul advises those who contribute to do so liberally; those who give aid, to be zealous about it; and when one is merciful, to be cheerful (Rom. 12:8). Such an attitude reflects God's generosity and Christ's self-sacrificing love, and they become characteristics of God's presence among the members of the universal and local body of the church. Furthermore, when one considers how these attitudes were to characterize the mutual sharing of financial resources discussed in 2 Corinthians 8–9, it becomes clear that the sharing itself not only promotes justice; it also manifests the fidelity to their relationships, which the members of the house churches of Paul's day (as well as ours) were to pledge to one another that extended beyond their own local communities into other parts of the empire.

Sandra Hack Polaski writes, "The *collection* symbolizes this unity-in-diversity in a way that no other act could." She notes that "the collection functions as an example in letters in which unity of Jews and Gentiles in Christ is a theme, such as Galatians, where Paul stridently opposes divisions between Jew and Gentile, and Romans (15.25-29), where Paul theologizes most fully about Jews and Gentiles together in Christ." She shows that this goal of intra- and intercommunal solidarity, which was so close to Paul's heart as an exemplification of the core meaning of the gospel, "explains why Paul must deliver the collection to Jerusalem himself, despite what he recognizes beforehand is great personal risk." She concludes,

> The collection emblematizes *his* gospel; he will carry it out in person. His person and his gospel are so closely linked that no other way will do. Paul, here, participates in a discourse of power, but he cannot control its results. Because Paul's personal identity, his gospel, and the collection are bound up together, Paul must make a difficult choice: either to deliver the collection to Jerusalem, or to compromise his gospel. Apparently he chose to go; Acts narrates the perilous journey.[54]

As I understand the teachings, writings, and comments of Pope Francis, in a world where there is so much inequality with regard to wealth, income, wages, and even education, we are in need of a new kind of economic solidarity that goes beyond the collection of one group more economically

---

54. Sandra Hack Polaski, *Paul and the Discourse of Power* (Sheffield: Sheffield Academic Press, 1999), 99.

secure on behalf of their brothers and sisters in other house churches. This demands a new kind of justice in the form of structural economic reform that will result in a political economy that reflects the Trinitarian economy of God and God's just relationships within the Godhead as they have been revealed in Jesus Christ and the community he envisioned and mystically experienced by Paul. This demands a totally new social order not defined by any kind of disparity—be it grounded in ethnicity (Jew/Gentile), economics (slave/free), gender (male/female), or disparity of any other kind as well.

The faith that does justice demands nothing less.

Chapter 13

Cultivating Self-Control as a Sign of Be(com)ing Free in the Spirit's Love

In Chapter 4, I outlined how I would attempt to develop elements of a mystical stance toward life, the pursuit of which represents the heart of this book. I noted there that I believe the seed of any developed "fruit" of the Spirit originally at the core of the Big Bang continues to evolve in various ways in everyone and everything. Thus, honoring the axiom that "grace builds on nature," I promised to try to address wherever I could the evidence we have about the fruit in question from what we know of science, especially biology and neuroscience. As I begin this last chapter, it should be clear that this has not proven to be the case for some of the manifestations of the fruit of love in our lives. However, self-control as a fruit of love is one of the exceptions because of its neurological connection.

In one of David Brooks's many insightful columns addressing what I consider to be the science/faith nexus, "The Deepest Self: What Is at the Core of Your Being," he noted that a good part of "a large literature on the chemistry and biology of love and sex" seems to reduce "the profound and transformational power of love into a series of mating strategies." However, he immediately adds that neuroscience is telling us something more. I think this insight can help lay a solid foundation in science as we consider Paul's notion of "self-control."

Brooks notes that the literature of psychology and cognitive science "these days, reinforces a specific view of human nature" as well. This points to the data showing that we humans have two systems within ourselves, one on top of the other. He explains, "Deep in the core of our being there are the unconscious natural processes built in by evolution. These deep unconscious processes propel us to procreate or strut or think in certain ways, often impulsively." However, the second "system" is at the top where "we have our conscious, rational processes. This top layer does its best to exercise some restraint and executive function." This, I believe, represents a contemporary understanding of the function of Paul's notion of self-control, which can also be called "self-restraint." Brooks calls this form of self-control or self-restraint the process of character formation that results in "the deepest self." He writes,

> When we say someone is deep, that they have a deep mind or a deep heart, we don't mean that they are animalistic or impulsive [i.e., operating from the lower, unconscious level]. We mean the opposite. When we say that someone is a deep person, we mean they have achieved a quiet, dependable mind by being rooted in something spiritual and permanent.
>
> A person of deep character has certain qualities: in the realm of intellect, she has permanent convictions about fundamental things; in the realm of emotions, she has a web of unconditional loves; in the realm of action, she has permanent commitments to transcendent projects that cannot be complete in a single lifetime.

Brooks noted that such findings from science "should cause us to amend the System 1/System 2 image of human nature that we are getting from evolutionary biology," especially in ways that "should cause us to make a sharp distinction between origins and depth." And, that echoes what we identified in Chapter 5 with Paul's kenotic spirituality of self-emptying that learns obedient love through suffering for a cause bigger than ourselves (the gospel). Brooks concludes,

> So much of what we call depth is built through freely chosen suffering. People make commitments—to a nation, faith, calling or loved ones—and endure the sacrifices those commitments demand. Often this depth is built by fighting against natural evolutionary predispositions . . . the suffering scours away a floor inside themselves, exposing a deeper level, and then that floor gets scoured away and another deeper level is revealed. Finally, people get down to the core wounds and the core loves.[1]

In the previous chapter I discussed the insight of Jonathan Haidt and other neuroscientists who have shown that our morality is grounded in deep emotions. In turn, these are articulated in diametrically opposed

---

1. David Brooks, "The Deepest Self: What Is at the Core of Your Being," *New York Times,* March 14, 2014, A21.

notions regarding the way we reason morally. Having such seminal, pre-existing mindsets, beliefs, or what psychologists and neuroscientists call "motivated reasoning" explains why people organize themselves into groups that become so polarized around their beliefs that evidence to the contrary becomes discounted. This realization has relevance when we consider its application to the contemporary issues of race and class, climate change and evolution, as well as the role of authority in the church.[2] One of these writers, I noted in a footnote in the previous chapter, is Daniel Kahneman, author of *Thinking, Fast and Slow.* Herein he shows that we are more ready to react emotionally (i.e., "fast") and then use our reasoning powers (slowly) to determine our ultimate reaction.

In Chapter 8, on "patience," I referenced the famous "marshmallow experiment," which tested children's efforts to exercise self-control. The main author of the marshmallow experiment, Walter Mischel, wrote a follow-up book in 2014, *The Marshmallow Test: Mastering Self-Control.*[3] It showed that scans of the brain actually manifest different activity when what he calls "the cool system" stimulates children to wait for the extra marshmallow in a way that reveals that self-control may be affected by our genes ("nature"). In studying what happened in later life to those who practiced self-control, the data shows they did much better in areas considered by society to truly matter, including jobs, making money, and other forms of "worldly" success. In support of the idea that people make moral judgments quickly and emotionally, he agrees with the data from science that reveals that moral reasoning is "mostly just a post hoc search for reasons to justify the judgments people had already made."

In the previous pages, however, I did not articulate how these polarized emotions get articulated between the "left" and the "right" in ways that help us understand our differences, especially the political divides we hear from many commentators on Fox News and MSNBC or the approaches to authority of Culture I and Culture II Catholics evidenced on the pages of the *National Catholic Register* and the *National Catholic Reporter.*

---

2. George Lakoff argues in a similar way from his findings on moral reasoning. He divides the two basic stances in life as representing in people's "strict father" and "nurturing parent" images. See George Lakoff, *Moral Politics: How Liberals and Conservatives Think* (2nd ed.; Chicago: University of Chicago Press, 2002), 245-62, For more on this, see my *Repair My House: Becoming a "Kindom" Catholic* (Maryknoll, NY: Orbis Books, 2012), 38-40.

3. Walter Mischel, *The Marshmallow Test: Mastering Self-Control* (New York: Little, Brown, 2014).

This invites us to return to Jonathan Haidt. He makes a persuasive argument that, while both those on "the left" and "the right" are grounded in notions of doing good and avoiding evil involving similar attitudes around care/harm and fairness/cheating, unlike those on "the left" (i.e., Democrats) those on 'the right" (i.e., "Republicans") evidence strong convictions around three other moral stances: loyalty/betrayal, authority/subversion, and sanctity/degradation. Not surprisingly, when I apply Haidt's moral foundations of loyalty, authority, and sanctity to Catholics, it becomes understandable how their forms came to be highlighted in the pontificates of popes John Paul II and Benedict XVI in ways that promoted the kind of authoritative patriarchal clericalism that I've called canonical nomism. This became ideologically reinforced when those Catholic theologians who dissented from almost any teachings of the Roman Curia or bishops were labeled as disloyal and subversive; further, Catholicism's episcopal structure and dynamics had become virtually equated with holiness and sanctity.

While it would be fascinating to discuss these findings and how they play out in our different political and religious stances (a key purpose of Haidt's book), Haidt also notes one other difference between those on the left and the right regarding their different ways of understanding what the left calls freedom and the right calls liberty that has important significance for the way we will approach Paul's notion of self-control (*egkrateia*). I want to show how a deeper understanding of *egkrateia* depends on Paul's notion in Galatians of freedom or liberty (*eleutheria*), especially Galatians, where it is used four times (2:4; 5:1; and 5:13 [2x]). Despite its minimal use, as Carolyn Osiek notes in the beginning paragraph of her commentary on Galatians, a misunderstanding of *eleutheria* can result in what we have called covenantal and canonical nomism as well as the kind of selfishness that undermines the necessity of the Spirit's power of self-control, which will be the main concern of this chapter. She writes,

> Galatians is a letter that is concerned from start to finish with a question that is timely in any age: the freedom of the Christian. Paul was aware that this freedom must be fought for simultaneously on two fronts. It must be defended against laws and restrictions imposed from without. At the same time, freedom is equally threatened from within by the innate human tendency to abuse it as an excuse for selfishness.[4]

---

4. Carolyn Osiek, R.S.C.J., *Galatians* (Dublin: Veritas Publications, 1980), 1.

I have already noted that an understanding of *egkrateia* hinges on Paul's notion of freedom/liberty (*eleutheria*), especially in Galatians.[5] Carolyn Osiek writes that the word (notion) "is the heart and soul of the Epistle to the Galatians." This is especially necessary for us in the United States who approach the notion of *eleutheria* with a grounding not so much in the Word as in our differing ideologies of "left" (freedom) and "right" (liberty).

The differences in meaning that we bring to Paul's notion of *eleutheria* were developed in an October 2014 issue of *First Things*, a journal addressing issues around religion and public life. Its author, Yuval Levin, argues that both the left (whom he calls "liberals" or "progressives," who stress the freedom of individuals to choose) and the right (whom he calls "conservatives," who stress the liberty of individuals stemming from [property] rights), are misguided, though not in "exactly the same way" because they "both tend toward radically deficient visions of the life of a liberal society."[6] He insists that "their confusions stem from a shallow and emaciated notion of the human person, albeit one that masquerades as a moral ideal."[7]

While noting that the "conservative" stress on liberty promotes individualism (more so than the liberal or progressive stance, I would add), he says that both approaches view the common good as grounded in "balanced or coordinated self-interest" in ways that have been "facilitated by modern political philosophy's lowering of the goals of social life."[8] Consequently, he concludes (and I agree), we must abandon both approaches if we are to come to understand the self-control that reflects that authentic moral living that must be cultivated for the common good, as Paul promoted it for the Galatian house churches. Rodrigo Morales writes,

> The Galatians need have no fear that Paul's talk of "freedom" and "following the spirit" will leave them without moral direction in a structureless existence doing whatever they want. In other words, one might paraphrase the last half of Gal 5:17 as follows: "these [i.e., the Spirit and the flesh] are opposed to one another, so that (despite your freedom!) you are not free to do whatever you want."

---

5. Ibid., 4.

6. Yuval Levin, "Taking the Long Way," *First Things* 246 (October 2014), 25. David Brooks gave this article his coveted annual award for best articles in 2014: "The Sidney Awards, Part II," *New York Times*, December 30, 2014, A19, http://www.nytimes.com.

7. Levin, "Taking the Long Way," 26.

8. Ibid., 27.

This broader interpretation would obviously also exclude the desire of the flesh, but only insofar as it excludes complete autonomy.[9]

In Paul's lexicon, the notion of "flesh" evokes the fundamentally selfish desires that are fostered by the pressures of sin, to which the inauthentic are enslaved. Through their incorporation into the community, believers are freed of this pressure; but in order to give reality to this freedom they must acquire mastery over the instincts of their bodies. On account of their long domination by forces outside themselves, whether this bondage came from the Anatolian cult of the Mother of the Gods or the codes around the Mosaic law, they have to learn self-control (Gal. 5:23). Such a fruit of the spirit of love stands as the antithesis of the kind of self-gratification that would enslave them all over again.

In Paul's wisdom, self-control frees; self-gratification enslaves. Self-restraint liberates; self-centeredness separates. When the Galatians were "enslaved to the elemental spirits of the world" (4:4), whether these be the their previous observance of their Anatolian worship or under the influence of the Teachers, who wanted them to observe "the law," Paul invited the Galatians to become free of such enslaving yokes. However, because Paul knew that some might interpret his stress on their need to become free from the law as freedom to do whatever they wanted in a way that their "opportunity to live by the Spirit" might become "an occasion for self-indulgence," as Frank Matera notes, Paul plays "on the concept of slavery" in order to urge "those who have been set free to 'enslave' themselves to one another through loving service (5:13)."[10] We will consider this key element after we examine more closely Paul's notion of *egkrateia,* self-control.

Paul's Notion of Self-Control

Due in part to polarization around notions of freedom and liberty, arguably no other manifestation of the fruit of love is more misunderstood than the final one in Paul's litany: self-control. This problem is compounded when we realize that self-control (*egkrateia*) is used only once, in Gal. 5:23, as one of the manifestations of the Spirit's fruit of love in the lives of the members of the house churches. In preparing this chapter, my understanding of *egkrateia* was further frustrated by the fact that I could find very little

9. Rodrigo I. Morales, *The Spirit and the Restoration of Israel: New Exodus and New Creation Motifs in Galatians* (Tübingen: Mohr Siebeck, 2010), 147.

10. Frank J. Matera, *New Testament Theology: Exploring Diversity and Unity* (Louisville: Westminster John Knox Press, 2007), 164.

extended development of the notion in Paul's authentic writings, except for helpful insights in the doctoral dissertation on *egkrateia* by D.S.M. Bredenkamp, a South African; unfortunately, it was written in Afrikaans![11]

The challenge is compounded when we look at the other three uses of *egkrateia* in the authentic Pauline corpus. All of these are found in 1 Corinthians (7:5, 9; 9:25). The first two mentions of self-control flowed from Paul's conviction regarding how the Christians were to live in light of what he thought was the imminent return of Jesus Christ. Given his belief that the end of the world was imminent, self-control meant virtual genital abstinence (1 Cor. 7:5, 9). (The third use, in 1 Cor. 9:25, speaks of Paul's reference to the need for athletes to train for the race to come.)

Because Paul shared in the adapted worldview of Second Temple Judaism that Christ was going to return to earth from which he had ascended into heaven, Paul's Letter to the Galatians and First Letter to the Corinthians were written from his belief that Christians should not be distracted from anything lest they be found wanting on the Day of Hope. Consequently, although he did not denounce matrimony, it was Paul's opinion that, "in view of the impending crisis" (i.e., the end of the world [1 Cor. 7:26]), the Spirit had given his audience the power to easily control sexual desires. Thus Paul advised them to be celibate in order that they might be free to devote themselves more wholeheartedly to God's service.

This is the kind of freedom that Hans Dieter Betz insists "is the central theological concept which sums up the Christian's situation before God as well as in this world." He states, "It is the basic concept underlying Paul's argument" not only here, but "throughout the letter."[12] From this perspective, it is not surprising that, as he discusses the meaning of self-control (*egkrateia*), Betz also states that among the last three of the fruits of the Spirit's love (gentleness, faithfulness, and self-control), self-control is "especially important." He reasons as follows:

---

11. D. S. M. Bredenkamp, "EGKRATEIA in die Pauliniese hoofbriewe (EGKRATEIA in the Principal Pauline Letters)," Ph.D. diss., University of Pretoria, 2001, http://repository.up.ac.za.

12. Hans Dieter Betz, *Galatians: A Commentary on Paul's Letter to the Churches in Galatia* (Philadelphia: Fortress Press, 1979), 255. In commenting on this passage from Betz, Carolyn Osiek writes that Paul's notion of freedom is, "I believe, the keynote and central theme of Paul's whole theology, the point around which all else revolves. Because of this fundamental conviction nothing, including the Mosaic law, can come between Christ and those who believe in him" (Osiek, *Galatians*, 59-60). As I note in this chapter, she writes that "Christ has freed us *from* something *for* a purpose" (60).

Socrates had introduced it into Greek ethics, and by the time of Paul it was a central concept of Hellenistic ethics, whence it was taken up by Jewish and Christian writers. In Paul, it appears in the context of radical asceticism. Its place at the end of the list in v 23 is conspicuous, and this is certainly intended; it stands in juxtaposition to love (v 22). The concept of self-control in the present context implies the claim that Christian ethics is the fulfillment not only of the Torah (cf. 5:14), but also of the central demand of Greek ethics. The gift of the Spirit and the "fruit of the Spirit" reach their climax in the fulfillment of the old Greek ideal of self-control. This outstanding position of self-control is unique in Paul.[13]

Bredenkamp does not agree wholeheartedly with Betz regarding Paul's understanding of *egkrateia* insofar as he argues that Paul was influenced by its use as a key part of character formation in Greek thinking (which interpreted it as temperance and thus included it among the four cardinal virtues along with prudence, justice, and fortitude). In his mind, for Paul, *egkrateia* was not primarily a personal characteristic that resulted from discipline; rather it characterized the restrained and sacrificial managing of rights and privileges among all the Christians' interactions within the faith community. Thus he notes,

> It was not the classical or Hellenistic interpretation of *egkrateia* that influenced him. While the Hellenized Judaism of the Septuagint formed Paul's concept of *egkrateia*, his utilization of the term was innovative and original: by angling the Christian view away from the Hellenistic self-centeredness, and focusing it on a loving and altruistic managing of rights and liberties, he thoroughly Christianized the term.[14]

True to the underlying assumption of this book, that love grounds all its various expressions as a "fruit" of the Spirit, Bredenkamp notes that an exegetical analysis of Paul's use of *egkrateia* in 1 Cor. 7:5, 9, and 9:25, as well as in Gal. 5:23 makes it clear that the term represented the dynamics associated with the love with which believers serve one another, within the freedom to which God called them to be part of the body of Christ. In other words, *egkrateia* not only represents the fruit of love (which is clear from

---

13. Betz, *Galatians*, 288.
14. For quotations from Brdenkamp, see n. 11 above.

Gal. 5:23-24); even more so, for our purposes in this chapter, it represents the way everyone in the church is called to live in authentic freedom.

When we consider Paul's notion of *eleutheria,* whether we call it freedom or liberty in the context of our polarized politics and church in the United States, whatever approach we take cannot be divorced from its original context in Paul's day around conflicts regarding the law. In this sense another South African, Gys M. H. Loubser, writes,

> Too often the subject of freedom in Galatians is restricted to freedom from law. In view of the above, we must think of freedom as freedom from a total symbolic universe encapsulating humankind's whole being in bondage, slavery, tutelage and immaturity. We must think of freedom as freedom from an outdated age which was without Christ and his Spirit—so radically different and bent into itself that a new life and way of living had to be revealed into it by God's Son. It was something of such tremendous impact that the result was not a mutation of the old, but its replacement by a new creation. We must understand Paul's view of freedom as eschatological freedom—the freedom of the time inaugurated by advent of Christ and his Spirit![15]

Unfortunately, Bredenkamp notes, the church over the centuries moved away from the Pauline notion of love and freedom as the underpinning of *egkrateia* to concentrate on forms of self-discipline that promoted celibacy as a sexual ideal that undermined what was intended (by God) for males and females.[16] This kind of self-control also seems diametrically opposed to the kind of self-control that Evelyn Underhill describes in her *Mysticism.* Whether "under one symbol or another," she writes, what Paul called self-control represents the mystic's consciousness, "the need of that long slow process of transcendence, of character building, whereby she is to attain freedom, become capable of living upon high levels of reality."[17]

Another unfortunate result of misunderstanding the true meaning of *egkrateia* has been the promotion of an asceticism that idealized obedience but which, in effect, promoted forms of that kind of legalism that we have

---

15. Gys M. H. Loubser, "About Galatians, Apocalyptic and the Switching of Paradigms," *Acta Theologica* 2014, Supplement 19, 181.

16. For more on this, see Michael H. Crosby, *Rethinking Celibacy: Reclaiming the Church* (Everett, WA: Wipf & Stock, 2004).

17. Evelyn Underhill, *Mysticism: A Study in the Nature and Development of Man's Spiritual Consciousness* (New York: New American Library, 1974), 198. In Underhill's mind this involves what has traditionally been called the Way of Purification (198ff.).

called canonical nomism in ways that ensured submission to those who defined themselves as God's unique representatives. The result occurred in such a way that self-control became a highly misunderstood virtue in the church. In the process, it also led to a misunderstanding of the notion of freedom itself, which Paul interpreted to be at the core of the believer's true freedom. Thus, while Paul in 1 Corinthians 7 says he had no command from the Lord about being celibate, the "freedom" to be celibate when it is canonically commanded for priests in the church can easily become another form of the enslavement from which Paul was trying to get his audiences to escape.

In his day Paul railed against another negative consequence of our contemporary form of covenantal nomism: an interpretation of canon law in ways that minimize, if not effectively eliminate, the ultimate freedom: an informed conscience. This has occurred (and is still being played out) in the different approaches to authority (of the organization led by the clerics or the individual with the primacy of conscience) that have been so divisive in the Roman Church today. These have been well articulated by Michael G. Lawler and Todd A. Salzman.[18] They note that what we have called Culture I Catholicism sees freedom as a commitment to authoritative teaching, as St. John Paul II envisioned it, wherein "conscience is ultimately about obedience to church teaching." On the other hand, in what is called Culture II Catholicism, the teaching of Joseph Ratzinger is quoted: "Over the pope as the expression of the binding claim of ecclesiastical authority there still stands one's own conscience, which must be obeyed before all else, if necessary even against the requirement of ecclesiastical authority."[19] However, they argue that beyond these polarities and, ideally, reconciling them, the role of the Holy Spirit as ultimate articulator has been best summarized by Pope Francis in his *Evangelii Gaudium*:

> Different currents of thought in philosophy, theology, and pastoral practice, if open to being reconciled by the Spirit in respect and love, can enable the church to grow, since all of them help to express more clearly the immense riches of God's word. For those who long for a monolithic body of doctrine guarded by all and leaving no room for nuance, this might appear as undesirable and leading to

18. Michael G. Lawler and Todd A. Salzman, "Following Faithfully: The Catholic Way to Choose the Good," *America* 212.3 (February 2, 2015), 16-20.
19. Ibid., 16.

confusion. But, in fact, such variety serves to bring out and develop different facets of the inexhaustible riches of the Gospel.[20]

As we move into Paul's understanding of self-control, we do well to see how, even though he believed the end of the world was around the corner, he did not want to use his authority in the community to restrain their conscience (1 Cor. 7:35). The restraint involved in authoritative teaching must always be subservient to the self-control that originates in true freedom, which arises from an informed conscience within the whole community of believers.

Cultivating Self-Control as a Form of Personal and Social Identity-Marker

We have already seen that, because they are all facets of love, all the manifestations of the fruit of love are facets of each other as well. This is especially true when we understand self-control as a dimension of the gentle life that is to be practiced in the church, especially in the restraint that is used by those in leadership when they correct those they consider to be erring members. Thus, Bernard Ukwuegbu describes the kind of communal correction in gentleness that is found in Gal. 6:1-10. Declaring that this section of Galatians "penetrates the heart of what it means to be 'in Christ' (6:10)," he also shows that self-control is a personal and social identity-marker of what it means not only to be "in Christ" but to be "in community." He notes that this section becomes a kind of expansion on what Paul has written earlier about the fruit of love itself:

> Paul's advice here is better seen in the context of his providing a practical way to act out the fruit of the Spirit. Christians who have sinned against fellow members should be restored to fellowship by those who have been tamed by the Spirit and have allowed God to rein in their wilder natures, so they do not react impulsively against a brother or sister.

Expanding then on the subsequent discussion of Paul which follows his narration of the works of the flesh and the fruit of the Spirit, Ukwuegbu notes that, in 6:1-10 Paul offers advice on how ethically appropriate behavior can be encouraged so that the right type of identity will be guaranteed.

First, he advocates peer pressure (6:1), as one would expect in Mediterranean society, given its strongly corporate nature and the

---

20. Pope Francis, *Evangelii Gaudium*, IV, 40, http://w2.vatican.va.

pressure customarily brought to bear on wayward group members to conform. Personal relationships are enhanced by the gentleness (*praüs*) that Paul employs, an attitude usually seen among one's own household. In the Hellenistic world, gentleness is a quality of a person who is in control of his or her own emotions and can choose to act with mildness in dealing with others.[21]

At the level of one's individual self, the opposite of self-control would be "self-interest"; however, in the same way, it might be argued, at the level of group, the opposite of group restraint would be group interest, or ethnocentrism. Since a key element behind Paul's understanding of the gospel that he had proclaimed was undermined by the kind of covenantal nomism that justified group interest at the expense of communal solidarity, it follows that his vision of the new creation would find all isolationistic forms of group antithetical to the gospel of Jesus Christ and the new creation this envisioned in which there would be neither Jew nor Gentile, slave or free, woman or man (3:28).

It is evident that, quite possibly given the "countergospel" of those we have called Teachers, Paul was confronted with the need to clearly develop the theological rationale for why gentiles entering the community must be considered equal to the Jews, not based on any notion of Jewishness (which might reinforce group interest) but on the basis of their personhood, for they were "in Christ" not as Jews or gentiles but as individuals baptized into Christ. If this is so, one might ask why Paul did not promote the same theological rationale for the equality of slave and free as well as women and men, especially if that new creation would represent an apocalyptic new social order in society.

It could be argued that Paul did not address what we have called the *injustice* of the Roman social system, which dominated his world; to directly confront it would have brought down its wrath. However, this did not mean that Paul did not promote the kind of redeemed relationships among the members of the house churches that would find them voluntarily creating a new model of household wherein all members would forgo all forms of social stratification. This involved a new way of addressing the culture of slavery by having all members of the household churches become slaves to one another out of love. We know this from Paul's Letter to Philemon: He

---

21. Bernard O Ukwuegbu, "Paraenesis, Identity-defining Norms, or Both? Galatians 5:13–6:10 in the Light of Social Identity Theory," *Catholic Biblical Quarterly* 70 (2008): 552.

urged Philemon to receive Onesimus as his equal in Christ insofar as, in Christ, Philemon had committed himself to be a slave!

If it seems that Paul's approach to justice between those structured as slave and free, in Christ, would be countercultural in the way a new ordering of the house (*oikonomia*) would be structured around relationships of equality, can the same be said of the alternative way Paul addressed the role of women in the house churches? Did he treat them as equals even though society had codes that made them virtual slaves of the men, especially if they were daughters of fathers or wives of husbands?

First of all, it is clear that subordination was not to take place among any members of the house churches if those house churches corporately consisted of those who were all slaves of one another in love. However, more specifically, how might this apply to female/male relationships themselves?

It is clear from the main form of address that Paul gave to his audience in the house churches that he regarded their members as constituting a new kind of household or family within the imperial, house-based social order. This was not to reflect the family dynamics of a human *pater familias*.[22] Rather, it was to be a family of siblings: brothers and sisters. The kind of self-control the members of the household churches should manifest was ultimately "other-concern," such as would be evidenced by siblings toward one another for the sake of the common good of the family, and which would give good example to outsiders. Reidar Aasgaard (who notes that *adelph-*, the root word for a sibling, is not only used metaphorically 120 times in Paul's seven letters but is also used as the most common metaphor for fellow Christians) writes,

> There are many indications that the sibling metaphor has a central place in Paul's ecclesiology and in his perception of Christian identity: he views individual Christians as brothers or sisters, and the Christian fellowship as a group of siblings, a siblingship. This suggests that his understanding of Christians as a family of siblings will play a role in his *ethical* thinking and praxis: *what* they are (i.e. siblings) has consequences for *how* they are (their ethical praxis), i.e. for the way in which they behave towards one another, and perhaps even for the way in which they behave vis-à-vis outsiders in the society in which they live.[23]

---

22. For more on this, see Kathy Ehrensperger, *Paul and the Dynamics of Power: Communication and Interaction in the Early Christ-Movement* (New York: T & T Clark International, 2009), 117ff.

23. Reidar Aasgaard, "'Role Ethics' in Paul: The Significance of the Sibling Role for Paul's Ethical Thinking," *New Testament Studies* 48 (2002): 517.

For those concerned that Paul did not more directly challenge inequality in his house churches (which were expected to "fit in") as part of the overall imperial body or household, Aasgaard helpfully notes that Paul did not try to abolish existing differences; rather he tried to persuade his family/household/churches to function in such a way "that their negative side-effects be reduced by means of mutual tolerance and generosity."[24]

Besides appreciating the sibling context that served as the environment for Paul's reflections, it is also clear in his letters (with some apparent anecdotal exceptions [such as his command that women not have their heads uncovered]) that Paul did not distinguish between women and men in that key area to which he felt all those "in Christ" were called: to be coworkers with him in the proclamation and living out of the gospel. Paul did not view women and their ministry as separate or complementary vis-à-vis their male coworkers. As Lisa Marie Belz writes, "On the contrary, they are coworkers with Paul whom he describes as having "labored side by side with me in the gospel together with Clement and the rest of my fellow workers, whose names are in the book of life." Indeed, Belz writes, "Paul writes about them in such a way as to give the impression that they are [not only] on the same level as their male colleagues,[25] but that a careful reading of Paul's genuine letters leads to the inescapable conclusion that he values women leaders in his churches."[26] Going even further, in a powerful insight that begs for further development, Belz clearly states that "Paul never situates any of these women in their relation to a man, their father, brother, husband or son."[27] In Paul's church the identity of women and men is the same: to be "in Christ."

Citing the images that point to equality among all women and men in the Christian household in their roles as brothers/sisters, Belz notes how Paul "describes women as his 'sisters,' his co-workers and fellow apostles,

---

24. Ibid., 522. This was especially apropos in the way he expected those who were stronger to be at the service of those who were weaker (1 Cor. 8).

25. As Wendy Cotter has observed, "the respect Paul exhibits toward each woman's position, and the level of concern he shows in making a public appeal to them, suggests that both Euodia and Syntyche hold some office of distinction in the Philippian community." See Cotter, "Women's Authority Roles in Paul's Church: Countercultural or Conventional?," *Novum Testamentum* 36.4 (1994): 353.

26. For a thorough summary of Paul's views regarding women, see Lisa Marie Belz, Chapter 5, "Paul's Views on Subordination, Marriage, and Gender Relations in His Undisputed Letters," in Belz, "The Rhetoric of Gender in the Household of God: Ephesians 5:21-33 and Its Place in Pauline Tradition," *Dissertations*, Paper 502 (Chicago: Loyola University, 2013), http://ecommons.luc.edu/luc_diss/502, 194.

27. Cotter, "Women's Authority Roles," 354.

even church office holders whose ministerial gifts and leadership are of tremendous benefit to the nascent church." More specifically, she concludes that "from 1 Cor. 11:5, we know that in the churches that Paul founded, women have a role as prophets. And while Paul's instructions to the women prophets in 1 Cor. 11:5 have to do with proper and modest dress, he places no limits on their speech."[28]

Cultivating Self-Control as a Key Character Trait of a Mystical Stance

Core to our understanding of a mystical stance in life, we have found that one's personal identity is not defined by self-referencing but by self-giving; rather than being centered on what can come to one's self, the concern is what one's self can give to the community. Rather than being defined by the law and its rituals, there is to be one law: that of self-giving (sacrificing) cruciform love as a sign of the Spirit's power in the lives of all the members of the community. In support of this approach, Bruce Longenecker writes,

> Paul expects Christian moral identity to be exhibited in patterns of life that evidence the working of the Spirit. The embodiment of the Spirit within Christians results in the promotion of wellbeing both within and beyond the boundaries of the Christian community. Moreover, the law finds its proper fulfillment in Christian self-giving, an eschatological trait enabled exclusively by the power of God. In short, Paul envisages divine triumph to have as its corollary a transformation in the moral identity of God's people, a transformation at odds with the patterns that characterize life beyond the boundaries of the new creation.[29]

We have already seen that Paul's understanding of self-control has a uniquely Christian "spin" to it; therefore it cannot be understood in Hellenistic terms, which interpreted it as the supreme virtue.

> Rather, it is about the willingness and ability to set one's own needs secondary to those of others. In terms of the very central notion of freedom in Galatians it is about the willingness to lovingly curb

---

28. Belz, "Paul's Views on Subordination," 194-95.
29. Bruce W. Longenecker, *The Triumph of Abraham's God: The Transformation of Identity in Galatians* (Nashville: Abingdon Press, 1998), 71-72.

one's freedom if it imposes on the freedom of another. Betz is correct that ἐγκράτεια is in juxtaposition to ἀγάπη. Paul, so to speak, wraps his list of virtues in ἀγάπη and ἐγκράτεια. It is about loving-service. In other words, the way Paul structures the list of virtues, beginning with love and ending with self-sacrifice, rings very well with Gal. 6:2. Christ's *love* for mankind *required* of Him to bear its burden of living the present evil age even to the point of *sacrificing his life.*"[30]

Any interpretation of self-control that limits it to the individual rather than community is not aware of Paul's warning to the members of the Corinthian house churches: "You are not your own" (1 Cor. 6:19b). Paul's words to Christians in Galatia seem to have an extended significance as a resource for consideration about modern society. In Paul's analysis, the "present age of evil" is sponsored by what he calls the "flesh," which he characterizes as "self-conceit," resulting in the provocation of others (5:26). A community or society motivated by the "flesh" ends up devouring and consuming its own members and destroying itself (5:15). A dysfunctional threadbare moral fabric within society is, then, not without precedent in Paul's theological imagination.

Against this background, Paul urges his readers to be enlivened by character that runs contrary to all this. He holds out a formula that he expects will infuse health and well-being into the Christian communities in Galatia, and spill over with beneficial effect on society as a whole (6:1). In contrast to the human propensity toward self-referentiality (whether ego- or ethnocentrism), Paul posits a scenario where social relationships are characterized by the volunteering of self for the benefit of others, the offering of one's resources and energies for the nurturing of others. In contrast to our modern times, when freedom, social liberties, and personal rights have become the mainstay of so much of the Western developed world, Paul's theology of freedom translates into the practice of responsibility toward and love for others in a network of mutual care and support.[31]

In Galatians, Paul is not asking the community to do something he has not tried to do in his own life. Indeed, given the transformative experience of Damascus, he had the boldness to offer his own example as a model to be imitated by the members of the house churches. Recalling

---

30. Gys M. H. Loubser, "Life in the Spirit as Wise Remedy for the Folly of the Flesh," *Neotestamenica* 43.2 (2009): 363.

31. Longenecker, *The Triumph of Abraham's God*, 185.

what we discussed in Chapter 13 on *gentleness* regarding imitation (*mimesis*), we can see why self-control might be another word for the kind of *character* or *authenticity* Paul was trying to model to his audience (and which should be the challenge to all of us as we live in our communities). Thus Longenecker writes, "When Paul writes his first imperative of the letter, 'Become like me' (4.12a), he has his autobiographical sketch of Galatians 1–2 primarily in mind, where his own life is presented as a demonstration of Christian commitment and resilience. What he means in 4.12a is best paraphrased as, 'Become resilient in your commitment to the gospel, just as I am.'"[32]

Authenticity as Self-Control:
Faith Working through Self-Giving Love

Throughout this book, I have promoted the need for us to *choose* to live and walk by the Spirit by cultivating attitudes and practices that reveal the Spirit's fruit of love in our lives and relationships at all levels of life. I believe such self-control is not self-defeating; on the contrary, it represents the heart of what it means to live an authentic life in society.

In Chapter 2 I noted that while we might not live in Second Temple Judaism with its eschatological expectations of the end of one age and the beginning of another, today's warnings about climate change make us realize we are at the end of the age of consumerism, which has helped create it. In addition, as we see the increasing disparity of wealth and income among peoples both domestically and globally, we are challenged to find new ways to proclaim the gospel that will be "good news" to those who are the victims of society's structural forms of poverty and inequality. This calls for a new kind of responsibility to bring about a new creation in the face of this geological apocalypse never imagined by Paul.

More and more scientists are embracing the notion (which I discussed in Chapter 2) that we have entered a new epoch and that this epoch is the "Anthropocene,"[33] a term originally (and arguably) coined by the Pontifi-

---

32. Ibid., 157.

33. For the past 12,000 years, including the age of Jesus and Paul, scientists called these centuries the Holocene because the period was marked by a stable and moderate climate. However, because humans have impacted the climate so severely, many scientists have stated that we have entered a new geological age, the Anthropocene (*anthropos* = human and *cene* = new). This is hardly the new creation that Paul envisioned. While addressed in some books, notably Mark Lynas, *The God Species: Saving the Planet in the Age of Humans* (London: Fourth Estate, 2012), and Gaia Vince, *Adventures in the Anthropocene: A Journey to the Heart of the Planet We Made* (Minneapolis: Milkweed Editions,

cal Academies of Science and Social Sciences.[34] The calamitous effects of human exploitation of the planet make a demand on us, that like the Galatians, we move from all forms of our own contemporary *stoicheia,* especially the consumerism, classism, and clericalism that have created a globalization of indifference that threatens the survival of people and the planet, and instead proclaim the gospel of love with power (and grace). In the church, as we face our own apocalyptic losses of members on most of the continents, we also face the need to imagine what it means to be the body of Christ for the life of the world.

Given the above, it should not be surprising that Paul would end his list of the fruit(s) of the Spirit with self-control, because it can be seen as a mystical stance that summarizes the whole transformation of character that Paul envisioned as the lifestyle that would somewhat mystically mirror the core of the gospel he experienced on the way to Damascus and, in the process, encapsulate the totally new social order that he envisioned, in Christ, to be identified with the new cosmic order of creation. Living in the reign of this God rather than under any other powers (*stoicheia*), be they our contemporary "isms" of consumerism, classism, and clericalism (with their manifestation in other "isms" such as sexism and racism, ethnocentrism and tribalism in society and curialism and careerism in the church), brings about what Bruce Longenecker calls "a sphere marked by unprecedented intimacy with God and multi-racial association." He concludes, "Those whose lives have been caught up in this sphere embody the triumph of God in their transformed patterns of life. By means of the Spirit, the pattern of self-giving that characterized the faithful son of God eradicates self-referential patterns of life that mark out the age of evil."[35]

While authentic Christian living was the evangelical ideal, Paul himself acknowledged the challenge such an ideal made to those who sought to live their lives "in Christ" in the midst of competing "gospels" in society and even in the house churches (i.e., different negative expressions of covenantal nomism with its contemporary echoes of canonical nomism in our church today). This conflict is perennial; thus, what Longenecker wrote of

---

2014), "Anthropocene" became mainstream with a cover article, "Welcome to the Anthropocene: Geology's New Age," in *The Economist* in its May 28–June 3, 2011, edition (11, 81ff.). For a brief popular overview of the term and another determination of its origin and historical foundation, see Anjana Ahuja, "The Muddle over the Moment Mankind Made Its Mark," *The Economist,* January 23, 2015.

34. Andrew C. Revkin, "Tracing the Roots of Pope Francis' Climate Plans for 2015," *New York Times,* December 31, 2014.

35. Longenecker, *The Triumph of Abraham's God,* 173.

the challenge facing Paul is the same challenge facing everyone trying to cultivate lives that bear witness to the forms of love that are called the "fruit of the Spirit":

> The success of Paul's case in Galatians depends upon the connection that he establishes between (1) one's pattern of life and (2) the suprahuman powers with which one is inevitably aligned. The contrast between opposing types of suprahuman powers is most clearly articulated in 4.1-11, where Paul sets out two categories of spiritual influence. On the one hand, there is the Spirit of Christ who lives in the hearts of Christians (4.6). On the other hand, there are the "elements of the world" (4.3, 9), "beings that by nature are no gods (4.8)—spiritual forces who lead their underlings away from true knowledge of God, who enslave them and who, in contrast to the sovereign God, are weak and beggarly.[36]

In his classic study of Paul's Letter to the Galatians, Hans Dieter Betz notes that, for Paul, human life was "a way of life"[37] that was to be led by the Spirit so that the Christ might be formed in every member of the community. Both individual and communal life involves ways of being led by the Spirit that will be fruitful for one's own personal and communal life. The goal of all of this is meant was to create authentic human beings formed in the image of the Christ through the power of the Holy Spirit. In this sense Jerome Murphy-O'Connor writes,

> Christ's self-giving is the creative act, which is the essence of authentic humanity. . . . Creative love is what makes a person both human and Christian; it is the law of the believer's being. Thence Paul is led to the conclusion that the law is Christ, "Bear one another's burdens and so fulfil the law of Christ" (Gal. 6:2). Christ's comportment exemplifies authentic behaviour. This is the true answer to the Galatian's question: how do we know what to do?[38]

Noting that "life" is "the Pauline term for authenticity," Jerome Murphy-O'Connor writes that such Pauline authenticity "cannot be conferred. It can only be chosen. The human creature, if it is to be true to its own nature,

---

36. Ibid., 157.

37. Hans Dieter Betz, *Galatians: A Commentary on Paul's Letter to the Churches in Galatia* (Philadelphia: Fortress Press, 1979), 277.

38. Jerome Murphy-O'Connor, OP, *Paul: A Critical Life* (Oxford: Oxford University Press, 1996), 204-5.

must decide for authenticity."[39] This process involves the kenotic process of moving from self-interest to other-interest through self-emptying because of authentic love that becomes ever less exclusive and ever more expansive (toward everyone and everything).

Teilhard de Chardin found in God's self-giving love and loving the core principle or energy of the universe. However, he was convinced that because "*the world is filled* with the absolute" and to "see this is to be made free," he also believed that the mystic who sees in this way not only becomes free but is free in a way that must give way to "*the effort to feel and to surrender.*"[40] In this understanding, Teilhard's words place him among those who realize that love and self-giving, freedom and surrender (*kenosis*) constitute the core of authentic Christian mysticism. The result is self-control.

As Longenecker makes so clear (without noting so directly), the notion of self-control represents the kind of *character* or *authenticity* that Paul envisioned for the members of the house church. A proper understanding of it thus links self-control with self-giving in a way that restrains one's own interests so that one can be at the service of the community. However, lest this be considered quite impossible, since self-control was one of the key identity-markers of the believers not only individually but communally, Paul envisioned all the members practicing self-control with the result that self-sacrificing love would become their new identifier and key to each community's character. For Paul, inauthenticity in the community was being promoted by appeals to a covenantal nomism that, instead of creating a more loving community as intended, would divide the members of the body of Christ. Such "inauthentic existence" meant the continuity, Jerome Murphy-O'Connor writes, "of opposed pairs, Jew against Greek, slave against free, male against female. In the new mode of being these divisions no longer exist, and it is in order to get this point across that Paul employs a variety of different expressions to evoke the communal nature of authentic existence: 'in Christ,' 'putting on Christ,' 'belonging to Christ,' and most dramatically 'you are all *one man* in Christ Jesus.'" He concludes, "No words could express more graphically the radical difference between the inauthentic and the authentic modes of being."[41]

---

39. Jerome Murphy-O'Connor, OP, *Becoming Human Together: The Pastoral Anthropology of St. Paul* (Wilmington, DE: Michael Glazier, 1984), 142.

40. PierreTeilhard de Chardin, *Writings in Time of War* (trans. René Hague; New York: Harper & Row, 1968), 124.

41. Murphy-O'Connor, *Becoming Human* Together, 175.

The Cruciform Life of Faith Working through Self-Giving Love

Throughout this book we have seen that to be "in Christ" and to have Christ be "in" our lives is the heart of Pauline theology. These terms, Bruce Longenecker writes, are not simply "synonymous with the adjective 'Christian'"; much more they represent "an elaborate network of ideas that cohere around the image of union with, participation in, and incorporation into, Christ." All of this is thoroughly eschatological, as is clear from 2 Cor. 5.17, where Paul links the theme of new creation with that of being "in Christ" in a way similar to Gal. 5:6 and 6:15: "Therefore if anyone is in Christ, new creation [literally]; the old has passed away, behold the new has come." In other words, if the church is going to be an evangelical microcosm of the new creation, its members must continue growing in conformity to Christ crucified whose death and resurrection has brought about this new order.[42]

Probably Paul's most clear articulation of his own self-control that led to choices that he made that were consequent to his realization of the need to mirror Christ through his own faith that was revealed in self-giving love is found in his testimony, "I have been crucified with Christ; it is no longer I who live, but Christ who lives in me; and the life I now live in the flesh I live in faith in the Son of God, who loved me and gave Himself for me" (2:20). Seen from this life, the equivalent form of authenticity for Paul had to be cruciformity in the lives of his audience then and now. This cruciformity invites all of us, as it did St. Francis of Assisi, to find the face of the Crucified One in the lepers of his day.

Paul's self-control was modeled on that of Christ, whose fidelity to the gospel of the kingdom of God, which was to bring good news to the poor and those considered "socially inferior," led him to the cross. Consequently, for Paul, only cruciform loving expressed in self-giving service to the members of the body of Christ would evidence his authenticity regarding such a claim as he made above. However, Paul's proclamation is to be evidenced in every one of our lives as well. Thus Loubser has written:

> The very basis of Christian life is that it is founded on and drenched in the love of Christ as illustrated on the Cross. It is not only about Him and his Cross as foundation of the believer's new life, but equally about partaking in Christ's life and cross. If salvation flows forth from Christ's loving-service and sacrifice, the ethic emanating from it must equally portray that attitude.

---

42. Longenecker, *The Triumph of Abraham's God,* 65..

What is this attitude? Loubser says simply that Paul has made it clear: "It is about faith working through love (πίστις δι' ἀγάπης ἐνεργουμένη— Gal. 5:6); about finding oneself in the disposition of faith and under the impulse to love others. It is the vocation of Christians to live freely, but in such a fashion that they 'through love serve one another (διὰ τῆς ἀγάπης δουλεύετε ἀλλήλοις).'"[43] In such loving service of all the members toward one another we find manifested the fruit of love called self-control, which invites the faithful Christian to replicate in his/her life the fidelity to the gospel that models that of Jesus. Thus Richard B. Hays writes, "For Paul, Jesus's death on the cross is an act of loving, self-sacrificial obedience that becomes paradigmatic for the obedience of all who are in Christ."[44]

I have always had a problem with statements such as these, mostly because they are often interpreted improperly. The stress is on the cross rather than on fidelity to a way of life that stands counter to the gospel of the prevailing structures of society that will incur its cross. Thus the cross is the consequence of faithful obedience to the gospel of the "kingdom/kindom" of God that Jesus preached. Today the embrace of suffering for proclaiming and practicing a gospel that reflects what we know to be God's Trinitarian household of equality impacting all relationships will necessarily produce resistance and even contemporary forms of rejection or crucifixion. But this is the obedience that is demanded: to the gospel, even if it took Jesus to the cross and will take us to the cross as well.

I believe that one of the few Pauline theologians writing this way is Kathy Ehrensperger. She states that "nowhere in the Pauline letters are suffering and weakness perceived as essential to faith in Christ in an ontological sense. The cross of Christ was a Roman cross, thus the actual historical context of his suffering and death cannot be ignored."[45] From this perspective she links the fidelity of Jesus to the proclamation of the gospel of the kingdom of God that took him to the cross to the equal challenge to every disciple of Jesus who must proclaim that same gospel in every age. She writes,

> A Jewish messianic movement like the early Christ-movement which witnesses to one crucified by Rome as resurrected by God, and thereby implicitly proclaimed that a kingdom other than the kingdom of the Caesars was in the process of dawning, was an

---

43. Loubser, "Life in the Spirit," 361.

44. Richard B. Hays, *The Moral Vision of the New Testament: Community Cross, New Creation, A Contemporary Introduction to New Testament Ethics* (San Francisco: HarperSanFrancisco, 1996), 27.

45. Ehrensperger, *Paul and the Dynamics of Power*, 115.

implicit threat to Roman imperial order. To remain faithful to God who resurrected Christ crucified, thereby confirming his promises of life and justice, rendered Christ-followers not prone to persecution but vulnerable to all sorts of trouble. Thus suffering and weakness were a consequence of life lived by faith in God through Christ, but not the essence nor the goal of this way of life.[46]

The essence of faith for the Christian is to reflect the essence of the faithfulness of Christ: to live a life of love expressed in self-giving even unto the cross. Any self-control of the disciple, thus, is to reflect that self-giving love (which has already been discussed in Chapter 5 of this book).

The combined religious and political powers of that area of the Roman Empire conspired to kill Jesus because he was a threat to their control over the people. Consequently, on the cross Christ became crucified not only by the world but to the world. The same cruciformity is the challenge of everyone who is "in Christ." If Paul could say "I have been crucified with Christ," so everyone else who is "in Christ" must be able to say that they are among "those who belong to Christ Jesus [because they] have crucified the flesh with its passions and desires" (5:24). To be "in Christ" involves the witness of a cruciform life that has overcome the flesh and is under the power of the Spirit.

Bruce Longenecker notes that "Paul does not offer his Galatian audience a recipe for Christian behavior other than the patter of cruciform existence. Prescriptive ethical regulations delimiting specific practices and behaviour have little to do with this text. Instead Paul seeks to exercise the imagination of the Galatians in order that they, enlivened by the Spirit of Christ, might be conformed to the model of Christ."[47]

Self-Restraint as Self-Control:
The *Sine Qua Non* in Apocalyptic Times

In the 2011 book *We Have Met the Enemy: Self-Control in an Age of Excess*,[48] Daniel Akst argues that the aggregate result of the lack of individual self-control is a troubled society. In it he distinguishes between "first order desires" (our emotions) and "second order desires" (the way our reason puts

---

46. Ibid., 116. For further elaboration on this, see 184-85.

47. Longenecker, *The Triumph of Abraham's God*, 186.

48. Daniel Akst, *We Have Met the Enemy: Self Control in an Age of Excess* (New York: Penguin Press, 2011).

controls on our "first order desires"). In a world where self-restraint is in short supply, he argues for the value of that kind of self-control offered by religious asceticism (such as I've tried to promote in this book, through the development of a mystical stance in life) that finds us rejecting immediate comforts with an eye toward eternity and supplying a supportive community to help sustain its members in the struggle. His argument about keeping an eye on eternity was later buttressed by a Queen's University study that showed people are actually better able to resist their temptations when they think about God![49]

Earlier, in 1999, Peter N. Stearns published a book entitled *Battleground of Desire: The Struggle for Self-Control in Modern America*. He showed that, at the turn of the twentieth century, inflexible and often-imposed moral codes (such as those identified with the Victorian Era) were replaced by a set of informal controls, imposed from within. While commenting on the merits of the book, David Brooks criticized it for its lack of critique about such codes in people themselves. He wrote, "It's indeed a virtue to practice self-control. It's a greater virtue to practice self-control for the sake of something that really matters."[50]

During the time that I was writing this book, it became clear from several sources that it "really matters" that we take Paul's understanding of self-control and put it into practice individually, communally, and organizationally. For example, the Intergovernmental Panel on Climate Control issued in 2014 its most dire warning about the future of life on our planet. The findings indicated that only by self-control in the form of self-restraint in order to bring about the rapid reduction of greenhouse gasses at all levels of human activity will we have hope for a viable future. The *New York Times* reported in a 2015 article that "the 80 wealthiest people in the world altogether own $1.9 trillion. This is nearly the same amount shared by the 3.5 billion people who occupy the bottom half of the world's income scale," and that "the richest 1 percent of the population, who number in the millions, control nearly half of the world's total wealth."[51] Pope Francis has spoken of

---

49. For a popular report on the findings, see Jonah Lehrer, "A Divine Way to Resist Temptation: Thinking of God Helps People to Assert Self-Control—Even if They're Atheists," *Wall Street Journal*, May 12-13, 2012. Also John Tierney, "For Good Self-Control, Try Getting Religious about It," *New York Times*, December 30, 2008.

50. David Brooks, *"Holding Back, Letting Go,"* a review of Peter N. Stearns, *Battleground of Desire: The Struggle for Self-Control in Modern America* (New York: New York University Press, 1999), in *Wall Street Journal*, June 8, 1999.

51. Patricia Cohen, "Study Finds Global Wealth Is Flowing to the Richest," *New York Times*, January 19, 2015, B6.

the "globalization of indifference" that exists because of our own consumerism and materialism with one understandable result: the breakdown of compassion. His encyclical on the environment (*Laudato Si*) developed this thought even further.

We have shown that, in effect, what Paul meant by the "works of the flesh" entailed all those negative dynamics or spirits in the world that vitiated against the gospel of life that was revealed in the death, resurrection, and empowerment of the faithful by the Holy Spirit. What was true of the *stoicheia* of Paul's day is true in the echoes of our own.

Noting that some religions will try to address the crises through a contemporary application of the Golden Rule, Sallie McFague invites us to return to Paul's core notion of *kenosis,* or self-emptying, as the way we Christians will develop the necessary self-restraint in our relationships and communities.[52] Noting the two great planetary crises I also have mentioned above, climate change and the increasing disparity of wealth and income among people domestically and globally, McFague writes that "what is needed is not more information but the will to move from belief to action, from denial to profound change at both personal and public levels." This demands, she writes, that we move from our culture's individualistic model promoting "market-oriented accumulation" and consumerism "to a model that sees self and planetary flourishing as independent." Such an independent model demands self-emptying (Christian *kenosis*) or "great compassion" (Buddhism) on the part of the well-to-do, so that all human beings and other life forms may live just, sustainable lives."[53]

In response to the individualism that has been so instrumental in creating our crises, McFague suggests self-restraint in a way that recognizes that the need of the common good surpasses that of individual self-interest. Given the issues I have addressed in this book, especially around the gap between rich and poor, our consumerism, which blinds us, and climate change, which threatens our very future, McFague calls self-restraint "the most significant challenge the religions could undertake for the well-being of our planet and its habitants."[54] Building on the "self-emptying" or *kenosis* of that God of love revealed in Jesus Christ, which Paul described in his canticle in Philippians, McFague applies its vision to our own lives:

---

52. Sallie McFague, *Blessed Are the Consumers: Climate Change and the Practice of Restraint* (Minneapolis: Fortress Press, 2013), xi.

53. Ibid., xii. McFague suggests "the kenotic paradigm as a way of loving the neighbor, a process in which God's own self may also be seen at work" (xiv).

54. Ibid., x.

What we see here is not an ascetic call for self-denial to purify ourselves or even a moral injunction to give others space to live; rather,
it is more basic. It is an invitation to imitate the way God loves the
world. In the Christian tradition, kenosis, or self-emptying, is a
way of understanding God's action in creation, the incarnation,
and the cross. In creation, God limits the divine self, pulling in, so
to speak, to allow space for others to exist. God, who is the one in
whom we live and move and have our being, does not take all the
space but gives space and life to others. This is an inversion of the
usual understanding of power as control; instead, power is given
to others to live as diverse and valuable creatures. In the incarnation, as Paul writes in Philippians 2:7, God "emptied himself, taking the form of a slave," substituting humility and vulnerability for
our insatiable appetites. In the cross, God gives of the divine self
without limit to side with the poor and the oppressed. God does
not take the way of the victor, but like Jesus and the temptations,
rejects absolute power and imperialism for a different way. Therefore, Christian discipleship becomes a "Cruciform" life, imitating
the self-giving of Christ for others.[55]

Building on this notion of cruciformity, McFague envisions a fourfold
plan that will move believers to action on behalf of the threatened people
involved and the planet itself:

1. Following the example of three "saints" of the past such as John
   Woolman, Simone Weil, and Dorothy Day, we must have *"experiences
   of 'voluntary poverty'"*;
2. We must find ways to "focus [our] attention on the needs of others";
3. In ways that lead to a "gradual development of a 'universal self'"
4. That "operates *at both the personal and public levels.*"[56]

In reading McFague's four points to help ensure a planetary future based
on self-restraint, I find concrete echoes of what I have tried to articulate in
these pages of the mystical stance that will not only offer a viable way of
life to any exclusivist form(s) of covenantal nomism but offer a concrete
response to Karl Rahner's challenge for the "devout Christian of the future":
we will be mystics—those who have experienced something—or be irrelevant. As I noted, key to that experience is the all-pervasive sense that we are

---

55. Ibid., 7-8.
56. Ibid., xii-xiii.

connected to everyone in Christ and thus must work to create in, among, and around us relationships that reflect that faith working through ever-increasing forms of all-inclusive love.

The "something" that we have experienced might not be mystical, like Paul's Damascus experience, but our effort to develop and practice a mystical stance that reflects it will find us assured with absolute conviction that this is the gospel that Paul proclaimed and that our future as devout Christians demands that we work to enable it to continue to be embodied in all peoples and the planet if the new creation is to be realized. If we do not promote this future, we will, as Christians, be increasingly irrelevant. Not only this, we may have no future at all.

Bibliography of Scriptural Sources

Aasgaard, R. *My Beloved Brothers and Sisters: Christian Siblingship in Paul.* London: T & T Clark, 2004.

———. "'Role Ethics' in Paul: The Significance of the Sibling Role for Paul's Ethical Thinking." *New Testament Studies* 48.4 (2002): 513-20.

Adolphe, Jane, Robert Fastiggi, and Michael Vacca, eds. *St. Paul, the Natural Law, and Contemporary Legal Theory.* Lanham, MD: Lexington Books, 2012.

Arnold, Clinton E. "Returning to the Domain of the Powers: *Stoicheia* as Evil Spirits in Galatians 4:3, 9." *Novum Testamentuum* 38.1 (1996): 55-76.

Asano, Atsuhiro. *Community-Identity Construction in Galatians: Exegetical, Social-Anthropological and Socio-Historical Studies.* London and New York: T & T Clark International, 2005.

Bachmann, Michael. *Anti-Judaism in Galatians? Exegetical Studies on a Polemical Letter and on Paul's Theology.* Translated by Robert L. Brawley. Grand Rapids, MI: Eerdmans, 2008.

———. "Identität bei Paulus: Beobachtungen am Galaterbrief." *New Testament Studies* 58.4 (2012): 571-97.

Becker, J. Christiaan. *Paul the Apostle: The Triumph of God in Life and Thought.* Philadelphia: Fortress Press, 1980.

———. *The Triumph of God: The Essence of Paul's Thought.* Translated by Loren T. Stuckenbruck. Minneapolis: Fortress Press, 1990.

Belz, Lisa Marie. "The Rhetoric of Gender in the Household of God: Ephesians 5:21-33 and Its Place in the Pauline Tradition." Dissertation Papers 502. Chicago: Loyola University, 2013.

Bertschmann, Dorothea H. "The Good, the Bad and the State—Rom 13.1-7 and the Dynamics of Love." *New Testament Studies* 60 (2014): 232-49.

Betz, Hans Dieter. *Galatians: A Commentary on Paul's Letter to the Churches in Galatia.* Philadelphia: Fortress Press, 1979.

Bird, Michael F., and Preston M. Sprinke, eds. *The Faith of Jesus Christ: Exegetical, Biblical, and Theological Studies.* Peabody, MA: Hendrickson, 2009.

Borg, Marcus J., and John Dominic Crossan. *The First Paul: Reclaiming the Radical Visionary behind the Church's Conservative Icon.* New York: HarperOne, 2009.

Bossmann, David M. "Paul's Fictive Kinship Movement." *Biblical Theology Bulletin* 26.4 (1996): 163-71.

Boyarin, Daniel. *A Radical Jew: Paul and the Politics of Identity.* Berkeley: University of California Press, 1994.

Brandos, David A. *Paul on the Cross: Reconstructing the Apostle's Story of Redemption.* Minneapolis: Fortress Press, 2006.

Byrne, Brendan, SJ. "Jerusalems Above and Below: A Critique of J. L. Martyn's Interpretation of the Hagar–Sarah Allegory in Gal 4.21–5.1." *New Testament Studies* 60 (2014): 215-31.

Callan, T. "The Style of Galatians." *Biblica* 88.4 (2007): 496-516.

Campbell, Douglas A. *The Deliverance of God: An Apocalyptic Rereading of Justification in Paul.* Grand Rapids: Eerdmans, 2009.

Choi, Hung-Sik. "ΠΙΣΤΙΣ in Galatians 5:5-6: Neglected Evidence for the Faithfulness of Christ." *Journal of Biblical Literature* 124.3 (2005): 467-90.

Cohen, Shaye J. C. "The Letter of Paul to the Galatians." In *The Jewish Annotated New Testament,* 332-44. Edited by Amy-Jill Levine and Marc Zvi Brettler. Oxford: Oxford University Press, 2010.

Cosgrove, Charles H. "Did Paul Value Ethnicity?" *Catholic Biblical Quarterly* 68 (2006): 268-90.

Cromhout, Markus. "Resurrection in Paul as Both Affirmation and Challenge to the Israelite Cycle of Meaning." *Neotestamentica* 45.1 (2011): 29-48.

Das, A. Andrew, *Paul and the Jews.* Peabody, MA: Hendrickson, 2003.

De Boer, Martinus C. *Galatians.* Louisville: Westminster John Knox, 2008.

de Villers, Pieter G. R., and Jan Villem van Helen, eds. *Coping with Violence in the New Testament.* Leiden: E. J. Brill, 2012.

Dewey, Arthur J., Roy W. Hoover, Lane C. McGaughey, and Daryl D. Schmidt. *The Authentic Letters of Paul: A New Reading of Paul's Rhetoric and Meaning. The Scholars Version.* Santa Rosa, CA: Polebridge, 2010.

Dodd, C. H. *Gospel and Law.* Cambridge: Cambridge University Press, 1963.

Dunn, James D. G. *The Epistle to the Galatians.* Peabody, MA: Hendrickson, 1993.

———. *Jesus, Paul, and the Gospels.* Grand Rapids: Eerdmans, 2011.

———. *The New Perspective on Paul.* Revised edition. Grand Rapids: Eerdmans, 2008.

———. "The Theology of Galatians: The Issue of Covenantal Nomism." In *Pauline Theology I: Thessalonians, Philippians, Galatians, Philemon.* Edited by Jouette M. Bassler, 125-46. Minneapolis: Fortress Press, 1991.

———. "Works of the Law and the Curse of the Law (Galatians 3:10-14." *New Testament Studies* 31 (1985): 523-42.

Eastman, Susan. *Recovering Paul's Mother Tongue: Language and Theology in Galatians.* Grand Rapids: Eerdmans, 2007.

Edwards, James R. "Galatians 5:12: Circumcision, the Mother Goddess, and the Scandal of the Cross." *Novum Testamentum* 53 (2011): 319-37.

Elliott, Mark W., Scott J. Hafemann, N. T. Wright, and John Frederich, eds. *Galatians and Christian Theology: Justification, the Gospel, and Ethics in Paul's Letter.* Grand Rapids: Baker Academic, 2014.

Elliott, John H. "Paul, Galatians, and the Evil Eye." *Currents in Theology and Mission* 17 (August 1990): 262-73.

Elliott, Neil. *Liberating Paul: The Justice of God and the Politics of the Apostle.* Sheffield: Sheffield Academic Press, 1995.

Elliott, Susan. *Cutting Too Close for Comfort: Paul's Letter to the Galatians in Its Anatolian Cultic Context.* New York: T & T Clark International, 2003.

Ellis, Peter F. "Galatians." In *Seven Pauline Letters,* 174-99. Collegeville, MN: Liturgical Press, 1984.

Ehrensperger, Kathy. *Paul and the Dynamics of Power: Communication and Interaction in the Early Christ-Movement.* New York: T & T Clark International, 2009.

———. "Speaking Greek under Rome: Paul, the Power of Language and the Language of Power." *Neotestamentica* 46.1 (2012): 9-28.

———. *That We May Be Mutually Encouraged: Feminism and the New Perspective in Pauline Studies.* New York: T & T Clark International, 2004.

Esler, Philp F. *Galatians.* London: Routledge, 1998.

———. "Making and Breaking an Agreement Mediterranean Style: A New Reading of Galatians 2:1-14." *Biblical Interpretation* 3.3 (1995): 285-314.

Fitzmyer, Joseph, S.J.. "A Life of Paul." In *The Jerome Biblical Commentary,* 215-22. Edited by Raymond E. Brown, S.S., Joseph A. Fitzmyer, S.J., and Roland E. Murphy, O.Carm. Englewood Cliffs, NJ: Prentice-Hall, 1968.

———. *Paul and His Theology: A Brief Sketch.* Second edition. Englewood Cliffs, NJ: Prentice Hall, 1989.

———. *Romans.* New York: Doubleday, 1993.

Freed, Edwin D. *The Morality of Paul's Converts.* London: Equinox, 2005.

Gabrielson, Jeremy. *Paul's Non-Violent Gospel: The Theological Politics of Peace in Paul's Life and Letters.* Eugene, OR: Pickwick Publications, 2013.

Gaventa, Beverly Roberts. "The Singularity of the Gospel: A Reading of Galatians." In *Pauline Theology I: Thessalonians, Philippians, Galatians, Philemon,* 147-59. Edited by Jouette M. Bassler. Minneapolis: Fortress Press, 1991.

Goh, David T. "Creation and the People of God: Creation Tradition and the Boundaries of the Covenant in Second Temple Jewish Writings and in Paul's Letter to the Galatians." Ph.D. diss., University of Durham, 1994.

Gorman, Michael J. *Cruciformity: Paul's Narrative Spirituality of the Cross.* Grand Rapids: Eerdmans, 2001.

Hahn, Scott W. "Covenant, Oath, and the Aqedah: Διαθήκη in Galatians 3:15-18." *Catholic Biblical Quarterly* 67.1 (2005): 79-100.

Hansen, Bruce. *"All of You Are One": The Social Vision of Galatians 3:28, 1 Corinthians 12:13 and Colossians 3:11.* London: T & T Clark, 2010.

Hays, Richard B. *Echoes of Scripture in the Letters of Paul.* New Haven: Yale University Press, 1980.

———. *The Faith of Jesus Christ: The Narrative Substructure of Galatians 3:1–4:11.* Second edition. Grand Rapids: Eerdmans, 2002.

———. *Galatians.* Nashville: Abingdon Press, 2000.

―――. *The Moral Vision of the New Testament: Community, Cross, New Creation; A Contemporary Introduction to New Testament Ethics*. San Francisco: HarperCollins, 1996.

Horsley, Greg. "Anatolia, from the Celts to the Christians." *Buried History: Quarterly Journal of the Australian Institute of Archeology* 36.1-2 (March-June 2000): 49-55.

Hunn, Debbie. "'Why Therefore the Law?' The Role of the Law in Galatians 3:19-20." *Neotestamentica* 47.2 (2013): 355-72.

Hurtado, Larry W. "Convert, Apostate or Apostle to the Nations: The 'Conversion' of Paul in Recent Scholarship." *Studies in Religion* 22.3 (1993): 273-84.

―――. "Jesus as Lordly Example in Philippians 2:5-11." In *From Jesus to Paul*, 113-26. Edited by Peter Richardson and John C. Hurd. Ontario: Wilfred Laurier University, 1984.

Jackson, T. Ryan, *New Creation in Paul's Letters: A Study of the Historical and Social Setting of a Pauline Concept*. Tübingen: Mohr Siebeck, 2010.

Jewett, Robert K. *Paul's Anthropological Terms: A Study of Their Use in Conflict Settings*. Leiden: E. J. Brill, 1971.

Kahl, Brigitte. *Galatians Re-Imagined: Reading with the Eyes of the Vanquished*. Minneapolis: Fortress Press, 2010.

Karris, Robert J. *Galatians and Romans*. Collegeville, MN: Liturgical Press, 2005.

Kerry, S. "An Exegetical Analysis of Galatians 3:1-5, with Particular Reference to Pneumatological Themes That Relate to the Onset and Continuation of Christian Identity, with Respect to Law and Gospel." *Journal of Biblical and Pneumatological Research* 2 (2010): 57-86.

Kim, Yung Suk. *Body in Corinth: The Politics of a Metaphor*. Minneapolis: Fortress Press, 2008.

Lategan, Bernard C. "Reconsidering the Origin and Function of Galatians 3:28." *Neotestamentica* 46.2 (2012): 274-86.

Lee, Michelle V. *Paul, the Stoics, and the Body of Christ*. Cambridge: Cambridge University Press, 2008.

Lennox, Stephen J. "'One in Christ': Galatians 3:28 and the Holiness Agenda." *Evangelical Quarterly* 84.3 (2012): 195-212.

Levison, John R. *Filled with the Spirit*. Grand Rapids: Eerdmans, 2009.

Longenecker, Bruce W. *The Triumph of Abraham's God: The Transformation of Identity in Galatians*. Nashville, Abingdon Press, 1998.

―――. "'Until Christ Is Formed in You': Suprahuman Forces and Moral Character in Galatians." *Catholic Biblical Quarterly* 61 (1999): 92-108.

López, René A. "Paul's Vice List in Galatians 5:19-21." *Bibliotheca Sacra* 169 (January-March 2012): 48-67.

Lyons, George: *Galatians: A Commentary in the Wesleyan Tradition* (Kansas City, MO: Beacon Hill, 2012.

Malina, Bruce J. *The New Testament World: Insights from Cultural Anthropology*. Revised edition. Louisville: Westminster/John Knox Press, 1993.

Malina, Bruce J., and John J. Pilch. "Galatians." In *Social Science Commentary on the Letters of Paul*. Minneapolis: Fortress Press, 2006.

Maloney, Elliott C., OSB. *Saint Paul: Master of the Spiritual Life "in Christ."* Collegeville, MN: Liturgical Press, 2014.

Marohl, Matthew J. *Faithfulness and the Purpose of Hebrews: A Social Identity Approach*. Eugene, OR: Pickwick, 2008.

Martínez, Aquiles Ernesto. "Fe Christiana, Bautismo e Identidad Social. Diálogo con Gál 3, 26-29." *Revista Biblica* 73.3-4 (2011): 163-86.

Martyn, J. Louis. "Events in Galatia: Modified Covenantal Nomism versus God's Invasion of the Cosmos in the Singular Gospel: A Response to J. D. G. Dunn and B. R. Gaventa." In *Pauline Theology I: Thessalonians, Philippians, Galatians, Philemon*. Edited by Jouette M. Bassler, 160-79. Minneapolis: Fortress Press, 1991.

———. *Galatians: A New Translation with Introduction and Commentary*. The Anchor Bible. New York: Doubleday, 1997.

Matera, Frank J. *Galatians*. Collegeville, MN: Liturgical Press, 1992.

———. *God's Saving Grace: A Pauline Theology*. Grand Rapids: Eerdmans, 2012.

Matlock, R. Barry. "The Rhetoric of πίστις in Paul. Galatians 2:16, 3:22, Romans 3:22, and Philippians 3.9." *Journal for the Study of the New Testament* 30.2 (2007): 173-203.

Meeks, Wayne A. *The First Urban Christians: The Social World of the Apostle Paul*. New Haven: Yale University Press, 1983.

Miller, Colin. "The Imperial Cult in the Pauline Cities of Asia Minor and Greece. "*Catholic Biblical Quarterly* 72 (2010): 314-32.

Moo, Douglas. *Galatians*. Grand Rapids: Baker Book House, 2013.

Morales, Rodrigo I. *The Spirit and the Restoration of Israel: New Exodus and New Creation Motifs in Galatians*. Tübingen: Mohr Siebeck, 2010.

Murphy-O'Connor, J., OP, *Becoming Human Together: The Pastoral Anthropology of St. Paul*. Wilmington, DE: Michael Glazier, 1978.

———. *Paul: A Critical Life*. Oxford: Oxford University Press, 1997.

———. *Paul: His Story*. Oxford: Oxford University Press, 2004.

———"The Unwritten Law of Christ (Gal 6:2)." *Revista Biblica* 119.2 (2012), 312-31.

Neyrey, Jerome H. "Bewitched in Galatia: Paul and Cultural Anthropology." *Catholic Biblical Quarterly* 50 (1998): 72-100.

———. *Paul, in Other Words: A Cultural Reading of His Letters*. Louisville: Westminster/John Knox, 1990.

Oakes, Peter. *Galatians*. Grand Rapids: Baker Academic, 2015.

Osiek, Carolyn, R.S.C.J. *Galatians*. New Testament Message 12. Dublin: Veritas Publications, 1980.

Polaski, Sandra Hack. *A Feminist Introduction to Paul*. St. Louis: Chalice, 2005.

———. *Paul and the Discourse of Power*. Sheffield: Sheffield Academic Press, 1999.

Prokhorov, Alexander V. "Taking the Jews out of the Equation: Galatians 6:12-17 as a Summons to Cease Evading Persecution." *Journal for the Study of the New Testament* 36.2 (2013): 172-88.

Punt, Jeremy. "Cross-Purposes in Paul? Violence of the Cross, Galatians, and Human Dignity." *Scriptura* 102 (2009): 446-62.

———. "He Is Heavy . . . He's My Brother: Unravelling Fraternity in Paul (Galatians)." *Neotestamentica* 46.1 (2012): 153-54.

———. "Pauline Brotherhood, Gender and Slaves: Fragile Fraternity in Galatians." *Neotestamentica* 47.1 (2013): 149-69.

Riches, John. *Galatians through the Centuries.* Oxford: Wiley-Blackwell, 2008.

Rosner, Brian S. *Greed as Idolatry: The Origin and Meaning of a Pauline Metaphor.* Grand Rapids: Eerdmans, 2007.

Russell, Walter Bo, III, *The Flesh/Spirit Conflict in Galatians.* Lanham, MD: University Press of America, 1997.

Saldanha, Assisi, CSsR. "'The Faith of Christ.' The Objective Basis of the Unity between Jew and Greek." *Indian Theological Studies* 43.3-4 (2006): 425-69.

Sanders, E. P. "Jewish Association Gentiles and Galatians 2:11-14." In *The Conversation Continues: Studies in Paul and John in Honor of J. Louis Martyn.* Edited by R. T. Fortna and B. R. Gaventa, 170-88. Nashville: Abingdon Press, 1996.

———. *Paul and Palestinian Judaism.* Philadelphia: Fortress Press, 1977.

———. *Paul, the Law and the Jewish People.* Minneapolis: Fortress Press, 1983.

Schantz, Colleen. *Paul in Ecstasy: The Neurobiology of the Apostle's Life and Thought.* Cambridge: Cambridge University Press, 2009.

Schreiner, Thomas. *Galatians.* Grand Rapids: Zondervan, 2010.

Schüssler Fiorenza, E. "Rhetorical Situation and Historical Reconstruction in 1 Corinthians." *New Testament Studies* 33 (1997): 386-403.

Schweitzer, Albert. *The Mysticism of Paul the Apostle.* New York: Macmillan, 1956.

Stirewalt, Jr., M. Luther. *Paul the Letter Writer.* Grand Rapids: Eerdmans, 2003.

Still, Todd D. "In the Fullness of Time (Gal. 4.4), Chronology and Theology in Galatians." In *Galatians and Christian Theology: Justification, the Gospel, and Ethics in Paul's Letter.* Edited by Mark W. Elliott, Scott J. Hafemann, N. T. Wright, and John Frederich, 249-57. Grand Rapids: Baker Academic, 2014.

Swartley, Willard M. *Covenant of Peace: The Missing Peace in New Testament Theology and Ethics.* Grand Rapids: Eerdmans, 2006.

Tatum, Gregory, OP. *New Chapters in the Life of Paul: The Relative Chronology of His Career.* Catholic Biblical Quarterly Monograph Series 41. Washington, DC: Catholic Biblical Association of America, 2006.

Theissen, Gerd. *The Social Setting of Pauline Christianity: Essays on Corinth.* Edited and translated by John H. Schütz. Philadelphia: Fortress Press, 1989.

Tibbs, Clint. "The Spirit World and the (Holy) Spirits among the Earliest Christians: 1 Corinthians 12 and 14 as a Test Case." *Catholic Biblical Quarterly* 70 (2008): 313-30.

Tsang, S. "Aramaic-Speaking Gentiles? 'Abba' Metaphor as Spiritual Experience of the Jesus Tradition" (Chinese). *CGST Journal* 42 (2007): 113-33.

Ukwuegbu, Bernard O. "Paraenesis, Identity-Defining Norms, or Both? Galatians 5:13–6:10 in the Light of Social Identity Theory." *Catholic Biblical Quarterly* 70 (2008): 538-59.

Van Voorst, Robert E. "Why Is There No Thanksgiving Period in Galatians? An Assessment of an Exegetical Commonplace." *Journal of Biblical Literature* 129.1 (2010): 153-72.

White, Joel R. "'Peace' and 'Security' (1 Thess 5.3): Roman Ideology and Greek Aspiration." *New Testament Studies* 60 (2014): 499-510.

Wiley, Tatha. *Paul and the Gentile Women: Reframing Galatians.* New York: Continuum, 2005.

Wilson, Todd A. "Wilderness Apostasy and Paul's Portrayal of the Crisis in Galatians." *New Testament Studies* 50 (2004): 550-71.

Woyke, Johannes. "Nochmal zu den 'schwachen und unfähigen Elementen' (Gal 4.9): Paulus, Philo und die στοιχεῖα τοῦ κοσμοῦ." *New Testament Studies* 54 (2008): 221-34.

Wright, N. T. *Paul and the Faithfulness of God,* Books I and II. Minneapolis: Fortress Press, 2013.

———. *Pauline Perspectives: Essays on Paul, 1978–2013.* Minneapolis: Fortress Press, 2013.

Witherup, Ronald D. *Galatians.* Grand Rapids: Baker Book House, 2008.

Index of Biblical Passages

Index of Subjects